THE PERFORMANCE APPRAISAL SOURCEBOOK

THE PERFORMANCE APPRAISAL SOURCEBOOK

Editors:

- **Lloyd Baird**
  Boston University
- **Richard W. Beatty**
  University of Colorado
- **Craig Eric Schneier**
  University of Maryland

Human Resource Development Press
Amherst, Massachusetts

ISBN Number: 0-914234-57-9 College Edition
0-914234-56-0 Professional Edition

First printing
Second printing 4/83
Third printing 1/84
Fourth printing 2/85

Manufactured in the United States of America

CONTENTS

PREFACE

This book deals with performance appraisal and how it is used to manage and improve individual and organizational performance. It is the result of the authors' common research, teaching, and consulting interests. Each of us has clients and students who are constantly asking for materials on designing, implementing, and evaluating performance appraisal systems. We find ourselves referring them to references scattered throughout the library or handing them stacks of readings out of our files. Checking around, we found other trainers, consultants, managers, professors, and students with the same problem. A sourcebook of readings, exercises, and training aids seemed like a natural way for us to integrate our own material and provide a valuable resource for those responsible for implementing and using performance appraisal systems in organizations.

This book contains materials that can assist both those in classrooms who are learning about performance appraisal systems and those in organizations who are designing and implementing them. We have included materials that we and others have found useful in planning, developing, and instituting appraisal systems in organizational settings of all types. These materials consist of role-plays, cases, questionnaires, checklists, and other materials, all of which can be made into overhead transparencies or duplicated to use as handouts for those attending briefings, orientation programs, workshops, or training sessions in appraisal.* These materials make this a *sourcebook* for appraisal that can be consulted to help solve the problems and issues of performance appraisal in business, industry, and government.

We do not view this as a completed project. We hope to update these materials as the field changes. If there is anything you have found particularly useful and would like to share with the rest of us we would welcome your contributions to an update. Feel free to send it to any one of us. Our own contributions and involvement have been equal and therefore the sequence of authors is alphabetical.

Lloyd Baird
School of Management
Boston University
212 Bay State Rd.
Boston, MA 02215

Richard Beatty
Graduate School
of Business Administration
University of Colorado
Boulder, CO 80302

Craig Eric Schneier
College of Business
and Management
University of Maryland
College Park, MD 20742

We would like to acknowledge the organizations and practitioners, too numerous to mention individually, that have given us the opportunity to work on their appraisal systems. This and our classroom experience have helped develop and refine our perspectives on appraisal and have served as stimuli for this book. We are also indebted to the authors and publishers who have allowed us to include their materials. They have made a major contribution to this book.

LSB
RWB
CES

1981

*The student edition of this book contains only the source readings.

INTRODUCTION TO THE PURPOSE AND USE OF THE PERFORMANCE APPRAISAL SOURCEBOOK

Performance appraisal—the identification, evaluation, and development of individual performance in organizations—has always been a critical component of management practices. Appraisals are used by managers as they make vital decisions in the areas of selection, placement, training, compensation, and promotion, among others. Yet performance appraisal is also a problematic and difficult managerial activity. Human judgment, inescapable in appraisal, is often fallible and influenced by factors other than the behavior of those being rated. The effective use of an appraisal system requires considerable time, energy, and commitment.

There are two recent changes in the work environment that have increased concern about performance appraisals. First, because of the ever increasing importance of human resources to what an organization can accomplish, more and more managers and organizations are realizing how critical a motivated, skilled workforce can be to their success. At the same time that an awareness of the importance of human resources is increasing, so are its costs in terms of salaries, benefits, etc. This makes it even more important that human resources be used properly. Contribution to organizational goals should be the basis for decisions about human resources. This is possible only if the results of appraisals are accurate, reliable, and available.

The second change in the work environment which places increasing emphasis on appraisals is the attention government officials are giving to the performance appraisal process. This attention has taken two forms: court action and management guidelines. The courts were initially concerned with "tests" (defined to include performance appraisals) used for hiring people. Laws were passed and executive orders issued essentially requiring that tests be accurate measures of future performance. The concern was that they not unfairly discriminate against categories of people specifically protected by law (e.g., women, aged, handicapped, racial groups, etc.). The courts quickly broadened their concern beyond the selection decisions to include any management decision which could affect the future employment status of an individual. The result was that management is now legally responsible for developing accurate measures of performance and using them properly.

The other form of government pressure for accurate performance appraisals has come from Executive Orders issued by presidents of the United States, procedures established by government agencies and issued as *Guidelines,* and the Civil Service Reform Act of 1978 which specifically addresses performance appraisal. Each of these has viewed performance appraisal as the basis for management decision making and requires that the appraisal be an accurate measure of performance, as well as providing additional requirements in terms of implementation and uses of appraisals.

The courts and the government are simply asking for sound human resources management practices. If the objective is to measure or improve performance, it is logical to suggest that decisions be based on accurate measures of that performance. The courts and the laws have heightened the awareness of performance appraisal, but effective managers have long recognized the importance of accurate, useable performance appraisals for improving their organizations.

HOW TO USE THIS BOOK

This book approaches performance appraisal as part of the continuing management process. Appraisal is not merely the measurement or evaluation of performance, but a series of continuing management responsibilities that help direct performance. These responsibilities include the following: definition and development of what will be measured (i.e., the criteria); design of appropriate appraisal formats to measure the criteria; implementation of the system (to include setting and communicating expectations, monitoring performance, coaching, counseling, providing feedback about performance, and training those who will use the system); evaluation of the appraisal system; and use of the results of the system for human resource decision making.

In this sourcebook we present six types of materials useful for each of these activities: readings, questionnaires, transparency masters/overheads, role-plays, cases, and outlines for presentations and workshops. These are described below. *

Part I: Sources

Source readings were selected in six areas: introduction to performance appraisal, defining and developing criteria, designing appraisal systems, implementing the performance appraisal process, evaluating the performance appraisal system, and using appraisal for human resource management. In each area the reading selections are organized to reflect the logical sequence for making useful performance appraisals in organizations. Readings were selected which met the following set of criteria:

1. views performance appraisal as part of a continuing management activity and an integral part of management;
2. up-to-date with current legal and professional guidelines;
3. applicable to the practicing manager;
4. readable and clearly presented; and
5. consistent with current research results.

If you are using this book to set up a new performance appraisal system we suggest that you follow the sequence in which the articles are presented. This will help you understand the basis of performance measurement and the nature of your organization's needs before you attempt to devise the actual format for performance appraisals and/or implement them.

If you are using this book as the basis for a training program, Part VI outlines a complete training program utilizing material in this book which can be duplicated for handouts. Also, there is a brief paperback *trainee* version of this sourcebook which includes just the source readings. This version, available from the publisher, together with the materials you duplicate, constitutes a complete training program.

If you are using the book to analyze and improve your present appraisal system, you may want to go directly to the sections that are the most important. To help you understand what is covered in each section, we present below a brief summary and a series of questions that each section in the readings is designed to answer.

Section 1: Introduction to Performance Appraisal

Topics

A brief introduction to the purpose and problems of managing performance; its importance, utility, and timeliness in the 1980s (e.g., EEO Laws and court cases, Civil Service Reform Act, expectations of workers for feedback and career development). The focus is on performance *management,* as opposed to simply performance *appraisal.* Performance appraisal is considered as part of the management process.

Questions Addressed

1. What is performance appraisal?
2. What are the many uses of performance appraisal?
3. How does performance appraisal relate to other human resource management programs?

Section 2: Defining Performance and Developing Criteria

Topics

Reviews why accurate measures are so important.

Considers criteria and criteria development.

Questions Addressed

1. Why are accurate measures so important?

*The student edition of this book contains only the source readings.

2. How should performance be defined so that it can be measured accurately?
3. What are the steps for developing accurate measures?

Section 3: Designing the Performance Appraisal System

Topics

The purposes of appraisal systems. How to adjust appraisal systems to fit the characteristics of the organization. The various formats for measuring and analyzing performance.

Questions

1. What are the characteristics of a good performance appraisal system?
2. What is a job analysis and how does it relate to performance appraisal?
3. What should be the format and content of performance appraisal?

Section 4: Implementing Performance Appraisal

Topics

Who evaluates? How to train raters. Documenting employee performance. The importance of preparation for appraisal. How to conduct the appraisal session.

Questions

1. Who evaluates?
2. How should performance be documented?
3. How should those doing the rating be trained?
4. How should performance interviews be conducted?

Section 5: Evaluating Performance Appraisal Systems

Topics

The legal and managerial requirements for a performance appraisal system.

Questions

1. What does the law require of a performance appraisal system?
2. What do managers need from a performance appraisal system?
3. What has research found about performance appraisal?

Section 6: Using Appraisal for Human Resource Management

Topics

Linking performance appraisal to continuing managerial activities and other human resource management programs.

Questions

1. How does performance appraisal relate to ongoing management activities such as solving performance problems, compensation decisions, information systems, and personal career development?

Part II: Questionnaires

The first step in designing and implementing an effective performance appraisal system is to assess existing individual and organizational characteristics. If the objective is to implement a performance appraisal system in an organization, the organization and its members must be analyzed to determine how best to proceed. If the objective is to help employees or students learn good performance appraisal practices, there should be a needs assessment of the individual.

The questionnaires were chosen because of their usefulness in individual needs assessment and organizational diagnosis. They may be used in all types of organizations at all levels. They have been used for both developing training programs and implementing performance appraisal in organizations. Feel free to duplicate them as they are or modify them in any way to fit the needs of your situation.

Part III: Role-Plays

Performance appraisal is a process people learn by doing. They must practice and receive feedback. Role-plays have proven to be valuable tools for training. This part of the sourcebook includes:

1. A brief description of what role-plays are and how they are to be done. You might want to review this with the participants in a training session before they do the role-plays.
2. A suggested method for running role-plays in triads.
3. Observer worksheet. The observers in a role play are critical. It is best to structure their observations so they can give the participants feedback that will be the most useful. The observer worksheet asks questions relevant to each stage of the performance appraisal process.
4. Role-plays. There are numerous role-plays included. We have selected ones that focus on problems which exist in most organizations. Remember the purpose of the role-plays is to learn the process of performance appraisal.
5. A description of how the role-plays may be used as a part of a workshop.

Part IV: Case Studies

Cases are excellent ways of learning how performance appraisal fits into the regular activities of organizations. The ones we have chosen are short, may be used in a variety of formats, and focus on many aspects of performance appraisal. In addition to the cases we have included a structured questionnaire which can be used to analyze performance situations.

Part V: Transparency Masters/Overheads

There are many times when you will need to explain performance appraisal in a concise form. This may be in an academic and teaching situation or it may be in a briefing in an organization. We have found overheads and transparencies valuable tools. Those we have included are a mixture from all portions of the performance appraisal process. They are organized in the order in which they might be used in a briefing or workshop. Again, you may duplicate, make transparencies, modify, rearrange, etc., these materials in any way that will be useful to you.

Part VI: Sample Topical Outlines for Briefings and Workshops

We have included topical outlines to facilitate presentations and workshops. The order of the outlines follows the sequence of the readings. The outlines provide an overview of the development and implementation of performance appraisal systems. These will be useful in briefings to explain the steps necessary to design PA systems or as guides for developing workshops, classes, or other training sessions. The readings provide the background material explaining each of the topics and much of the material needed for training sessions. Modify the outlines and workshops to fit your situation.

SUMMARY

All of these materials are included to help you understand, analyze, and practice good performance appraisal. Performance appraisal is such a critical part of the management process that it cannot be left to chance. It must be consciously managed. Use these materials in any way that they will help you do that.

PART ONE
SOURCES

SOURCES SECTION ONE

INTRODUCTION TO PERFORMANCE APPRAISAL

What Is Performance Appraisal?
by Craig Eric Schneier and Richard W. Beatty

- Defines performance appraisal
- Identifies the objectives and uses of performance appraisal
- Discusses the problem areas in performance appraisal

What Is Performance Appraisal?

by Craig Eric Schneier and Richard W. Beatty

Performance appraisal or evaluation is the process of identifying, measuring and developing human performance in organizations. An effective appraisal system must not only accurately measure current performance levels, but also contain mechanisms for reinforcing strengths, identifying deficiencies and feeding such information back to ratees in order that they may improve future performance. This second, developmental aspect of appraisal is as important as the measurement aspect.

The term performance itself denotes judgement—behavior which has been evaluated. Performance appraisal is thus the process of observing and identifying, measuring and developing human behavior in the organization. These activities are described as follows:

- *Observation and identification* refers to the process of viewing or scrutinizing job behaviors. It consists of choosing what job behaviors to look at among all that are emitted by a ratee, as well as how often to observe them. The choices inherent in this process add subjectivity to appraisal.
- *Measurement* refers to ascertaining the extent, degree, level, etc., of a behavior. After raters choose what information to examine, they compare this information about ratee behavior against a set of organizational or personal expectations for each job. The degree to which observed behavior meets or exceeds the expectations determines its desirability, or the level of performance it reflects, such as excellent or satisfactory.
- *Development* refers to performance improvement over time. An appraisal system must contain mechanisms to communicate the expectations and measurement process to persons being appraised, motivate them to remove any deficiencies uncovered and reinforce them to build on strengths in order to improve future performance.

When PA is considered in terms of its utility to an organization, several operational PA objectives seem critical. These include 1) the ability to provide adequate feedback to employees to improve subsequent performance, 2) the identification of employee training needs, 3) the identification of criteria used to allocate organizational rewards, 4) the validation of selection techniques to meet Equal Employment Opportunity (EEO) requirements and 5) the identification of promotable employees from internal labor supplies (see Figure 1). In order to accomplish these objectives, the PA system must, of course, be an accurate measure of performance.

A PA's adequacy to provide feedback and improve performance requires that it possess the following characteristics: be unambiguous and clearly specify the job-related performance expected, use behavioral terminology, set behavioral targets for ratees to work toward and use a problem-solving focus which culminates in a specific plan for performance improvement. If PAs are to identify training needs, the format must specify ratee deficiencies in behavioral terms, include all relevant job dimensions, and identify environmental deterrents to desired performance levels.

PAs are also used in the allocation of organizational rewards such as merit pay and punishments, such as disciplinary actions. Effective reward allocation may require a valid PA which ranks employees according to a quantifiable scoring system. Sufficient variance in scores is esential to differentiate across performers. In allocating rewards, PAs must have credibility with employees. The same PA format must also be used for disciplinary action, which may range from warnings to termination. Thus, the documentation required for such decisions must also be facilitated by the PA format. With the recent passage of Civil Service Reform Act and its provisions typing performance to merit pay and bonuses, the importance of PAs in the public sector has been greatly heightened.

PAs must be designed to facilitate the validation of selection techniques. The process requires, in general terms and at a minimum, measures of employee output or job-related dimensions that tap the behavioral domain of the job analysis, the facilitation of inter-rater reliability measures, professional and objective administration of the PA and continual rater observation of ratee performance.[1]

The identification of promotion potential requires that job-related PAs have several dimensions in the incumbent's

Reprinted from "Integrating Behaviorally-Based and Effectiveness-Based Methods" in the July, 1979 issue of *Personnel Administrator,* copyright, 1979, the American Society of Personnel Administration, 30 Park Drive, Berea, Ohio 44017.

[1]See "Uniform Guidelines on Employee Selection Procedures," *Federal Register,* December 30, 1977; D. B. Schneier, "The Impact of EEO Legislation on Performance Appraisal," *Personnel,* 1978, 55 (4), 24–34.

job, the same, or similar to, the job to which the incumbent may be promoted. This indicates the incumbent's ability to assume increasingly difficult assignments. The PA must also rank ratees comparatively, measure the contribution to departmental objectives and perhaps capture a ratee's career aspirations and long-term goals.

The final but perhaps most important PA objective is its accuracy in measuring performance. In some ways, it could be conceived as essential for meeting the PA objectives mentioned above. The issues of concern here would include PA formats which minimize rater response set errors (e.g., leniency, restriction of range, halo), those which agree with other measures of performance using alternative formats (e.g., direct indices such as salary or number of promotions), those which obtain reliability across raters, those which have the flexibility to reflect changes in the job environment and those possessing credibility with raters such that they complete the format seriously.

Thus, there are several criteria which PAs should meet to be fully operational. But which types of formats—those which measure worker behavior or those which measure the outcomes of that behavior—are more effective? No simple answer is available, but the utility of various types of behavior-based formats can best be ascertained by comparing them against the PA objectives identified above.

COMPARISON OF FORMATS

Global ratings. The first PA format alternative is a uni-dimensional, global rating which uses a rater's overall estimate of performance without distinguishing between critical job elements or dimensions. There are numerous problems in the use of uni-dimensional formats and when compared to the six PA objectives described above, they generally fall far short (see Figure 2). Uni-dimensional PA formats are also questionable as measures of performance (i.e., criteria) from a legal standpoint because they are not based on job analysis and thus are not job-related.

Trait-based scales. There are numerous multi-dimensional (or graphic) approaches to measuring performance. They are more useful than global scales because they recognize that job performance consists of separate dimensions, or job elements. The first of these is the familiar trait-based scale using dimensions such as loyalty, dependability, etc. Other dimensions traditionally found on these formats are cooperation, initiative and self-confidence. There are problems in the use of trait-based scales centering around potential ambiguity and subjectivity. That is, specifically what is meant by "lack of cooperation?" Thus, many trait-based scales are generally evaluated as only poor to fair relative to PA objectives. Further, and perhaps most important, trait-based scales are typically not sufficiently job-related or based on a thorough job analysis. Thus an organization's vulnerability to Equal Employment Opportunity (EEO) litigation is not alleviated.

Behavior-based scales. A significant step beyond global and trait-based scales. These are based upon a job analysis and attempt to determine what an employee actually *does* at work. A behavior-based scale provides specific feedback to employees because it is based on the activities required of the job. It captures specific information across employees for reward allocation and about each employee specifically in the assessment of training needs because it identifies the activities (dimensions) in which an employee may be deficient. For promotion potential, a dimension-based scale can certainly be useful because it may specify the kinds of behaviors incumbents are to demonstrate in their present jobs. Performance on these dimensions can then be compared to the dimensions required in the next job level (for which the employee is a promotion candidate). Behavior-based scales are often seen as more accurate than the previous two PA formats because of their job-relatedness and specificity. Thus we can expect less rater error and higher interrater agreement (and/or reliability). Finally, because dimension-based scales can meet the legal requirements for criterion measure, these certainly can be an improvement for the validation of selection procedures.

The major drawback with dimension-based scales is that although they provide specification of the particular activities of an employee, the scale points are of limited use if they are only numerically and/or adjective-anchored. They provide little specific feedback on what behavior led to the particular rating given, even though the area of performance deficiency has been identified. Thus, a dimension-based PA may be deficient in assessing an employee's specific behaviors within the job dimensions since only adjective or numerical anchors are used.

Behavioral expectation scales or *behaviorally-anchored rating scales (BARS)* are also dimensional scales.[2] The scale points are behavioral statements illustrating various degrees of performance, not merely adjectives or numbers. Thus, BARS are far more specific in terms of identifying employee behavior relative to performance on a specific job dimension. These are also more sophisticated than dimension-based formats and require more time to develop.

Behavior-based scales seem to provide excellent feedback to employees in specifying not only what activities employees are to engage in, but also the behaviors a rater perceives that a ratee has demonstrated during the per-

[2]The development and utility of BARS is the subject of Part II of this series of three articles. See also C. E. Schneier and R. W. Beatty, *Personnel Administration Today* (Reading, Massachusetts: Addison-Wesley, 1978) and S. J. Carroll and C. E. Schneier, *Performance Appraisal* (Goodyear Publishing Company, forthcoming).

FIGURE 1
Objectives of Performance Appraisal Systems

1 *Feedback/development requires:*	2 *Assessing training needs/requires:*	3 *Identifying promotion potential requires:*
Specifying behavioral terminology on the format. Setting behavioral targets for ratees to work toward. Job-related, problem-solving performance review which ends with a plan for performance improvement. Reducing ambiguity/anxiety of ratees regarding job performance required and expected by raters/organization.	Specifying deficiencies in behavioral terms. Rating on all relevant job dimensions. Identifying motivation/attitude and environmental conditions as causes of inadequate performance.	Job-related criteria. Job dimensions dealing with ability to assume increasingly difficult assignments built into the form. Ability to rank ratees comparatively. Measuring of contribution to organization/department objectives. Assessing of ratee's career aspirations and long-range goals.

formance period. In fact, performance improvement has been demonstrated through the use of behavior-based systems.[3]

Effectiveness-based systems. Another multi-dimensional system is results, or effectiveness, based scaling. Effectiveness-based scales attempt to provide "objective" indicators for levels of performance and are, of course, typically called Management by Objectives (MBO) systems.[4] Although it is a multi-dimensional approach in that there are often many objectives which are to be accomplished, effectiveness-based scaling is unique in that what it provides is a measure of an employee's *contribution,* not an employee's *activities or behaviors.*

Ratees evaluated with effectiveness-based scaling are being evaluated not on what they *do* but what they *produce;* not on how they spend their time, but what they contribute. This is an important difference and a major shortcoming of the previously discussed PA approaches. Obviously, it is difficult to develop specific indicators of employee contribution, but it can be done for many jobs. It is accomplished with more ease in lower level jobs and entry-level jobs within an organization than in higher level jobs.

Thus, effectiveness-based scales offer something that is critical and often overlooked in the assessment of performance appraisals. MBO systems are often used to measure unit productivity to which a manager presumably makes a contribution.

WHAT ARE THE CAUSES OF PROBLEMS?

Regardless of what format is used, problems can deter PA system effectiveness. The cause of the ineffectiveness of any particular PA system is a function of many variables, acting singly or in groups, which characterize the job, organizational setting and users. However, most often specific causes are located within the following broad problem categories: human judgment, raters, criteria and formats, organization policy, legal requirements and Equal Employment Opportunity (EEO) legislation and inflexibility. Each of these six broad categories contains several possible sources of PA problems (see Figure 3), discussed briefly below.

Problems in a PA system ultimately can only be judged as to their degree of severity and dysfunctional consequences in light of the original objectives developed for each system. For example, a PA system may sacrifice some degree of applicability across job-type (and would, possibly, have higher developmental costs) in order to have a greater amount and specificity of information about performance available to a certain group of ratees. Hence, it may have greater ability to pinpoint performance deficiencies and thus reduce costs of unnecessary training programs. If the objectives of a PA system are predetermined and prioritized, the system can be designed to make such trade-offs rationally and at minimal cost. Further, after PA design and implementation, problems diagnosed can be judged as to seriousness and corrective action planned in light of objectives. This relationship between PA objectives and both the design and revision of PA systems, while considering various PA problems, is emphasized in the discussion to follow.

---

[3] R. W. Beatty, C. E. Schneier and J. R. Beatty, "An Empirical Investigation of Perceptions of Ratee Behavior Frequency and Ratee Behavior Change Using Behavioral Expectation Scales (BES)," *Personnel Psychology,* 1977, 30, 647–658.

[4] See S. J. Carroll and H. Tosi, *Management by Objective* (New York: Macmillan, 1973).

4 *Rewards allocation requires:*	5 *Validation of selection techniques requires:*	6 *Measurement accuracy requires:*
Ability to rank order ratees or results in quantifiable, performance scores. Facilitating a variance or spread of scores to discriminate between good, bad, fair, etc., ratees. Measuring contributions to organization/department objectives. Accuracy and credibility with employees.	Job relatedness and a comprehensive list of dimensions tapping the behavioral domain of the job. Systematic job analysis to derive criteria. Assessing interrater reliability. Professional, objective administration of format. Continual observation of ratee performance by raters.	Reducing rater response set errors (e.g., leniency, restriction of range, halo). Agreeing with other performance measures not on the format (e.g., direct indices such as salary, number of promotions.) Reliability across multiple raters. Flexibility to reflect changes in job or environment. Job-related criteria. Commitment of raters to observe ratee performance frequently and complete format seriously.

Problem no. 1: Human judgment. A fundamental source of problems in PA is the *subjectivity and individuality* which accompanies the human judgment process. Individual differences among people influence their attitudes, values, perceptions, behavior and judgment, a fact as true in the PA setting as it is in all others. Intelligence, cognitive style, amount of education, age, sex and self-esteem are but a few of the individual level characteristics which have been found to influence the making of judgments of others. The expectations raters' supervisors hold for them, as well as a rater's own level of job performance and competence, have also been found to effect ratings.[5]

All of these factors, however, act in an implicit manner. They reflect "honest" or legitimate differences in personality, background or ability between participants in PA which influence their perception—their view of reality—and thus perceptions of the behavior of ratees. While these individual differences typically do not result in deliberate attempts to bias or prejudice ratings, their result on PA (e.g., inaccuracies) is similar.

Besides these *unintentional* PA errors resulting from individual differences, are those overt, deliberate attempts to distort PAs based upon personal prejudices and biases against others of a certain religion, national origin, race, sex, age, political ideology, etc. The result can be the setting of different performance standards for two people performing the same job or the distorting of PA results upward or downward to correspond to one's prejudices. Even when performance criteria are quantifiable and visible, figures

[5]See e.g., C. E. Schneier, "The Psychometric Characteristics and Operational Utility of Behavioral Expectation Scales (BES): A Cognitive Reinterpretation," *Journal of Applied Psychology,* 1977, 62, 541–548.

FIGURE 2
Generalized Evaluation of PA Formats Compared to PA Objectives

Objective / *Format*	*Feedback/ development*	*Assessing training needs*	*Identificatoin of promotion potential*	*Reward allocation*	*Selection system validation*	*Measurement accuracy*
Global	Poor	Poor	Poor to Fair	Poor	Poor	Poor
Trait-based	Poor	Poor	Poor to Fair	Poor to Fair	Poor to Fair	Poor to Fair
Behavior-based (if behaviorally-anchored)	Very Good to Excellent	Very Good	Very Good	Very Good	Very Good to Excellent	Good
Effectiveness-based	Fair to Good	Fair to Good	Fair to Good	Very Good to Excellent	Fair to Good	Very Good to Excellent

FIGURE 3
Sources of Problems in Appraisal Systems

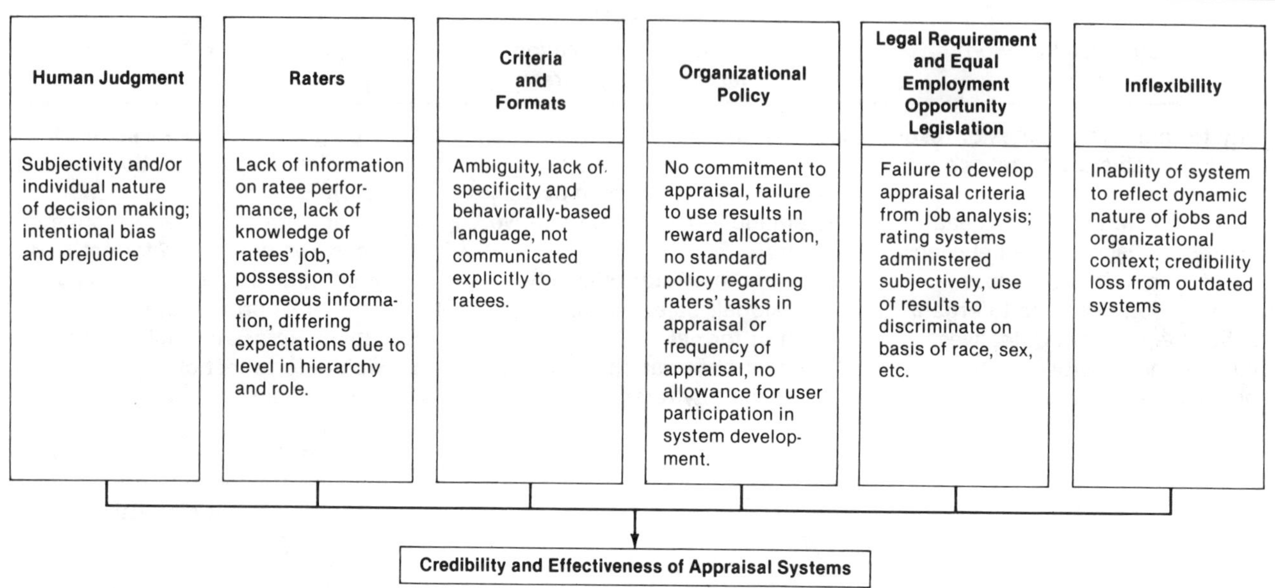

can be distorted or interpreted erroneously by such judgmental factors as perceived amount of effort or initiative and hence intentional bias still enter the process.

Problem no. 2: Raters. PA problems stem from conscientious raters who possess *inadequate and/or erroneous information* about ratee performance. Many supervisors, due to their own job duties which may physically separate them from their subordinate ratees, are able to observe ratee performance too infrequently to accurately judge typical performance over a long period. But non-representative sampling or allowing a typical positive or negative performance occurring during their infrequent observation periods to bias their judgments of performance over the entire period can lead to inaccurate appraisals.

In addition, members of each hierarchical level within an organization may view a ratee's performance from a different vantage point or hold differing expectations for desired performance based upon their roles.[6] Thus a ratee's supervisor may be in an excellent position to judge the ratee's technical competence, but not his or her ability to effectively interact with others. Peer raters may possess the best information regarding a ratee's interpersonal effectiveness. Supervisors of ratees, as critics and evaluators of their subordinates, typically judge performance more harshly than do job incumbents themselves.

Problem no. 3: Criteria and PA formats. The identification of specific, consistent, performance criteria is the first objective of a PA system, as discussed earlier. The easiest way to assure that a ratee's performance can be evaluated based upon only the whim of a rater is of course to keep the criteria ambiguous and/or secret, to change them capriciously, or never to develop them at all! As discussed above, each type of appraisal format has advantages and disadvantages relative to this issue of defining the criteria against which to base evaluations. The overall objective, of course, is to develop a format which identifies and defines the criteria in explicit, concrete terms.

Problem no. 4: Organizational policy. Problems in PA systems arise from the relationship between organizational policies regarding performance, promotion, merit raises and other decisions and the uses for which PA results are intended. If these types of decisions are actually to be made on the basis of performance, rather than on the basis of seniority or other criteria, results of a PA obviously assume a great deal of importance. Here problems arise when PA formats are ambiguous, criteria are not communicated to raters and ratees and/or if each of several degrees of performance (e.g., good, fair, etc.) do not have observable, behavioral referents.

For example, if a supervisor (rater) is given the authority to set merit raises for a group of subordinates (ratees) and the PA format which is used to measure performance is of the global type involving overall ranking, the supervisor can easily feel trapped. Of course, the supervisor might have a definite and accurate overall impression as to the relative performance of his or her ratees and can easily discriminate between the excellent and average performers. But if the top performers are given merit raises and the others are not, the supervisor needs a rationale for this action to give to those who were denied the merit raise. The global

[6]See C. E. Schneier and R. W. Beatty, "The Influence of Role Prescriptions on the Performance Appraisal Process," *Academy of Management Journal*, 1978, 21, 129–134.

PA format provides little help since it does not specify and define the exact criteria used in PA or the different levels of performance within each criterion. To develop a formal, written rationale for each rating may not only be seen as too bothersome for many raters but they may find it difficult to articulate the exact criteria to ratees. The result is often that either extreme leniency is used on many ratings or that all ratees are rated about the same and hence each receives a smaller merit raise. Thus, expediency rather than discriminability between good and poor performers characterizes the PA system and its credibility is destroyed.

Problem no. 5: Legal requirements and Equal Employment Opportunity (EEO) legislation. The risk of precipitating charges of discrimination as a result of policy decisions based upon PA results is now itself a serious cause of problems in PA systems. The ramifications of subjective, unsubstantiated PAs can be devastating to an organization. Recently, through several pieces of legislation, court decisions and guidelines of various federal agencies, the issue of discrimination in employment as a result of PAs has become more visible and spelled out in more detail than ever before.[7]

Organizations must present PA forms and any instructions given to raters as part of the evidence for the validity of such selection techniques as employment tests. Thus, the use of, for example, an application blank, would be judged acceptable in certain situations only if answers to particular items on the blank were found to correlate highly with the probability of future job "success" of workers in the job. Job "success" is demonstrated typically by results of a PA system. The PA system is thus open to scrutiny by the courts and must therefore be thorough and as bias-free as possible.

Violation of civil rights legislation can also come from the use of PAs directly in promotion decisions. The following excerpts from discussions of recent court cases involving PAs illustrate the potential consequences of an inadequate system.

The court found the following as a basis for discrimination: Recommendations by foremen were based on standards which were vague and subjective and were made without written instructions concerning qualifications necessary for promotion... one company was required to offer training programs to upgrade personnel, to provide foremen with written instructions delineating objective criteria.... The other company was ordered to post announcements of pre-foremen training classes, to post notices of qualifications required for salaried positions....

Using performance ratings for determining personnel layoffs was found to be in violation of Title VII of the Civil Rights Act when an employer failed to validate the appraisal methods according to EEOC guidelines. The evaluations were judged invalid because they were based on subjective observations (two of three evaluators did not observe the employee on a daily basis), evaluations were not administered and scored under controlled and standardized conditions.... The courts ordered the company to reinstate the employees with nominal back pay and required the company not to use performance ratings until they had been validated.[8]

Problem no. 6: Inflexibility. The final cause of problems in PA systems is the dynamic nature of jobs and job performance and the static nature of any written PA document typically developed several months before it is to be used. As job responsibilities, duties, requirements and job environments change over time, a PA format may become obsolete before it is even used! Further, as workers' performance levels change over time, perhaps due to training and experience, the standards set in PA formats may be too low, geared only for newer workers. Even the same jobs within classes are not identical.

One solution is, of course, to continually develop new PA formats as all of the above factors change and to develop separate PA formats for each and every position. But this solution is an economic impossibility. A solution often used by organizations is to develop a few categories of formats—perhaps one format for operating level workers, one for clerical workers, one for technical workers, and one for managers. A reasonable solution? Yes, provided raters are knowledgeable, competent, use identical standards, observe performance equally, are generally bias-free and are provided with specific, detailed criteria. But in the all too often instances when the "ideal" rater is unavailable, PA formats applicable across job types may lead to subjectivity and possibly to litigation for discrimination.

The view of PA systems presented above is, admittedly, problematic. Yet it is a realistic one as many organizations find their appraisal system to be the source of continual problems. As discussed, no system is capable of alleviating all appraisal problems completely. Yet there are a few things which can be done to enhance a system's effectiveness.

The first way to improve appraisal systems is to recognize that the appraisal process entails far more than measurement and the use of a form. It also includes observation and identification of performance, as well as development of performance. As discussed, PA systems have several objectives. They must be developed in light of both the trade-off between these objectives and the potential problem sources in appraisal.

The second mechanism for improved appraisal is to integrate the best aspects of the various formats. Behavior-

[7]See W. H. Holley and H. S. Feild, "Performance Appraisal and the Law," *Labor Law Journal*, July, 1975, 423–429; "Uniform Guidelines on Employee Selection Procedures," op. cit.; C. E. Schneier, "Psychometric Characteristics."

[8]Holley and Feild, "Performance Appraisal and the Law," pp. 427–428.

based systems, such as Behaviorally-Anchored Rating Scales (BARS), specify criteria in very concrete terms to improve accuracy, provide detailed feedback to ratees and help comply with legal requirements due to the job-relatedness of criteria. Effectiveness-based systems, such as Management by Objectives (MBO) are very popular due to their ability to measure and quantify results, redirect effort to important tasks and allow for ratee participation in goal-setting.

SOURCES SECTION TWO

DEFINING PERFORMANCE AND DEVELOPING CRITERIA

THE PURPOSES OF MEASURING PERFORMANCE

Why Worry About Accurate Measures?

by Lloyd S. Baird

- Describes from a managerial and legal perspective why valid measures are important.
- Lists characteristics of good criteria.
- Analyzes the common reasons people give for not having good measures of performance.

DEVELOPING MEASURES

Developing Performance Measures Which Are Consistent with the Mission of the Organization

by Richard Henderson

- Shows how the mission of the organization is translated into productive employee work effort.
- Describes why performance appraisal is the critical component necessary to translate organization mission into productive employee work effort.

Essentials of Criterion Development

by Wayne Cascio

- Describes the steps for developing performance criteria.
- Lists characteristics which criteria should have.
- Answers the question "Should one or many criteria be used?"

THE LIMITATIONS OF QUANTITATIVE MEASURES

Humanistic Numbers

by John E. Jones

- Explains why quantitative numbers may not be enough to measure and describe people.
- Suggests some activities for training programs to demonstrate the uses and limitations of numbers.

Why Worry About Accurate Measures?

by Lloyd S. Baird

The ultimate management practice would be to know what needs to be done and to have perfectly accurate measures of everything that is happening. In reality, we rarely have perfectly accurate measures but operate at various levels of ignorance, each involving different types of risks and costs. Let us review the levels of ignorance and then see how they affect our ability to manage.

LEVEL 1: TOTAL DARKNESS

When we are in total darkness we don't know what is to be accomplished. At this level the manager and the subordinates can look very busy and may even accomplish something. The problem is, of course, that they don't know when, how, or what they've accomplished or how to change and improve their performance.

LEVEL 2: GOOD OBJECTIVES BUT BAD MEASURES

At this level, we know where we would like to go but are using inaccurate measures of progress. From a management perspective, this is often worse than not knowing what is to be accomplished. We may know what should be done and be working towards objectives, but our measures of progress are inaccurate. When these measures indicate that our efforts are not paying off, we make changes and focus our efforts in different directions. The measures may then indicate performance is up but when we look around, we know that just isn't true. Everything else indicates that real problems exist. Because our measures of performance are inaccurate, our energies have not been directed properly. In fact, the inaccurate measures focus all of our efforts away from performance. We would have been better off without any measures. At least then some of our random behavior might have proven beneficial.

LEVEL 3: I THINK I WANT TO GO THERE

The third level of ignorance is to know where we would like to go and to have a good measure of progress, while being a little unsure whether the specified goal is exactly where we want to go because we have never been there before. This is a much more acceptable way to operate and, in reality, is where we are most of the time. We have a goal, but there is really no way to tell whether this goal is exactly what we want until we reach it. So we start off. As we progress, we modify our approach based on what is happening.

LEVEL 4: EVERYTHING WORKS

This is a level that few ever reach. We know where we want to go and have accurate measures of our progress. In this case, all of our energies can be directed towards the proper results. This is the ideal—an ideal that is rarely reached. Few of us are ever absolutely certain what we want to accomplish. We never quite have perfectly accurate measures of our progress. Any measure, by its very nature, must be a summary of what is being done and accomplished. We couldn't possibly use measures that include everything in detail. They would be far too complex and involved to use in decision making. We need summaries of what is happening, and whenever information is summarized, something must be left out. It is probably more important that we continually evaluate the measures we are using and revise them when necessary than that we try to find the ultimate in valid and sophisticated measures. We try to dispel as much ignorance as possible and then take some risks.

WHY WORRY ABOUT ACCURATE MEASURES: THE MANAGERIAL PERSPECTIVE

It should be obvious from the above discussion that it is important to have as much accurate information as possible. Without it, management will make decisions that misdirect and obstruct good performance. To appreciate how crucial it is to have accurate measures, consider the impact that having poor measures would have at each stage of the human resource cycle (see Figure 1).

Selection

Hiring is the first step in the human resource cycle. This can either be done randomly or be based on what needs to be accomplished. The desired results become the basis for identifying the appropriate "predictors," i.e. the measures of individual characteristics such as skills, attitudes, behaviors, etc. that have proven to lead to high job performance. These predictors become the basis for selection decisions. If the

This article was prepared especially for this book.

FIGURE 1
The Human Resource Cycle

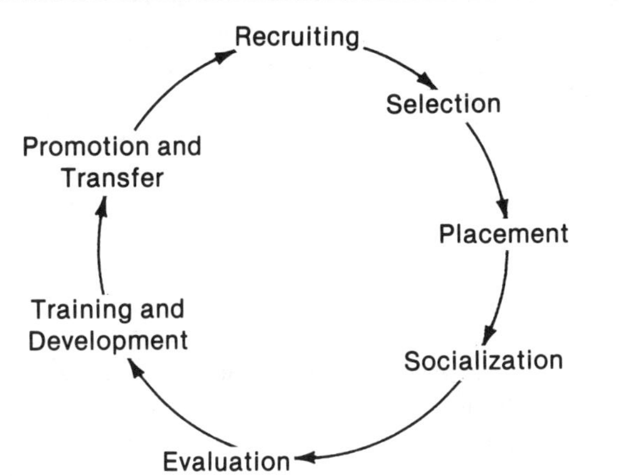

measures of performance are wrong, the predictors will be wrong, and the wrong people will be hired.

Placement

After being hired, employees are placed on a particular job and given a set of responsibilities. It is logical to suggest that employees be placed according to their potential to perform on a particular job. No amount of effort on the part of the employee will make up for a total lack of ability. Thus, placement decisions should be based on an understanding of the requirements of the job and how well the employees' abilities match them.

Socialization

When people are placed on jobs they have to learn what is expected of them. They have to learn the formal and informal rules of conduct. These rules should relate to productivity. Without appropriate goals and ways of measuring progress towards them, management asks the employee to "guess what we want" or, worse yet, tells the employee "We don't know what we want, but go do something and bring it back and then we will decide if we like it."

Evaluation

After people start working on a job, their progress has to be monitored and evaluated. Evaluation makes it possible to distribute rewards, establish training programs, make corrections, etc. Performance is best evaluated in relation to some pre-established definition of desired results. How we are doing is best determined by comparing it with what we want to achieve. It is senseless for employees to work toward one objective while being evaluated in terms of a totally different objective. Yet, this is exactly what often seems to happen. In the day-to-day work of organizations, managers are primarily concerned with concrete accomplishments such as sales, proposals, or contracts. Yet when the time comes for the yearly performance evaluation, managers will use measures related to something totally different, such as personal traits of initiative, promptness, or decorum.

Training and Development

If performance is deficient, one way to approach the problem is to establish training and development programs. The skills and behaviors dealt with in these programs should be determined by what is supposed to be accomplished on the job. They should be set up to help employees acquire skills and behaviors which will most likely lead to higher performance. Without the proper criteria, training will focus on the wrong skills.

Promotion and Transfer

Eventually performance may be so good that employees are promoted. Alternatively, performance on the job may be poor because the employees' skills don't match the demands of the job. These employees should be transferred to other jobs where they can perform better. If performance is poor because the employees refuse to work, dismissal may be the solution. Notice that each of these decisions has an explicit reference to performance, and that the measure of performance is the basis of the decision. If invalid measures are used, something other than performance will decide who will move and who will stay. Predictably, performance itself must suffer because some of the good performers will be moved for reasons other than performance.

Recruiting

Promotions and transfers create vacancies for which new employees must be recruited either internally or externally. If valid definitions and measures of good performance have been developed, they can be used to select new employees. Performance becomes the basis for identifying and recruiting people for the job.

WHY WORRY ABOUT VALID MEASURES: THE LEGAL PERSPECTIVE

Much of the impetus for developing accurate performance measures has come from court decisions about race and sex discrimination. The initial intent of the Equal Employment Opportunity Commission's (EEOC) *Guidelines on Em-*

ployee Selection Procedures and the Office of Federal Contract Compliance's (OFCC) *Order on Employee Testing and Other Selection Procedures* was to eliminate discrimination in the selection of employees. The basic purpose of both the EEOC and the OFCC was to insure that all tests (i.e. formal, scored, quantified, or standardized techniques of assessing job suitability) were accurate measures of potential job performance.

The courts very quickly went beyond this narrow concern for the use of performance measures only in selection decisions. They expanded the applicability of discrimination legislation to cases that went to the very heart of management practices. They expanded in two directions. First they became concerned about the measures themselves. If selection decisions were based on how well the person was expected to perform in the future, the court argued that the organization should have a good definition and measure of what future performance was expected. Unfortunately, too often the organization had only a supervisor's rating of performance based on a subjective trait scale, and, for all practical purposes, these subjective trait scales only measure how much the supervisor likes a subordinate or job candidates. The courts then asked "Are supervisor ratings actually ratings of performance and good descriptions of what a person is expected to do?" The answer was often, no. In their rulings the courts suggested that we ought to find out whether measures are accurate reflections of performance before they are used as the sole basis for decision making.

Second, the courts *broadened* their definition of a selection decision to include any decision that might affect the future employment status of an individual. This definition included the use of any formal or informal device for evaluating employees for such purposes as layoffs, transfers, or promotions. This quite clearly includes decisions made at all stages of the performance process. The following examples illustrate how the courts have gradually broadened their concern for accurate measures.

Griggs v. *The Duke Power Company* is perhaps the best example of the courts' initial interest in insuring that selection decisions be based on valid measures. In their decision the Supreme Court upheld the EEOC's view that employers who demand certain skills, educational level, or test scores must be able to demonstrate conclusively that the skills required are in fact needed on the job. If test scores are to be used, the employer must also demonstrate that the tests reliably measure the skills in question. The Duke Power Company had required applicants for certain jobs to have a high school diploma and to score above a certain level on an aptitude test. The tests were impartially administered but resulted in the hiring of very few blacks. The company argued that their intent was to raise the overall quality of the work force by using the education requirement and the aptitude test. It could not, however, demonstrate that the tests or the diploma had any direct relationship to the jobs being performed. The court ruled that these requirements had to be dropped and said that the employer had the burden of "showing that any given requirement had a manifest relationship to the employment in question."

Since then the courts have gradually included most personnel decisions in their rulings. When the Baltimore City Council could not verify that the efficiency rating system or the use of seniority credits for promotion were job related, it was found in violation of the equal protection clause of the Fourteenth Amendment. In the case of *Baxter* v. *Savannah Sugar Refining Company,* the courts found that promotions and transfers discriminated unjustly against minority employees. Recommendations by the company's foreman were based on standards which were vague and subjective "and were made without written instructions concerning qualifications necessary for promotion." In *Brito* et al. v. *Zia Company,* the use of performance ratings for determining personnel layoffs was found to be in violation of Title VII of the Civil Rights Act because they were based on subjective observations and were not administered and scored under controlled and standardized conditions.

There have been other court decisions that focused more specifically on the accuracy of the performance measures. The question of the validity of performance appraisals as criteria for personnel decisions was the basis of *Albermarle Paper Company* v. *Moody.* The case questioned the subjectivity of the company's performance ratings and the lack of any kind of job analysis as a basis for the ratings. The court found that employees were rated against a vague standard which was open to each supervisor's interpretation and that they had been ranked against one another even though their jobs were not comparable. The company had made no attempt to analyze each job and determine what constituted good and bad performance. The court stated, "There is no way of knowing precisely what were the criteria for job performance the supervisors were considering; whether, indeed, any of the supervisors actually applied a focused and stable body of criteria of any kind." Further, they said there is "no way to determine whether the criteria actually considered were sufficiently related to the company's legitimate interest in job-specific ability to justify a testing system with a racially discriminating impact."

The courts are now saying that if measures are used as decision-making tools for any personnel decisions and if the results have the potential to affect a protected group (e.g. minorities, the aged, or women) adversely, then the organization must justify the use of these measures. Also, if any type of test is used to rate accomplishments, the tests must be proven to be real measures of what has been done. The guidelines for validation established by the EEOC and the OFCC have set forth certain minimum standards for criteria. The major requirement is that the criteria "must represent major or critical work behavior as revealed by careful job analysis." For example, in *Albermarle Paper Company* v. *Moody,* the Supreme Court focused on the lack of job analysis and found that the ratings were being applied arbitrarily. Albermarle was using supervisors' subjective performance appraisals and had made no attempt to analyze the jobs to determine what type of job skills were required or what results were expected.

Another requirement specified by the guidelines is that the tests "must be administered and scored under controlled and standardized conditions." Standardization is a basic minimum requirement in testing. Without standardization it is hard to tell whether the scores obtained are measures of the individual being tested or simple indications of the methods of scoring and administering the test. In *Wade* v. *Mississippi Cooperative Extension Service,* a U.S. District Court found that the criteria used to appraise job performance unjustly discriminated against blacks. In its decision, the court stated that a major cause of this discrimination was the subjective supervisory evaluations, which had not been shown to be a measure of expected job accomplishment and which were not standardized. Another problem the court noted was the lack of a standard format for observing performance. A supervisor could base his or her evaluations on direct observation or on previous reports and subjective reactions to the subordinate's performance.

In its decision, the court stated that the so-called objective appraisal of job performance "is based upon scores received by subordinates rated by supervisors on an evaluation instrument according to a number of factors. For example, a substantial portion of the evaluation rating relates to such general characteristics as leadership, public acceptance, attitude toward people, appearance and grooming, personal conduct, outlook on life, ethical habits, resourcefulness, capacity for growth, mental alertness, and loyalty to organization. As may be readily observed, these are traits that are susceptible to partiality and to the personal taste, whim, or fancy of the evaluator. Thus, we must view these factors as presently utilized to be patently subjective in form and obviously susceptible to completely subjective treatment."

There have been other similar cases, for instance, *Row* v. *General Motors Corporation* in which the courts have focused on the standardization of performance criteria. In most cases, the courts have found that the "evaluations were based on the best judgments and opinions... but not on any identifiable criteria based on quality or quantity of work or specific performance that were supported by some kind of record," and that the tests (based on these criteria) were not "administered and scored under controlled and standardized conditions."

To summarize the results of these court cases, Thompson, Klasson and Lubben (1979) suggest that a performance appraisal process should have the following characteristics in order to meet the legal requirements. Note how closely they follow the proper steps for performance management.

1. The overall appraisal process should be formalized, standardized, and made as objective as possible.
2. The performance appraisal system should be as job-related as possible.
3. A thorough, formal job analysis for all employment positions being rated should be completed.
4. Although useful, subjective supervisory ratings should be considered as only one component of the overall evaluation process.
5. Evaluators should be adequately trained in the use of appraisal techniques that employ written qualification criteria for promotion or transfer decisions.
6. Evaluators should have substantial daily contact with the employee being evaluated.
7. If the appraisal involves various measures of performance, the weight of each measure in relation to the overall assessment should be fixed.
8. Opportunities for promotion or transfer should be posted and the information made available to all interested individuals.
9. An employee-initiated promotion/transfer procedure should be established that does not require the immediate supervisor's recommendation.
10. Whenever possible, the appraisal should be conducted by more than one evaluator. All such evaluations should be conducted independently.
11. The administration and scoring of the performance appraisal should be standardized and controlled.

IF IT IS SO IMPORTANT, WHY ISN'T IT DONE?

From both a managerial and legal perspective it is important to have accurate measures. That is the theory, what has been the practice?

As Guion (1961) points out, deciding what measures to use and how to collect them usually involves a series of judgments on the part of the personnel specialist (notice it's usually the personnel worker and not the manager), which culminates in the decision to use someone else's judgment (usually the superior's subjective performance appraisal). Not only have measures tended to be subjective, but as Wernimont and Campbell (1976) suggest, they have been oriented towards such personal characteristics as loyalty or creativity, instead of toward what the worker actually does or accomplishes.

There are important reasons for developing and using valid criteria. But if it's so important, why aren't more managers doing it? Let's look at some of the reasons people give for not developing and using valid performance criteria.

It Is Not Worth the Time, Nobody Will Use Them Anyway. Decisions Will Still Be Made Based on Who You Know and Who Likes You.

This, unfortunately, is too often the case. Good performance measures are not worth developing if they will not be used, but it is a fallacy to think that because good measures have not been developed, people are not using some sort of performance measurement in decision making. Of course they are; they have to use something to help make decisions. They probably use very subjective, ill-defined measures based on personal preference. Such measures will have just as much effect on what employees do as will any other measures. They will start orienting their actions towards them, their feelings of success will be determined by them, and they will be concerned about how the organization's rewards are related to them.

The question, then, is not "Why don't people use measures of performance in their decision making?" It is "Why don't they use measures of performance that are valuable to the organization and to the individual?" Here we get into a vicious circle. Valid measures are not used because they're not available. They are not available because they are not used. Some managers have not had the experience of having clear goals to work towards and good criteria to help them evaluate their employees. Those who have, don't have to be convinced of their value. Those who haven't, often have to be coaxed, cajoled, or forced into accepting them.

Another reason good performance criteria aren't used is that they are often not useful. Sometimes they are so complex that no one can understand or use them. Bellows (1954) and Tiffin and McCormick (1965) have developed a number of characteristics of useful criteria. Figure 2 lists and describes some of them. Some of these characteristics, such as reliable and free from bias, are statistical properties which would be of interest to the personnel psychologist who works with statistical evaluations. Others, such as reasonable in cost and useable, will determine whether the criteria are likely to be accepted and used by the organization. A statistically sophisticated measure that is costly and not understood has very little chance of affecting the performance process. That is why it is critical to involve management and employees in the development of performance measures. Besides the fact that they are people who know the most about the jobs, they are definitely the ones who will determine whether the criteria will be used. The best way to get understandable, useable criteria is to have the relevant managers and workers involved in the development process.

FIGURE 2
Characteristics of Useable Criteria

Reliable.	Measures must be consistent. They shouldn't change based on who is doing them or when they are done.
Representative.	The total performance cannot be measured. Samples must be taken. In order to be useable, these performance samples have to be representative of the whole.
Selective.	The purpose of evaluation is to separate the good from the bad. Measures indicate performance; they must sift the high from the low performers.
Unbiased.	Measures should vary only with performance. They should not be affected by other factors in the situation such as sex, race, religion, or national origin.
Reasonable in cost.	Information about performance is like any other type of information—it costs money to gather and maintain. The increases in performance gained from using accurate measures should outweigh the cost of developing the measures.
Useable.	The measures must be appropriate to the purpose for which they will be used.

I Can't Develop Hard and Fast Measures; Too Much of My Work Is Subjective.

It is often the case that much of what a person does is "subjective," that is, based on perceptions and personal interpretations. Many of management's problems will be interpersonal, and dealing with such problems is very much a subjective process. We react and make decisions based on our perceptions, but just because they are subjective doesn't mean they can't be described, summarized, and discussed. They can, but it is threatening. Once subjective measures are made public, others can disagree and challenge the manager. Which means the manager will have to defend the measure, and if it is not defensible, change it. This process will, in the best case, improve the measure. The worst that can happen is that a bad measure is not improved. The manager may continue to use it, but at least everyone will understand what it is and how it is being used and react accordingly.

It's Too Expensive.

It really depends on where you want to put your money. Accurate measures are likely to increase costs and they will probably be more expensive than what was previously available. In fact, they can become quite expensive, particularly if the organization has never done any previous analysis of performance measurement.

Recruiting, training, and evaluation—in fact most of the costs associated with human resources administration—will probably increase also because using accurate measures is likely to mean that more applicants will be rejected. Consequently, more time and money will have to be spent on recruiting. More money will be spent on training because more relevant weakness will have been identified. Evaluations will become more expensive because they will require a thorough understanding of the job and conscientious attention to the employee's performance.

At each stage of the human resource cycle, costs are likely to increase. Usually, however, there will be more than enough benefit in terms of increased productivity to offset these costs.

Running an organization without the use of accurate measures is also expensive, because management must pay the hidden costs associated with loss of productivity, waste, and hiring of the wrong people. Accurate measures will reduce these costs but increase immediate out-of-pocket expenses. When managers say that using accurate measures is expensive, they are focusing on the immediate costs and disregarding the hidden costs of lost productivity.

My Job Is Too Complex to Talk About Any Type of Outcome. I'm Doing Well Just to Keep Up.

Many jobs are undoubtedly complex. They have to deal with multiple input and multiple output. The challenge in developing valid performance measures is to identify the data which best describe what is to be accomplished on the job. It is better to try to deal with that complexity than to ignore it and make serious mistakes in evaluating performance.

SO WHY DO IT?

All of the above reasons have been offered at one time or another and none stands up to scrutiny. Managers are responsible for performance; they can manage it only if they have an accurate way to measure it. Developing accurate, useable measures may be costly and time consuming, but the potential benefits are tremendous. Not only are accurate measures of performance good management practice, but you are legally responsible for decisions made using invalid measures.

REFERENCES

- *Albermarle Paper Company* v. *Moody,* 442 U.S. 405 (1975).
- *Baxter* v. *Savannah Sugar Refining Company,* 350 F. Supp. 139 (1972).
- Bellows, R.M. *Psychology of Personnel in Business and Industry.* 2d ed. Englewood Cliffs, N.J.: Prentice-Hall, 1954.
- *Brito* v. *Zia Company,* 478 F. 2d. 1200 (1973).
- *Griggs* v. *Duke Power Company,* 401 U.S. 424 (1971).
- Guion, R.M. "Criterion measurement and personnel judgments." In *Personnel Testing.* New York: McGraw-Hill, 1965.
- *Row* v. *General Motors Corporation,* 457 F. 2d. 348 (1972).
- Lubben, G.; Thompson, D.; Klasson, C. "Performance Appraisal: The Legal Implications of Title VII." *Personnel,* 1980.
- Tiffin, J., and McCormick, E.J. *Industrial Psychology* 5th ed. Englewood Cliffs, N.J.: Prentice-Hall, 1965.
- *Wade* v. *Mississippi Cooperative Extension Service,* 372 F. Supp. 126 (1974).
- Wernimont, P.F., and Campbell, J.P. "Signs, Samples, and Criteria." *Journal of Applied Psychology* 1968, 52:372–376.

Developing Performance Measures Which Are Consistent with the Mission of the Organization

by Richard Henderson

Understanding how the mission of the organization becomes translated into productive work effort requires a knowledge and appreciation of the relationship among desired results, means for accomplishing the results, work to be done, actual results achieved, and the recognition and rewarding of employee efforts. Figure 1 identifies the major activities involved in translating the missions of the organization into productive employee work effort. In this model, a top-down approach to the identification and setting of goals, a *bottom-up* development and integration of functional job activities, and a *lateral* process that links job responsibilities and duties to identified objectives and goals ties the mission of the organization to job requirements. This system uses performance appraisal as the control

From *Performance Appraisal* by Richard Henderson (Reston, Va.: Reston Publishing Co., 1980). Reprinted with permission of Reston Publishing Company, Inc., a Prentice Hall Company, 11480 Sunset Hills Road, Reston, Virginia.

device to compare desired results (objectives and goals established in the top-down process) with the results achieved as employees perform job requirements. Figure 2 describes the role of performance appraisal as a control device in the process described in Figure 1.

MISSION OF THE ORGANIZATION

The mission statements identify and describe the reason for existence of the organization—what it is all about. Progressing from the dreams of one or more individuals, products and services desired by society are identified and produced through a combination of capital and technical and human resources. A framework that allows individuals with different levels of knowledge and skills and divergent desires and interests to work together for the common good includes (1) philosophy statements that establish what the owner-leaders identify as acceptable and unacceptable behaviors of the organization and its members and (2) policies that emanate from the philosophy established by the leaders of the organization that further define acceptable and unacceptable workplace behavior.

In the philosophy and policy of the organization, there is normally much room for variations in acceptable employee workplace behavior. Limitations on behavior are established by standing operating procedures, regulations, rules, and work methods. All of these behavior-related guidelines influence the types of programs that the organization implements to provide its desired outputs. The guidelines and programs in turn influence the capital outlays required to operate the organization. Various types of budgets identify the money needed and how it is to be allocated among the various resource areas to fund the programs that make the identified and desired outputs possible. The mission statements direct the efforts of all employees toward successful completion of the intended purposes of the organization.

CASCADE OF GOALS

Anthony P. Raia used the term *cascade of goals* to describe a goal-setting process that starts with the formulation of long-range objectives and moves down the organizational hierarchy to where these objectives are redefined in concepts and terms appropriate to the involved level or functional area of the organization.[1] Similar to the processes described in both Figures 1 and 2, Raia's cascade of goals model is circular in that information flows from one level or stage of the model to the next, thereby permitting redirection or modification where and when necessary. The important point here is that *initially* the identification and setting of goals is a top-down approach that allows all employees an opportunity to know what the organization desires from them at their particular level. This activity becomes the first step toward identifying, describing, and obtaining work effort that supports the overall mission of the organization.

FUNCTIONAL ACTIVITY STATEMENTS

The next step in the process of translating mission statements to productive work effort is to interpret goals into employee work activities. With the division of labor, employees specialize their efforts in specific areas of responsibilities. From the newly hired, unskilled laborer to the experienced Chief Executive Officer, the organization expects specific kinds and levels of work to be performed. One approach for identifying the work to be accomplished is through a bottom-up identification and integration of responsibilities and duties.

Once goals have been subdivided into the smallest practical parts, it is possible to interpret these goals as work requirements for specific groups and to define the work group requirements as job activities. (The models developed in Figures 1 and 2 are theoretical and idealistic in nature and will seldom, if ever, be followed in a step-by-step sequence by an organization. In most cases, organizations that wish to use the concepts, ideas, and tools proposed and developed in this book are already in existence and have implemented many of the steps. Newly developed organizations that could use these models in totality frequently do not have the sophistication or knowledge to recognize the need for them. Most new organizations have enough trouble surviving, let alone looking at ways and means for improving management skills. These models should be of immense value for use as check lists by operating organizations to see where they are today, to identify possible trouble areas, and to develop programs that will overcome deficiencies that are blocking effective use of their available resources.)

With the bottom-up approach to the identification and description of job requirements, it becomes easier to see whether each job is carrying its own weight. Is the job necessary? Should there be any redistribution or realignment of job activities? Do the jobs of the work group support each other? Do the job requirements of the supervisor successfully integrate and coordinate the requirements of his or her subordinates? If this questioning process is continued through to the highest level of the organization, the answers should result in a description of the responsibilities and duties of the Chief Executive Officer that support and mesh with the mission of the organization.

---

[1]Anthony P. Raia, *Management by Objectives* (Glenview, IL: Scott, Foresman and Company, 1974), p. 29.

FIGURE 1
Determining, Describing, and Measuring Mission-Related Work Efforts

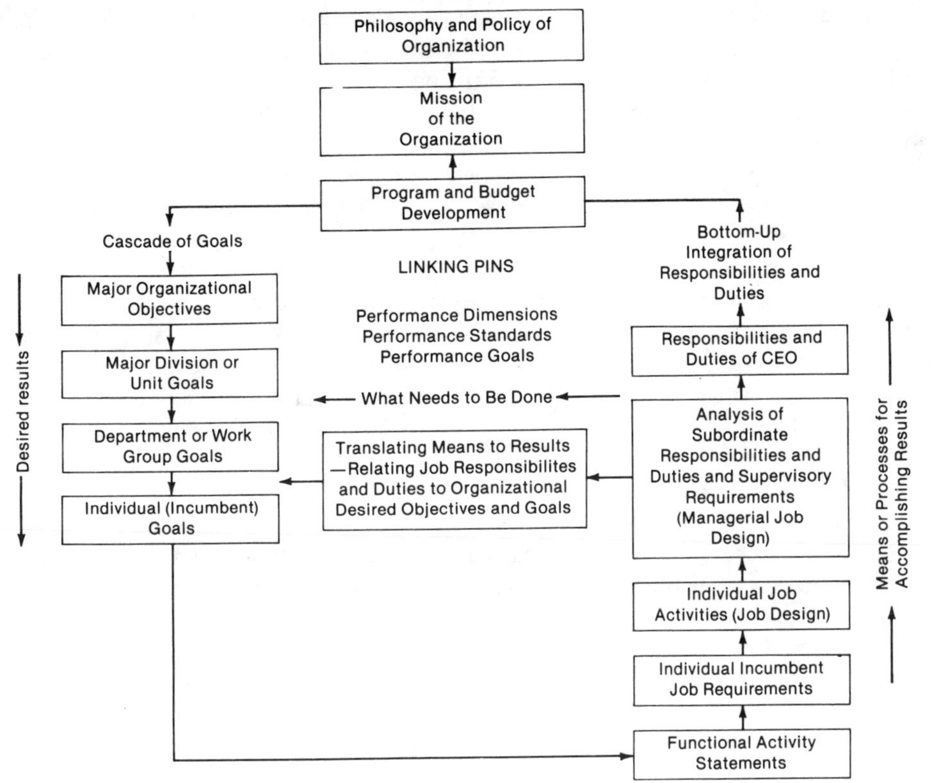

FIGURE 2
Tying Organizational Mission to Work Force Productivity

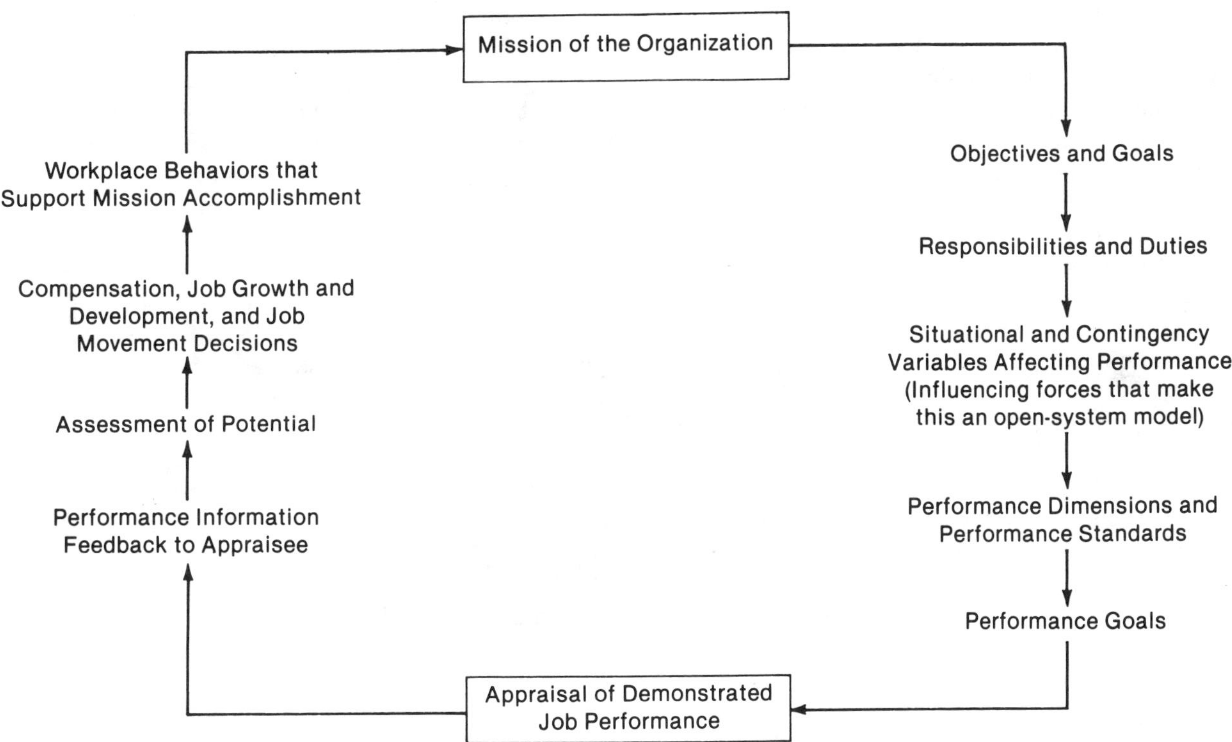

THE LINKING PINS

The circuitous route from mission statements through goals to responsibilities and duties and back to mission statements is insufficient in operating most complex organizations that hire hundreds, thousands, or tens of thousands of employees. Additional steps must be implemented to allow for more and improved integration between top-down set goals and bottom-up identified responsibilities and duties. This part of the process is frequently missing from many management planning, operating, and control systems.

Over the years, many specialists in workplace and job design have decried the need for extensive job analysis and the writing of soon-to-be obsolete job descriptions. These critics of job analysis and job descriptions say that the time that they consume and the costs involved are not worth the benefits gained. In my opinion these views are false; in fact, one of the principal goals of this book is to develop a sound foundation for justifying the expenditure of time and money on these efforts.

We will now investigate an approach available for linking responsibilities and duties to goals. This approach requires the maximum possible participation by affected employees and the commitment to the process by everyone in the organization. The transition stage involves the development of *performance dimensions,* the possible identification of *critical performance dimensions,* the establishment of *performance standards,* and the setting of *performance goals.* This stage also includes the identification of situational and contingency variables that can either assist or block goal achievement, and the appraisal of demonstrated workplace behavior.

Responsibilities and duties identify and describe the means or processes for accomplishing desired results (goals). Responsibilities and duties identify requirements void of unique individual qualities and the environmental factors (both internal and external to the organization) that influence the way an incumbent performs. For these reasons, procedures must be designed that recognize the impact of these critical areas.

Performance Dimensions

The transition to job requirements that recognize the influences of the individual jobholder and the various demands placed on the job by an ever-changing environment starts with the identification of performance dimensions. Through the use of performance dimensions, it is possible to recognize situational differences and to write job requirements in terms that relate to the incumbent. Similar to the closely related responsibilities and duties, performance dimensions describe processes that identify the specific knowledge, skills, efforts, and desires of the jobholder. Performance dimensions then integrate the unique qualities of the incumbent with the demands placed on the job by the situation. The fairly static responsibilities and duties are replaced by the more dynamic performance dimensions. These job-related qualities permit the development of job-related criteria that are useful in appraising employee job performance.

Performance dimensions can be very broad and relate to all jobs or they can be extremely narrow and relate to only one or a very small number of jobs. The broadest and most universal performance dimension is simply JOB PERFORMANCE. Although this dimension is certainly job related, it is extremely ambiguous and open to a wide variety of interpretations. In order for a performance dimension to be useful in the process developed in this and the following chapters, it must relate to a specific responsibility or duty and be precise enough to lead to explicit goals.

Criteria used for establishing performance dimensions can be broadly classified as human qualities and technical abilities. Human qualities may be further subdivided into categories such as personal traits and interpersonal skills. Personal traits include qualities such as dependability, resourcefulness, cooperation, and innovativeness, whereas interpersonal skills describe qualities such as the ability to promote and use feedback in group effort, to organize group activities, and to respect individual differences. Technical abilities include mechanical skills and conceptual aptitudes. Mechanical skills relate to the operation of a specific piece of equipment, the handling of various materials, and/or the processing of inputs that may range from the assembly of a manufactured product to coding, storing, or retrieving of data, etc. The ability to identify problems and the willingness to accept and understand responsibility requirements within a variety of risk-taking situations are but two examples of conceptual aptitudes.

Performance dimensions are variables useful for measuring individual workplace behaviors or for profiling incumbent performance. For these reasons, performance dimensions must (1) accurately describe major or significant behaviors required in the successful performance of the job, (2) be amenable to scaling, and (3) be able to be weighted, if necessary. Performance dimensions provide a degree of individual tailoring to each job since they set the stage for identifying the unique sets of behaviors that relate most appropriately to a specific job. Responsibilities and duties describe inputs into the work process; performance dimensions begin the movement toward identifying required outputs or outcomes by further describing processes required for carrying out a specific responsibility or duty.

When employees have the opportunity to provide the basic inputs to the development of responsibilities and duties and have a final sign-off on the description and the ordering of importance of these responsibilities and duties, there is a much greater likelihood of achieving a high degree of agreement between supervisor and subordinate as to the content of the subordinate's job. Using this as the foundation for the eventual measuring of employee performance is a rational and consistent approach for developing agreement and understanding and minimizing the fear, anxiety, and hostility that frequently accompany the appraisal of performance.

Linking performance dimensions to job responsibilities and duties establishes a first cut at prioritizing performance dimensions, which should equate to the importance of the associated job responsibility and duty. Although this may not always be true, when work demands and situational variables require changes in performance dimension priorities, a basis for priorities has already been established. Reasons acceptable to both supervisor and subordinate can then be identified, assisting both parties to understand more clearly why and how work efforts should be redirected.

Critical Performance Dimensions

Critical performance dimensions are those components of job performance that are systematically determined to be the pivotal behaviors required for the successful accomplishment of the job. Failure to achieve results related to these dimensions outweighs satisfactory achievement of results related to other dimensions. Here again, situational variables and changing organizational demands influence the identification of critical performance dimensions.

A quick review of the numbers involved in moving from responsibilities and duties to performance dimensions assists in identifying the need for establishing critical performance dimensions. Most jobs have from four to seven responsibilities. A complete description of a responsibility normally requires the identification of three to seven duties. For each duty, there may be one or more performance dimension. It is impractical and unwieldy to appraise an employee relative to 15 to 30 or more performance variables. It makes far more sense to select the four to ten variables (performance dimensions) that, over an appraisal period, will identify successful job performance.

This does not mean that it is acceptable to ignore noncritical performance dimensions. What this permits is the use of a simple acceptable—unacceptable rating scale relative to these noncritical variables. Unacceptable performance in one or more of these noncritical dimensions is a flag item that requires further investigation by the supervisor and discussions with the employee.

Number of variables to use. To improve the identification and measurement of employee performance, managers and personnel specialists develop models. Appraisal forms and their various components are models of reality. Like all models, if they are too simple, they fail to improve recognition, understanding, and measurement. On the other hand, if they are too complex, those using the model will be unable to comprehend its various parts and the interactions between the parts, and they will find the model to be of little to no use. A useful model must be a valid representation of reality; and it must be neither overly simple nor overly complex.

Performance appraisal instruments must provide sufficient measurement criteria and measurement scales if they are to be useful in synthesizing the critical features of individual performance. Remember, these instruments are models of reality. In this case, reality is the actual demonstrated behavior of the involved employee.

Performance appraisal measurements depend primarily on observation. Most appraisal observations rely on transient information, which is developed in real time (the here and now), requires short but specific spans of attention, and uses short-term memory.

Short-term memory involves concept identification. In concept identification, an individual learns to identify specific dimensions through learning and to select the correct dimension when facing specific stimuli. The appraiser is normally involved in complex situations with a short time to make observations. To be effective under such conditions, he or she must learn to classify stimuli. Most individuals can learn to respond almost perfectly to a reasonable number of previously learned and classified stimuli.

Research by George A. Miller recognized that there are severe limits to the capacity of the short-term memory.[2] He concluded that the short-term memory is used primarily for identifying lists of unconnected events. (In the world of the appraiser, these unconnected events are demonstrated behaviors of subordinates.) Short-term memory not only uses few items for measurement but also operates on a "push-down" principle for retrieving information stored in the human brain (Last-In, First-Out, is an example of the "push-down" principle).

Miller theorizes that most people can work concurrently with five to nine different items of information (e.g., criteria, dimensions, variables) when making decisions. The more different items with which an individual works concurrently and the more input information required for analysis and discrimination purposes, the greater is the likelihood of making errors. When appraising performance relative to one variable—for example, observed performance—it is possible to misidentify or inconsistently appraise certain performance features. On the other hand, too many variables overly complicate the recognition and appraisal processes, leading to ineffective or risky uses of appraisals.

Over the years, Miller and other researchers have noted that individual short-term perceptual and memory abilities normally permit discrimination of about seven variables. Most people can work with at least five variables. Using less than five may unduly restrict an individual's

---

[2]George A. Miller, "The Magical Number Seven Plus or Minus Two: Some Limits On Our Capacity For Processing Information," *The Psychological Review*, March, 1956, pp. 81–97.

ability to discriminate and the result will not be as consistent as it should be. Using more than nine variables may result in an individual making discriminations that are too fine.

From his own research and that of others, Miller concludes that individuals possess finite and rather small capacities for making unidimensional judgments. An underlying reason for this characteristic is that human survival depends on adaptability which requires a little bit of information about a lot of things. The measuring of employee performance, however, requires considerable information about relatively few things. It is for this reason that essential job requirements (responsibilities and duties) and distinctive features of an employee's job performance (performance dimensions) are grouped into rather small units for identification and observation purposes.

Performance Standards

Criteria for differentiating the level or degree of results are provided by the performance standards. To describe results, measurement terms of how much, how well, when, and in what way are used and may be further identified through (1) quantity of output, (2) quality of output, (3) timeliness of output, (4) effectiveness in use of resources, (5) positive and negative effects of effort, (6) manner of performance, and (7) method of performing assignments.

When performance standards are developed, quantitative measures may be identified through statements such as:

- No more than (quantity or quality measures)
- No less than (quantity or quality measures)
- Within (a time measure)
- By (a time measure)
- No later than (a time measure)

Measures must be achievable, but they should relate to a scale of performance whereby the organization identifies an acceptable performance that it expects most employees to meet. These measures may also identify an achievable performance that requires employees to put forth extra effort, to stretch themselves; only a few employees will perform to these above-expected standards. These measures permit the identification of performance where employees are failing to meet expected standards. Some employees will, at times, fall into these categories. When standards are established and identified, care must be taken to ensure that they are stated in specific, understood terms and are attainable and valid.

Performance Goals

The setting of performance goals follows the identification and description of performance dimensions and performance standards. This step in the transition process leads to further personalization of job requirements. Goals are specific outcomes or desired results from incumbent workplace behavior. They must be observable and measurable, preferably in quantitative terms, but qualitative measurements are satisfactory in some cases. Goals may be classified as follows:

- *Routine goals:* those that ensure a continued level of performance;
- *Emergency goals:* those required to meet a specific crisis;
- *Special goals:* those required to satisfy particular situations or contingency demands;
- *Innovative goals:* those that promote new and vital actions; and
- *Personal development goals:* those that foster individual growth.

Similar to responsibilities and duties, there is a limit to the number of goals that a person can work toward achieving at any one time. Since most formal performance appraisal programs cover a period of one year, it is unlikely that it would ever be wise to set more than ten goals during an appraisal period.

In moving from duties to performance dimensions, it is possible to identify 15 to 20 goals. When this occurs, goals should be prioritized, and only those that meet certain criteria should be used for appraisal purposes. In developing a list of goals by order of importance, the following criteria are useful:

1. Represents full range of job responsibilities;
2. Covers important aspects of job;
3. Is appropriate to work required;
4. Is meaningful to work required;
5. Is challenging to the incumbent; and
6. Is feasible and attainable.

The setting of performance goals requires the involvement of both supervisor and subordinate. The goals relate to the performance dimensions that come from the duties. For the goals to be valuable to both the employee and the organization, they must be understood and accepted by the employees and must fit into the overall purposes of the organization. In addition to identifying results that are observable, goals should be measurable preferably in quantitative terms. This is not always possible however, and in these cases, qualitative measurements are acceptable.

Performance goals provide the critical link back to the top-down goals identified for accomplishing the mission of the organization and represent only one of a number of checks and balances built into the performance appraisal process. Establishing performance goals attempts to ensure (1) that all goal-directed work effort relates to the achievement of the mission of the organization and (2) that the goals of each individual and the work group are compatible with and supportive of results to be achieved by other organizational groups and units.

Non-responsibility, duty-related goals. it is quite possible that certain performance goals may be related to job responsibilities and duties, an example of which is a growth or development goal. Among the essential responsibilities and duties of a job, there is seldom one that relates to personal growth. This type of goal may be set and used as a critical measure of job performance. Involvement in and successful completion of a wide range of training and development programs may be a critical goal. There is no problem, including these and other types of goals, that does not relate directly to responsibilities and duties. The problem that may develop is the weighting of these goals related to those evolving from specific responsibilities and duties. Here again, final weighting may best be accomplished through supervisor subordinate discussion and negotiation.

The concept of adding goals beyond those related to job responsibilities is similar in nature to a statement found in most job descriptions, "and other duties as assigned." Neither case is meant to be a "catch 22"—placing the incumbent in a compromising situation. Both are necessary because job requirements must be flexible enough to meet demands of a constantly changing environment. The nagging, truthfully unanswerable issue is how to identify what is sufficient flexibility.

Attainment steps. Before actually appraising employee performance, attainment steps must be identified. This activity is by far the most personal and highly individualized portion of the entire process. Here, supervisor and subordinate discuss the various actions that the subordinate will implement in order to achieve a goal. The attainment steps provide both diagnostic and monitoring opportunities for the supervisor and subordinate. The attainment steps permit identification of:

1. Subordinate strengths and weaknesses;
2. Barriers to goal attainment;
3. Opportunities for goal attainment; and
4. Degree of progress.

During the discussion of attainment steps, supervisors identify how they will assist their subordinates to attain their established goals. Opportunities for documentation and review of both supervisor and subordinate behavior occur at this point. Although general goals may be set on an annual basis, attainment steps and specific goals may be set for a two- or three-month period with specific goals and attainment steps reset at the conclusion of a bimonthly or quarterly review session.

AVAILABLE OPTIONS

The step-by-step process from organizational goals to job responsibilities, duties, performance dimensions, performance standards, and performance goals can be shortened. It is certainly possible to develop three to five responsibilities in very general terms, i.e., supervision, quality of work, quantity of work, affirmative action, etc., and to go from these directly to goals. It is also possible to measure results directly by reviewing how well employees have performed relative to the assigned job duties. Another option is to develop a performance dimension profile and to select the element in the profile that most closely relates to the demonstrated workplace behavior of the appraisee.

A *performance dimension profile* is a set of behaviors within a specific performance dimension that provides a scale, degree, or range of behaviors that act as standards or reference points for identifying and measuring demonstrated employee behaviors. The critical point on a performance dimension profile is the break point that describes a minimum level of competency for that dimension. Requiring a "yes" or "no" response for the break point profile statement signifies either that the behavior did or did not occur. A useful profile provides a set of behaviors ranging from unacceptable to acceptable to mastery and possibly to superior mastery.

The following is an example of a performance dimension profile:

Performance Dimension

- Provides sufficient on-the-job training to ensure efficient use of equipment and input materials in producing a timely and quality output.

Performance Dimension Profile

- Ignores agreed-upon training procedures.
- Frequently has insufficiently trained employees to fill all key jobs.
- *Explains how to do the job, describes why things went wrong, but does not explain why or check to see if employees understand the reason for doing something in a prescribed manner.
- Provides minimal follow-up after training an employee.
- Ensures that employees know how to do their jobs but there is no inventory of available skills.
- Ensures that employees know their jobs, and jobs of others in work group and can provide adequate support under most circumstances.
- Uses slack time to cross train employees.
- Promotes skill development and continuous training is promoted within work group.

---

*Breakpoint statement describing minimum level of competency.

A specific selected profile statement provides information useful for identifying training, coaching, and counseling needs and for relating demonstrated behaviors to the rewards provided by the organization. Developing performance dimension profile statements to identify and measure performance requires more of the time and effort of skilled professionals, but less time of the supervisor and subordinate than does the establishment and use of performance goals. In many jobs, however, appraising performance relative to a set of statements that profile a specific performance dimension would be more appropriate. These jobs are those:

1. that are routine in nature and require repetitive work effort;
2. that permit employees little opportunity to participate in decisions that affect them;
3. in which work rules, methods, and procedures closely define work to be done; and
4. in which authority is centralized and autonomy limits the appraisal process.

A possible area of confusion occurs when differentiating between a performance dimension profile and a performance profile. As mentioned, a performance dimension profile describes a complete range of behaviors that employees may exhibit when performing their job assignments related to a specific dimension. A performance profile, on the other hand, is a set of performance dimensions that fully describes or forms the composite criterion—job performance.

The dimensions included within a performance profile should consist only of those essential to the performance of a job and should comprehensively describe it. Performance dimensions should be conceptually different, requiring different knowledge and skills to perform properly. Performance dimensions, like job responsibilities, have a tendency to deteriorate over time. Like all aspects of job requirements, they require review and reevaluation.

Essentials of Criterion Development

by Wayne F. Cascio

Criterion development is fundamentally a rational, nonempirical procedure, and even if it never gets beyond a precise statement of the conceptual criterion, such a statement alone will aid in the development of useful criterion measures (Astin, 1961). Conceptual criteria depend upon prior value judgments about what forms of behavior or results of behavior are good or desirable, and what behaviors or results are more or less equally desirable compared with others (Guion, 1961). Entire programs of personnel research will stand or fall upon the adequacy of these initial judgments.

Clearly, then, the role of the conceptual criterion is to provide a conceptual framework from which operational criteria (acceptable to the investigator or sponsoring organization as having intrinsic importance) can be derived (Astin, 1964). The actual process of criterion selection and development begins, therefore, with a statement of the conceptual criterion. Criterion elements, however, must be derived from statements of organizational needs (e.g., from worker-oriented job analysis).

A five-step procedure for criterion development has been outlined by Guion (1961). It includes:

1. Analysis of job and/or organizational needs.
2. Development of measures of actual behavior relative to expected behavior as identified in job and need analysis. These measures should supplement objective measures of organizational outcomes such as turnover, absenteeism, production, etc.
3. Identification of criterion dimensions underlying such measures by factor analysis, cluster analysis, or pattern analysis.
4. Development of reliable measures, each with high construct validity, of the elements to be identified.
5. Determination of the predictive validity of each independent variable (predictor) for each one of the criterion measures, taking them one at a time.

In Step 2, behavior data are distinguished from result-of-behavior data or organizational outcomes, and it is recommended that behavior data supplement result-of-behavior data. In Step 4, construct valid measures are advocated. Construct validity is essentially a judgment that a test or other predictive device does, in fact, measure a specified attribute

---

From *Applied Psychology in Personnel Management* by Wayne F. Cascio, © by Reston Publishing Company, Reston, Virginia, 1978, pp. 45–56. Reprinted with permission of Reston Publishing Company, Inc., a Prentice Hall Company, 11480 Sunset Hills Road, Reston, Virginia.

or construct to a significant or appreciable degree, and that it can be used to promote the understanding or prediction of behavior (Guion, 1965a). These two poles, *utility* (i.e., the researcher attempts to find the highest and therefore most useful validity coefficient) versus *understanding* (in which construct validity is advocated), have formed part of the basis for an enduring controversy in psychology over the relative merits of the two approaches. We shall examine this in greater detail in a later section.

EVALUATING CRITERIA

A frontal assault on the perennial "criterion problem" requires that the problems of reliability of performance and its observation, job performance multi-dimensionality, and intra-individual contributions to criterion performance be dealt with adequately. In addition, we need to apply certain yardsticks in evaluating the usefulness of any single criterion measure.

Relevance

The principal requirement of any criterion is its judged relevance (i.e., it must be logically related to the conceptual criterion). Hence, it is essential that the conceptual criterion be set forth clearly. For example, if our immediate problem is to compare two or more alternative automobile assembly methods with profit being the more general organizational goal, then we may choose as our conceptual criterion the production/cost ratio. Criterion measures such as speed of production and dollar costs of rejected or faulty work may be judged relevant because of their logical relationship to the conceptual criterion.

Much of the controversy surrounding the alleged differential prediction of tests for whites and blacks essentially reduces to the nature of the criteria used in different studies to evaluate test fairness. For example, one study may use attendance or turnover as a criterion, while another uses a measure of job proficiency. As Bray and Moses (1972) pointed out, however:

> A well-designed study using turnover as a criterion which shows different relationships between test scores and termination for black and white groups may well be a study of practical significance. It would obviously have strong implications for the organization hiring and attempting to retain members of both groups. But when the study is said to prove differential validity of the tests, then one may object that the criterion is irrelevant (p. 553).

Indeed, the American Psychological Association (APA) Task Force on Employment Testing of Minority Groups (1969) specifically emphasized that the most appropriate (i.e., logically relevant) criterion for evaluating tests is a direct measure of the degree of job proficiency developed by an employee after an appropriate period of time on the job (e.g., six months to a year). To be sure, the most relevant criterion measure will not always be the most expedient or the cheapest. A well-designed work sample test or performance appraisal system may require a great deal of ingenuity, effort, and expense to construct. Although turnover or output statistics (in which job proficiency is confounded with numerous other factors) are easily made available, they generally do not provide representative samples of the universe of relevant job behaviors. By themselves, therefore, they are deficient as criteria. Regardless of how many criteria are used, if, when considering all the dimensions of job performance, there remains an important aspect that is not being assessed, then an additional criterion measure is required.

Sensitivity or Discriminability

In order to be useful, any criterion measure must also be sensitive—that is, capable of discriminating between effective and ineffective employees. Suppose, for example, that quantity of goods produced is used as a criterion measure in a manufacturing operation. Such a criterion is frequently used inappropriately when, because of the technology in the plant, everyone doing a given job produces about the same number of goods. Under these circumstances there is little justification for using quantity of goods produced as a performance criterion, since the most effective workers do not differ appreciably from the least effective workers. Perhaps the amount of scrap or the number of errors made by workers would be a more sensitive indicator of real differences in job performance. Thus, the use of a particular criterion measure is warranted only if it serves to reveal discriminable differences in job performance.

Practicality

It is important that management be thoroughly informed of the real benefits of using carefully developed criteria. Management may or may not have the expertise to appraise the soundness of a criterion measure or a series of criterion measures, but objections will almost certainly arise if record keeping and data collection for criterion measures become impractical and interfere significantly with ongoing operations. Overzealous personnel researchers sometimes view organizations as ongoing laboratories which exist solely for their purposes. This should not be construed as an excuse for using inadequate or irrelevant criteria. Clearly a balance must be sought, for the personnel department occupies a staff role, assisting through more effective manpower utilization those who are directly concerned with achieving the organization's primary goals of profit, growth, or service. Keep criterion measurement practical!

COMPOSITE VS. MULTIPLE CRITERIA

Most applied psychologists agree that job performance is multi-dimensional in nature, and that adequate measurement of job performance requires parallel multi-dimensionality in criteria. The next question is what to do about it. Should one combine the various criterion measures into a composite score, or should each criterion measure be treated separately? If the investigator chooses to combine the elements, what rule should he use to do so? As with the utility vs. understanding issue, both sides have had their share of vigorous proponents over the years. Let us consider some of the arguments.

Composite Criterion

The basic contention of Toops (1944), Thorndike (1949), Brogden and Taylor (1950a), and Nagle (1953), the strongest advocates of the composite criterion, is that the criterion should provide a yardstick or overall measure of "success" or "value to the organization" of each individual. Such a single index is indispensable in decision making and individual comparisons, and even if the criterion dimensions are treated separately in validation, they must somehow be combined into a composite when a decision is required. Although this may be (and often is) done subjectively, a quantitative weighting scheme makes objective the importance placed on each of the criterion elements.

For example, suppose there are only two criterion elements involved in the job of assembler of kitchen appliances, (say, total number of appliances produced and number of errors). Perhaps the firm views errors as more important than quantity of output because errors (especially undetected errors) result in reworks, loss of customer goodwill, high cost of warranty maintenance, etc. Assume further that each non-defective appliance is worth $15 to the company (from which the worker is paid $1), but each error costs the worker $2. If a worker produces 50 appliances in a single day, but also makes 10 errors, his total worth to the organization on that day is 50 times $1 minus 10 times $2, or $30. This simple weighting scheme, using the common metric of dollar value to the firm, can now be applied across occasions and decision makers (Brogden and Taylor, 1950a). In fact, Nagle (1953) outlined seven different methods of combining subcriteria into a composite, assuming, of course, prior acceptance of the underlying philosophy and assumptions of the composite criterion approach.

Multiple Criteria

Advocates of multiple criteria contend that measures of demonstrably different variables shouldn't be combined. As Cattell (1957) put it, "Ten men and two bottles of beer cannot be added to give the same total as two men and ten bottles of beer" (p. 11). Consider a study of proofreaders by Lawshe and McGinley (1951). In measuring the proficiency of proofreaders, it was found that speed, accuracy, and versatility were all important and related to success. It was also found, however, that the three dimensions were unrelated to each other—that is, the fastest proofreader was not necessarily the most accurate, nor the most versatile. Under these conditions, combining the measures leads to a composite that is not only ambiguous, but also psychologically nonsensical. Guion (1961) brought the issue clearly into focus:

> The fallacy of the single criterion lies in its assumption that everything that is to be predicted is related to everything else that is to be predicted—that there is a general factor in all criteria accounting for virtually all of the important variance in behavior at work and its various consequences of value (p. 145).

Schmidt and Kaplan (1971) subsequently pointed out that combining various criterion elements into a composite does imply that there is a single underlying dimension in job performance, but it does not, in and of itself, imply that this single underlying dimension is behavioral or psychological in nature. A composite criterion may well represent an underlying economic dimension, while at the same time being essentially meaningless from a behavioral point of view. Thus, Brogden and Taylor (1950a) argued that when the criteria are all relevant measures of economic variables (dollars and cents), they can be combined into a composite, regardless of their intercorrelations.

Differing Assumptions

As Schmidt and Kaplan (1971) have noted, the two positions differ in terms of: (1) the nature of the underlying constructs represented by the respective criterion measures, and (2) what they regard to be the primary purpose of the validation process itself. Let us consider the first set of assumptions. Underpinning the arguments for the composite criterion is the assumption that the criterion should represent an economic rather than a behavioral construct. The economic orientation is illustrated in Brogden and Taylor's (1950a) "dollar criterion": "The criterion should measure the overall contribution of the individual to the organization" (p. 139). Brogden and Taylor argued that overall efficiency should be measured in dollar terms by applying cost accounting concepts and procedures to the individual job behaviors of the employee. "The criterion problem centers primarily upon the quantity, quality, and cost of the finished product" (p. 141).

In contrast, advocates of multiple criteria (Ghiselli, 1956b; Dunnette, 1963a; Guion, 1965a) argued that the criterion should represent a behavioral or psychological construct, one that is behaviorally homogeneous. Haire (1960) contended that in order to understand business as a social institution, applied psychologists must attempt to frame psychological problems in that special context and not simply in terms of management (i.e., economic) problems.

With regard to the goals of the validation process, advocates of the composite criterion assume that the validation process is carried out only for practical and economic reasons, and not to promote greater understanding of the psychological and behavioral processes involved in various jobs. Thus, Brogden and Taylor (1950a) clearly distinguished the end products of a given job (job products) from the job processes that lead to these end products. With regard to job processes they argued: "Such factors as skill are latent; their effect is realized in the end product. They do not satisfy the logical requirements of an adequate criterion" (p. 141).

In contrast, the advocates of multiple criteria view increased understanding as an important goal of the validation process, along with practical and economic goals:

> The goal of the search for understanding is a theory (or theories) of work behavior; theories of human behavior are cast in terms of psychological and behavioral, not economic constructs. (Schmidt and Kaplan, 1971, p. 424).

Resolving the Dilemma

Clearly there are numerous possible uses of job performance and program evaluation criteria. In general, they may be used for research purposes or operationally as an aid in managerial decision making. When criteria are used for research purposes, the emphasis is on the psychological understanding of the relationship between various predictors and separate criterion dimensions, where the dimensions themselves are behavioral in nature. When used for managerial decision-making purposes such as job assignment, promotion, or evaluation of the cost effectiveness of recruitment, training or advertising programs, criterion dimensions must be combined into a composite, representing overall (economic) worth to the organization. Combination may be done *subjectively,* in which case, as Schmidt and Kaplan (1971) have indicated, the bases for assignment, the relative sizes, and the reliabilities of the weights are unknown. Combination may also be done *objectively,* by using, for example, a unit weighting scheme where each criterion element is given equal weight, or by using a multiple regression analysis in which statistically optimal weights for each criterion element are derived, based on relationships with some overall criterion.

In summary, the resolution of the composite vs. multiple criterion dilemma essentially depends upon the objectives of the investigator (Schmidt and Kaplan, 1971). Both methods are legitimate for their own purposes. If the goal is increased psychological understanding of predictor-criterion relationships, then the criterion elements are best kept separate. If managerial decision making is the objective, then the criterion elements should be weighted, regardless of their intercorrelations into a composite representing an economic construct of overall worth to the organization.

Ultimately, the issue will probably not be resolved as long as both sides insist on using one *or* the other method of validation. Criterion measures with theoretical relevance should not replace those with practical relevance, but rather should supplement or be used along with them (Guion, 1961; Wallace, 1965). The real hope lies in finding a happy medium—that is, utility *and* understanding.

REFERENCES

- Astin, A.W. Criterion-centered research. *Educational and Psychological Measurement,* 1964, 24, 807–822.
- Bray, D.W. & Moses, J.L. Personnel selection. *Annual Review of Psychology,* 1972, 23, 545–576.
- Brogden, H.E. & Taylor, E.K. The dollar criterion—applying the cost accounting concept to criterion construction. *Personnel Psychology,* 1950, 3, 133–154 (a).
- Cattell, R.B. *Personality and Motivation Structure and Measurement.* New York: Harcourt, Brace & World, 1957.
- Dunnette, M.D. Personnel management. In P. R. Farnsworth, O. McNemar, & Q. McNemar (eds.) *Annual Review of Psychology,* 1962, 13, 285–314.
- Ghiselli, E.E. Dimensional problems of criteria. *Journal of Applied Psychology,* 1956, 40, 1–4 (b).
- Guion, R.M. Criterion measurement and personnel judgements. *Personnel Psychology,* 1964, 14, 141–149.
- Guion, R.M. *Personnel Testing.* New York: McGraw-Hill, 1965 (a).
- Haire, M. Business is too important to be studied only by economists. *American Psychologist,* 1960, 15, 271–272.
- Lawshe, C. H. & McGinley, A. D. Job performance criteria studies: The job performance of proofreaders. *Journal of Applied Psychology,* 1954, 35, 316–320.
- Nagle, B.F. Criterion development. *Personnel Psychology,* 1953, 6, 271–288.
- Schmidt, F.L. & Kaplan, L.B. Composite vs. multiple criteria: A review and resolution of the controversy. *Personnel Psychology,* 1974, 24, 419–434.
- Thorndike, R.L. *Personnel Selection: Test and Measurement Techniques.* New York: Wiley, 1949.
- Toops, H.A. The criterion. *Educational and Psychological Measurement,* 1944, 4, 410–418.
- Wallace, S.R. Criteria for what? *American Psychologist,* 1965, 20, 411–417.

Humanistic Numbers

by John E. Jones

A basic human tendency in our culture is to enumerate our experiences. Because people attempt to abstract those elements that they recognize as repeatable, they often end by describing their experiences in terms of "how much" or "how many." This tendency to attach numbers to observations of everyday life, however, has some inherent dangers.

The tendency to oversimplify is one danger. Another is to imagine that experience can be accumulated, as if one experience is equal to another. Yet another danger occurs when we enumerate the characteristics and experience of others. That is, in describing other people numerically, we summarize their experiences, characteristics, and behaviors in terms of linear scales. A fourth danger is that we forget to look at human beings and look instead at quantities.

Numbers, best thought of as symbols or as abstract concepts, are a very useful device. When we assign a numerical value to some event, behavior, observation, or pattern of tick marks on an answer sheet, we are symbolically representing a human process. Counting may be done mechanically or electronically, but the schema is an extension of the thought process of some person or persons. Numbers can be talked about, manipulated statistically and arithmetically, and seen in an abstract, conceptual way. The primary value of numbers, then, is to extrapolate from and summarize human experience.

In practice, however, there is a tendency to assign more value to our numbering than to the quality of human interaction needed to solve social problems. The logic of numbers is not the syntax of human experience, even though ample evidence exists that we treat people as though they were numbers. Persons who feel they are being subjected to such inhumanity are almost uniformly offended by it. When a person feels that he has been treated with less dignity than that accorded to punched cards, he usually feels helplessness and bitterness. A few years ago a joke among college and university students was "I am an IBM card. Do not fold, spindle, or mutilate me."

HUMANISTIC PRINCIPLES

The use of numbers in human relations—in organization surveys, in instrumentation, in counting—is best carried out in ways that are consistent with humanistic values. The following principles are concerned with the relationship between using numbers in human relations and acknowledging the worth and dignity of individual people.

1. *No number or array of numbers can capture the essence of a human being.* People do not *experience* numbers, but we do *use* numbers to abstract some principles or frequencies from what we see. The complexity of the individual human being far exceeds our ability to describe human traits, their interrelationships, or their patterns of interaction with the environment.

2. *It is possible and desirable to conceptualize experience both numerically and nonnumerically.* The traditional notion held by many psychometricians is that "If a thing exists, it exists in some amount. If you have not measured it, you do not know what you are talking about."

In human relations, we are concerned with what could be termed "soft" variables, that is, those characteristics and interactions of human beings that cannot be described very precisely. For example, we often talk about such concepts as trust, openness, self-actualization, interdependence—concepts that are neither precisely defined nor accurately measured. While it is useful to posit these human characteristics in order to improve the ways people relate to each other, it is important for us to recognize that the attempts that have been made represent the crudest form of measurement. To say, for example, that a person who scores 8 on a 9-point synergy scale has an unusually high ability to see "the opposites of life as meaningfully related" is as indefensible as to say that unless we have mapped that characteristic of his, we cannot discuss it with any usefulness.

3. *Numbers do not have meaning; only people experience meaning.* There are no inherent values in numbers. We impute, or assign, to these symbols meanings that may be idiosyncratic. Just as words are symbols, numbers are symbols used to simplify, arrange, and collect our experience. When we use them in communication, we have many of the same problems we have in using other symbols, such as words. People do not attach the same meanings to the same symbols, though we often assume that they do (Jones, 1972).

4. *There is no such thing as objectivity.* Far enough behind any set of numbers will be the subjective impressions, feelings, attitudes, theories, hunches, and assumptions of one or more human beings. It is self-deceiving to imagine that one can be objective in relation to oneself, other people, or even the physical universe. "Scientific" observations are inevitably clouded by our ability to con-

---

Reprinted from J. E. Jones and J. W. Pfeiffer (eds.), *The 1975 Annual Handbook for Group Facilitators.* San Diego, CA: University Associates, 1975. Used with permission.

ceptualize experience and observations. In human relations it is important to accept that we are first, last, and always subjective. Thus we need to accept responsibility for our biases, prejudices, and favorite ways of looking at the world.

5. *The most difficult number problem is counting.* A great many people experience anxiety with regard to numbers, arithmetic, and especially statistics. Many people are awed by the complexity of mathematical operations. It is almost as though these number systems had a reality to be discovered and mastered. The application of numerical processes, however, cannot be more useful than the observations on which the processes are based. The manipulation of frequencies, or counts, do not *add* validity to the basic observations that are assigned numerical value.

6. *More of a good thing may be too much; human relations are not necessarily linear.* One human tendency, especially in our Western culture, is to think of things as if they existed on a linear scale. For example, we imagine intelligence (a desired quality) to be a linear trait. Thus, the more intelligence, the better. Since openness in human relations is held to be desirable, we have a tendency to think that our activities in relation to each other would be most profitable if we had completely open human interaction. It is useful, however, to think of extremes—such as being completely open or being completely closed—as equally dysfunctional (Pfeiffer & Jones, 1972).

7. *When numbers become labels for people, individuals begin to be seen as static.* Although we usually think of people as being dynamic and changing, we tend to oversimplify each other and to assume that our human characteristics are unchangeable. Assigning numbers to the amounts of our hypothesized traits strengthens this tendency. It is more useful, then, to consider numerical designations of observed human behavior as short-term indicators. In training we are interested in helping persons change their behavior. Using numbers in that context suggests that intra-individual dynamics are more important than characteristics that the individual cannot change.

8. *The things that can be measured precisely are relatively unimportant in human relations.* Physical characteristics, certain personality traits, and some aspects of the physical environment can be specified with considerable precision. These considerations, however, cannot adequately account for the wide individual differences in human interaction.

CONCLUSION

The dilemma in using numbers to foster human and organizational growth and development, then, is that we have to allow for our subjectivity while we are attempting to amass a reliable body of useful knowledge and information. In this process it is critical, however, that we avoid committing the error implied in the old adage "Don't throw out the baby with the bath water."

People are not numbers, but their experience can nevertheless, to a degree, be collected, accumulated, and used as a basis for prediction. The important humanistic consideration is that in using numbers we not violate the integrity of the people whose human experience we are abstracting.

SUGGESTED ACTIVITIES

The facilitator can request a count of the political party affiliations of participants, asking them to classify themselves according to the major parties. Those persons who cannot classify themselves in such a way should consider themselves "independents." A discussion could follow on how this arbitrary categorization oversimplifies the wide range of political differences among people.

The number of pennies in the pockets of participants is averaged to five decimal places. The facilitator leads a discussion of the meaning of the average.

The facilitator asks participants to pair off and to estimate each other's I.Q.'s. He encourages them to explore their emotional reactions to having themselves labeled with a number, and he asks them to specify what they believe to be the optimal intelligence quotient.

REFERENCES

- Jones, J. E. Modes of communication. In J. W. Pfeiffer & J. E. Jones (Eds.), *The 1972 annual handbook for group facilitators.* La Jolla, Ca.: University Associates, 1972.
- Pfeiffer, J. W., & Jones, J. E. Openness, collusion, and feedback. In J. W. Pfeiffer & J. E. Jones (Eds.), *The 1972 annual handbook for group facilitators.* La Jolla, Ca.: University Associates, 1972.

SOURCES SECTION THREE

DESIGNING THE PERFORMANCE APPRAISAL SYSTEM

CHOOSING THE RIGHT FORMAT

Performance Appraisal: Match the Tool to the Task

by John D. McMillan and Hoyt W. Doyel

- Suggests that the uses of the appraisal program (salary, incentives, promotions) should determine what format is chosen and how it is used.
- Reviews the purposes for which four common formats are best suited.

FITTING THE INSTRUMENT INTO THE ORGANIZATION

The Environmental Context of Performance Evaluation and Its Effect on Current Practices

by Harvey Kahalas

- Discusses how performance evaluation has been affected by the context within which it was done.
- Explains how performance evaluation must fit the context.
- Lists a sequence for developing, implementing, and maintaining an effective evaluation program.

Job Analysis and Performance Appraisal

by Richard W. Beatty

For any performance appraisal system to work, job content must be exhaustively examined. Certainly the determination of job content is of obvious importance but is frequently overlooked or not effectively assessed in the development of performance appraisal instruments. The following excerpt from a court case involving performance appraisal shows how this can occur.

> ... the analyst did not verify the description by making an on-site inspection of the employee who actually performed the job.... The former procedure was flawed insofar as it created the possibility of inconsistent descriptions, over- or under-inflation of job duties or requirements, and was associated with the lack of employee awareness of the evaluation procedure.... The criteria actually employed by the defendants were not developed by professional consultants, but rather adapted from a commercially-available method of job analysis from which Defendants borrowed what they believed to be pertinent to their needs. (*Greenspan* v. *Automobile Club of Michigan,* 1980, p. 195)

This excerpt from a judge's opinion raises several questions that most laypersons would raise if they were to consider what procedures might be attempted in capturing and understanding the content of a job such that an organization could use the information for performance appraisal as well as for determining selection requirements, wage and salary levels, and the identification of relevant internal labor supplies. The major points concern the collection of data which is relevant to the job in question by on-the-job observation (i.e. with job incumbents). Questionnaires like those found in Figure 1 are often used in the collection of job content information.

The major issue in job content identification for performance appraisal purposes is to insure that the information collected enables the job analyst to identify tasks, personal characteristics, or behaviors which are required on the job. For performance appraisal, the identification of relevant tasks should occur first, followed by training of managers to identify the varying levels of performance for these tasks, ranging from excellent to unacceptable, for jobs in which performance must be measured on tasks which cannot be precisely or quantitatively measured (e.g. customer relations). For such tasks a behavioral approach to job performance is necessary, whereas in jobs in which specific contributions are attributable to an individual (e.g. number of pieces welded and passing quality control), the job analysis need only focus on the desired *results* of a job.

These points are clearly demonstrated in the following statements from the *Uniform Guidelines on Employee Selection Procedures* (1978):

> *Criterion measures.* The bases for the selection of the criterion measures should be provided, together with references to the evidence considered in making the selection of criterion measures (essential). A full description of all criteria on which data were collected and means by which they were observed, recorded, evaluated and quantified should be provided (essential).
>
> *Job analysis or review of job information.* A description of the procedure used to analyze the job or group of jobs, or to review the job information should be provided (essential). Where a review of job information results in criteria which may be used without a full job analysis (see section 14B(3)), the basis for the selection of those criteria should be reported (essential). Where a job analysis is required a complete description of the work behavior(s) or work outcome(s) and measures of their criticality or importance should be provided (essential). The report should describe the basis on which the behavior(s) or outcome(s) were determined to be critical or important, such as the proportion of time spent on the respective behaviors, their level of difficulty, their frequency of performance, the consequences of error, or other appropriate factors (essential).

As noted above, job analysis is the systematic collection of job-related information for each unique job, including what is to be done (physical and mental responses); how it is to be done (tools, equipment, methods, judgments, calculations, etc.); and why it is to be done (overall purposes and how tasks relate to one another).

Task analysis, the Position Analysis Questionnaire, and the numerous quantitative job analysis methodologies all provide useful approaches to job analysis although questions have been raised as to the reliability of these techniques (Milkovich, 1979; Schwab, 1979).[1] There are also difficulties in deciding what levels of job analysis should be pursued (e.g., task, position, job, occupation, or family level). These are difficult and still unresolved issues

This article was prepared especially for this book.

[1] For research results and citations to other research, see R. Richard Hackman and Greg R. Oldman, "Development of the Job Diagnostic Survey," *Journal of Applied Psychology* 60 (April 1975), pp. 159–170; G. Douglas Jenkins Jr., David A. Nadler, Edward E. Lawler III and Courlendt Cammann, "Standardized Observations: An Approach to Measuring the Nature of Jobs,"

FIGURE 1
An Example of a Job Analysis Questionnaire

GENERAL DATA

1. Department Unit Name:
2. Name:
3. Position Title:

I. ORGANIZATION RELATIONSHIPS

4. Employees supervised—title
   A)
   B)
   C)
   D)
   E)
   F)
   G)
   H)
   I)
   J)

7. Organization of department (sketch an organization chart for the incumbent's part of the organization)

5. Total number supervised

6. Supervision received

8. Department title

II. DUTIES OF THE POSITION

9. A)
   B)
   C)

D) ______________________________

E) ______________________________

F) ______________________________

G) ______________________________

H) ______________________________

I) ______________________________

J) ______________________________

10. Major outputs of the unit supervised

III. QUALIFICATIONS REQUIRED BY THE POSITION

11. Education required ______________________________

12. Experience required ______________________________

13. Other requirements (specify) ______________________________

14. Required knowledge, skills, and abilities

A) ______________________________

B) ______________________________

C) ______________________________

D) ______________________________

E) ______________________________

From *Personnel Administration: An Experiential/Skill-Building Approach,* 2d ed. by Richard W. Beatty and Craig Eric Schneier, Addison-Wesley, Reading, MA, 1981, 91–92.

(Pearlman, 1980). There is also the possibility that the sex of the job analyst may interfere with the accurate assessment of job content (Schwab, 1979).

Common methods of job analysis can be divided into qualitative and quantitative approaches and include the following:

Qualitative

Task analysis (U.S. Department of Labor, 1972). Questionnaires and interviews with job knowledge experts are used to analyze jobs into component tasks. Job analysts assign ratings to tasks on a number of scales that reflect the abilities, personal traits, and physical demands required of a worker in performing tasks. Tasks are grouped into similar functions.

Critical incidents (Flanagan, 1954). Job knowledge experts delineate important job dimensions and describe incidents of job behavior illustrative of poor, average, and exceptional performance on that dimension.

Quantitative

Job elements (Primoff, 1975). In group sessions, job knowledge experts generate skills, knowledges, abilities, and other worker characteristics (the job elements) required to perform the job in question. Experts assign ratings to the elements on a set of scales designed to assess each element's relative importance for selection. Analysis of the ratings yields the most important elements.

Position Analysis Questionnaire (PAQ) (McCormick et al., 1972). Job knowledge experts complete a structured, commercially available questionnaire. The responses are analyzed by computer into a number of job dimensions (e.g., processing information) based on previous research with the PAQ.

For large organizations the best approach to job analysis may be a quantitative one. A quantitative job analysis (QJA) system has several advantages such as permitting the comparability of job content for the design of performance appraisal formats as well as for base wage determination, and the identification of the relevant internal labor supplies. To develop a quantitative job analysis system, job analysts should use existing job content information such as job descriptions, job evaluation documents, or previous performance appraisals. If this information does not exist, the functional language technique (Department of Labor, 1972) should be used to collect basic data on job content. A very useful source of job content information is

FIGURE 2
Sample Jobs from the *Dictionary of Occupational Titles*

612.685-010 LEVER-TENDING (forging)
Tends power hammer or power press that forges metal stock. Moves levers, upon signal from HEAVY FORGER (forging), to control force and frequency of hammer blows, or ram pressure to shape forging. May be designated according to equipment tended as FORGING-PRESS-LEVER TENDER (forging). HAMMER DRIVER (forging).

612.685-014 SPRING TESTER (spring)
Tends power press that tests resiliency of spiral springs and that compresses them to specified length. Positions spring over mandrel of press table and places metal plate over end of spring. Pulls lever that forces plunger of machine against plate to compress spring. Measures compressed length of spring, using, micrometers, calipers, and gages. Releases press and measures uncompressed length of spring. Inserts metal wedge between spring coils and taps spring with mallet to adjust spring to specified length and pitch.

612.687-010 HEAT READER (forging)
Compares glow inside forge shop furnace with color intensity chart to determine internal temperature of furnace, using pyrometer. Looks through pyrometer into furnace and compares intensity of light generated by furnace with chart depicting color at various temperatures to determine internal furnace temperature. Informs specified forging personnel of observed temperature to permit designated adjustment to furnace controls, maintenance work, and production rescheduling.

612.687-014 HEAVY-FORGER HELPER (forging)
Assists HEAVY FORGER (forging) in shaping hot metal on power hammer or press equipped with open dies, working as member of crew. Pulls work piece from furnace with tongs and positions and turns it on hammer anvil. Removes scale from metal and anvil during forging using compressed air or broom. May assist in forging unheated metal. May be designated according to worker assisted as HAMMERSMITH HELPER (forging). PRESS-SMITH HELPER (forging). Performs other duties as described under HELPER (any ind.).

Journal of Applied Psychology 60 (April 1975), pp. 171–181; E. McCormick, P. R. Jeanneret and R. C. Mecham, "A Study of Job Characteristics and Job Dimensions as Based on the Position Analysis Questionnaire (PAQ)," *Journal of Applied Psychology* 56 (August 1972), pp. 347–368. This study compared the reliabilities of different persons (incumbents, supervisors and job analysis). Sample sizes were so small, however, that the findings may have little generality. Kenneth N. Wexley and Stanley B. Silverman, "An Examination of Differences Between Managerial Effectiveness and Response Patterns on a Structured Job Analysis Questionnaire," *Journal of Applied Psychology* 63 (October 1978), pp. 646–649. See also citations in Walter W. Tornow and Patrick R. Pinto, "The Development of a Managerial Job Taxonomy: A System for Describing, Classifying and Evaluating Executive Positions," *Journal of Applied Psychology* 61 (August 1976), pp. 410–418. Richard D. Arvey, Emily M. Passino and John W. Lounsbury, "Job Analysis Results as Influenced by Sex of Incumbent and Sex of Analyst," *Journal of Applied Psychology* 62 (August 1977), pp. 411–416.

FIGURE 3
An Example of a Quantitative Job Analysis Worksheet

A. Tasks required	*A* *Check (✓) if required*	*B* Importance *Criticalness of this task as relative to other tasks* *1 = unimportant* *2=minor importance* *3=important* *4=very important* *5=critical* *(insert number below)*	*C* Frequency *Time spent relative to other tasks* *1 = much less time* *2=less time* *3=about the same time* *4=more time* *5=much more time* *(insert number below)*
1. Delegate authority to subordinates			
2. Exercise general supervisory and appointing authority over all department employees			
3. Organize the department into organizational units			
4. Employ and fix the compensation of employees			
5. Purchase or lease personal property			
6. Purchase services and lease real property			
7. Issue and enforce orders and instructions to assure compliance with the provisions of law			
8. Conduct studies in appropriate operational activities			
9. Provide courses of instruction and practical training for employees			
10. Prepare an annual budget of the department			
11. Cooperate with attached agencies and adjunct agencies			
12. Appoint a "director" for each division			
13. Apply for and receive any public or private funds			
14. Recommend appropriate legislation			
15. Make and adopt department rules and regulations			

FIGURE 4
An Example of a Quantitative Job Analysis Worksheet

A. Tasks required	*A* Check (✓) *if required*	*B* Importance *Criticalness of this task as relative to other tasks* *1=unimportant* *2=minor importance* *3=important* *4=very important* *5=critical* *(insert number below)*	*C* Frequency *Time spent relative to other tasks* *1=much less time* *2=less time* *3=about the same time* *4=more time* *5=much more time* *(insert number below)*	*D* Error Consequences *Probability of a serious consequence resulting if task not done correctly* *1=low* *2=same* *3=average* *4=high* *5=certainty* *(insert number below)*
1. Install and adjust new rollers and passes				
2. Monitor condition of rollers and other equipment				
3. Determine when passes need to be replaced				
4. Determine if machine breakdowns are electrical or mechanical problems				
5. Inspect quality of product being produced				
6. Monitor safety hazards				
7. Monitor work of crew members				
8. Diagnose machine/equipment breakdowns				
9. Instruct crew members on new jobs and safety				

the *Dictionary of Occupational Titles* (Department of Labor, 1978). This book lists over 35,000 jobs and the tasks associated with each (see Figure 2). Once a list of tasks is obtained, the list can be distributed to all job incumbents requesting them to identify which tasks are more important, more frequently performed, more critical, and have a greater error consequence.[2] Incumbents are asked to review all the tasks found in the organization. Incumbents then indicate which tasks comprise their job. The maximum number is usually ten to twelve. A system for scoring these tasks can then be devised (e.g. multiplying the importance

[2]If the job analyst believes that some organizational tasks have been omitted, the questionnaire could ask workers to add tasks to the list and assess each new task on the same criteria. See the quote from the *Uniform Guidelines on Employee Selection Procedures* for the criteria to be used in ranking the tasks found in a job.

FIGURE 5
The Quantitative Job Analysis (QJA) Scoring System

Table of means for the following job title:
2 Key entry operator II
based on responses from 7 cases

Variable	*Label*	*Mean*
451	Key data from written mat onto cards—etc	19.0000
164	Perform data entry-verification of input	17.8571
450	Verify recorded info for accuracy	14.1429
165	Transfer data disk to tape for ADPD	10.0000
455	Maintain discs-cards and tapes	10.0000
340	Process documents	9.4286
145	Distribute workload to employees	8.7143
166	Maintain control of input-output docum	8.1429
449	Operate data in-put equipment	8.1429
167	Adopt forms used with data processing	6.4286
234	Maintain logs	6.4286
163	Maintain data processing equip	6.2657
129	Revise forms-reports-records in the dept	5.8571
219	Process taxpayer records	5.8571
156	Acquire data processing equipment	5.7143
367	Answer phone + refer calls	5.7143
199	Carry out special assignments-projects	5.4286
205	Maintain daily records + totals of paymt	5.2857
146	Trans + oper mag tape-card-disc typewrts	5.1429
452	Locate data	5.1429
463	Maintain good working relationships	5.1429
512	Load input-out units with mat of oper rn	5.1429
151	Design-analyze-document computer systems	5.0000
369	Sort-arrange-file materials	4.8571
402	Operate computers + peripheral equipment	4.8571
157	Develop + maintain docum of computers	4.5714

times the frequency scores). The tasks which can then be identified as the most important ones are used to assess each incumbent in the job title in question. Examples of such quantitative approaches to job analysis are shown in Figures 3 and 4. The ranking of the tasks is shown in Figure 5.

Once the tasks are identified for each job title a system for evaluating each incumbent's performance on each task can be devised. The tasks are entered on a form and supervisors are requested to record observations of incumbent performance in behavioral terms and then rate/evaluate these behaviors. Such a system should meet at least the minimal expectations of the *Guidelines* as well as the objectives of a performance appraisal system such as to provide feedback for developmental purposes; to identify training needs; to identify promotable employees; and to identify employees eligible for merit pay increases.

Although the preceding discussion demonstrates some of the problems in job analysis methods and the inconsistency of the courts in ruling on job analysis questions, effective performance appraisal requires that quality efforts be given to the capture of job content information. There is no alternative in the design of performance appraisals to do other than identify the tasks critical for effective performance; weigh each of these tasks as a proportion of the total job; demand that supervisors record their observations of employee behaviors on each task; and then evaluate the effectiveness of each employee's behaviors. Such a procedure obviously cannot occur without an exhaustive analysis of the employee's job.

Although the court rulings on job analysis seem to be inconsistent, it appears as though they have generally been lenient in their demands for rigorous analysis of job content. In a review of legal cases (Kleinman and Faley, 1978),

FIGURE 6
An Example of a Dimensionalized Performance Appraisal Procedure with Documentation

Appraisal Date ______

Name ______ Job Title ______

Dept. ______ Supervisor ______

Period Reviewed: From ______ To ______

Length Of Time Employee In Position: ______

Full-Time ______ Part-Time ______

Reason For Appraisal (check one)

_____ Regular Interval _____ Counseling Only

_____ Probationary _____ Discharge

Instructions: After reviewing the description for this job, supervisors and subordinates should have agreed on the dimensions (or job related tasks) to be included and the weights assigned to each dimension. Both raters and ratees are to review the job-related work behaviors of the ratee. These job-related work behaviors are to be described for each dimension in the spaces provided below. This behavior is to be descriptive and typical of the ratee on this dimension during the rating period. Once this behavior has been described, it is to be evaluated for each dimension on the scale provided on page 36. Examples of behaviors for various managerial jobs are printed on page 36.

JOB RELATED BEHAVIORS

DIMENSION: ______ DIMENSION WEIGHT: ______ %

TASK DEFINITION: ______

JOB-RELATED EXAMPLES OF EMPLOYEE'S BEHAVIORS DURING THE PERFORMANCE PERIOD:

______

______

RATING OF EMPLOYEE'S BEHAVIORS DURING THE PERFORMANCE PERIOD: Unacceptable _____

Poor _____ Fair _____ Average _____ Good _____ Very Good _____ Excellent _____

DIMENSION: ______ DIMENSION WEIGHT: ______ %

TASK DEFINITION: ______

JOB-RELATED EXAMPLES OF EMPLOYEE'S BEHAVIORS DURING THE PERFORMANCE PERIOD:

______

______

RATING OF EMPLOYEE'S BEHAVIORS DURING THE PERFORMANCE PERIOD: Unacceptable _____
Poor _____ Fair _____ Average _____ Good _____ Very Good _____ Excellent _____

DIMENSION: ______________________ DIMENSION WEIGHT: ______ %

TASK DEFINITION: ______________________

JOB-RELATED EXAMPLES OF EMPLOYEE'S BEHAVIORS DURING THE PERFORMANCE PERIOD:

____

____

RATING OF EMPLOYEE'S BEHAVIORS DURING THE PERFORMANCE PERIOD: Unacceptable _____ Poor _____ Fair _____ Average _____ Good _____ Very Good _____ Excellent _____

_____ SUPERVISOR'S EVALUATION SIGNATURE: ______________

_____ EMPLOYEE'S SELF-EVALUATION DATE: ______________

_____ __________ EVALUATION

_____ FINAL EVALUATION

it was reported that of the thirty-one cases reviewed, in only eleven did defendants conduct job analysis (*Davis; Chance* (Appeals); *Western Addition Community Organization; Qwarwen Addition Community Organization* (Appeals); *Commonwealth; Jones; Bridgeport Guardians* v. *Police Department; U.S.* v. *City of St. Louis; U.S.* v. *City of St. Louis* (Appeals); and *Shield Club*). In the twenty other cases, the court either assumed knowledge of the job requirements or relied on either expert testimony or pre-existing information, such as job descriptions or specifications which were developed for other purposes. Despite the fact that job analysis is essential to validity, the study found the fact that no formal job analysis had been conducted had little effect on the rulings. In only three cases did a judge rule against a defendant for failure to perform an adequate job analysis: *Western Addition Community Organization; Vulcan Society;* and *Kirkland.* Kleinman and Faley concluded that "in the vast majority of cases,...the courts failed to consider the issue" and that the courts' evaluations were based upon whatever job information was available, regardless of how it was obtained.

What basis do the courts use, then, to evaluate job analysis? It appears that job analysis may be accepted if it is done in "good faith," or by obtaining a statement of the duties prior to performance appraisal by consulting with a subject matter expert (e.g., job incumbents, job analysts, and supervisors) to determine the most significant responsibilities of the job.

REFERENCES

- Arvey, Richard D., Emily M. Passino and John W. Lounsbury, "Job Analysis Results as Influenced by Sex of Incumbent and Sex of Analyst," *Journal of Applied Psychology* 62 (August 1977), pp. 411–416.
- *Bridgeport Guardians* v. *Police Department,* 16 FEP 486.
- *Chance* v. *Board of Examiners* (Appeals), 4 FEP 556.
- *Commonwealth of Pennsylvania* v. *Flaherty,* 11 EPD 10, 624.
- *Davis* v. *Washington,* 5 FEP 293.
- Flanagan, J.C. "The Critical Incident Technique," *Psychological Bulletin,* 1954, 51, 327–358.
- *Greenspan* v. *Automobile Club of Michigan,* 22 FEP, 195.
- Hackman, Richard and Greg R. Oldman. "Development of the Job Diagnostic Survey," *Journal of Applied Psychology* 60 (April 1975), pp. 159–170.
- Jenkins, G. Douglas Jr., David A. Nadler, Edward E. Lawler III and Courtlendt Cammann. "Standardized Observations: An Approach to Measuring the Nature of Jobs," *Journal of Applied Psychology* 60 (April 1975), pp. 171–181.
- *Jones* v. *New York Human Resources Administration,* 11 EPD 10.664.
- *Kirkland* v. *Department of Correctional Services,* 7 FEP 694.
- Kleinman, L.S. and R.H. Faley. "Assessing Content Validity: Standards Set by the Court," *Personnel Psychology,* 31, 4, 1978.
- Krzytofiak, F.J., J.M. Newman and G. Anderson. "A Quantified Approach to Measurement of Job Content: Procedures and Payoffs," *Personnel Psychology.* Summer 1979.
- Levine, E.L., R.A. Ash and N. Bennett. "Exploratory Comparative Study of Four Job Analysis Methods," *Journal of Applied Psychology,* Vol. 65, 1980, pp. 524–535.
- Lindsay, C.M. "Equal Pay for Comparable Worth," *Economic Analysis of a New Anti-Discrimination Doctrine.* University of Miami Law and Economic Center, 1980, p. 18.
- McCormick, E., P.R. Jeanneret and R.C. Mechan, "A Study of Job Characteristics and Job Dimensions as Based on the Position Analysis Questionnaire (PAQ)," *Journal of Applied Psychology* 56 (August 1972), pp. 347–368.

- Milkovich, George T. "Wage Differentials and Comparable Worth: The Emerging Debate." Washington, D.C.: Equal Employment Advisory Council, *Review of Comparable Worth.* 1980.
- Pearlman, K.R. "Job Families," *Psychological Bulletin,* 1980, pp. 1–23. Vol. 87, No. 1.
- Primoff, E.S. *How to Prepare and Conduct Job Element Examinations.* Washington, D.C.: U.S. Government Printing Office, 1975. (GPO No. 006-000-00893-3).
- Records of the City and County of Denver Career Service Authority, 1977.
- Schwab, Donald P. "Intra-Organizational Pay Setting and Comparable Worth." Washington, D.C.: Equal Employment Advisory Council, *Review of Comparable Worth.* 1980.
- *Shield Club* v. *City of Cleveland,* 13 FEP 533.
- Tornow, Walter W. and Patrick R. Pinto. "The Development of a Managerial Job Taxonomy: A System for Describing, Classifying and Evaluating Executive Position," *Journal of Applied Psychology* 61 (August 1976), pp. 410–418.
- *U.S.* v. *City of St. Louis* (Appeals), 14 FEP 1486.
- U.S. Department of Labor, *Handbook for Analyzing Jobs.* Washington, D.C.: U.S. Government Printing Office, 1972. (GPO No. 029-000-00131-6).
- U.S. Department of Labor, Bureau of Labor Statistics, *Length of Working Life for Men and Women, 1970,* Special Labor Force Report No. 197. Washington, D.C.: U.S. Government Printing Office, 1977.
- U.S. Department of Labor, Bureau of Employment Security, *Dictionary of Occupational Titles,* 4th ed., Washington, D.C.: U.S. Government Printing Office, 1977.
- *Uniform Guidelines on Employee Selection Procedures, Federal Register,* August 25, 1978.
- *Vulcan Society* v. *Civil Service Commission,* 6 FEP 1945.
- Wallace, Marc J., Jr. and Ralph E. Steuer. "Satisfying Job Centered and Employee Centered Objectives in the Design of Internal Wage Structures." Paper presented to the National Academy of Management Meetings, Detroit, 1980.
- Wegener, E. "Comparable Worth: EEOC's Issue of the 80s?" *The Personnel Administrator* (May 1980), pp. 38–43.
- *Western Addition Community Organization* v. *Alioto,* 4 FEP 772.
- *Western Addition Community Organization* v. *Alioto* (Appeals), 6 FEP 85.
- Wexley, Kenneth N. and Stanley B. Silverman, "An Examination of Differences Between Managerial Effectiveness and Response Patterns on a Structured Job Analysis Questionnaire," *Journal of Applied Psychology* 63 (October 1978), pp. 646–649.

Types of Performance Measures

by Wayne Cascio

OBJECTIVE MEASURES

Performance measures may be classified into two general types: objective and subjective. *Objective performance* measures include production data (dollar volume of sales, units produced, number of errors, amount of scrap) as well as personnel data (accidents, turnover, absences, tardiness). These variables directly define the goals of the organization, but they often suffer from several glaring weaknesses, the most serious of which are performance unreliability and modification of performance by situational characteristics. For example, dollar volume of sales is influenced by numerous factors beyond a particular salesperson's control—for example, territory location, number of accounts in the territory, nature of the competition, distances between accounts, price and quality of the product, and so forth. Our objective in performance appraisal, however, is to judge an individual's *performance,* not factors beyond his or her control. Moreover, objective measures focus not on behavior, but rather on the outcomes or results of behavior. Admittedly, there will be some degree of overlap between behavior and results, but the two are qualitatively different (Levinson, 1976). Finally, in many jobs (e.g., those of middle managers), there simply are no good objective indices of performance, and in the case of personnel data, variables in this category are usually present in less than 5% of the cases examined (Landy & Trumbo, 1976). Hence, they are often useless as performance criteria. In short, although objective measures of performance are intuitively attractive, theoretical and practical limitations often make them unsuitable. Although they can be useful when used as supplements to supervisory judgments, correlations between objective and subjective measures are often low (Cascio & Valenzi, 1978) and when used as bases for personnel decisions, the combination of such measures may be weighed differently for different ethnic groups (Bass & Turner, 1973).

From *Applied Psychology in Personnel Management* by Wayne Cascio (Reston, Virginia: Reston, 1978) pp. 317–336. Reprinted with permission of Reston Publishing Company, Inc., a Prentice Hall Company, 11480 Sunset Hills Road, Reston, Virginia.

SUBJECTIVE MEASURES

The disadvantages of objective measures have led researchers and managers to place major emphasis on *subjective measures* of job performance. However, since subjective measures are dependent upon human judgment, they are prone to certain kinds of errors associated with the rating process. To be useful, they must be based on a careful analysis of the behaviors viewed as necessary and important for effective job performance.

We will have more to say about developmental procedures for rating formats in a later section, but for the present, it is important to point out that there is enormous variation in the types of subjective performance measures used by organizations. Some use a long list of elaborate rating scales; others use only a few simple scales; still others require managers to write a paragraph or two concerning the performance of each of their subordinates.

In addition, subjective measures of performance may be *relative* (in which comparisons are made among a group of ratees) or *absolute* (in which a ratee is described without reference to others). Regardless of their form, however, subjective performance appraisals frequently suffer from various behavioral barriers which limit their effectiveness.

SYSTEMATIC APPROACHES TO SUBJECTIVE APPRAISAL

Performance appraisal systems were classified earlier as either relative or absolute. Within this taxonomy, the following methods may be distinguished:

Relative	*Absolute*
Rank order	Essays
Paired comparisons	Behavior checklists
Forced distribution	Critical incidents
	Graphic rating scales

Relative Rating Systems (Employee Comparisons)

Simple ranking requires only that a rater order all ratees from highest to lowest, from "best" employee to "worst" employee. *Alternation ranking* requires that the rater initially list all ratees on a sheet of paper. From this list the rater first chooses the best ratee (#1), then the worst ratee (#n), then the second best (#2), then the second worst (#$n - 1$), and so forth, alternating from the top to the bottom of the list until all ratees have been ranked.

Both simple and alternation ranking implicitly require a rater to compare each ratee with every other ratee, but systematic ratee-to-ratee comparison is not a built-in feature of these methods. For this we need *paired comparisons.* The number of pairs of ratees to be compared may be calculated from the formula $[n(n-1)]/2$. Hence if 10 individuals were being compared, $[10(9)]/2$ or 45 comparisons would be required. The rater's task is simply to choose the better of each pair, and each individual's rank is determined by counting the number of times he or she was rated superior.

Employee comparison methods are easy to explain and are helpful in making personnel decisions. They also provide useful criterion data in validation studies, for they effectively control leniency and central tendency errors. Like other systems, however, they suffer from several weaknesses which should be recognized.

Employees are usually compared only in terms of a single overall suitability category. The rankings, therefore, lack behavioral specificity, and may be subject to legal challenge (as in *Albemarle Paper Company* v. *Moody,* 1975).[1] Halo is merely obscured, not eliminated (Guion, 1965), and in addition, employee comparisons yield only ordinal data—data which give no indication of the relative distance between individuals. Moreover, it is often impossible to compare rankings across work groups, departments, or locations. The last two problems can be alleviated, however, by converting the ranks to normalized standard scores which form an approximately normal distribution.

A further problem stems from the tendency of employee comparison methods to reward members of an inferior group and penalize members of a superior group. Finally, as ratee group size decreases, error increases, inversely as the square root of group size (Duffy & Webber, 1974). Reliability also may suffer, for when asked to re-rank all individuals at a later date, the extreme high or low rankings will probably remain stable, but the rankings in the middle of the scale may shift around considerably.

A final employee comparison method, the *forced distribution,* has been discussed previously. Its primary advantage is that it controls leniency and central tendency errors rather effectively, but it assumes that ratees conform to a normal distribution. This may introduce a great deal of error if a group of ratees, *as a group,* is either superior or substandard. In short, rather than eliminating error, forced distribution may simply introduce a different kind of error!

Absolute Rating Systems

Absolute rating systems enable a rater to describe a ratee without making direct reference to other ratees. Perhaps the simplest absolute rating system is the *narrative essay,* in which the rater is asked to describe, in writing, an individual's strengths, weaknesses, and potential together with suggestions for improvement. The assumption underlying this approach is that a candid statement from a rater who is

---

[1]This will not always be the case, especially when behaviorally anchored paired comparisons are used.

knowledgeable of a ratee's performance is just as valid as more formal and more complicated appraisal methods.

The major advantage of narrative essays (when they are done well) is that they provide detailed feedback to ratees regarding their performance. On the other hand, essays are almost totally unstructured and they vary widely in length and content. Comparisons across individuals, groups, or departments are virtually impossible since different essays touch on different aspects of ratee performance or personal qualifications. Finally, essays provide only *qualitative* information; yet in order for the appraisals to serve as criteria or to be compared objectively and ranked for the purpose of a personnel decision, some form of rating which can be *quantitied* is essential. Behavioral checklists provide one such scheme.

When using a behavioral checklist, the rater is provided with a series of descriptive statements of job-related behavior. His task is simply to indicate ("check") which of the statements are descriptive of the ratee in question. In this approach raters are not so much evaluators as they are reporters of job behavior. Moreover, ratings which are descriptive are likely to be higher in reliability than ratings which are evaluative (Stockford & Bissell, 1949).

To be sure, some job behaviors are more desirable than others; checklist items can, therefore, be scaled by using attitude scale construction methods (cf. Edwards, 1957). In one such method, the Likert method of *summated ratings,* a declarative statement (e.g., "she follows through on her sales") is followed by several response categories, such as "always," "very often," "fairly often," "occasionally," and "never." The rater simply checks the response category which he feels best describes the ratee. Each response category is weighted—for example, from 5 ("always") to 1 ("never") if the statement describes desirable behavior, or vice versa if the statement describes undesirable behavior. An overall numerical rating for each individual can then be derived by summing the weights of the responses which were checked for each item, and scores for each performance dimension can be obtained by using item analysis procedures (cf. Anastasi, 1976).

The selection of response categories for summated rating scales is often made arbitrarily, with equal intervals between scale points simply assumed. Scaled lists of adverbial modifiers of frequency and amount are available, however, together with statistically optimal 4–9 point scales (Bass, Cascio, & O'Connor, 1974). Scaled values are also available for categories of agreement, evaluation, and frequency (Spector, 1976). A final issue concerns the optimal number of scale points for summated rating scales. Although several investigations have concluded that reliability is generally independent of the number of scale points used (Komorita & Graham, 1965; Matell & Jacoby, 1971), Lissitz and Green (1975), using a Monte Carlo approach, have shown that for relatively homogeneous items, reliability increases up to five scale points, and levels off thereafter.

Checklists may also be constructed using Thurstone's method of *equal-appearing intervals.* First, a large number of statements which describe both desirable and undesirable job behaviors are generated, and judges sort the statements into piles representing steps along 7-, 9-, or 11-point scales of desirability. Means and standard deviations are then computed for each statement. Mean judgments represent scale values, while the standard deviations of judgments represent measures of statement ambiguity. Statements with large standard deviations are discarded, for they apparently mean different things to different people. Unambiguous statements representing the full range of scale values are then assembled into a checklist for rating. Fortunately, this rather laborious preliminary effort is not really necessary since Uhrbrock (1950, 1961) has published lists of 724 and 2000 scaled items, each with mean and standard deviation. An independent check on the stability of these scale values, using a different sample of judges and a different technique, correlated .97 with those reported by Uhrbrock (Prien & Campbell, 1957).

An example of an equal-appearing intervals scale is presented in Table 1; in practice, however, raters would not be shown statement means and standard deviations. They simply check as many statements as apply to describe a particular ratee, and an individual's overall rating is equal to the sum of the scale values of the items checked.

The item "has surly attitude" would ordinarily be dropped from the scale because it is ambiguous (S.D. = 12.1). This ability to evaluate statement ambiguity is clearly the main advantage of the equal-appearing intervals approach.

Halo has not been a serious problem with checklists since they yield only an overall summary rating. However, there is no control for leniency, although special scoring procedures can be developed for this purpose (Bass, 1956). Despite these advantages, it is sometimes difficult for a rater to give diagnostic feedback based on checklist ratings, for he does not see the scale values of the items he chooses. On balance, the many advantages of checklists (developed either by Likert or Thurstone scaling procedures) probably account for their widespread popularity in organizations today.

Forced-Choice Systems

A special type of behavioral checklist is known as the forced-choice system—a technique developed specifically to reduce leniency errors and to establish objective standards of comparison between individuals (Sisson, 1948). In order to accomplish this, checklist statements are arranged in groups, from which the rater chooses statements which are most or least descriptive of the ratee. An overall rating (score) for each individual is then derived by applying a special scoring key to the rater's descriptions.

TABLE 1
Sample Equal-Appearing Intervals Scale*

Item	*Mean*	*S.D.*
Is a dynamic leader who stimulates enthusiasm	109.4	2.4
Is very well informed on all phases of work	99.4	7.5
Conveys ideas well to others	89.4	5.6
Learns quickly	78.8	5.9
Doesn't waste much time	68.1	6.3
Makes occasional errors and mistakes	58.1	3.9
Wanders from subject in conversation	48.8	4.8
Is slow	37.5	5.6
Too often needs to be shown what to do next	28.1	6.3
Has surly attitude	18.8	12.1
Cannot be trusted	10.6	2.4

*Adapted from Uhrbrock, R.S. 2000 scaled items. *Personnel Psychology,* 1961, *14,* 375–420.

Forced-choice scales are constructed according to two statistical properties of the checklist items: (1) *discriminability,* a measure of the degree to which an item differentiates effective from ineffective workers, and (2) *preference,* an index of the degree to which the quality expressed in an item is valued (i.e., is socially desirable) by people (Guilford, 1954). The rationale of the forced-choice system requires that items be paired so that they appear equally attractive (socially desirable) to the rater. Theoretically, then, the selection of any single item in a pair should be based solely upon the item's discriminating power, not its social desirability.

Although many different item arrangements have been used, Berkshire and Highland (1953) found optimal a form which included four statements, all favorable (and equally socially desirable), from which the rater selects the two statements most like the ratee. It was most resistant to deliberately induced bias, it demonstrated adequate reliability and validity, and it was one of the two forms most preferred by the raters. For example, in rating Air Force instructors, the following tetrad was used by Berkshire and Highland (1953):

a. Patient with slow learners.
b. Lectures with confidence.
c. Keeps the interest and attention of class.
d. Acquaints classes with the objective for each lesson in advance.

All four statements are approximately equal in preference value, but only *a* and *c* were found to be characteristic of effective instructors. Modifications of this basic forced-choice system have been tried (Kay, 1959; Obradovic, 1970), with mixed success.

The main advantage claimed for forced-choice scales is that a rater cannot distort a person's ratings higher or lower than is warranted since he or she has no way of knowing which statements to check in order to do so. If the rater deliberately attempts to be positively lenient in assigning ratings, he or she is most likely to choose statements which are socially desirable, but which can also be said of almost everyone and, therefore, do not discriminate effective from ineffective performers. Hence, leniency should theoretically be reduced. However, when forced-choice scales have been administered first under guidance conditions and later under employment selection conditions, marked distortion in a positive direction has been observed (Hedberg, 1962; Mahler, 1959), although this is not always the case (Gordon & Stapleton, 1956).

Forced-choice scales can always be beaten by using an "ideal employee" strategy. When a rater wants to give average employee Linda Middle a high rating, the rater simply describes the very best employee he knows on Linda Middle's forced-choice form. Forced-choice systems do not, in general, control for halo. They usually give only a single, global indication of merit, rather than ratings of specific dimensions of performance. Sets of items are usually not developed for specific dimensions because a great deal of time and effort is required to write and scale items and then to develop tetrads which: (1) are matched on social desirability, and (2) discriminate adequately among individuals.

There are two further problems with forced-choice scales. The most serious is rater resistance. Since control is removed from the rater, he or she cannot be sure just how she rated a subordinate. Raters often become irritated with forced-choice scales; they want to say openly how they rate someone and not be second-guessed or tricked with making "honest" appraisals (Oberg, 1972). Finally, forced-choice forms are of little use (and may even have a negative effect) in performance appraisal interviews, for the rater is unaware of the scale values of the items he chooses. In order to overcome these difficulties, some form of critical incident scale may be used.

Critical Incidents

This method of performance appraisal has generated a great deal of interest in recent years, and several variations of the basic idea are currently in use. As described by Flanagan (1954b), the critical requirements of a job are those behaviors which make a crucial difference between doing a job effectively and doing it ineffectively. *Critical incidents* are simply reports by knowledgeable observers of things employees did that were especially effective or ineffective in accomplishing parts of their jobs. Critical incidents are recorded for each employee by supervisors, as they occur. Thus, they provide a behaviorally based starting point for appraising performance. For example, in observing a police officer chasing an armed robbery suspect down a busy street, a supervisor recorded the following:

June 22, officer Mitchell withheld fire in a situation calling for the use of weapons where gunfire would endanger innocent bystanders.

Critical incidents typically provide information on both the static and dynamic aspects of a job. These little anecdotes force attention on the situational determinants of job behavior and also on ways of doing the job successfully that may be unique to the person described (individual dimensionality). The critical incidents method looks like a natural for performance appraisal interviews because supervisors can focus on actual job behavior rather than on vaguely defined traits. Performance, not personality, is being judged. Ratees receive meaningful feedback and they can see what changes in their job behavior will be necessary in order for them to improve. While the ratee may not agree with his supervisor's standards, at least he knows what those standards are (Oberg, 1972). In addition, when a large number of critical incidents are collected, abstracted, and categorized, they can provide a rich storehouse of information about job and organizational problems in general and are particularly well-suited for establishing objectives for training programs (Flanagan & Burns, 1955).

As with other approaches to performance appraisal, the critical incidents method also has its drawbacks. First of all, it is time-consuming and burdensome for supervisors to record incidents for all of their subordinates on a daily or even weekly basis. Feedback may, therefore, be delayed. Moreover, the rater sets the standards by which subordinates are judged; yet subordinates are likely to be more motivated if they have some say in setting their own behavioral standards. Finally, in their narrative form, incidents do not readily lend themselves to quantification, which, as we noted earlier, poses problems in between-individual and between-group comparisons as well as in statistical analyses.

For these reasons two variations of the original idea have been suggested. Kirchner and Dunnette (1957b), for example, used the method to develop a behavioral checklist (using the method of summated ratings) for rating sales performance. After incidents were abstracted and classified, selected items were assembled into a checklist. For example,

Gives good service on customers' complaints

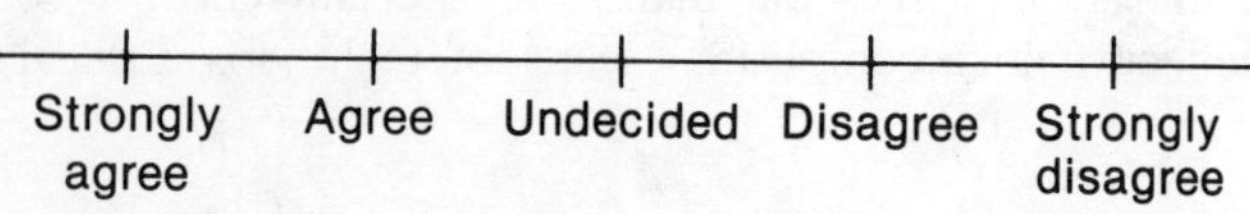

A second modification has been the development of behaviorally anchored rating scales, an approach we will treat more fully in the next section.

Graphic Rating Scales

Probably the most widely used method of performance appraisal is the *graphic rating scale.* Landy and Trumbo (1976), for example, reported that 72% of the validation studies published in the *Journal of Applied Psychology* between 1955 and 1975 relied on some form of rating scale, examples of which are presented in Fig. 1.

In terms of the amount of structure provided, the scales differ in three ways: (1) the degree to which the meaning of the response categories is defined, (2) the degree to which the individual who is interpreting the ratings (e.g., a personnel manager or researcher) can tell clearly what response was intended, and (3) the degree to which the performance dimension being rated is defined for the rater.

On a graphic rating scale each point is defined on a continuum. Hence, in order to make meaningful distinctions in performance within dimensions, scale points must be defined unambiguously for the rater. This process is called *anchoring.* Scale *a* uses qualitative end anchors only, while scale *b* includes numerical anchors as well. These anchors are almost worthless, however, since what constitutes high and low quality is left completely up to the rater. A "4" for one rater may be a "2" for another. Scale *c* is a slight improvement, but scale *h* is even better; it is clear and easy to use.

The scales also differ in the relative ease with which a person interpreting the ratings can tell exactly what response was intended by the rater. In scale *a,* for example, the particular value which the rater had in mind is a mystery. This is also true of scales *b, c, d,* and *i.* Scales *e, f,* and *g* are less ambiguous in this respect.

Finally, the scales differ in terms of the clarity of the definition of the performance dimension in question. In terms of Fig. 1, what does *quality* mean? Is *quality* for a nurse the same as *quality* for a quality control inspector? In Fig. 1, it is more desirable to speak of quality in terms of errors and mistakes as in scales *d* and *h,* or accuracy, economy, and neatness (though these may be independent dimensions) as in scales *f* and *i.* On the other hand, scales *a, b, e,* and *g* offer almost no help to the rater in defining just what is to be rated.

In constructing rating scales, intensive research (Barrett, 1966; Edwards, 1957; Guilford, 1954) and experience lead to the following suggestions:

1. Performance dimensions should be factorially pure (i.e., only homogeneous clusters of activities should be grouped together).
2. Performance dimensions should be behaviorally based. The rater should be able to support all ratings with objective, observable evidence.

FIGURE 1
Examples of Graphic Rating Scales

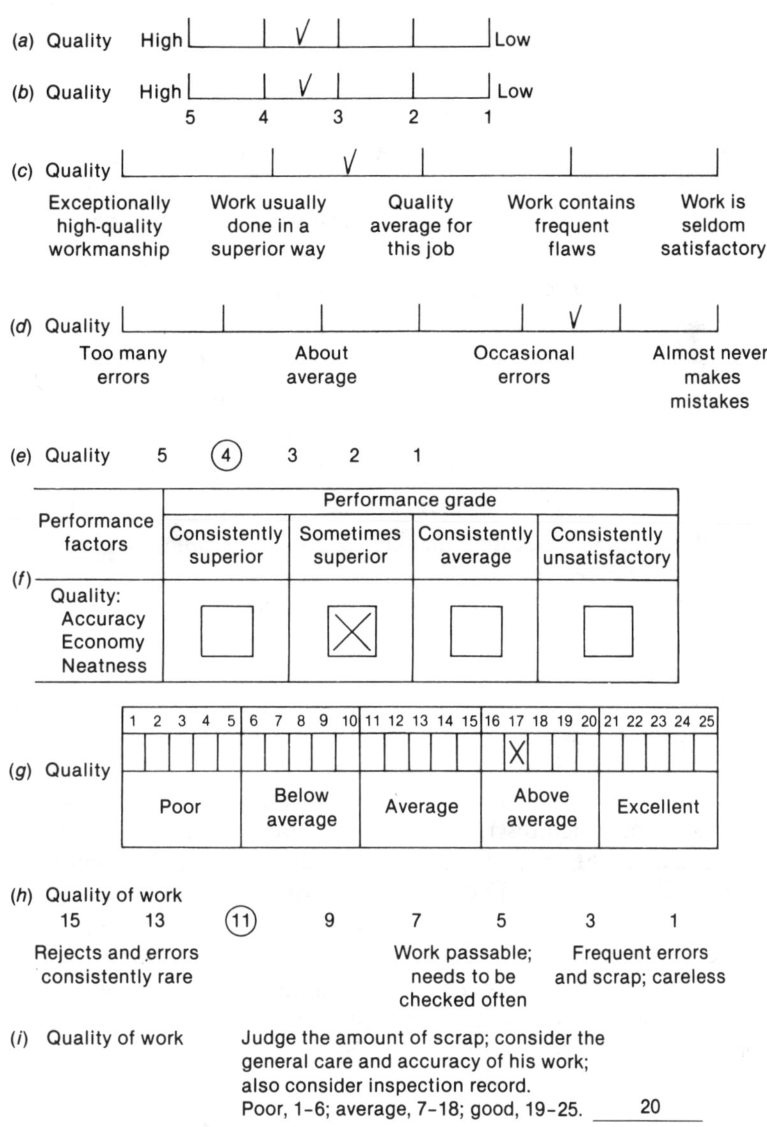

Source: Guion, R.M. *Personnel Testing,* New York: McGraw Hill, 1965.

3. Abstract trait names such as loyalty, honesty, and integrity should be avoided unless they can be defined in terms of observable behaviors.
4. Anchors should be brief, unambiguous, and relevant to the dimensions being rated. For example, in rating a speaker's flow of words, it is preferable to use anchors such as "fluent," "easy," "unimpeded," "hesitant," and "labored," rather than "excellent," "very good," "average," "below average," and "poor."
5. Avoid double negatives or logical inconsistencies which make interpretation difficult.

Graphic rating scales may not yield the depth of narrative essays or critical incidents, but they: (1) are less time-consuming to develop and administer, (2) permit quantitative results to be determined, (3) are dimensionally heterogeneous, and (4) are standardized and, therefore, comparable across individuals. On the other hand, graphic rating scales give maximum control to the rater, thereby exercising no control over leniency, central tendency, or halo errors. For this reason, they have been widely criticized. Nevertheless, when simple graphic rating scales have been compared against more sophisticated forced-choice ratings, the graphic scale consistently proved just as reliable and valid and was more acceptable to raters (Berkshire & Highland, 1953; Taylor & Wherry, 1951). Recently, however, there have been two exciting innovations in graphic rating scales—mixed standard scales and behaviorally anchored rating scales.

FIGURE 2
Mixed Standard Rating Scale Where I, II, and III Represent the Dimensions of Efficiency, Self-Confidence, and Report Making, Respectively, and "G", "A", and "P" represent good, average, and poor performance.

		Rating
II.	1. Has normal self-confidence, with only occasional uncertainty. He usually is open and assured. (A)	0
I.	2. There is some lack of efficiency on his part. He may take too much time to complete his assignments, and sometimes he does not really finish them. (P)	+
III.	3. Both his written and oral reports are well formulated, thorough, and well thought out. They rarely need additional explanation. (G)	+
II.	4. He is a little shy and uncertain. Occasionally avoids situations which require him to take a position. (P)	+
I.	5. He is efficient enough, usually getting through his assignments and work in a reasonable time. (A)	+
III.	6. Sometimes his reports are so incomplete and poorly organized that they are of little value, or must be done over. (P)	+
I.	7. He is quick and efficient, able to keep his work on schedule. He really gets going on a new task. (G)	0
II.	8. Behaves confidently. Reacts in all situations without hesitation and assurance. (G)	−
III.	9. His reports are useful and meaningful, but they usually require some additional explanations. (A)	+

Adapted from Blanz, F., Ghiselli, E.E. The mixed standard scale: A new rating system. *Personnel Psychology,* 1972, *25,* 185–199.

Mixed standard scales. These are designed specifically to minimize halo and leniency errors, and to permit evaluations of the reliability with which each individual is rated, each scale rates, and each rater rates (Blanz & Ghiselli, 1972). The procedure is as follows. Items which discriminate effective from ineffective performance are first obtained from knowledgeable persons (usually supervisors). For each performance dimension to be rated, three items are chosen which represent good, average, and poor performance, respectively. These are "standards" or degrees of performance, and the rater must respond to each standard, indicating whether he considers the ratee to be better than the description (+), to fit the description (0), or to be worse than the description (−).

The performance dimensions and the standards describing them are then randomly mixed so that no clear order-of-merit descriptions exist for each dimension. A mixed standard scale using only three (of the 18) dimensions used by Blanz and Ghiselli (1972) is presented in Fig. 2.

If all ratings are assigned accurately, then whenever the rater checks one statement as "fits the ratee" (0), all statements in that scale which describe superior behavior should be checked as "the ratee is poorer than this statement" (−), and all those which describe inferior behavior should be checked as "the ratee is better than this statement" (+). If all three standards in a scale are checked (+), then in the rater's opinion, the ratee is truly exceptional on this dimension since he or she exceeds even the best of the three standards. On the other hand, if all three standards are checked (−), then according to the rater the ratee is very poor since his or her performance is worse than even the poorest of the three standards. According to the scoring scheme in Fig. 3, the individual in Fig. 2 received a score of 6 on dimension I (efficiency), a 4 on dimension II (self-confidence), and a 7 on dimension III (report-making).

Obviously, not all raters will respond accurately and logically. For example, a rater might say that an individual was worse than the "poor" statement but better than the "average" statement. In this case, the scoring scheme in Figure 3 would not apply. Blanz and Ghiselli (1972) have developed a scoring scheme which will handle such logically inconsistent errors, but empirical evidence on its effectiveness is not yet available.

The rationale for mixing standards stems directly from the logic of forced-choice formats—namely, that halo and leniency are likely to be reduced if ratings are not made on a scale with statements arranged in an obvious order-of-merit hierarchy. Empirical findings lend support to these hypotheses (Saal & Landy, 1977). In addition, raters tend to use all seven scale points. A final advantage of mixed standard scales, and one which is not to be taken lightly is that they are capable of providing indices of the extent of error for different raters and ratees and for different scales.

Mixed standard scales are not without their disadvantages, however. Completion of each statement for each ratee is a painstaking task. When a large number of statements must be responded to individually, negative rater reaction may be anticipated, and inter-rater reliabilities may be low (Saal & Landy, 1977). Scoring may also be time-consuming (although computer scoring is possible). Finally, since items and dimensions are both scrambled, mixed standard scales may not be very useful in performance appraisal interviews. Nevertheless, the mixed

FIGURE 3
Scoring Scheme for a Mixed Standard Scale.

Statements			*Points*
G	A	P	
+	+	+	7
0	+	+	6
–	+	+	5
–	0	+	4
–	–	+	3
–	–	0	2
–	–	–	1

+ = the ratee is better than the statement
0 = the statement fits the ratee
– = the ratee is worse than the statement
(Adapted from Blanz & Ghiselli, 1972.)

standard format is well suited for other uses of performance appraisals; hopefully, its advantages will stimulate further development and more widespread use in the future.

Behaviorally anchored rating scales. So far, it seems that the performance appraisal systems which are most acceptable to raters (e.g., narrative essays, employee comparisons, graphic scales) are often least acceptable in terms of their psychometric characteristics. Conversely, those which are psychometrically acceptable (e.g., forced-choice scales) are often resisted by raters. Where is the happy medium? According to Smith and Kendall (1963):

> Better ratings can be obtained, in our opinion, not by trying to trick the rater (as in forced-choice scales) but by helping him to rate. We should ask him questions which he can honestly answer about behaviors which he can observe. We should reassure him that his answers will not be misinterpreted, and we should provide a basis by which he and others can check his answers. (p. 151)

Their procedure is as follows. At an initial conference, groups of workers and/or supervisors attempt to identify and define all of the important dimensions of effective performance for a particular job. Graphically:

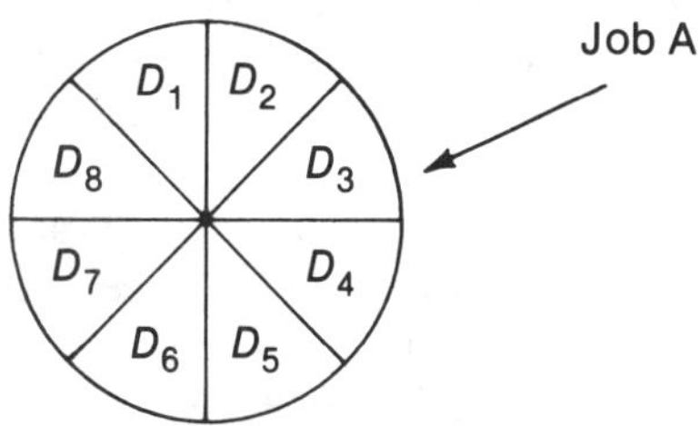

A second group then generates, for each dimension, critical incidents illustrating effective, average, and ineffective performance. A third group is then given a list of dimensions and their definitions, along with a randomized list of the critical incidents generated by the second group. Their task is to sort or allocate incidents into the dimensions which they best represent. Graphically:

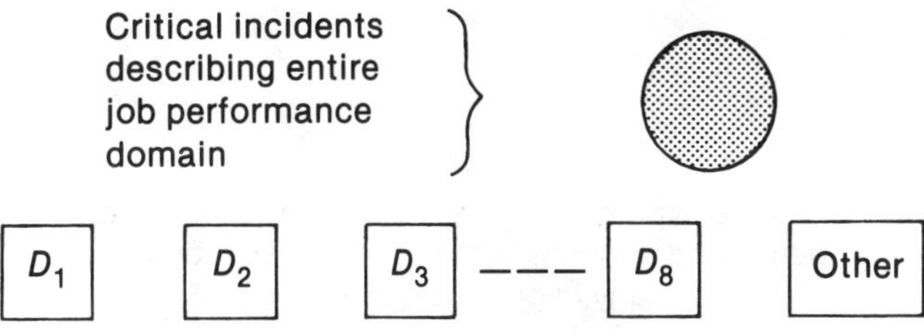

This procedure is known as *retranslation* since it resembles the quality control check which is used to insure the adequacy of translations from one language into another. Material is translated into a foreign language and then retranslated back into the original by an independent translator. In the context of performance appraisal, this procedure ensures that the meaning of both the job dimensions and the behavioral incidents chosen to illustrate them is specific and clear. Incidents are eliminated if there is not clear agreement among judges (usually 60–80%) regarding the dimension to which each incident belongs. Dimensions are eliminated if incidents are not allocated to them. Conversely, dimensions may be added if many incidents are allocated to the "other" category.

Each of the items within dimensions that survived the retranslation procedure is then presented to a fourth group of judges, whose task is to place a scale value on each incident (e.g., in terms of a 7- or 9-point scale from "highly effective behavior" to "grossly ineffective behavior"). Graphically:

D_1	D_2	. . .	D_8
7 C.I.	7 C.I.		7 C.I.
6 C.I.	6 C.I.		6 C.I.
5 C.I.	5 C.I.		5 C.I.
4 C.I.	4 C.I.		4 C.I.
3 C.I.	3 C.I.		3 C.I.
2 C.I.	2 C.I.		2 C.I.
1 C.I.	1 C.I.		1 C.I.

Means and standard deviations for each incident are then computed. Items in the final scale for each dimension must have mean scale values covering the entire range of performance and low standard deviations. The end product looks like that in Fig. 4.

Finally, the behaviorally anchored rating scales (BARS) are pilot-tested with a sample of supervisors who are asked to rate their subordinates on each of the dimensions. Each subordinate is rated independently by at least two raters, and the ratings are correlated to provide an estimate of inter-rater reliability. Scale scores are also intercorrelated as a check on dimension independence. Periodically thereafter (e.g., annually), the behavioral anchors are checked for their continued relevance, clarity, and scale values.

BARS development is a long, painstaking process which may require many individuals. Moreover, separate

FIGURE 4
Scaled Expectations Rating Scale for the Effectiveness with Which the Department Manager Supervises His Sales Personnel.

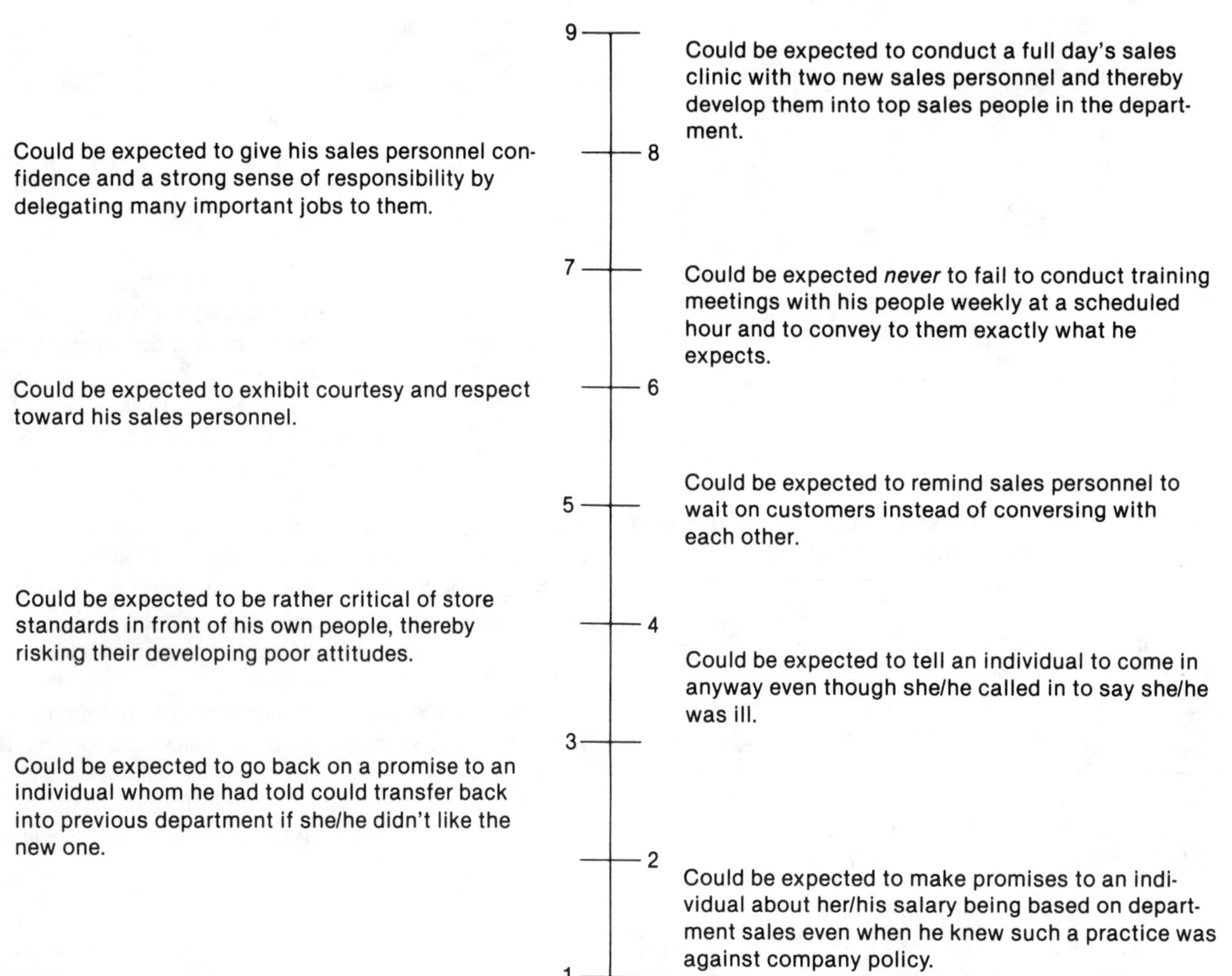

From Campbell, J.P., Dunnette, M.D., Arvey, R.D., & Hellervik, L.V. The development and evaluation of behaviorally based rating scales. *Journal of Applied Psychology,* 1973, *57,* 15–22. *Copyright ©1973 by the American Psychological Association. Reprinted by permission.*

BARS must be developed for dissimilar jobs. Consequently, this approach may not be practical for many organizations. As BARS grow in popularity and use, however, it is likely that scales which have generality across organizations (e.g., BARS for computer programmers, purchasing agents) will be developed.

The retranslation approach to developing job behavior rating scales holds considerable promise and many advantages are claimed for it. BARS are rooted in, and referable to, actual job behavior, not vaguely defined personality traits. A second advantage may be attributed to an aspect of the developmental procedure which is unrelated to the measurement of performance *per se*—namely, intense rater–ratee involvement throughout all phases of BARS development. High participation serves a dual purpose: (1) it ensures acceptability of the resulting scales and a commitment to make them work, and (2) it guarantees that the scales are relevant to the jobs in question. Performance dimensions and behavioral anchors are rigorously defined and can be distinguished from one another easily and accurately. Moreover, the scales are phrased in the jargon of the users, not the jargon of the psychologist or scale developer. Finally, even though specific behaviors may be observed in different situations, they are referred to a common set of expectations which serve as a mutual frame of reference (Smith & Kendall, 1963).

How have BARS worked in practice? Evaluative research seems to be organized around three main areas: (1) effects of rater participation, (2) differences in developmental procedures, and (3) comparisons of BARS with other rating systems.

REFERENCES

- Anastasi, A. *Psychological Testing* (4th edition). New York: Macmillan, 1976.

- Barrett, R.S. *Performance rating.* Chicago: Science Research Associates, 1966.
- Bass, A.R. and Turner, J.N. Ethnic group differences in relationships among criteria of job performance. *Journal of Applied Psychology,* 1973, *57,* 101–109.
- Bass, B.M. Reducing leniency in merit ratings. *Personnel Psychology,* 1956, *9,* 359–369.
- Bass, B.M., Cascio, W.F. and O'Connor, F.J. Magnitude estimations of expressions of frequency and amount. *Journal of Applied Psychology,* 1974, *59,* 313–320.
- Berkshire, J.R. and Highland, R.W. Forced-choice performance rating: A methodological study. *Personnel Psychology,* 1953, *6,* 355–378.
- Blanz, F. and Ghiselli, E.E. The mixed standard scale: A new rating system. *Personnel Psychology,* 1972, *25,* 185–199.
- Campbell, J.P., Dunnette, M.D., Arvey, R.D. and Hellervik, L.V. The development and evaluation of behaviorally based rating scales. *Journal of Applied Psychology,* 1973, *57,* 15–22.
- Cascio, W.F. and Valenzi, E.R. Relations among criteria of police performance. *Journal of Applied Psychology.* In press.
- Duffy, K.E. and Webber, R.E. On "relative" rating systems. *Personnel Psychology,* 1974, *27,* 307–311.
- Edwards, A.L. *Techniques of attitude scale construction.* New York: Appleton-Century-Crofts, 1957.
- Flannagan, J.C. The critical incident technique. *Psychological Bulletin,* 1954, *51,* 327–358 (b).
- Flannagan, J.C. and Burns, R.K. The employee performance record: A new appraisal and development tool. *Harvard Business Review,* 1955, *33,* 95–102.
- Gordon, L.V. and Stapleton, E.S. Fakability of a forced-choice personality test under realistic high school employment conditions. *Journal of Applied Psychology,* 1956, *40,* 258–262.
- Gordon, L.V. and Medland, F.F. The cross-group stability of peer ratings of leadership potential. *Personnel Psychology,* 1965, *18,* 173–177.
- Guilford, J.P. *Psychometric methods* (2nd edition). New York: McGraw-Hill, 1954.
- Guion, R.M. *Personnel testing.* New York: McGraw-Hill, 1965.
- Hedberg, R. More on forced-choice test fakability. *Journal of Applied Psychology,* 1962, *46,* 125–127.
- Kay, B.R. The use of critical incidents in a forced-choice scale. *Journal of Applied Psychology,* 1959, *43,* 269–270.
- Kirchner, W.K. and Dunnette, M.D. Identifying the critical factors in successful salesmanship. *Personnel,* 1957, *34,* 54–59.
- Komorita, S.S. and Graham, W.K. Number of scale points and the reliability of scales. *Educational and Psychological Measurement,* 1965, *4,* 987–995.
- Landy, F.J. and Trumbo, D.A. *Psychology of work behavior.* Homewood, Illinois: Dorsey, 1976.
- Levinson, H. Appraisal of *what* performance? *Harvard Business Review,* 1976, *54,* 30–32, 34, 36, 40, 44, 46, 160.
- Lissitz, R.W. and Green, S.R. Effect of the number of scale points on reliability: A Monte Carlo approach. *Journal of Applied Psychology,* 1975, 60, 10–13.
- Maher, H. Studies of transparency in forced-choice scales: I. Evidence of transparency. *Journal of Applied Psychology,* 1959, *43,* 275–278.
- Matell, M.S. and Jacoby, J. Is there an optimal number of alternatives for Likert scale items? Study I: Reliability and validity. *Educational and Psychological Measurement,* 1971, *31,* 657–674.
- Oberg, W. Make performance appraisal relevant. *Harvard Business Review,* 1972, *50,* 61–67.
- Obradovic, J. Modification of the forced-choice method as a criterion of job proficiency. *Journal of Applied Psychology,* 1970, *54,* 228–233.
- Prien, E.P. and Campbell, J.T. Stability of rating scale statements. *Personnel Psychology,* 1957, *10,* 305–309.
- Saal, F.E. and Landy, F.L. The mixed standard rating scale: An evaluation. *Organizational Behavior and Human Performance,* 1977, *18,* 19–35.
- Sisson, D.E. Forced choice, the new Army rating. *Personnel Psychology,* 1948, *1,* 365–381.
- Smith, P.C. and Kendall, L.M. Retranslation of expectations: An approach to the construction of unambiguous anchors for rating scales. *Journal of Applied Psychology,* 1963, *47,* 149–155.
- Spector, P.E. Choosing response categories for simulating rating scales. *Journal of Applied Psychology,* 1976, *61,* 374–375.
- Stockford, L. and Bissel, H.W. Factors involved in establishing a merit rating scale. *Personnel,* 1949, *26,* 94–116.
- Taylor, E.K. and Wherry, R.J. A study of leniency in two rating systems. *Personnel Psychology,* 1951, *4,* 39–47.
- Uhrbrock, R.S. Standardization of 724 rating scale statements. *Personnel Psychology,* 1950, *3,* 285–316.
- ———. 2000 scaled items. *Personnel Psychology,* 1961, *14,* 375–420.

MBO as an Approach to Performance Appraisal

by George Labovitz and Lloyd S. Baird

A continuing theme in management literature today is that the MBO approach to managing people is a process of continually structuring expectations through mutual goal setting with subordinates, establishing action plans and target dates, reaching objectives, and providing feedback. This is a way of managing subordinates that permits them to meet their personal needs for responsibility, freedom of

---

This article was prepared especially for this book.

action, and recognition. At the same time the MBO approach provides a supervisor with an element of control, and changes his or her role from police officer to colleague or coach.

THE PROCESS OF MANAGING BY OBJECTIVES

Any time a manager defines responsibilities and expectations with subordinates, sets target dates and interim check points, and provides feedback, he or she is managing by objectives. The supervisor is also going a long way toward establishing a relationship with his or her subordinates that dramatically eases the pain of the traditional, yearly, quantitative evaluation or appraisal process. Involvement with subordinates as they begin to understand their responsibilities, collaborating with them on how those responsibilities will be met, and providing the kind of recognition and feedback that is directive and useful all help to create a good relationship between superior and subordinate. The goal of this relationship is to permit the subordinate to view his or her boss as a facilitator rather than an evaluator. Such a relationship opens channels of communication, reduces cognitive dissonance or rationalizations for inadequate performance, and establishes a work climate in which both the superior and the subordinate can maximize their potential.

There are two dimensions to managing people by objectives. The first deals with a more formal relationship in which responsibilities between superiors and subordinates are clearly defined. The second deals with the supervisor's role in removing obstacles to the subordinate's productivity.

The Formal Relationship

One of the most important things to understand about MBO is that it is a *process* of setting goals and providing feedback. Formal MBO systems often break down because they are not seen as a continuing process. Goals are set and then immediately forgotten until the next year when new goals arc set. Goal setting becomes independent of the work. The key, then, to making an MBO approach work is to understand goal setting as part of the process. Employees and supervisors should leave a goal-setting session understanding the goals, the priorities among the goals, how progress toward the goals will be measured, when and how the employee will receive the feedback necessary to manage the work, and when the employee will be accountable for the results. Then the supervisor and employee must work together on a regular basis to achieve the results.

These goal-setting sessions afford an employee the chance to express his or her own priorities and to disagree with those of the supervisor. The process cannot go forward until mutual agreement on priorities is reached. Goal setting should thus be viewed as an opportunity to negotiate job matters requiring the agreement of both supervisor and subordinate.

Finally, the goal-setting interview gives an employee a chance to promote his or her career development directly. Employees may elicit a superior's analysis of their job performance and competence in the light of the objectives they have established. This will also highlight the need for additional training or experience. It is a chance to indicate what other training or education would forward an employee's career goals.

From the manager's standpoint the goal-setting session affords the opportunity to receive feedback on his or her performance as the boss. Too often this information is not available to superiors. By making these sessions as objective and unemotional as possible, both sides can discuss the other's performance and areas of strength and weakness, and agree about future goals.

Three aspects of performance should be considered in these discussions.

1. *Normal work output*—What products or services constitute the normal work output? What are the measurable units for these products or services? How many and what type of production will be required during the next period?
2. *Normal work output improvements*—What are the areas of performance in which improvement is necessary or desirable? How much improvement is realistic and achievable over the next review period?
3. *Personal or organizational improvements*—What are the current individual or organizational capabilities? What improvements would result in the greatest overall benefit to the organization and individuals concerned? How much improvement is realistic and achievable during the forecast time period?

The purpose of a goal-setting session is to establish goals which are useful not only for performance evaluation at the end of the review period but for managing the work process during that period as well. In order to be useful for management and evaluation goals should:

1. *Identify specific results desired and actions to be taken*—The purpose of goals is to focus activities. Specific targets not only direct effort but provide a concrete basis for measuring accomplishment.
2. *Set time limits*—Specify when an objective should be accomplished. The target date of some objectives will logically fall at the end of the review period; they can be reviewed at that time. Others, however, will require that completion dates and intervals at which to monitor progress be agreed upon during the goal-setting session. This will insure that problems arising during the review period will be identified and corrected.
3. *Specify costs*—The acceptable cost of each objective should be specified. Cost includes money, the price of

human resources, raw materials, technology, and opportunity.

4. *Make your objectives measurable*—In order to determine if objectives have been achieved, they have to be measurable. This does not mean that objectives should always be quantified. There are some very important results that can't be measured in dollars and physical amounts. In objectives involving attitudes, personal improvement, relationships, etc., subjective measures are appropriate. The point is to make them as measurable and useable as possible so that feedback can continue through the performance period.
5. *Make your objectives realistic and attainable*—A good objective should be challenging but attainable.
6. *Be consistent with organization plans, policies, and procedures*—Objectives are established to help people contribute to an organization. They should therefore be consistent with the goals of management.

In setting goals that meet these criteria, standards for performance appraisal during and at the end of the review period will also be established. With these goals, feedback can be a continuing process. The performance review will then be a time to discuss successes and failures and plan for the next period. There is no need to dwell on appraising performance against goals. Because feedback has been constantly received and goals specified, both parties know how performance has been. The only case where actual appraisal—identifying performance and judging the level—will need to take place is where objectives have been set for improvement or in areas where subjective measures are appropriately used. The rest of the time can be spent on solving performance problems and planning for the future. Table 1 details the steps that should be taken in a goal-setting interview which will serve as the basis for future performance appraisals.

This approach to managing by objectives is far less formal than others that have been discussed, but it touches most directly on the modern manager's role as integrator or coordinator, rather than police officer.

Removing Obstacles to Productivity

Removing the obstacles to your subordinate's productivity through the use of MBO as part of a goal-setting and performance appraisal process involves manager and subordinate working together on a continuing basis. It consists of the following steps:

1. *Define the job*—Many recent studies have indicated that it is common for subordinates and superiors to have different perceptions about the nature of the subordinate's role and the evaluation process. Therefore, the first step in helping your employees become more productive is to agree on the exact dimensions of their jobs. Ask your subordinates to list the major functions of their work, as they see them.
2. *Agree on priorities*—Ask your subordinate to list approximately how much time he or she devotes to each of the major functions of the job, and what priorities are as he or she sees them.
3. *Establish performance expectations*—It is at this stage that the supervisor can ask a key question in human resources management: "How do you know you're doing a good job?" At this point expectations for work and performance as well as evaluation must be jointly established. There are many aspects of work in which responsibilities can be specific and measurable. There are many jobs, especially supervisory ones, in which performance is hard to evaluate. How can you evaluate the performance of a manager—especially if you cannot measure the output of his or her department? In such a case, even if you cannot enumerate output, you can certainly measure those things that reflect on your subordinate's management responsibilities. Turnover, absentee rate, complaints, and costs all reflect an individual's ability to manage. As the manager of a person who manages other people, there's a good chance that you have an understanding of acceptable performance in those areas that reflect your subordinate's ability to supervise. At this stage, you can jointly establish reasonable expectations for good performance as measured by productivity, turnover, absentee rate, complaints, etc.
4. *Compare current performance to expected performance on a regular basis*—When job dimensions are laid out in this way, it becomes apparent that most people perform some portions of their responsibility well, while other aspects of their performance can stand some improvement. When comparing actual with expected performance, the result will often provide an opportunity to offer positive as well as negative feedback to employees, to comment not only on their areas of weakness but on their strengths as well. This is a continuing process of working together to establish organizational objectives. Corrections are best made as they are discovered rather than saved till the end of the period.

THE PROBLEMS WITH MBO AS THE BASIS OF APPRAISALS

One common reason the MBO process doesn't work as a basis for performance appraisal is because the manager is focusing on one component and forgetting the total process of management. Goals are set but never pursued. Evaluations are made before goals have been specified. Activities are planned with no understanding of or concern

TABLE 1
Three Checklists For The Objective Setting-Interview

Checklist 1—Before the Interview

What the Subordinate Should Do

Develop preliminary objectives that have a clear performance standard and completion deadline.

Provide the superior with a copy of the preliminary objectives prior to the interview.

Prepare supporting data for each objective.

Decide what resources and coordination will be necessary.

List questions and problems for discussion with the superior.

What the Superior Should Do

Decide whether each preliminary objective represents a priority need.

Check for technical completeness of objectives. Is there a clear performance standard, completion deadline, and method of checking results?

Judge whether performance standards are realistic (not too easy, not too difficult).

Decide if the subordinate has sufficient authority in the objective area.

Specify any required personnel coordination needed to achieve an objective.

Determine if needed resources can be provided.

Note whether foreseeable contingencies should be recognized.

Consider the extent of personal support that the subordinate will require for improved performance.

Examine the subordinate's other job responsibilities to see if any are being neglected.

Determine whether additional objectives are appropriate.

Insure that there are neither too few nor too many objectives in total.

Checklist 2—During the Interview

What the Superior Should Do

Select a convenient interview location and stress the meeting's importance. Be prompt and allocate sufficient time for an uninterrupted discussion.

Begin with small talk to set the subordinate at ease; tailor the approach to the individual.

Request that the subordinate explain each objective. Provide ample opportunity for developing insight into the objectives. Listen with interest and understanding.

Ask questions based on prior preparation and new information. Encourage subordinate to respond and ask his own questions.

Ask how superior can help subordinate do an even better job. Take notes on agreed support.

Avoid placing the subordinate in a defensive position. Keep advice to a minimum. Avoid clashes over personality differences, weaknesses, and past mistakes; avoid arguments.

Provide positive comments whenever possible. Be open about ideas. Seek self-awareness and mutual understanding. Help him gain insight into his behavior and its consequences. Concentrate on anticipated performance. Future improvement should be the focus.

See that final objectives meet technical requirements (clear performance standard, completion deadline, and method of checking).

Remember that setting objectives is a joint process. Compromise when possible. Be willing to change viewpoints.

Be willing to resolve serious controversies (in the final analysis, there must be a boss).

What the Subordinate Should Do

Present objectives vigorously.

Be thorough and confident in discussing each objective.

Accentuate the positive by emphasizing what should be done.

Listen carefully to the superior's responses, both positive and negative. They are important indications of his priorities and perception of career development.

Insist on final agreement. Do not leave questions hanging in the air. Use the opportunity to bring differences out into the open and resolve them.

Checklist 3—After the Interview

What the Subordinate Should Do

Set up a method for regularly reviewing progress toward objectives.

Renegotiate objectives when major changes occur.

Let the superior know when progress is lagging.

Let the superior know when a lack of coordination or resources requires action.

What the Superior Should Do

Maintain a historical and current file on each subordinate's objectives.

Develop checks and reminders for using with each subordinate to insure continuous progress.

In a timely and informal way, let subordinates know that he is interested in week-to-week progress (however, avoid nagging).

Source: From Slusher, E.A. and Sims, H.P., Jr. Commitment through MBO interviews, *Business Horizons,* April, 1975, 5–12.

for what they are supposed to accomplish. MBO as a performance appraisal system only works if all of the components work together.

When Peter Drucker formulated the concept of MBO in his book *The Practice of Management*[1], he was defining a formal system of management, not an appraisal system. Appraisal was a key component, but only one component. Because setting objectives is only one component of an overall system, it must relate to the other parts of the system. Objectives must provide the basis for:

1. adequate feedback to employees on the quality of their work based on a comparison of their actual performance with previously set goals of what was expected;
2. identifying training needs;
3. assessing promotion potential;
4. establishing a basis for distributing organizational rewards;
5. validating hiring techniques; and
6. developing future goals.

Clearly, all of these cannot be accomplished at the same time. Some of them may even be in conflict. Consider for example the judgmental vs. developmental uses of performance appraisal.

Judgmental and Developmental Uses of Performance Appraisals

When objective-setting and performance appraisal are used judgmentally they enable the manager to discriminate among employees for the purpose of making administrative decisions. This places the manager in an evaluative role; he or she must therefore use such dimensions as good or bad, effective or ineffective, strong or weak, correct or incorrect in assessing the subordinate's performance. On the other hand, when objective-setting and performance appraisal are used developmentally, they aid in improving an individual's skills and effectiveness. This places the manager in a counseling, non-evaluative role in a subordinate-centered, helping relationship. Table 2 contrasts the judgmental and the counseling roles in performance appraisal.

If the goal-setting and performance-appraisal system cannot be used for both judgmental and developmental purposes, it is doomed to failure. Both purposes are necessary for attaining higher productivity from workers. But, it is precisely because both purposes must be served that the MBO/appraisal process is so often resisted by managers. In their book *Performance In Organizations*[2], Professors Cummings and Schwab list three primary reasons why managers frequently resist this appraisal process.

Role conflict. It is impossible for managers to play simultaneously the two roles necessary to the appraisal process. Each demands behavior inconsistent with the other. Because of this it would be better to face the problem squarely and establish two distinct systems dealing with the two different sets of problems and opportunities involved in each purpose.

Lack of a conceptual model. A manager may not understand how appraisals fit into the management system. This problem is particularly acute among managers without formal training in personnel administration. Knowing where appraisal fits into the system and how it contributes to effective recruitment, selection, placement, training, utilization, and maintenance of personnel will increase the frequency and the quality of its use.

Lack of a behavioral framework. The manager often has no conceptual framework for integrating performance appraisal into his knowledge of organizational behavior. Therefore, appraisal can erroneously be seen as a mere tool for administrative manipulation with little or no link to the causes of human behavior in organizations. This also means that the manager may not see appraisal as a constructive force for behavioral change.

These problems can only be solved if the purpose of management by objectives/performance appraisal (MBO/PA) is to improve the motivation, involvement, and most importantly, the productivity of people on a continuing basis. To meet these objectives MBO/PA must obviously be a regular activity. If MBO becomes the basis of the yearly evaluation, and only that, it is doomed to failure. Helping subordinates understand their responsibilities, collaborating with them to decide on the way those responsibilities will be met, and providing the kind of recognition and feedback that is directive, useful, and educational is the daily responsibility of management. MBO/PA must become a way of managing the work process rather than just a stick to beat the employees with when they don't reach objectives at the end of the year.

When MBO/PA is an accepted part of the manager's daily activities, it is possible to fulfill both the developmental and judgmental roles. Then there is time to work toward solving problems, developing skills, and planning the future. A relationship is established between manager and employee wherein each is concerned enough about

[1]Drucker, Peter F., *The Practice of Management* (New York: Harper & Row, 1954).

[2]Cummings, L. L. and Schwab, Donald P., *Performance in Organizations* (Glenview, Illinois: Scott, Foresman and Company, 1973).

TABLE 2
Comparison of the Judgmental and Counseling Roles in Performance Appraisal

	Judgmental Role in Appraisal	*Counseling Role in Appraisal*
Focus:	Past performance	Improvement of future performance
Objective:	To improve performance by more effective personnel administration	To improve performance through learning and growth
Method:	Variety of rating and ranking procedures	Series of developmental steps as reflected in management by objective
Role of Superior:	To judge and evaluate	To counsel, help, or guide
Role of Subordinate:	Passive or reactive, frequently defensive	Acting involvement in learning

Source: From Cummings, L.L. and Schwab, Ronald P., *Performance in Organizations* (Glenview, Illinois: Scott Foresman and Company, 1973).

performance to ask continually, "How are we doing?" Problems can be solved as they occur; skills can be developed as they are needed rather than at a time of crisis.

If feedback and development are continuing activities, the year-end evaluation shouldn't contain any surprises. The employee will already know where he or she stands. The formal year-end evaluation will provide a chance to make a summary evaluation of the past and start planning for the future. If everything is saved until the end of the year, however, there won't be enough time to accomplish anything; there will be too many competing objectives; opportunities will have passed; and much of the feedback will be too late to serve both developmental and evaluative ends. In summary then, MBO is a valuable tool for performance appraisal if it is used properly. It must become part of the continuing management process.

Developing Behaviorally-Anchored Rating Scales (BARS)

by Craig Eric Schneier and Richard W. Beatty

For several years organizations have been moving toward goal-setting, results-oriented performance appraisal systems, such as Management by Objectives (MBO). While certainly useful, goal-setting performance programs can easily fall into the trap of concentrating too heavily on final *results* or objectives and ignoring the *methods* required to achieve objectives. First, a "results at any price" philosophy often rewards behaviors which can be harmful to an organization in the long run, but which may facilitate short-run goal attainment. Second, guidelines in terms of specific behaviors are seldom given employees in the goal-setting sessions, thus the opportunity to improve effectiveness through engaging in alternative (i.e., more desirable) behaviors is often not provided. In short, a question coming up with increasing frequency among professionals in appraisal is "How do we use MBO to set goals *and* develop specific information on how to attain them?"

Identifying those desired behaviors necessary to attain both long and short-run objectives is the function of the action planning phase of goal-setting or MBO programs. The action planning process is difficult, but can be aided by using Behaviorally-Anchored Rating Scales (BARS), a recently developed technique which offers a systematic pro-

Reprinted from the August, 1979 issue of *Personnel Administrator*, copyright, 1979, The American Society for Personnel Administration, 30 Park Drive, Berea, OH 44017.

FIGURE 1
Example of a Behaviorally-Anchored Rating Scale

Job Dimension: Planning, Organizing and Scheduling Project Assignment and Due Dates	
7 [ ] EXCELLENT	Develops a comprehensive project plan, documents it well, obtains required approval and distributes the plan to all concerned.
6 [ ] VERY GOOD	Plans, communicates and observes milestones; states week-by-week where the project stands relative to plans. Maintains up-to-date charts of project accomplishments and backlogs and uses these to optimize any schedule modifications required. Experiences occasional minor operational problems, but communicates effectively.
5 [ ] GOOD	Lays out all the parts of a job and schedules each part; seeks to beat schedule and will allow for slack. Satisfies customers' time constraints; time and cost overruns occur infrequently.
4 [ ] AVERAGE	Makes a list of due dates and revises them as the project progresses, usually adding unforeseen events; instigates frequent customer complaints. May have a sound plan, but does not keep track of milestones; does not report slippages in schedules or other problems as they occur.
3 [ ] BELOW AVERAGE	Plans are poorly defined; unrealistic time schedules are common. Cannot plan more than a day or two ahead; has no concept of a realistic project due date.
2 [ ] VERY POOR	Has no plan or schedule of work segments to be performed. Does little or no planning for project assignments.
1 [ ] UNACCEPTABLE	Seldom, if ever, completes project because of lack of planning and does not seem to care. Fails consistently due to lack of planning and does not inquire about how to improve.

cedure for identifying desired behavior. With BARS, MBO programs are not only able to specify desired ends, but also provide the parameters of the means used to reach those ends.

Management by Objectives (MBO) is a firmly established and well-supported technique for improving performance, reducing role ambiguity and redirecting effort to important organizational goals. MBO has been used successfully in organizations of all types and sizes as a general planning process, a control technique and a form of individual performance appraisal.[1]

Most MBO programs have three basic phases. First, goals or objectives are jointly set by superiors and subordinates. Second, action plans are developed (often by the employee alone) to meet objectives, giving people considerable freedom to perform their tasks. Third, performance is reviewed in order to ascertain the degree to which objectives were attained. While there are innumerable variations of MBO programs in actual practice, all incorporate these three essential activities in some form. The first and third phases of the typical MBO process have received a great deal of attention. Many guidelines are available for setting specific, quantifiable and/or challenging goals and discussions note the importance of mutual (i.e., supervisor and subordinate) goal setting.[2] The various types of goals which can be used in MBO, including personal growth goals, performance goals and staff development goals have been frequently stressed.

Further, there are available in the MBO literature several useful discussions regarding the problems and pitfalls of MBO review sessions. Allowing for authentic subordinate input, using a problem-solving orientation, ending with an action plan and using non-threatening language to reduce defensiveness have all been suggested and used successfully. Making salary and promotion actions contingent upon performance would also facilitate the motivational impact of the review session.

However, little has been written and few guidelines have been offered to those implementing MBO programs concerning the second phase of MBO noted above, action planning. In fact, contributors to the field generally feel that the method of goal accomplishment should largely be left to the subordinate. But action planning can be of obvious importance when it refers to the identification and definition of specific activities necessary to accomplish goals. In short, action planning is the "how do we get there" phase of MBO. Not everyone possesses the skills required to determine which are the most appropriate and efficient methods for accomplishing objectives. Further, newer or inexperienced workers typically welcome assistance in planning how to attain their goals effectively. Because it is often difficult to translate objectives into specific actions in an MBO program, guidelines for the action planning phase of MBO are offered in this discussion.

Several authors have recognized the importance of the action planning phase of MBO and have noted the neces-

[1]See e.g., S. J. Carroll and H. Tosi, *Management by Objectives,* NY:Macmillan, 1973.

[2]For example see Exercise 6 in R. W. Beatty and C. E. Schneier, *Personnel Administration: An Experiential/Skillbuilding Approach,* Reading, MA: Addison-Wesley, 1977.

FIGURE 2
Example of a Behaviorally-Anchored Rating Scale

Job Dimension: Knowledge and Use of Job Control Language (JCL)

EXCELLENT	• Has used or has knowledge of the majority of important JCL statements, systems function better since is able to take advantage of the computer's ability through JCL, new situations are little or no problem due to abundant knowledge. • Can solve the most complicated JCL problem and writes simple JCL so others can follow it. • Knows JCL and SSG, and creates smooth running streams for every run, always willing to try out new phases of JCL and SSG.
VERY GOOD	• Uses JCL effectively and efficiently, may review job streams to upgrade systems, pays particular attention to newer methods of using JCL. • Utilizes JCL very effectively both from machine and operator viewpoint. • Is aware of good JCL technique, makes JCL efficient and easily followed by others who might use it. Tries to keep up to date with knowledge of JCL.
GOOD	• Has few problems with JCL and causes few operations problems. • Creates good JCL job streams and will upgrade them when and if necessary, needs little help.
SLIGHTLY BETTER THAN AVERAGE	• JCL works and follows standards. • Able to write JCL that works correctly.
AVERAGE	• Can make a JCL job stream for usual type jobs, can maintain existing JCL jobs with some help. • Knows how to set up standard, or relatively simple job stream.
SLIGHTLY LESS THAN AVERAGE	• Does not make maximum use of JCL, has limited knowledge of JCL. • Does not assign files correctly and leaves some files on desk at end of job.
POOR	• Possesses little kowledge of JCL, quite often runs have to be killed due to impossible situations, such as requesting the same tape on different drives at the same time. • Needs constant supervision to write JCL.
VERY POOR	• This programmer's knowledge of JCL is virtually nonexistent, runs consistently error off or else have to be killed by the operator. • Avoids use of JCL if at all possible.
UNACCEPTABLE	• Unwilling to learn the most basic JCL commands.

sity of specifying those activities which lead to objective attainment.[3] But few suggestions are offered. Actually specifying activities when MBO is implemented is a difficult and time-consuming process if attempted without a detailed procedure. When we see what the action planning phase entails, the problems become obvious reasons why it is often the most neglected aspect of the MBO system. For example, defining the duties and responsibilities of one's job in order to specify action plans makes conflicts between subordinates and supervisors explicit. Such potential conflicts are not often confronted and MBO systems become ineffective.

DIVERGENCE IN ROLE PRESCRIPTIONS

Supervisors and subordinates operate from different perspectives, in large part due to their divergent role prescriptions. Supervisors may evaluate technical aspects of the job as these seem to reflect outputs directly, outputs against which they themselves may be evaluated. On the other hand, subordinates may perceive cooperation and interpersonal aspects of the job as primary since, as they deal with their peers, these factors influence their ability to perform.[4] Such differences are identified as goals and are mutually set in MBO. Further, the process of planning how objectives will be met may point out ambiguous and inconsistent organizational policy regarding performance or can pinpoint the failure of superiors to communicate that policy across levels of the organizations. These potential problems can thwart an MBO effort by amplifying conflict and-lessening commitment before the program is even under way.

[3]Among these are Carroll and Tosi, *Management by Objectives,* and A. P. Raia, *Managing by Objectives,* Glenview, IL: Scott Foresman, 1974.

[4]See C. E. Schneier and R. W. Beatty, "The Influence of Role Prescriptions on the Performance Appraisal Process", *Academy of Management Journal,* 1978, *21,* 129–134; C. E. Schneier, "Performance Appraisal: Does the Use of Multiple Raters Groups Help or Hinder the Process?", *Public Personnel Management,* 1977, *6* (1), 13–20.

FIGURE 3
Example of a Behaviorally-Anchored Rating Scale

Job Dimension: Centrifuge Operation

Scale	Anchor
7	This operator could be expected to: vary the centrifuge speed in order to obtain the best speed for unfamiliar material, constantly monitor evenness of cake.
6	This operator could be expected to: contact superiors immediately when material does not spin, install bags correctly and quickly, wash cake evenly and completely.
5	This operator could be expected to: determine correct rate of spin by material appearance, not wash product over basket, always check effluent for solids when starting to spin.
4	This operator could be expected to: dig out cakes too slowly, load properly but incorrectly judge the amount in centrifuge versus the amount in pot to obtain correct number of spins, never try to spin without turning on pump, occasionally let cakes run down too long, cause centrifuge to wobble resulting in uneven wet cake.
3	This operator could be expected to: wash cake at such a speed such that only part of the cake gets washed, forget to blow down hose from bottom of pot after loading each spin.
2	This operator could be expected to: select wrong washing material, forget to place honey cart under centrifuge when digging it out, run effluent over top of bag, overrun centrifuge, or overrun surge tank.
1	This operator could be expected to: forget to turn on centrifuge pump or open proper outlet valves, frequently tear bags or not report holes in them until end of shift.

CRITIQUE OF MBO

The action planning phase of MBO has often been the focus of criticism of MBO programs.[5] The criticism can be explained by recalling the following three definitions. Most MBO objectives are measures of *effectiveness.* That is, they are designed to measure a person's contribution to the attainment of organization goals or overall effectiveness. When objectives are stated in overtime units, in terms of cost reductions, in deadlines met, or in profit margins, they refer to indices of effectiveness. *Behavior,* on the other hand, refers simply to work activity on the job—what people *do* at work (hopefully in pursuit of objectives). Behaviors are *how* objectives are accomplished while the objectives are *what* is accomplished. When this behavior is evaluated or measured in an organization, it is called *performance.* For example, if a salesperson meets with a client (a behavior) and their behavior in the meeting facilitates a sales quota being met (a measure of effectiveness), the behavior would be termed excellent performance. If the customer is lost as a result of certain behaviors exhibited in the meeting (e.g., abrasiveness, incorrectly citing product characteristics), performance would be poor.

[5]See R. W. Beatty and C. E. Schneier, "A Case for Positive Reinforcement", *Business Horizons,* Vol. 18, No. 2 (April, 1975), 57–66.

The Cost of "Results at Any Price"

The relationship between behavior, performance and effectiveness and their meaning in an MBO program help explain the criticism of MBO noted above. MBO concentrates heavily on effectiveness or results. While this concentration on results is of obvious use since it redirects efforts toward key performance areas, an overemphasis on results can lead to undesirable outcomes. For when performance objectives are stated only as effectiveness indices (e.g., profit margins) and behaviors or the *means* to attain these objectives are ignored, people could be damaging the organization in the long run in order to meet short-run effectiveness objectives.

To illustrate, consider the example of a manager who has attained an objective of reduced delivery times (an effectiveness index) but has done so only by using extremely punitive supervision of his subordinates (a behavior). If the behavior which led to the goal attainment was ignored, long-run problems such as employee dissatisfaction may manifest themselves in increasing organizational costs through absenteeism, turnover, poor quality work and perhaps sabotage.

Thus, the "results at any price" philosophy often comes at an extremely *high* price. That is, possible undesired behaviors (e.g., a punitive supervisory style in the example above) are reinforced by the organization. This occurs when the undesired or potentially harmful behaviors lead to

FIGURE 4
Steps Required to Develop BARS and Approximate Time Required

1. Orientation to BARS purpose and terminology: Meetings of about two hours for each group uses. Groups of 20 to 30 are most effective.
2. Identification of all relevant job dimensions: Meetings of about two hours for each group of 20 to 30 used.
3. Writing behavioral anchors for each job dimension illustrative of various degrees of performance: About one hour for each participant for *each* job dimension.
4. Attach randomized group of anchors back to job dimensions: About two hours for each participant.
5. Deciding on scale values for remaining anchors: About two hours for each participant. (Can be combined with step 4 above.)
6. Computing percentage of participants who agree on placement of anchors to job dimensions and mean scale value given each anchor by participants: Time required varies depending on number of anchors and participants. (Electronic calculators simplify the process greatly.)
7. Arranging anchors surviving step 6 above on scales according to appropriate scale value and job dimension: time required depends on number of anchors and job dimensions.
8. Reading over final scales to assure proper terminology, adding any necessary anchors, final editing, etc.: Time required varies according to number of job dimensions used and number of people involved in this stage.

short-run objective attainment. But consider the possible long-run consequences. Since close supervision, a behavior, led to rewards, that behavior will be used again and again by the manager because it worked. By simply looking at results (ends) and not behavior (means to reach ends), the possible undesired means used to reach a desired end are not uncovered in MBO and thus will persist.

Ignoring Desired Behavior

If an MBO program is too heavily oriented toward results, it might also fail to recognize behaviors which are desired, but which did *not* lead to goal attainment. For example, a manager may have used desirable behaviors which characterize discretion and judgment in handling a delicate customer complaint or may have been innovative in devising a problem solution, but if the customer still returned the merchandise or the innovative solution was not implemented due to budget cuts, overall effectiveness—or results—may still look poor. Thus, the effectiveness index used in MBO may not be totally within the worker's control, as in the cases when general economic conditions, prevailing interest rates, or product demand affect a worker's or a department's goal attainment. Again, desired behaviors may go unnoticed if only results are evaluated in MBO.

A Systematic Procedure for the Action-Planning Phase of MBO

Outlined below is a systematic procedure for identifying desired behavior which can also facilitate the attainment of objectives in MBO. It is a performance appraisal technique called Behaviorally-Anchored Rating Scales (BARS) developed to specify desired behavior in an organization and to judge the level of performance certain behaviors indicate. BARS can supply managers attempting to implement MBO with a procedure whereby action plans can be developed in specific terms and MBO programs can be developed with an emphasis on desired behavior, as well as results or effectiveness. BARS can thus help fill a gap in the guidelines available for the important action-planning phase of MBO.

BARS are a technique used to specify the behaviors required to attain objectives—they supply the means necessary to attain ends. The BARS process can be used after major objectives are set and desired behavior or activities needed to meet objectives are required.

FIGURE 5
BARS Anchor Worksheet

Instructions: After you have inserted the appropriate job title and job dimension in the spaces below, write at least three specific behavioral statements for good performance, three for fair performance, and three for poor performance on this sheet. These are examples of what people in the job actually *do* which you feel can be judged as good, fair, or poor performance. Please be very precise.

Job title ______________________

Job dimension: ______________________

Anchors for GOOD Performance

1.
2.
3.

Anchors for FAIR Performance

1.
2.
3.

Anchors for POOR Performance

1.
2.
3.

FIGURE 6
Suggestions For Developing Useful Behavioral Anchors For BARS

1. Use specific examples of behavior, not conclusions about the "goodness" or "badness" of behavior.

   Use this: This supervisor could be expected to tell a secretary when the work was to be completed, the degree of perfection required, the amount of space it must be typed within and the kind of paper necessary.

   Not this: This supervisor could be expected to give very good instructions to a secretary. Instructions would be clear and concise.

2. Avoid using quantitative values (numbers) within anchors.

   Use this: This accountant could be expected to submit reports on time which contain no misinformation or mistakes. If discrepancies occur on reports from the last period this accountant knows the cause.

   Not this: This accountant could be expected to meet 90 percent of deadlines with 95 percent accuracy.

3. Avoid using *adjective qualifiers* in the anchor statements, use descriptions of actual behavior.

   Use this: This supervisor can be expected to understand employees such that the supervisor can repeat both the employee's communication and the intent of the message. They also make certain they talk in private when necessary and do not repeat the conversation to others.

   Not this: When supervising associates this supervisor does a good job of understanding their problems. This supervisor is kind and friendly.

4. Avoid using anchors which make assumptions about employee *knowledge* about the job, use descriptions of behavior.

   Use this: This employee can perform the disassembly procedure for rebuilding a carburetor by first removing the cap and then proceeding with the internal components, gaskets, etc. If in doubt about the procedure the mechanic will refer to the appropriate manual.

   Not this: This mechanic knows how to disassemble a carburetor and will do so in an efficient and effective manner.

What Are BARS?

BARS were designed as a behaviorally-based performance appraisal tool.[6] They are a set of scales—one scale for each major job dimension, or broad class of duties, responsibilities, or activities of a job. Placed on the scales are a set of anchors, or statements illustrative of worker behavior on the particular job dimension. There are usually several such anchors attached to each scale. The anchors illustrate specific degrees of performance, ranging, for example, from *Excellent Performance,* noted at the top of the scale, to, *Unacceptable Performance* noted at the bottom of the scale.

Figure 1 is an example of one such scale. The scale was written for a job dimension found in many managerial jobs which can be called "planning, organizing and scheduling project assignments and due dates". On the left of the scale are the scale values illustrated by the anchors. The values on this scale run from seven (Excellent) to one (Unacceptable). The behavioral anchors appear on the right side of the scale. These are the brief statements of actual worker *behavior* which, when exhibited on the job, indicate the degree of performance on the scale opposite that particular anchor. Figure 2 is an example of a scale written for a computer programmer/systems analyst position, whereas Figure 3 is an example of a scale developed for a chemical plant worker. Each is different, but possesses the salient features of the behaviorally-anchored format. BARS can be designed for any position—clerical, technical, staff, executive, or operating level.

To rate someone's performance with BARS, raters read through the list of anchors on each scale until they find the group of anchors most typical of the ratee's job behavior during the performance period. The performance level opposite those anchors is then checked. This procedure is followed for each job dimension identified for the job and a total numerical score can be obtained by summing the scale values checked across all dimensions.

Some Terminology

There are a few key terms which must be clearly understood in order to use BARS effectively. Job *dimensions* are those broad categories of duties or responsibilities which comprise a job. If a job is comprised of six separate dimensions, there will be six separate scales with anchors used to describe total performance on that job. *Anchors* are those very specific statements generated to illustrate various degrees of performance along each scale. They are behaviors, or worker activity. As they appear beside each level or degree of performance, they are said to "anchor" each of the scale values along a scale. The BARS rate worker *behavior,* not contribution to department or organization goals (i.e., effectiveness). Measures of effectiveness are best typified in the objectives themselves in an MBO program, not in the action plan.

How Are BARS Developed?

BARS are typically developed through a series of small group discussions which include both superiors and subordi-

[6]See W. J. Kearney, "The Value of Behaviorally Based Performance Appraisals", *Business Horizons,* Vol. 19, No. 6 (June, 1976), 75–83; Beatty and Schneier, Personnel Administration, *op. cit.;* C. E. Schneier and R. W. Beatty, *Personnel Administration Today,* Reading, MA: Addison-Wesley, 1978.

FIGURE 7
BARS Anchor Reassignment and Scale Value Worksheet

Instructions: Randomly order all anchors below in the right hand column. Then put all of the job dimensions in the middle column. Ask participants to decide which job dimension each anchor most clearly illustrates by placing an "x" in one and only one job dimension column. Then participants note the degree of performance they feel is illustrated by each anchor by placing an "x" in one of the columns numbered 1–7. (Five, nine, or four point scales can also be used.)

	Job Dimensions							*Scale Values*						
								Excellent	*Very Good*	*Good*	*Average*	*Below Average*	*Very Poor*	*Unacceptable*
Behavioral Anchors	*No. 1*	*No. 2*	*No. 3*	*No. 4*	*No. 5*	*No. 6*	*etc.*	*7*	*6*	*5*	*4*	*3*	*2*	*1*
1.														
2.														
3.														
4.														
5.														
6.														
7.														
8.														
9.														
10.														
11.														
12.														
13.														
14.														
15.														
etc.														

nates.[7] Figure 4 contains an outline of the major steps in developing BARS, along with approximate time frames for each. The following discussion details these steps.

Step one in the procedure is usually a brief orientation in which the terminology and purposes of BARS are discussed. In step two, several of the job incumbents and their supervisors (the eventual reviewers of performance in an MBO program) meet to discuss the job in question. Their task is to identify all of the relevant job dimensions for the job. It is best either to compare such a list with that generated by another group of subordinates and superiors or to ask the initial group to review their list after a few days in order to make sure all of the relevant job dimensions were identified. Step three is to write the behavioral anchors for each of the job dimensions. A work sheet with good, fair and poor performance written along the left margin can be used for each dimension and should be given to several superiors and subordinates (see Figure 5). As many anchors as possible should be written for each level of performance on each dimension.

Writing anchors is not an easy task for some people as they typically think of job performance in terms of *results* rather than *behavior*. Using as many job incumbents as possible as suppliers of anchors not only helps assure a large and representative pool of behaviors, but also facilitates the participation of a wide number of people in the development of *their* appraisal system. Such participation fosters commitment.

Anchors should not contain such words as feel, think, know, expect, or other psychodynamic concepts which cannot be explicitly ascertained. For example, to assess whether someone knows a work procedure, we must observe it being done, ask to have it explained, etc. Anchors are behavioral statements and thus should contain action verbs. Figure 6 contains some characteristics of useful anchors and offers suggestions for their development.

[7]For a more detailed explanation, see Exercise 5 in Beatty and Schneier, *Personnel Administration.*

In step four of the BARS process, the users must reach consensus as to which job dimension each anchor most clearly illustrates. If there is disagreement among as to which job dimension an anchor best illustrates, even though the anchor's original author intended it for a specific dimension, the anchor is probably too ambiguous to be meaningful. Consensus as to the dimension which an anchor best illustrates is accomplished by randomly ordering all anchors written by participants in step three above, after any redundancies have been removed and any minor editing required has been performed. The entire group of randomly ordered anchors is given to several participants who are asked to indicate which job dimension each anchor illustrates. A sample worksheet used for this process appears as Figure 7. As a general rule, any anchor which 75 percent or more of the particpants have not agreed to as a job dimension should be discarded due to ambiguity. In addition, dimensions which have very few or no anchors attached to them should be eliminated, reworded and/or combined into others.

Step five in the BARS process consists of deciding exactly what scale value (one through seven when a seven-point scale is ued, one through five when a five-point scale is used, etc.) each of the anchors remaining after step four best illustrates (see Figure 5). Here the anchors are attached to their job dimensions and participants are asked to indicate the scale value each should be given. The mean scale value given by the group is used as the final scale value. This would be an "average" of the group's opinion.[8]

The anchors are then placed on the appropriate scales according to their exact mean group scale values or the values can be rounded to the nearest whole number and attached to the scale opposite the scale value (see Figures 1 to 3). Finally, the scales are read carefully by the members of the groups and top management to be sure that the job incumbent's terminology was used in the anchors, that any additional anchors required to illustrate certain performance levels are added and that all anchors reflect the organization's policy regarding performance.

USING BARS IN AN MBO PROGRAM

As noted earlier, a major use of BARS in MBO programs would be to specify those desired behaviors which can be used by workers to reach objectives, or the means to reach their ends. For example, if a performance objective for a manager was to reach a certain level of competence in "planning, organizing and scheduling project assignments and due dates" (see Figure 1), the BARS would help specify *how* the goal is to be reached, or what specific behaviors are required, expected and necessary in order to reach the goal. These behaviors appear as the anchors in BARS.

Many MBO authorities have pointed out that one key motivational aspect of MBO is that workers are typically given the freedom, within certain limits, to perform in those ways which facilitate objective attainment. The many behavioral anchors listed on BARS, as well as the process of writing anchors itself, can facilitate the identification of several possible behavioral strategies or action plans which can attain objectives.

Because BARS may precisely specify how objectives are to be reached, they enable barriers to goal attainment to be uncovered, such as impractical time frames or inadequate staffs. BARS aid in specifying the degree to which goal attainment might involve help from other persons, they offer a way to estimate resource and time requirements in quantitative terms and they may identify areas in which superiors' help is required in order to reach goals. The behaviors specified by BARS reduce role ambiguity for workers in that they help pinpoint their responsibilities and authority.

An Aid in the Performance Review Phase of MBO

Any MBO program requires a review of performance and a method by which goal attainment can be measured. BARS help in this process by providing performance standards in the form of behavioral anchors against which performance can be judged. The scales also serve as cues to reviewers as to what behaviors to observe as they evaluate a ratee. Typical ratee behaviors can be noted and anecdotal records can be kept by raters in MBO to facilitate fair and comprehensive evaluation at the end of review periods.

Further, BARS serve as a focal point for discussion in the MBO performance review session. They provide job-related, specific behavioral statements which can be used to discuss actual performance in a problem-solving manner. BARS offer a way to provide specific feedback to ratees in MBO. Rather than evaluating goal attainment as merely good, fair, or poor, BARS enable raters to pinpoint ratee strengths and weaknesses and to show ratees exactly where they excelled or were deficient. The scales enable the parties to end the review session with a plan indicating what behaviors are necessary to reach goals and to gain commitment both to the plan and to performance improvement itself by stressing specifically which behaviors on the form need to be improved.

Employees usually know when their performance was deficient and may fear the performance review session because they feel their deficiencies are over-emphasized. With BARS the supervisor can offer suggestions in terms of how workers may improve as he or she notes specific behaviors on the form which would lead to improvement.

---

[8]Anchors with standard deviations of 1.5 or greater (on a seven-point scale) should be discarded as the large standard deviation indicates the group varied considerably in their opinions of what degree of performance a behavior illustrated.

Further, if an innovative procedure or unusual effort has led to accomplishment beyond set goals, the BARS system is flexible enough to build in these new behaviors. New behaviors can be added as BARS anchors any time they are identified and it is often wise to leave space on the BARS to insert them. BARS, like MBO itself, must be a dynamic, not a static, system and must recognize changes in worker behavior, jobs and job environments over time.

An Aid in the Goal-Setting Phase of MBO

BARS can improve the goal setting process of MBO by bringing differences of opinion between parties into the open as job dimensions and anchors are developed. Superiors and their subordinates often have differing expectations regarding desired performance, responsibility and authority boundaries, as noted above. Such ambiguities and conflict can be resolved as the BARS process forces a thorough job analysis which makes duties, responsibilities and authority explicit. Further, BARS can pinpoint ambiguities in job objectives themselves. For if parties in MBO are unable to list and agree upon the desired way to reach an objective (i.e., if they cannot write behavioral anchors for BARS), the objective itself may be at fault and thus needs to be reworded as it is perceived differently by different people.

General Performance Improvement Technique

Any performance appraisal technique, including MBO, would seem to have two objectives. It must be able to accurately measure present performance and must be able to help develop or improve future performance. There is empirical evidence that BARS can lead to improved performance.[9] Its motivational base is essentially that of MBO and hence its compatibility to MBO is enhanced.

Essentially, BARS can improve performance at two different time periods. After job dimensions are identified and anchors are written and scaled, ambiguity regarding performance is reduced. Employees now have a clear statement of what aspects of job performance are required. The anchors are essentially behavioral goals which, when set explicitly, can improve performance by redirecting effort to important job duties. As BARS are used in the MBO review session, the feedback generated by comparing performance to targets, and hence identifying specific behavioral deficiencies, has a motivating effect. This goal-seting and feedback on performance model has been well documented as a facilitator of performance improvement.[10]

An Aid to Personnel Programs in Addition to MBO

BARS can facilitate effective training programs as the behavioral deficiencies which are noted in performance review sessions can serve as objectives around which training program content is built. BARS aid selection programs as jobs are analyzed carefully and major duties and responsibilities are identified which can be translated into realistic selection criteria. In addition, the behavioral anchors specified by BARS themselves can be used as selection criteria which are job-related. Hence validity studies are more feasible. Wage and salary administration can be improved as the job dimensions derived in BARS for each job can be compared to those in other jobs so as to rank the jobs in importance, complexity, or skill requirements. Relative wage and salary levels can then be calculated for different jobs and a rational, data-based wage structure can be developed in an organization. Motivation programs can also be designed which tie rewards to those specific desired behaviors identified in the BARS procedure.

POTENTIAL PROBLEMS

Like other appraisal techniques, BARS are not problem-free, either when used in conjunction with MBO or alone. The information derived in BARS can be biased if too few participants are used or if participants come from only one level in the hierarchy. In addition, BARS can be difficult to develop. Because they are so detailed and thorough, because they are tailormade for one type of job and because they require much subordinate and superior participation, they may be time consuming and thus costly. For jobs which have only one or a few incumbents, developing the BARS can place a large burden on these people. Identifying job dimensions and numerous specific behavioral anchors requires concentration and serious commitment. Some persons may find it difficult to generate anchors and to make the many, fine discriminations required as raters.[11] This commitment to the development and use of BARS must begin at the top of the organization and be carried downward in order for the data to be effectively used. But for MBO programs, as well as for other personnel activities,

---

[9]See R. W. Beatty, C. E. Schneier and J. R. Beatty, "An Empirical Investigation of Ratee Behavior Frequency and Ratee Behavior Change Using Behavioral Expectation Scales (BES)", *Personnel Psychology,* 1977, *30,* 647–658.

[10]See e.g., E. A. Locke, N. Cartledge and C. S. Knerr, "Studies in the Relationship Between Satisfaction, Goal-setting and Performance", *Psychological Bulletin,* 1968, *70,* 474–485; Carroll and Tosi, *op. cit.*

[11]See C. E. Schneier, "The Operational Utility and Psychometric Soundness of Behavioral Expectation Scales (BES). A Cognitive Reinterpretation", *Journal of Applied Psychology,* 1977, *62,* 541–548.

BARS seem to be worth the effort. Many organizations are finding that the job-related, behaviorally-based information generated by BARS outweighs their initial cost.

Behaviorally-based appraisal systems have advantages regarding relevance and job-relatedness. If developed according to the procedure outlined here for Behaviorally-Anchored Rating Scales (BARS), commitment of raters is built through their participation in the system's development.

BARS facilitate the action planning phase of Management by Objectives (MBO) by specifying what behavior is desired by the organization in order to attain objectives. It thus details *how* to become effective once the goals in MBO have specified *what* outcomes are expected.

BARS can also facilitate performance review sessions as specific feedback is available to ratees regarding what behaviors deterred or facilitated the attainment of their objectives. Ratee strengths and weaknesses can be identified, developmental or remedial task assignments can be made and behaviorally-based job-related data on the form assist raters in presenting a rationale for their ratings. Such a rationale helps alleviate halo and leniency in judgments.

A behaviorally-based appraisal system such as BARS augments other human resource programs. It can identify training needs, provide a content-valid criterion for validation of selection systems and form a basis for wage, salary, benefit and promotion decisions. While more time-consuming to develop than other types of scales, BARS have several operational advantages as an appraisal system and as a technique for the management of performance.

Performance Appraisal: Match the Tool to the Task

by John D. McMillan and Hoyt W. Doyel

Developing an effective performance appraisal program is one of the most difficult areas for organizations. Management can define the duties and specifications for each position, establish competitive pay levels through salary grades and ranges, and establish a stated policy of "merit pay" or "pay for performance." But where it all comes together is in the performance appraisal program, and in most personnel systems that is the weakest link. Indeed, performance appraisal is widely recognized as the "Achilles' heel" of the personnel function.

DEFINING THE PURPOSE

Performance appraisal programs serve a wide range of purposes in organizations and, in many, a single performance appraisal program serves multiple purposes. Many performance appraisal programs encounter difficulty in attempting to serve more than one purpose—when, for example, a supervisor "backs into" a performance appraisal rating based on a desired salary increase.

The first step in developing an effective program is to define the *purpose* for, or use of, the performance appraisal program. The authors' experience suggests that the most effective programs are those focused on a single, clearly defined purpose. This means that *separate* appraisal programs may be required to address separate purposes.

The primary purposes of performance appraisal are:

- *Salary administration.* Performance appraisals are used in determining salary increases for employees. (This is probably the most frequent purpose.) Such appraisals should focus on performance in relation to ongoing requirements of the position and in relation to other employees in similar functions or at the same organizational level.
- *Incentive award determination.* Performance appraisals are also frequently used to determine bonus payments. Such use tends to focus on accomplishment of specific, short-term objectives.
- *Promotability assessment.* Performance appraisals also are used in determining an employee's suitability for promotion.

Because of these different purposes, the authors believe companies should develop separate performance appraisal programs to serve each. Too often, one "off the

Reprinted, by permission of the publisher, from *Personnel,* July–August, 1980,

shelf" appraisal form is used for every purpose, and with predictable results.

FREQUENT PITFALLS

When developing a new program, it is often useful to review problems and pitfalls other organizations have encountered. The following issues are frequent sources of difficulty:

- *Defining "performance."* Particularly where one purpose of the program is to support compensation decisions, it is critical to differentiate what constitutes the "performance" that is being "appraised." Unless clearly defined, "performance" often means "results" to top management and "effort expended" to employees and first-level supervisors. Similarly, there is the question of how "learning, gaining good experience" is to be rated relative to "fully proficient" levels of performance—is it "progress" or "proficiency" that is to be rated? (The answer will depend on the purpose of the program.)
- *Defining factors to be rated.* Good management practice dictates that employees should be rated on factors relevant to their jobs. As a minimum, virtually all companies with performance appraisal programs use separate appraisal forms for management and nonexempt employees. Many organizations, in fact, find it well worth the effort to develop separate appraisal forms specific to each job or at least to each function, such as sales or accounting. Making appraisals job-specific allows ratings to be more objective and more pertinent to the employee; it also allows management to be more specific in defining performance levels.
- *Defining "rating scales" or "standards of comparison."* Effective performance appraisal programs require clear standards of comparison to keep supervisors from taking the stance that "all my people are outstanding." Some appraisal programs typify ratings in such terms as "outstanding," "above average," and others that can carry different meanings among various departments. Other programs define performance in terms of specific objectives or performance standards. Whichever method is used, the "rating scale" must be consistent with the factors being rated, and this relationship should be clear both to the rater and to the employee being rated.
- *Training supervisors.* Too often, companies believe development of the performance appraisal program is finished when the appraisal forms are developed. Successful appraisal programs, however, encompass the training of supervisors who carry out the appraisals—including both initial programs and ongoing reviews that assess how well supervisors are rating their employees.

TIMING OF PERFORMANCE APPRAISALS

Practices vary widely not only in the *type* of appraisal used, but also in the frequency of appraisal. It is important that the timing be consistent with the type of appraisal used. The most common practices are as follows:

- *Annual/fiscal year.* Conducting annual appraisals covering fiscal year performance is best for programs using actual-versus-budget (sales, profit) results as one measure of performance, or for programs in which it is important to get a clear picture of how the performance among a group of employees compares at one particular point in time. The principal disadvantage of this approach is that all appraisals become due at the same time, but this is an administrative problem that can be overcome with minimal effort.
- *Annual anniversary date.* Conducting appraisals on the employee's anniversary date of hire (or last merit raise or last promotion) gives the appraisal a personal characteristic that is important in the employee development type of appraisal programs. However, this approach is extremely difficult to use if actual-versus-budget results are measured, since the budget/monitoring cycle rarely aligns with the anniversary review dates of most employees.
- *Semiannual/quarterly.* Using either fiscal or anniversary cycles, certain companies prefer to monitor performance quarterly or semiannually, often on an informal basis.
- *Project completion.* Many companies operate on a "project" basis, measuring performance upon completion of each major project.
- *Critical incident.* One method of appraisal involves continuous monitoring of performance and the recording of how the employee handled certain critical incidents—those that demonstrated either "good" or "bad" performance.

Also, the authors' experience suggests that, regardless of which review cycle is used, employees should not be told about any salary increases at the time that their performance reviews are conducted. Their performance can be discussed much more thoroughly and constructively by removing the salary increase issue and focusing the discussion solely on job performance. Furthermore, real performance improvement is achieved only through ongoing coaching of the employee, in which the supervisor provides *immediate* feedback (either positive or negative). Supervisory training should stress this fact.

PERFORMANCE-BASED RATING SCALE

Performance-based rating scales (also called "behaviorally anchored" rating scales) are a fairly new development that

FIGURE 1
Level of Performance by Performance-Based Criteria

Criteria	Level of performance		
	Outstanding	*Superior*	*Competent*
Production as a percentage of budget ("Quantity of Work")	120% or more	110%–120%	100%–110%
Quality control reject percentage "Quality of Work")	.05% or less Anticipates problems and takes preventive action.	.05%–1% Recognizes source of all problems and can take corrective action.	1%–2% Recognizes source of most problems and is able to correct using standard procedures.
Percentage of jobs shipped on time	100%	98%	95%
Supervision	Subordinates are well trained and motivated; team effort evident; no wasted effort.	Subordinates are trained and motivated individually but not working as a team; occasional duplication of effort.	Subordinates are trained but not working together as a team; occasional duplication of effort.

could greatly increase the effectiveness of most appraisal programs. Most appraisal forms use the standard terms "outstanding," "superior," "competent," and so on for rating employee performance. MBO programs often establish target performance, but no range of performance above or below the target to indicate how high performance must be to be "outstanding." Free-form programs don't use such definitions at all.

A performance-based rating scale defines the performance level in terms of the work task itself (or in terms of the actions or "behavior" involved). For example, the performance descriptions shown in Figure 1 could be used in rating a production manager—showing first the *performance-based criteria* and, below them, the traditional "trait checklist" terms where these would be different.

The performance-based rating scale is clearly superior to the normal "outstanding/superior/competent" scale, but it is difficult to implement because separate rating forms are required for each position covered. A principal application of this approach is in jobs with large numbers of employees where it is feasible to establish such clear performance expectations. Also, this is where it is important to do so because employees are being rated by different supervisors, each with his or her own concept of what constitutes an "outstanding" employee.

THREE COMMON METHODS—AND AN UNCOMMON ONE

The three most common methods of appraisal are trait checklist, MBO, and free form. A relatively uncommon approach is "responsibility rating"—the method that's best suited for exempt salary administration, in the authors' opinion. The four types of appraisal programs may be, and often are, combined in various combinations in one appraisal form (most frequently a checklist form with space for comments). The checklist type of appraisal is most prevalent—undoubtedly because of its ease of installation and administration rather than its effectiveness. The relative values of each of the four methods is shown in Figure 1.

Now let's take a detailed look at the characteristics and advantages of each.

Trait Checklist

Characteristics of the trait checklist appraisal method are:

- *Key features.* Standardized rating forms are used for broad groups of employees, such as all "nonexempt" or "exempt" employees. For each group, qualities or "traits" of employee performance are listed, such as:

Quantity of work	Job knowledge
Quality of work	Cooperativeness
Dependability	Planning
Effort	Timeliness
Initiative	Attitude

  Supervisors rate employee performance on each trait, generally using a predetermined scale such as: outstanding—superior—above average—average—be-

FIGURE 2
Value of Characteristics in Four Appraisal Methods

	Methods of Appraisal			
Characteristics	*Trait Checklist*	*Responsibility Rating*	*MBO*	*Free Form*
Appropriate for:				
Salary administration	2	1	3	4
Incentive awards	4	2	1	3
Employee development	4	2	3	1
Promotability assessment	4	3	2	1
Job-related	4	1	2	3
Minimize "halo effect"	3	2	1	4
Objective	3	2	1	4
Ease of installation	1	3	4	2
Ease of administration	1	2	4	3

Rating: 1 = Best; 2 = Second Best; and so on.

low average—unsatisfactory. Narrative support for ratings may or may not be required.

- *Advantages.* This method is extremely easy to install and administer since relatively few forms are required and a number of such forms are commercially available. All employees are rated on the same factors and on the same scale. The checklist allows a wide latitude for the supervisor's interpretation of terms. It is equally suited to anniversary date or fiscal year appraisal cycles.
- *Disadvantages.* The traits are general and don't relate specifically to job performance—thus they are particularly susceptible to varying standards of comparison being used by various raters. The tendency of those using this method is to focus on personal characteristics rather than job performance results. And because the factors rated are general, there is a tendency for ratings to reflect the "halo effect." This method makes no sense when different levels in a job family are rated on the same form. A senior accountant, for example, should be expected to rate higher on "job knowledge" and "quality of work" than an entry-level accountant, but the appraisal form doesn't reflect this expectation.
- *Best applications.* This method may be appropriate for salary administration that depends on a management philosophy of paying for personal *effort* rather than proficiency. The method may also be appropriate for low-level positions for which it's impractical to set targets and measure performance against targets. As a variation, separate trait checklists can be developed for individual jobs or functional areas to overcome most disadvantages of generalized trait checklist programs.

Responsibility Rating

Characteristics of the responsibility rating appraisal method are:

- *Key features.* The firm develops or alters position descriptions for each position to include all major responsibilities and, where appropriate, standards of performance. Supervisors review position descriptions with employees each year and set standards as needed. Periodically throughout the year, expectations and results are reviewed. Supervisors rate employees on responsibilities identified on the position description. Rating forms consist of responsibilities from position description, anticipated achievement levels, space for "actual" versus "budget," and an "outstanding-superior-average" rating scale with space for comments.
- *Advantages.* Rating factors are specific to the job and rating scales are the same for all employees. Where standards of performance are included in the position description, employees see a direct relation between superior performance and superior rating (or poor performance and poor rating). This overcomes the "standard of comparison" problem. Responsibility rating involves little incremental effort to install once satisfactory position descriptions have been developed. The system forces a review of position descriptions annually, and it encourages updating.
- *Disadvantages.* This method may lead to proliferation of position descriptions (to make duties and performance standards apply specifically to each employee). Unlike the trait checklist method, responsibility rating requires specific job descriptions (and,

ideally, performance standards) and the communication of objectives to employees at the start of the review period.

- *Best applications.* This method is useful for companies with well-written position descriptions that include performance standards or in situations where performance expectations can be added to position descriptions. It is also useful for positions in which duties are largely repetitive and where it is necessary to establish standards of performance for many jobholders. It's appropriate for salary administration, but not for promotability assessment because ratings apply to present positions.

MBO (Management by Objectives)

Characteristics of MBO performance appraisals are:

- *Key features.* Employee suggests, and supervisor agrees on, employee's performance objectives for coming year. Objectives are stated primarily in terms of "business results" or performance standards, but "employee development" types of objectives may be included. Periodically throughout the year, employee and supervisor monitor progress against objectives. At year-end, employee and supervisor assess performance against each objective.
- *Advantages.* MBO focuses directly on the achievement of business results, not the personal characteristics that may contribute to results. The annual establishment of agreed-upon business and personal objectives adjusts the program to changing business needs and personal development requirements.
- *Disadvantages.* Under this program, each employee is rated on different factors and on different scales. This could lead employees to perceive inequity in the system. Furthermore, the system is susceptible to the use of varying standards to establish performance objectives. The MBO approach is very difficult to install and very time-consuming to administer properly. It requires extensive training in goal setting and is subject to all the difficulties of forecasting. And it is very difficult to use if appraisals are tied to employee anniversary dates.
- *Best applications.* This method could be used for senior-level positions that warrant individual goal setting and performance measurement. It could also be used for appraisals for the purpose of making incentive awards.

Free Form

Characteristics of the free-form performance appraisal method are:

- *Key features.* Supervisors rate subordinates with little or no prescribed format. Three principal variations are pure free form, prompted free form, and critical incident. In pure free form, supervisors write a narrative description and assessment of an employee's overall performance. In prompted free form, supervisors write narrative assessments of employee performance/development needs in such preselected areas as: What are the employee's strengths? In which areas does the employee need to improve? In the critical incident format, supervisors record employee performance throughout the year in "critical incidents"—that is, high pressure, particularly sensitive, or especially important situations in which the employee demonstrated accomplishment or need for improvement.
- *Advantages.* Supervisors are free to rate performance directly without being forced to rate aspects/attributes (as in trait checklists) or normal responsibilities (as in responsibility rating). All three formats (but especially the critical incident format) allow supervisors to emphasize and demonstrate when and how employees either "really came through" or "really fell down."
- *Disadvantages.* These methods are totally susceptible to varying standards of comparison problems because employees are rated without either common rating factors or rating scales. Free-form methods aren't conducive to reaching the reliable overall ratings that might be needed for salary administration. The process encourages, rather than inhibits, the "halo effect" and depends heavily on the writing ability of supervisors.
- *Best applications.* Appraisals for the purpose of employee development and promotability assessment should probably use prompted free form for at least part of the appraisal process. Free form is not particularly well suited for salary administration or incentive types of appraisal. Including free-form ratings in employee development appraisals is useful for all levels of employees, subject only to the writing ability of supervisors.

CONCLUSION

Each of the four principal types of appraisal program has valid applications. The authors' experience suggests that the trait checklist approach is too often used where one of the other approaches would yield significantly better results. The typical trait checklist forms are poorly suited to their assigned tasks. Where salary administration is the primary use of the appraisal, responsibility rating would yield significantly more useful appraisals and also improve supervisory and employee attitudes toward the program itself.

The Environmental Context of Performance Evaluation and Its Effect on Current Practices*

by Harvey Kahalas

Performance evaluation (also commonly called performance appraisal or performance review) is the personnel activity by means of which an organization determines the extent to which employees are performing their jobs effectively. It is impossible to manage an organization without information on how well employees are performing. Judgments about performance will be made whether or not there is a formal program, and many will be erroneous. A formal program attempts to minimize errors and assure that the information obtained is useful for its intended purposes. Thus, formal performance evaluation is a conventional management activity in American business, and most surveys show that over three-fourths of United States business organizations have appraisal programs.

Yet, a recent Conference Board report of a survey of 293 firms concludes, "However necessary some formal appraisal system appears to be, current systems are still widely regarded as a nuisance at best and a dangerous evil at worst."[1] Performance evaluation is a personnel activity which, while not new, has not yet matured. Some significant studies have been done, but there are conflicting results, and a complete body of knowledge is still years away.[2]

However, environmental factors are beginning to exert pressures on performance evaluation programs. Social changes, government pressures, and new laws are requiring that programs be reexamined. This process will bring about a more mature and effective activity. Moreover, organizations will find it necessary to alter their performance evaluation practices in order to maintain or improve their human resource utilization and overall organizational effectiveness.

ORGANIZATIONS IN AN OPEN ENVIRONMENTAL SYSTEM

According to open system theory, an organization is just one element in a larger aggregate designated as an open environmental system.[3] Organizations obtain inputs from the environment and transform them into outputs, which are judged acceptable or unacceptable by the numerous forces constituting the environment. Information concerning the outputs or the process of the system is fed back as input into the system, perhaps leading to changes in the transformation process and/or future outputs. Thus, with the proper degree of openness, a system may remain in dynamic equilibrium through the continuous exchange of materials, energy and information.

An organization is continually dependent upon inputs from the environment and this inflow—including human energy—is not constant or guaranteed. The organization lives only so long as people are induced to be members and to perform as such.[4]

Thus, organizations do not live in a static world. The surrounding environment, including its social, political, and legal components, is constantly changing, and a rigid organization cannot survive. While the pressure for change may be communicated most sharply to the organization when there is no market for its output, it may also be communicated more subtly by a gradual deterioration in the quality of its maintenance inputs which are necessary to retain and motivate employees. An organization may discover that it is unable to recruit or retain the quality of human resource it needs or to motivate its members to perform their expected activities effectively.

PRESSURES FROM THE SOCIAL SYSTEM AND THEIR EFFECTS

The current social pressures on performance evaluation practices stem largely from changing attitudes about work, including an increasing concern about the quality of work-

Reprinted from *Human Resource Management,* Vol. 19 No. 3, Fall, 1980, pp. 32–40. Graduate School of Business Administration, University of Michigan, Ann Arbor, MI 48109.

*Thanks should be given to Mr. Ernest Canfield, a graduate student, who helped with some general issues that are discussed in this work.

[1]Robert I. Lazer and Walter Wikstrom, *Appraising Managerial Performance: Current Practices and Future Directions* (New York: The Conference Board, 1977), p. 1.

[2]William F. Glueck, *Personnel: A Diagnostic Approach* (Dallas: Business Publications, 1978), p. 285.

[3]Daniel Katz and Robert Kahn, "Open-System Theory," in *Readings in Organization Theory: Open-System Approaches,* ed. John G. Maurer (New York: Random House, 1971), pp. 13–29.

[4]Ibid., pp. 14–15.

ing life. To examine the effect of these pressures, it is helpful to first examine the integrated model of the determinants of performance described by Cummings and Schwab.[5]

Employee performance is seen as most directly a consequence of the employee's ability and motivation to perform. Motivation is affected by personal goal aspiration, satisfaction, personal goal attainment, intrinsic outcomes and extrinsic outcomes. Organizational variables influence goal aspirations, ability, the relationship between successful performance and the individual's ability and motivation to perform, and extrinsic outcomes.

Formal and informal performance evaluation impacts on most of these constructs and relationships. It influences the definition of the following constructs as seen by the performer: performance itself, intrinsic outcomes, extrinsic outcomes, personal goal attainment, personal goal aspirations, and satisfaction. Likewise, it influences the performer's perceptions of the following linkages: ability-performance, motivation-performance, performance-intrinsic outcomes, performance-extrinsic outcomes, and personal goal attainment-personal aspirations.

Daniel Yankelovich, president of a large social research firm, claims that a major contributing factor to the recent decline in the productivity of American business is the change which is occurring in attitudes toward work.[6] His research suggests that people who work, especially younger, middle management people, are no longer motivated to work as hard and as effectively as in the past. In the late 1960's almost half of all employed Americans looked to their work as a source of personal fulfillment. Now that number has plunged to fewer than one out of four. In the 1960's, 58% believed that "hard work always pays off." Now those who hold this belief constitute only 43%. In short, people's attitudes, values, and motivations have changed faster than the incentives being used—creating a mismatch.

Yankelovich's research has identified two broad group of workers—those for whom the old incentives still work fairly well, about 56% of all workers, and those for whom the old incentives do not work, about 44%. Within the first group there are three subgroups: traditionalists (22%), strongly committed (19%), and young go-getters (15%). The traditionalists, who tend to be older and poorer, are not looking for meaning in their work. Work is just a habit and they want structure, guidance, clear-cut responsibilities, and job security. They just want to do what they think they can do well and have their good job acknowledged. The strongly committed are older, dedicated, and hard-working. Money is important to them, but not as important as the work itself. They are work-before-pleasure people who want to make a contribution and do a good job. The young go-getters are motivated primarily by money and getting ahead.

While not a problem for the three sub-groups just described, the mismatch between motivations and incentives is a problem for the remaining 44% of the working population, which contains two sub-groups: the turned-off (27%) and the self-fulfillers (17%). The turned-off are young, poor and poorly educated. Of all groups, they have the least internal motivation to do an outstanding job for its own sake. They are uncreative, hedonistic, and hungry for diversion from boredom and fatigue. The conventional roads to upward mobility in America—the acquisition of higher education, status, and money in exchange for substantial effort, discipline, dedication, subordination of self to a job—are clearly not for them. The last sub-group, the self-fulfillers, is the youngest and contains the largest proportion of college educated, white collar and middle-management professionals. Its members have the strongest creativity and achievement needs and are the most willing to sacrifice either money or job security in order to fulfill these needs. It is the group hungriest for responsibility, challenge, autonomy, informality, and less rigid authority in organizational structure. Not finding satisfaction in their work, these people are finding outlets in their leisure, hobbies, and new life styles.

While the above analysis is obviously not precise, and the distribution will vary from organization to organization, this study does give a very useful dimension to the problem of motivation. The key point is that we can no longer assume that the workforce is homogeneous with respect to motivations. Therefore, no single type of incentive—desire to work hard, money, fear of job loss, etc.—can motivate the entire spectrum of today's workforce. Incentives are comparable to the intrinsic and extrinsic outcomes in the Cummings and Schwab model. Thus, as the outcomes which employees desire (in return for their effective performance) change, the design, administration and uses of appraisal programs must also change. For example, an appraisal program which applies uniformly in purpose and method to all employees of an organization will become increasingly dysfunctional.

Many other related social changes are affecting appraisal programs. A cross-current through the Yankelovich study is what he calls the "demand for individualization of the work environment" and what Cavanaugh calls the "central role of the person."[7] Each type of worker increasingly views his personal goals as matters of *right.* In the changing social contract between workers and employers, the new

---

[5]Larry Cummings and Donald P. Schwab, *Performance in Organizations: Determinants and Appraisal* (Glenview, IL: Scott Foresman & Co., 1973), Ch. 5; also see Edward E. Lawler, "Job Attitudes and Employee Motivation: Theory, Research, and Practice," *Personnel Psychology,* Vol. 23, 1970, pp. 223–237.

[6]Daniel Yankelovich, "New Approaches to Worker Productivity" (A talk at the National Conference on Human Resource Systems, Dallas, Texas, October 25, 1978).

[7]Gerald F. Cavanaugh, *American Business Values in Transition* (Englewood Cliffs, N.J.: Prentice-Hall, 1976), pp. 188–191.

worker attitude can be best described as a demand that the job fit the worker's own life plan rather than the worker should adjust his/her life plan to fit the employer's needs. A corporation that is prepared to reward and promote only the "traditional" worker will bear the cost of losing a good deal of talent which could be highly motivated in an altered work context. Harry Levinson identified this conflict between personal goals and organizational goals in his classic article on "Management By Whose Objectives?"[8] He claims that appraisal systems, such as management by objectives, must be designed so that the employee's personal needs, values, and goals are considered first, before his or her work goals are set. Then, with the employee, the organization assesses how well they can be met within the organization, doing what the organization needs to have done. Few appraisal programs currently conform to this model.

A closely related trend is the increasing concern over workers' rights and civil liberties in the workplace.[9] According to David Sirota, the modern emphasis on this old idea stems from the fact that companies are just beginning to realize that they must view the attitudes and concerns of workers within the overall context of their social responsibility to the workforce. In the context of appraisals, workers feel they have a right to know how well they are performing, although the quality and level of interest in such feedback will vary with the type of worker. Marion Kellogg states that this "right to know" is the fundamental purpose of the annual appraisal discussion.[10] A candid appraisal discussion establishes the employee in a position of choice. If an employee does not know exactly how work is viewed, his/her choice is limited. If he/she knows what his/her manager feels are strengths and weaknesses and where the balance lies—regardless of how unfair or incorrect that judgment may be perceived—he/she has a choice: to cope as best he/she can, to try to change the manager's mind, to wait it out, or to make a job move. A recent national opinion survey by Louis Harris and Associates indicated that 88% of the responding workers felt they should have the right to look at and question supervisor's reports to management on their performance and promotability.[11]

A related social issue is the ethical concerns of managers about appraisals. For various reasons, such as lack of understanding or skill or poor program design, many managers resist doing appraisals because they feel that they are being forced to "play God," that they do not have the right to sit in complete judgment of another. For example, a manager may "fudge" a performance evaluation in order to justify a preconceived salary increase, and then later another manager may use that same appraisal to make a promotion or termination decision.

Another emerging social value is the desire for participation in decision making.[12] Workers are asking for a greater say in the decisions that affect their work environment. In European countries, worker participation is becoming a legal requirement. Participation is a form of what Thompson and McEwen describe as co-optation, the process of absorbing new elements into the policy—determining structure of an organization in order to avert threats to its stability or existence.[13] Participation increases the likelihood that organizations and employees, related to one another in complicated ways, will find compatible goals. Participation has significant implications for the appraisal process. While its usefulness will vary with the type of employee, in general, it is a method which is significantly related to effective interviews and subsequent performance improvement.[14]

Finally, another social trend which has implications for the appraisal process is the extensive activity of industry in the past 15 years in the area of job enrichment, designing work so that it can more effectively provide workers with the intrinsic outcomes they value.[15] While its usefulness varies with the type of employee, and the method must vary with the constraint of technology, many successful applications have been made. The essence of hundreds of studies is that organizations should attempt to design a job so that: (1) it is a complete piece of work, (2) the incumbent has as much decision-making control over his/her piece of work as possible, and (3) the individual receives frequent, direct feedback on performance.[16] Therefore, job enrichment is an organizational variable which may effectively mediate the relationship between successful performance and the individual's ability and motivation to perform.

All of these social trends have implications for the way organizations use performance evaluation programs to manage their human resources. While they obviously com-

---

[8]Harry Levinson, "Management by Whose Objectives?" *Harvard Business Review,* July–August 1970, pp. 125–134.

[9]David Sirota, "Employee Rights" (A talk at American Management Association's 50th Annual Human Resources Conference, New York City, March 1979) also see D. Quinn Mills, "Human Resources in the 1980's," *Harvard Business Review,* July–August 1979, pp. 158–159; and Mack Hanan, "Make Way for the New Organization Man," *Harvard Business Review,* July–August 1971, pp. 128–138.

[10]Marion S. Kellogg, *When Man and Manager Talk....A Casebook* (Houston, Texas: Gulf Publishing Co., 1969), pp. 87–91.

[11]"Policy Guide—The Privacy Issue," *Bulletin to Management* (Washington, D.C.: Bureau of National Affairs), May 10, 1979, p. 8.

[12]Cavanaugh, pp. 191–193.

[13]James D. Thompson and William J. McEwen, "Organizational Goals and Environment," in Maurer, pp. 448–458.

[14]Herbert H. Meyer, Emanuel Kay, and John R.P. French, "Split Roles in Performance Appraisal," *Harvard Business Review,* January–February 1965, p. 5; Ronald J. Burke and Douglas S. Wilcox, "Characteristics of Effective Employee Performance Review and Development Interviews," *Personnel Psychology,* Vol. 22, 1969, p. 300.

[15]J. Richard Hackman, Greg Oldham, Robert Janson, and Kenneth Purdy, "A New Strategy for Job Enrichment," *California Management Review,* Summer 1975, pp. 57–71.

[16]David A. Whitsett, "The Enriched Job," *The Personnel Administrator,* September–October 1972, p. 53.

plicate the work of the program administrator, they offer the prospect of program improvements which can bring about what McGuire calls a "more equitable distribution of organizational satisfaction."[17] Perhaps, too, they can have a positive effect on performance and productivity.

POLITICAL AND LEGAL PRESSURES AND THEIR EFFECTS

With the Age Discrimination in Employment Act Amendments of 1978 and the resulting increase to 70 in the mandatory retirement age permitted under federal law, increased attention has been focused on performance appraisal programs.[18] Personnel decisions such as terminations cannot be made on the basis of age, but must be made on the basis of job performance. Instead of carrying less productive older workers on the payroll, employers may begin to remove them earlier in an effort to deter age-discrimination charges. In defending age discrimination cases, employers will point to appraisals of poor performance; but whether a given appraisal program is a legally acceptable basis for making a particular personnel decision must be determined by the courts.

Court decisions in recent age discrimination cases indicate that accurate and substantiated evidence of individual performance is necessary as a basis for justifying personnel actions that adversely affect protected older employees. Where appraisals are general, informal, and subjective, there is a risk of age bias. Courts require, for example, that appraisals be based on "definite identifiable criteria based on quality or quantity of work or specific performances..." (*Mistretta* v. *Sandia Corporation*).[19] In other words, courts look for evidence that the measures of performance are job-related. Walker indicates the judicial discussions of appraisals and their validity suggest three essential program characteristics: reasonableness, relevance and reliability.[20]

Basnight and Wolkinson, in their review of applicable court cases, claim that managerial merit plans typically suffer from three weaknesses: vagueness of standards, subjectivity, and inconsistency among appraisers.[21] Both the Fair Labor Standards Act (FLSA) and Title VII of the Civil Rights Act of 1964 contemplate differences in pay based on merit considerations, but, for various reasons, there has been very little litigation involving merit systems under either statute. The issue has come into the courts, nonetheless, in cases involving nonmanagerial employees, as an outgrowth of investigations of other charges or as one item in a list of discriminatory practices being charged. Where such challenges have occurred, the courts have taken different approaches. In FLSA cases, they have tended to look to form; in civil rights cases, to substance. Systems challenged under FLSA have been scrutinized for little beyond uniformity of administration.

However, Basnight and Wolkinson claim that, "in light of Title VII decisions regarding other employment practices, the problems of vagueness of standards, subjectivity and inconsistency among appraisers will probably require substantial restriction—perhaps elimination—of the use of traditional, subjective performance evaluation in making both merit-pay and promotion decisions."[22] To protect itself from the thrust of the leading case in this area (*Rowe* v. *General Motors*), an employer might provide written instructions, with objective criteria, for the preparation of evaluations. However, if this evaluation program produces disproportionate numbers of merit increases and/or promotions for minority and female employees, it may still be found illegal under another landmark case (*Griggs* v. *Duke Power*) if it cannot be shown to be related to job performance.[23] Basnight and Wolkinson suggest that an appraisal technique such as "management by objectives" might better meet the Rowe standards by giving subordinates advance knowledge of the objective criteria to be used in evaluating their performance.[24]

Appraisal programs must also meet the requirements of EEOC's Uniform Guidelines on Employee Selection Procedures, which apply, under Title VII, to "tests and other selection procedures which are used as the basis for any employment decisions."[25] The Guidelines require that employers demonstrate the job relatedness of any device that is used in making employment decisions and that has an adverse impact on members of any race, sex, or ethnic group. Thus, if a company finds that its appraisals do have an adverse impact, then it must either cease using that procedure, find an alternative procedure which eliminates the adverse impact or validate the procedure—that is, determine statistically that the appraisal procedure yields results which are indicative of actual job performance.

If, for example, a firm's female or minority employees are not receiving salary increases or promotions at a rate

[17]Joseph W. McGuire, "The Changing Nature of Business Responsibilities (A paper presented at Oklahoma State University, Stillwater, Oklahoma, March 8, 1978), p. 10.

[18]James W. Walker and Daniel E. Lupton, "Performance Appraisal Programs and Age Discrimination Law," *Aging and Work*, Spring 1978, pp. 73–83; Jeffrey Sonnenfeld, "Dealing with the Aging Workforce," *Harvard Business Review*, November–December 1978, pp. 81–92.

[19]Walker and Lupton, p. 74.

[20]Ibid., pp. 78–79.

[21]Thomas A. Basnight and Benjamin W. Wolkinson, "Evaluating Managerial Performance: Is Your Appraisal System Legal?" *Employee Relations Law Journal*, Autumn 1977, p. 241.

[22]Ibid., p. 247.

[23]Ibid., pp. 250–251.

[24]Ibid., p. 253.

[25]U.S. Equal Employment Opportunity Commission, "Uniform Guidelines on Employee Selection Procedures," in *Daily Labor Report* (Washington, D.C.: The Bureau of National Affairs), August 25, 1978, p. 7.

comparable to white male employees, relative to their number in the firm's labor force, and these decisions are based in whole or part on a performance appraisal system, that appraisal system is heading for trouble. Obviously, a firm's first defense should be to make sure that its procedures do not result in adverse impact under the "bottom line" concept described in the Guidelines.[26] However, any one employee who feels he or she has been discriminated against as a result of a performance rating retains the right to file a complaint and proceed through the appropriate agency and into federal court. Thus, an organization may still be required to demonstrate the job performance relationship (validity) of its appraisal procedures even though those procedures otherwise meet the "bottom line" standard.

In regard to validation of appraisals, and measuring the extent to which performance ratings correspond to actual performance on the job, it is not yet clear what the acceptable methodology is for conducting such studies. W.B. Walker, President of Psycon, Inc., states, "I know of no studies to measure the validity of a performance appraisal procedure in an operational context."[27] In the recent Conference Board survey mentioned earlier, not one of the 217 companies with appraisal programs reported that they had completed such a study.[28] To the question of whether appraisals can be validated, Walker responds, "Outside of a controlled laboratory-type of experimental model, the answer, from the standpoint of practicality and financial feasibility, is probably 'No' for most organizations."[29] In most cases, it is difficult or impossible to find the ultimate objective criteria against which to validate subjective appraisals. If such criteria were identified, they would become the basis of the ongoing appraisal and move from the criterion to the predictor side of the equation.

One possible answer may be the use of content validity, a demonstration that the content of an appraisal procedure is representative of all important aspects of performance on the job.[30] Such a study involves a careful job analysis, which identifies all important observable work behaviors and shows how they are used in the job and how they relate to the content of the appraisal procedure. The strength of evidence of content validity depends on the proportion of critical work behaviors measured by the appraisal system. For highly populated jobs in large organizations, this is a feasible and probably cost effective approach. For positions which are unique and high in the organization, it may not be.

Thus, the effect of the new emphasis on validity of appraisals is to eliminate vague factors such as attitude, cooperation, dependability, initiative, and leadership. These are constructs, and psychologists have yet to agree on an acceptable methodology for conducting a construct validity study.[31] In general, the elimination of such vague constructs will be an improvement of the appraisal process. However, if this change prevents managers from considering certain behaviors or qualities which are highly important to the effective functioning of an organization, because they cannot be operationally defined, then this new emphasis will cause problems for organizations. Miner argues that the measurement of behaviors and qualities that are valied by an organization, often implicitly, may be more important to organizational effectiveness than the typical work objectives which are more amenable to measurement.[32] Effective organizations need an integrated value system that pulls people together, makes them think somewhat the same way, and makes them able to communicate with each other effectively. This conflict between implicitly valued behaviors and work accomplishments appears to be a central issue behind the recent negative reaction of President Carter's Cabinet to the staff evaluation form which was suddenly given to them to use in evaluating their key staff.[33] To the extent that such implicit factors as loyalty will be brought out in the open, defined, integrated with the work factors, and communicated in advance of their use, this new emphasis on validity will be positive for employees (such as by reducing value dissonance and hence stress) and for organizations. In most respects, this is what Harry Levinson means when he says that "current dissatisfactions with appraisal systems will continue until they are revised to accommodate the 'how' as well as the 'what' in performance."[34]

However, that appraisals cannot yet be acceptably validated does not mean that companies should eliminate their programs or that those which have not undertaken a program should not do so. There is a degree of risk either way. Most companies believe that they are better off in defending themselves against EEO discrimination charges if their personnel decisions are based on somewhat subjective standards than if based on no standards at all.

---

[26] Ibid., p. 2.

[27] N. B. Winstanley, W. B. Walker, John Miner and David Ackerman, "Performance Appraisal: The Barrier to Pay for Performance," *1978 National Conference Proceedings* (Scottsdale, Arizona: American Compensation Association, 1979) p. 43.

[28] Robert I. Lazer, "The Discrimination Danger in Performance Appraisal," *The Conference Board Record,* March 1976, p. 63.

[29] Winstanley et al., p. 44.

[30] "Validation of Performance Appraisal Systems" (Internal memorandum to U.S. consulting and support staff of Towers, Perrin, Foster, and Crosby, May 18, 1979).

[31] Ibid., p. 3.

[32] Winstanley et al., pp. 46–48.

[33] "Carter's Great Purge," *Time,* July 30, 1979, pp. 10–19.

[34] Harry Levinson, "Appraisal of *What* Performance," *Harvard Business Review,* July–August 1976, p. 30.

AN INTEGRATED PROGRAM OF PERFORMANCE EVALUATION

In concept, the actions which must be taken to redesign appraisal programs so they respond to these legal and social pressures are not much different from those which ought to be taken just to bring the state of the art to a more mature stage. Performance evaluation is obviously a highly complex activity and its effectiveness is determined by many key contingencies. In order to integrate and balance the many factors involved, the program administrator should give thought to four critical considerations—purpose, relevance, process, and program management.

Purpose

One of the basic problems with performance evaluations concerns their multi-purpose nature.[35] Much of the research literature on the subject indicates that performance evaluations serve two types of purposes—administrative and developmental—each of which may have a variety of sub-purposes. On one hand, performance evaluations provide information which managers need on performance to make human resource decisions on salaries, transfers, and terminations. They may also provide information on promotion potential for use in making decisions on promotions. Formal appraisals also provide documentation indicating that such decisions were not made on the basis of age, sex, race, etc., but rather on the basis of job performance. On the other hand, performance evaluations are also intended to stimulate performance improvement by providing feedback to employees on performance expected, performance achieved, promotion possibilities, and job skills to be improved.

This variety of purposes poses several problems. One is the possible conflict among program purposes. The dual goals of appraisal require managers to serve as both judge and counselor simultaneously, and inevitably one purpose will render the other ineffective. A program which is illegal for administrative purposes may be legal for developmental purposes. As a result, many firms are now developing separate programs for each of these two general purposes. To be achieved effectively, different purposes require different conditions and, hence, different appraisal techniques. Another problem is that program purpose may be vague and unrealistic. The courts favor the view that a performance appraisal program should be rational, that is that the program be designed for specific purposes which are reasonable and clearly identified, and that the techniques adopted have the capacity to achieve these objectives.[36] Further, separation and clearer definition and communication of purposes can do much to resolve the ethical dilemmas which managers face in regard to appraisals.

Relevance

The courts and EEOC's Uniform Guidelines also require that appraisal programs be relevant, that is, job related and based on clear and objective criteria. They must cover only those aspects of work that are important and must provide clear statements of job requirements and the kind of on-the-job behavior necessary for successful performance. To be job related, performance evaluations must be based on empirically derived job requirements. The process of job analysis, job description, and job evaluation as typically carried out for salary administration purposes is inadequate for performance evaluation. A different kind of job analysis is required—a kind directed at identifying specific, measurable job performance standards for both the 'what' and 'how' of job performance.[37]

Process

The design and management of performance evaluation programs must reflect the fact that performance evaluation is a process, that is, a continuous, systematic series of actions which must effectively integrate various related sub-programs. Failure to view the total integrated process can easily lead to many conflicts among the related human resource sub-programs and reduce a performance evaluation program to useless paperwork. Consideration of the process is essential in designing programs which respond to the social issues discussed earlier. For example, an effective approach is to permit employees to participate in each step of the process. Below is a description of the typical sequence of steps to be taken by a manager in carrying out the process.

1. *Establishing understanding of performance expected:* This is the process of determining what specific work results are to be accomplished and how well. Objectives and standards are set well in advance of any performance review and provide the basis for a fair evaluation.
2. *Establishing a development plan:* This is the process of determining what job skills are to be improved and

---

[35] Meyer et al.; Robert J. Hayden, "Performance Appraisal: A Better Way," *Personnel Journal,* July 1973, pp. 606–613.

[36] Walker and Lupton, p. 80.

[37] Craig E. Schneier, "Content Validity: The Necessity of a Behavioral Job Description," *The Personnel Administrator,* February 1976, pp. 38–44.

how. It should also be established well in advance of a performance review.

3. *On a continuous basis.*
   a. *Measuring performance:* This is the process of keeping record of an employee's results so that he/she can see on a daily basis how his/her performance compares with performance expected.
   b. *Updating understanding of performance expected:* This is the process of adding assignments, changing standards, etc., in the normal process of work.
   c. *Providing individual training and development programs.*
4. *As needed.*
   a. *Using performance information to make decisions on salaries, transfers, and terminations.*
   b. *Using information on promotability to make promotion decisions.*
5. *Preparing for a performance review:* This is the process of reviewing performance data, making a tentative evaluation, analyzing problems, and considering possible improvement plans. Understanding of job enrichment concepts can be especially useful here in identifying actions to facilitate development. A logical problem-solving approach, such as one which identifies performance problems caused not by a lack of knowledge, but by organizational factors which prevent effective performance, can also be helpful.[38]
6. *Conducting the appraisal discussion:* This is the process of discussing and comparing notes on performance, promotability, key problems, and improvement opportunities.
7. *Establishing understanding of performance expected:* This is a complete updating of the agreement established in Step 1.
8. *Establishing a development plan:* This is updating of the plan set in Step 2.
9. *Completing and submitting the appraisal form:* The last step in a complete work cycle is to complete a final copy of the required form, show it to the employee, and forward it through division management channels to Personnel.

PROGRAM MANAGEMENT

To be effective, a performance evaluation program must be not only well designed—in terms of purpose, relevance, and process—but also well managed. The role of a designated program manager is critical to an effective program and is comparable to the role of boundary personnel conceived by Katz and Kahn.[39] The program manager must be receptive not only to external forces (social, political, and legal) but also to internal forces (demands of the organization and its employees) and must mediate and balance these conflicting demands as conditions change. The following sequence of actions is recommended to develop, implement, and maintain an effective performance evaluation program.[40]

1. *Determine the type of program the organization climate will support.* An appraisal program must be consistent with company philosophy, method of operation, and objectives. Kast and Rosenzweig's contingency view suggests the type of analysis required.[41] The goals of organizations in more placid environments will be directed toward efficient performance, stability, and maintenance, while those in more turbulent environments will be directed toward effective problem-solving, innovation and growth.
2. *Obtain support of top management.* Top management must be willing to participate actively in the program, demonstrate its importance through personal example, and make use of its results. This can help to overcome the ethical dilemmas which managers may experience regarding appraisal situations which may otherwise seem to require unfairness or manipulation.[42]
3. *Determine what specific existing needs the program would fulfill,* i.e., determine the purpose of the program.
4. *Involve the users in the design.* User participation is helpful in obtaining commitment and assuring that practical purposes are served.
5. *Design a performance information system.* Performance information must be controlled in its content, flow, timing, etc., in order to assure its use for its intended decision-making purpose.
6. *Test the program.* A pilot program provides an opportunity to identify needed modifications.
7. *Develop policy, procedures, and guidelines in the form of an appraiser's manual.* The courts appear to favor appraisal programs that are systematically ad-

[38]Geary A. Rummler, "Human Performance Problems and Their Solutions," *Human Resource Management,* Winter 1972, pp. 2–10.

[39]Katz and Kahn, p. 17–18.

[40]Thomas N. Baylie, Carl J. Kujawski, and Drew M. Young, "Appraisal of 'People' Resources," in *PAIR Handbook,* Vol. 1, ed. Dale Yoder and Herbert G. Heneman (Washington, D.C.: The Bureau of National Affairs, 1974).

[41]Fremont E. Kast and James E. Rosenzweig, "General Systems Theory: Applications for Organization and Management," *Academy of Management Journal,* December 1972, pp. 459–463; also see Roger Harrison, "Understanding Your Organization's Character," *Harvard Business Review,* May–June 1972, pp. 119–128.

[42]Robert L. Bjorklund and Harvey Kahalas, "Ethical Value Congruence Among Engineers and Managers: A Look at Specific Ethical Constructs" (unpublished paper): Max S. Wortman and Agnes Missirian, "Ethics in the Organizational Microcosm: Suggestions for Research" (unpublished paper).

ministered.[43] A patterned, structured appraisal format has a positive effect on reliability and validity.

8. *Communicate the program.* Top management should explain the specific requirements to all affected, i.e., who, why, when, how, etc.
9. *Train supervisors.* As the previous discussion of process suggests, performance evaluation requires many different management skills, such as communicating, problem solving, developing people, and planning. Unless training is comprehensive and ongoing, the program will be less than fully effective. Surveys indicate that 25% to 50% of companies with appraisal programs provide no training whatsoever.[44] This is a critical need in view of the legal emphasis on consistent administration of appraisals. Marion Kellogg describes a very useful approach applicable to the various types of dialogues a manager must conduct at the different steps in the process cycle described above.[45]
10. *Orient subordinate employees.* The purpose and procedures of the program should be explained in advance to all who will be affected.
11. *Begin making appraisals.*
12. *Use the results in making salary, transfer, promotion, and termination decisions.*
13. *Monitor and revise the program.* The program manager must audit the quality of the program and how well it is achieving its intended purposes, provide program feedback to management, and be alert to ways the program might be improved. A critical aspect of this step is to monitor for adverse impact on protected classes.
14. *Orient new supervisors.* As new supervisors are appointed, they must be trained.

CONCLUSION

No mention has been made in this discussion of any of the many appraisal techniques in use.[46] This is because it is the manner of design, implementation, and administration that determines the effectiveness of an appraisal program more than it is the particular set of techniques adopted. What is needed is more of a systems approach. Appraisal techniques, like organizational structures, are merely tools for achieving organizational objectives. To remain effective, organizations must be open to input from the social, political, and legal areas of the environment. Since the appraisal process is a useful subsystem within an organization, it, too, must be dynamic and subject to change. What is required is a more pro-active, anticipatory, problem-solving role in administering appraisals. The potential payoffs are the avoidance of costly lawsuits; a more equitable distribution of job satisfactions; improved recruitment, motivation, utilization, and retention of personnel; and improved organizational effectiveness. Usually the benefits of an appraisal program are worth its costs. To achieve these benefits, organizations must implement programs that focus on purpose, relevance, process and program management.

[43] Walker and Lupton, p. 81.

[44] Lazer and Wikstrom, p. 39; Alan H. Locher and Kenneth S. Teel, "Performance Appraisal—A Survey of Current Practices," *Personnel Journal*, May 1977, p. 247.

[45] Kellogg, pp. 87–91.

[46] Baylie et al., pp. 185–200.

SOURCES SECTION FOUR

IMPLEMENTING PERFORMANCE APPRAISAL

CHOOSING WHO EVALUATES

Who Evaluates?
by L. L. Cummings and Donald P. Schwab

- Discusses five sources of evaluations.
- Presents advantages and disadvantages of each source.

TRAINING THE RATERS

Training Approaches and a Workshop to Minimize Rating Error
by Gary Latham and Kenneth Wexley

- Reviews common errors found in ratings.
- Discusses characteristics of unsuccessful rater training programs.
- Describes a workshop for rater training and compares it to a group discussion.

Discussion on Training Programs for Observers of Behaviors
by Mark D. Spool

- Lists characteristics of effective rater training programs.
- Reviews the four major activities of successful rater training programs.

OBSERVING PERFORMANCE AND DOCUMENTING IT SO THAT APPRAISALS ARE ACCURATE

Documenting Employee Performance
by Michael Smith

- Explains the purpose and use of documentation.
- Describes three characteristics documentation should have.
- Presents a self-test of your understanding of documentation.

GIVING PERFORMANCE FEEDBACK

Nonevaluative Approaches to Performance Appraisals

by Les Wallace

- Suggests ways of giving performance feedback so that it is accepted and used.
- Gives examples of effective and ineffective communication in performance appraisal.

Performance Interview Guidelines

by Walter Mahler

- Gives six ways to improve the performance appraisal interview.
- Provides a checklist for evaluating performance appraisal interviews.

Who Evaluates?

by L. L. Cummings and Donald P. Schwab

There are five possible parties that can do the appraising: (1) the superior(s) of the person to be appraised, (2) organizational peers of the appraisee, (3) the appraisee himself, (4) subordinates of the appraisee, and (5) persons outside the immediate work environment of the appraisee.[1] Each of these parties might be appropriate, depending on the purpose (evaluative or developmental) of the appraisal and the dimensions (either outcomes or methods) being appraised.

Figure 1 depicts the full array of possibilities when one combines the two broad purposes of appraisal with the general dimensions to which appraisal can be applied. There are four possibilities, corresponding to the four cells of Figure 1. Cell 1 shows that appraisal can be utilized to evaluate the methods individuals employ in their jobs. Illustrative of this would be an examination and appraisal of whether a salesman is following the prescribed procedure in illustrating the functioning of his product to a prospective customer. Cell 2 refers to the fact that appraisals may focus on evaluating whether desired outcomes were achieved. For example, in a sales context, Was a sale made? or How much was sold?

Cell 3 indicates that appraisal may be used to assist the employee in improving the method he uses to perform his job. For example, this might involve aiding a salesman in correcting what is thought to be a crucial mistake or omission in his sales presentation. He may be attempting to close the sale too quickly, thereby generating resistance by the customer and losing the sales opportunity. The focus of the appraisal here would be on assisting the salesman in (1) seeing the consequences of his overly aggressive approach, (2) providing him with more appropriate models to imitate, and (3) allowing him to practice his new response.

Cell 4 shows that appraisals can focus directly on the development of the ends or outcome to be achieved on the job. Illustrative of this use of appraisals would be an attempt to provide the salesman with feedback concerning his past goal accomplishment. As a part of this process he might be encouraged to establish outcome goals for the next performance period. Here the focus is on the motivating force that comes from (1) participating in the setting of one's own goals, and (2) publicly committing oneself to these goals.

We shall now integrate the issues raised to this point by discussing the advantages and disadvantages of having each of the five parties engage in the appraisal process. This discussion will involve both normative issues and empirical issues where research findings are available to aid us in assessing the value of having various parties engage in various types of appraisal activities.

SUPERVISORY APPRAISAL

There are two primary justifications for centering the appraisal process in the performer's superior. The hierarchy of formal authority which exists in most organizations legitimates the right of the superior to make both evaluative and developmental decisions concerning his subordinates. Indeed, it is his duty and obligation. To behave otherwise would violate the expectations of his own superior as well as those of most of his subordinates. In addition, the superior generally controls the magnitude and scheduling of many of the rewards and punishments received by his

FIGURE 1
Superior, Peer, Self, and Outside Appraisal in Relation to the Purposes and Dimensions of Appraisal

Purpose of Appraisal / Dimension of Appraisal	Evaluation	Development
Means (Method Used)	1: Superior, Peer, Self, Subordinate, Outsider	3: Superior, Peer, Self, Subordinate, Outsider
Ends (Outcomes Achieved)	2: Superior, Peer, Self, Subordinate, Outsider	4: Superior, Peer, Self, Subordinate, Outsider

[1]For empirical evidence on this issue see: Amir, Kovarsky, and Sharon (1970); Barrett (1961, 1963, 1964, 1966); Barrett, Parker, Taylor, and Martens (1958); Bassett and Meyer (1968); Berkshire and Nelson (1958); Campbell, Otis, Liske, and Prien (1962); Doll (1962); Doll and Longo (1962); Hanson, Morton, and Rothaus (1963); Kay, Meyer, and French (1965); Kirchner (1965); Kirchner and Reisberg (1962); Prien and Liske (1962); Rothaus, Morton, and Hanson (1965); Thorton (1968).

subordinates. To the extent that performance is enhanced when rewards are based on performance, then appraisal and reward-punishment power should be in the same hands. To separate these is to undercut the legitimacy of the appraisal process itself and/or the reward power of the superior.

The literature on appraisal suggests that the appraisal can be made more valid by the use of several superiors, at the same organizational level or at successive levels. This is true because it is unlikely that even the immediate superior will observe all the relevant dimensions of a subordinate's behavior or that he will weigh these dimensions in the same way as higher levels of management, in terms of their contribution to overall organizational goals.

A caution is appropriate however. There is evidence that the immediate supervisor's appraisal is highly related to the average evaluations across several appraisers and to objective measures of performance. This suggests that an appraisal by the immediate supervisor may function adequately in the absence of other assessments.

Several potential liabilities of appraisal by the superior have been studied and discussed in the literature. First, being appraised by a reward-and-punishment controller may threaten and subordinate. Moreover, the appraisal communication process often tends to flow only from the superior to the subordinate so that the latter feels he must defend himself and justify his actions. Often, little coaching and development seem to transpire.

In addition, the superior frequently feels uncomfortable in the appraisal role because: (1) the role demands skills which he does not possess, (2) he has an ethical objection to "playing God," (3) communication of negative appraisals may alienate subordinates, or (4) he realizes that in some cases the superior does not have sufficient reward-and-punishment power to implement the results of an appraisal even if he does a thorough job of it. As a consequence, the superior often avoids conducting the appraisal.

These potential liabilities have led some organizations to incorporate other persons in the appraisal process, such as subordinates' peers, self, and outsiders. Some organizations have also suggested that appraisals not be used for evaluation at all, but solely for purposes of development.

PEER APPRAISAL

Two considerations would seem to facilitate the effective use of peer appraisals: (1) a high level of interpersonal trust and sharing among peers, coupled with a noncompetitive reward system, and (2) situations where information about the appraisee's performance methods or outcomes are uniquely available to his peers. Peer appraisals are most frequently used in highly professional organizations where the above two conditions are most likely to be true; for example, among professors in universities, among physicians in clinics, or among scientists in industrial organizations.

Research on peer appraisals has shown them to be predictive of success or correlated with both objective and other subjective evaluations of success in naval flight training and performance, military officer performance, scholastic performance, field sales performance, performance as a first-level manufacturing supervisor, and middle-management performance.

This being the case, peer evaluations may be an appropriate alternative to supervisory evaluations, when one wants to reduce the threat associated with the status differentials and social distance built into the typical review by the superior. This in turn may act as a force toward honesty and open communication between the appraiser and the appraisee. Peer evaluations may also be appropriate when the supervisor is unable to effectively observe the behavior of his subordinates.

Peer appraisal and subsequent discussion may also be useful in uncovering communication and coordination problems among members of a work team. Mutual expectations and task interdependencies may be clarified so that self-control becomes more feasible.

There are also several potential liabilities associated with the use of peer appraisals. First, their value may be depreciated by the competitive nature of many organizational reward systems. A win-lose game among peers tends to inhibit honesty in evaluating perceived rivals. In addition, a highly competitive organizational reward system should suggest a caution of a different nature in the use of peers for appraisal. Such systems place an employee, when requested to evaluate his peers, into one or more of several possible psychological conflicts. For example, conflicts may arise between evaluating one's peer highly and maximizing one's own chances of a large salary increase or between evaluating him poorly and maintaining his friendship. It is for such reasons that peer appraisals have been found invalid, or even disruptive, in some organizations.

SELF-APPRAISAL

Self-appraisals appear justified where there are strong reasons to believe that the performer himself is in the best position to observe and evaluate his own methods of work and outcome; for example, where the performer is working under conditions of extreme physical isolation or is the unique possessor of a rare skill.

The most visible thrust for self-appraisals, however, comes from the trend, beginning in the 1960s, toward the use of a developmental focus or theme in performance evaluation. This theme places major emphasis on the personal growth, self-motivation, and organizational potential of the employee. Thus self-appraisals become an integral part of the feedback process to the employee.

Several positive results have been found to be associated with self-appraisal, including (1) more satisfying and constructive appraisal interviews, (2) less defensiveness by performers regarding the appraisal interviews as well as the overall appraisal process, and (3) improved job performance.

These advantages have to be countered by the evidence indicating several problems associated with the use of self-appraisals. First, several studies have found low agreement between self- and supervisory appraisals. These disagreements may pertain to the definition of the dimensions of the performer's job, the relative importance of the dimensions and the performer's achievements on these dimensions. In general, subordinates tend to evaluate their performance more favorably than do their superiors. Second, there is evidence to indicate that managers who overevaluate themselves, relative to their superiors' evaluations, tend to be judged as less promotable than their counterparts. This implies that the very persons who could benefit the most from developmental efforts are those who disagree with their superiors about their performance and may, therefore, be least likely to receive such development.

Third, there is some evidence indicating that what is evaluated influences the amount of agreement between the superior's and the subordinate's appraisals. Greater superior-subordinate agreement tends to be achieved when evaluating task-related (performance) characteristics than on personality and interpersonal characteristics. This may be because of the greater availability of behavioral anchors for such task-related characteristics on the job.

In sum, it would appear that self-appraisals are effective tools for programs focusing on self-development, personal growth, and goal commitment. On the other hand, it would also appear that self-appraisals are subject to systematic biases and distortions when used for evaluative purposes. As a final point, it should be noted that whether good or bad, some form of self-perception and self-appraisal is inevitable. Most employees can be expected to walk into a performance review session with their superior with some preconceived notion of how they feel they have performed. Disagreements between the superior's perceptions and those of the performer can (and should) form the basis for important discussions and, possibly, developmental efforts.

APPRAISAL BY SUBORDINATES

In most organizations the explicit appraisal of a superior by his subordinates would be perceived as unusual, or perhaps even illegitimate. There are circumstances, however, when subordinate appraisals can be useful. Some organizations utilize anonymous subordinate evaluations as one of several inputs into the development process for their managers. Knowing how one is perceived by his subordinates can be an important, although potentially stressful, ingredient into the change of a superior's behavior. Occasionally, organizations will utilize subordinate appraisals for purposes of assessing the leadership potential of their lower-level managers.

Some organizations have also encouraged subordinate appraisals of their superiors as a means of creating an atmosphere of power equalization and involvement on the part of lower organizational levels. A variation on this approach involved a program in a pharmaceutical firm (Cummings, in press) which had a group of operative employees aid in the development of an appraisal system in terms of defining performance dimensions, scales, and items. This involvement resulted in increased perceptions of clarity and meaningfulness regarding the appraisal process, as well as a closer perceived link between performance and pay.

There are, however, several significant disadvantages of bottoms-up appraisal. Studies have shown, for example, that some subordinates perceive it as illegitimate. They view a request to formally appraise their boss as threatening; that is, the boss may reprimand them for an honest, but unfavorable, appraisal. Of course, many superiors also view the process with suspicion. Subordinate appraisals tend to undermine the superior's legitimate, positional power, as well as his reward-and-punishment power.

Finally, there is the distinct possibility that the subordinate may base his evaluation on something other than the superior's contribution to the organization. There is some evidence to indicate that the subordinate will focus primarily on the extent to which his superior fulfills the subordinate's needs rather than on the organizational accomplishments of the superior. Ideally, these two foci would not be in conflict, but the possibility of inconsistency leads most organizations to exercise caution in the use of subordinate appraisals.

APPRAISAL BY OUTSIDERS

Organizations sometimes utilize specialists from the personnel department with expertise in performance assessment, and also external consultants (most likely psychologists), to engage in the appraisal process. Two general conditions would suggest the use of such outsiders: (1) the need for specialized expertise, either as a trained observer or in a substantive content area, and (2) where the objectivity of the appraisal process can be insured only through appraisal by someone without a vested interest in the outcomes of the appraisal (e.g., as in the case of a C.P.A. firm testifying to the general acceptance of the principles used in the financial statements of a client firm).

There is an increasing amount of evidence suggesting that persons outside of the superior-subordinate-peer triad can make valuable contributions to the *selection* of managers for increased responsibility. Most of this evidence is found in the literature and in practice under the rubric of the assessment center approach to managerial selection and promotion.[2]

One type of outside appraisal, usually referred to as the *field review,* focuses on the evaluation of performance for purposes of administering organizational rewards and punishments. In this technique, a specialist from the personnel department interviews the superior(s) of the person being evaluated. The focus of the interview is on the job content and job performance of the subordinate. The specialist typically summarizes the interview content into a general, overall assessment which is then discussed with the superior and possibly modified as a result of this discussion. The resulting appraisal becomes a part of the subordinate's personnel file. It may or may not be discussed with the subordinate.

Many managers find this use of an outside appraiser attractive since they feel it will save them time and will partially allow them to escape a distasteful chore. The other advantage frequently cited for this type of appraisal is that it reduces the variance in evaluations due to different appraisers using different dimensions and standards of performance. Presumably, the specialist utilizes a common frame of reference across similar jobs and situations.

There are several severe disadvantages to this approach. First, it encourages the superior to avoid an essential part of his managerial responsibility. Second, it is questionable whether meaningful conversations will take place between a superior and his subordinates about performance improvement if the evaluation process is conducted by an outside party. Third, it is inefficient to the extent that at least two representatives of management must spend time doing each appraisal. From an organizational point of view, what started out as a time-saver may end up consuming additional time and manpower.

SUMMARY

Organizational practice and empirical evidence would indicate that, most typically, the appraisal process is conducted by the immediate superior of the performer. The perceived threats and stress associated with this procedure as well as other problems have led some organizations to use peer, self, subordinate, and outside sources of appraisal. Appraisal by a performer's peers appears to be appropriate under conditions of high interpersonal trust, high visibility of performance to peers, and intensely specialized skills and abilities. Self-appraisal has been found useful where personal development is the goal and where a psychological acceptance of the appraisal is necessary to generate change by the appraisee. Appraisal by a manager's subordinates is helpful when the aims are the development of the manager's insight into how others see him and change in his behavior as a supervisor. Generally, subordinate appraisal is perceived with suspicion by superiors and some subordinates. Evaluation by outsiders is increasingly used in assessment for selection and in the identification of possible, long-term managerial talent. The field review by a personnel specialist can be useful as an evaluation technique, but may encourage the manager to neglect his basic responsibility to review the performance of his subordinates systematically and to discuss his review with them.

[2]In addition to several of the references in footnote 1 of this chapter, an excellent review of experience in this area can be found in Campbell et al. (1970, p. 36 and pp. 213–31).

REFERENCES

- Amir, Y., Y. Kovarsky, and S. Sharon. "Peer Nominations as a Predictor of Multistage Promotion in a Ramified Organization." *Journal of Applied Psychology,* 1970, *54,* 462–469. Sample of 3897 Israeli soldiers. Peer nominations obtained at early stages of training predicted promotion at several successive stages in the soldier's military career with a high degree of validity and correlations around .6 and .7. Predictions were valid for success within groups of different personnel, with different purposes, and with different criteria for achievement. Peer nominations were also found to contribute markedly to the predictive validity of conventional psychological screening measures, suggesting the value of combining psychometric and sociometric procedures for personnel selection.
- Barrett, R.S. "The Agreement Scale: A Preliminary Report." *Personnel Psychology.* 1961, *14,* 151–165.
- Barrett, R.S. "Performance Suitability and Role Agreement: Two Factors Related to Attitudes." *Personnel Psychology.* 1963, *16,* 345–357.
- Barrett, R.S. "Explorations in Job Satisfaction and Performance Rating." *Personnel Administration.* 1964, *27,* 14–21. Series of studies reported by Barrett in the early and mid-1960s on the determinants of supervisors' ratings and the agreement between perceived job requirements as seen by the supervisor and the subordinate.
- Barrett, R.S. "The Influence of the Supervisor's Requirements on Ratings." *Personnel Psychology.* 1966, *19,* 375–387. Study examines data relating to the following: (1) Do supervisors and their subordinates agree on job requirements? and (2) What differences exist in the job performance of those subordinates who are rated high versus those rated low?
- Barrett, R.S., E.K. Taylor, J.W. Parker, and L. Martens. "Rating Scale Content: I. Scale Information and Supervisory Ratings." *Personnel Psychology.* 1958, *11,* 333–346. Comparison of rating scales incorporating trait titles and behavioral descriptions between first- and second-level supervisors.
- Bassett, G.A., and H.H. Meyer. "Performance Appraisal Based on Self-Review." *Personnel Psychology.* 1968, *21,* 421–530. Study found that self-appraisal, as an input into appraisal discussions, compared to more boss-centered appraisals resulted in (1) more satisfying appraisal interviews, (2) less defensiveness by the subordinate, and (3) greater improvement in subsequent on-the-job performance.
- Berkshire, J.R., and P.D. Nelson. "Leadership Peer Ratings Related to Subsequent Proficiency in Training and in the

Fleet." Special Report 58-20, Naval School of Aviation Medicine, Pensacola, Florida, 1958. Study showing the favorable predictive power of peer ratings for subsequent performance.

- Campbell, J.P., M.D. Dunnette, E.E. Lawler, III, and K.E. Weick, Jr. *Managerial Behavior, Performance and Effectiveness.* McGraw-Hill, 1970. Comprehensive book describing industrial practice and empirical evidence in most of the personnel functions as well as several areas of organizational behavior.
- Campbell, J.T., J.L. Otis, R.E. Liske, and E.P. Prien. "Assessment of Higher-level Personnel: II. Validity of the Overall Assessment Process." *Personnel Psychology.* 1962, *15,* 63–74. Study concludes that psychologists are able to make predictions of successful and unsuccessful job performance, and that industrial supervisors are more lenient in their evaluations than outside industrial psychologists.
- Doll, R.E. "Peer Ratings: A Note on the Unrated Cases." *Personnel Psychology.* 1962, *15,* 419–421. Technical study examining the alternative procedures in allocating the average ratees in peer appraisal to various categories (rated average versus is not included in the distribution). Conclusion is that they should be included in the distribution as average.
- Doll, R.E., and A.A. Longo. "Improving the Predictive Effectiveness of Peer Ratings." *Personnel Psychology.* 1962, *15,* 215–220. Study showing that, whereas low scores on peer ratings of leadership potential predict failure in the U.S. Naval Air Training Program, low peer ratings based on "anti-social" personality traits are not predictive of training failure.
- Hanson, P.G., R.B. Morton, and P. Rothaus. "The Fate of Role Stereotypes in Two Performance Appraisal Situations." *Personnel Psychology.* 1963, *16,* 269–280. Study compares the stereotyped role attitudes of supervisors and subordinates during the course of traits-rating method and goals method of performance appraisal interviews.
- Kay, E., H.H. Meyer, and R.P. French, Jr. "Effects of Threat in a Performance Appraisal Interview." *Journal of Applied Psychology.* 1965, *49,* 311–317. Study that found if a subordinate perceives a performance appraisal interview as threatening to his self-esteem, then he becomes defensive with a less-favorable attitude toward the appraisal.
- Kirchner, W.K. "Relationships Between Supervisor and Subordinate Ratings for Technical Personnel." *Journal of Industrial Psychology.* 1965, *3,* 57–60. Study reports moderately high agreement between supervisors' and subordinates' ratings of the same technical personnel. The conditions for appropriate use of subordinate ratings are discussed.
- Kirchner, W.K., and D.J. Reisberg. "Differences between Better and Less-effective Supervisors in Appraisal of Subordinates." *Personnel Psychology.* 1962, *15,* 295–303. Study showed that better and less-effective supervisors differed in their range of rating subordinates and in regard to independence of action expected of subordinates. Better supervisors exhibited greater range of ratings and expected more independent action.
- Prien, E.P., and R.E. Liske. "Assessments of Higher-Level Personnel. III. Rating Criteria: A Comparative Analysis of Supervisory Ratings and Incumbent Self-Ratings of Job Performance." *Personnel Psychology.* 1962, *15,* 187–194. Research study reporting low agreement between supervisory ratings and self-ratings of job performance; self-ratings were generally more favorable.
- Rothaus, P., R.B. Morton, and P.G. Hanson. "Performance Appraisal and Psychological Distance." *Journal of Applied Psychology.* 1965, *49,* 48–54. Study investigated the rating attitudes of supervisors and their subordinates and their reactions during public- and private-performance evaluations. Supervisors were less favorable in their ratings. Public appraisals generated more negative reactions than private appraisals.
- Thornton, G.C. "The Relationship Between Supervisory- and Self-Appraisals of Executive Performance." *Personnel Psychology.* 1968, *21,* 441–455. Empirical study showing that (1) executives tend to rate themselves higher than they were rated by their supervisors, (2) this disagreement tended to be true in several areas of performance, and (3) executives who tended to overrate themselves were judged by their superiors to be least promotable.

Training Approaches and a Workshop to Minimize Rating Error

by Gary Latham and Kenneth Wexley

RATING ERRORS

Rating errors are errors in judgment that occur in a systematic manner when an individual observes and evaluates another. Rating errors may be defined technically as a difference between the output of a human judgment process and that of an objective, accurate assessment uncolored by bias, prejudice, or other subjective, extraneous influences (Blum & Naylor, 1968; Feldman, 1979). What makes these errors so difficult to correct is that the observers are usually

From Latham/Wexley, *Increasing Productivity Through Performance Appraisal,* © 1981, Addison-Wesley Publishing Company, Inc., chapter 5, pp. 100–111. Reprinted with permission.

unaware that they are making them. In those instances when they are aware of errors, they are frequently unable to correct them themselves (Wexley, Sanders, & Yukl, 1973). The unfortunate result can be an employee who is inappropriately retained, promoted, demoted, transferred, or terminated. The most common rating errors include contrast effects, first impressions, halo, similar-to-me, central tendency, and positive and negative leniency.

The *contrast effects* error is the tendency for a rater to evaluate a person relative to other individuals rather than on the requirements of the job (Wexley, Yukl, Kovacs, & Sanders, 1972). For example, think of the best looking man or woman you have known. Rate this individual on a 9-point scale with 9 representing outstanding in terms of physical attractiveness. Now, think of your favorite glamorous movie star. Rate that person on the same criteria by which you rated the previous individual. Now, rerate the first individual. If you are tempted to give that person a lower rating, you are on the verge of making a contrast error. The rating should be given on the basis of the attractiveness criteria that you established prior to the rating, *not* on the basis of a comparison with another individual. Similarly, employees should be rated on the degree to which they fulfill predetermined job requirements, not on how they compare with others.

Contrast effects occur most frequently in selection when a person interviews one or more highly qualified candidates for a job opening and then interviews one who is only average; or conversely, when a person interviews one or more very underqualified candidates followed by an interview with an average candidate. In the first case, the average applicant may be rejected only for looking bad relative to the two previous candidates. The candidate may very well have met the requirements of the job. If there were several job openings in the company, the rejection was the organization's loss and possibly a competitor's gain. In the second instance of contrast effects, the average candidate may get a higher rating than would be deserved simply due to the favorable comparison to much weaker candidates.

Contrast effects are particularly troublesome in performance appraisals because of the deeply imbedded assumption by many personnel people that the distribution of ratings should resemble a normal or bell-shaped curve. To automatically rate on a curve is not only in violation of the 1978 Civil Service Reform Act, but it is also absurd.

For example, work units that have experienced a series of economic recessions that resulted in layoffs may have only excellent employees remaining. It is unethical for a personnel officer to insist that at least some of them be given low ratings on the performance appraisal form. People should be evaluated on the degree to which they fulfill the requirements of their jobs, not on how well they do relative to other people. This point is especially true if the other people are doing different jobs. To do otherwise not only invites a possible lawsuit, but also can create havoc within the organization.

Consider the following incident. An individual in one department appeared to be outstanding relative to (in contrast with) the other people in the department. Consequently, the individual was promoted to a higher paying job in another work unit. The individual is presently a failure in the new job. This person has been promoted into incompetence. Why? Because no one asked whether that person could fulfill the requirements of the new job, let alone how well the requirements of the original job were being performed. Instead, everyone was impressed with how well the person was doing relative to the poor performers in that original department.

Another example of contrast effects that is dangerous from the standpoint of reducing an organization's productivity and increasing the chances of a lawsuit occurred when a company was recently experiencing the results of an economic recession. An average manager working in an exceptionally good department was laid off. An equally average manager doing the same exact job, but in a poor department, was given additional responsibility and subsequently promoted. Thus, even though these two individuals were comparable in terms of their job performance, one benefited from the mediocrity of peers while the other one suffered because the peers were exceptional. The moral for employees, as far as contrast effect errors are concerned, is to practice what we all can recall from school, namely, "be the smartest kid in the stupid class."

First-impression error refers to the tendency for a manager to make an initial favorable or unfavorable judgment about an employee, and then ignore (or perceptually distort) subsequent information, so as to support the initial impression. For example, the first month on the job one individual did outstanding work. For the next five months the person did at best average work. The manager committed first-impression error by continuing to give the individual a high rating despite the fact that once the employee knew that a good impression had been created, he decided to coast on the job. Conversely, another individual initially experienced difficulties on the job for a variety of nonjob-related (e.g., divorce) reasons. After three months this individual was doing extremely well, but the manager continued to assign mediocre ratings. The unfortunate result was that the challenging assignments were given to the first individual who was no longer performing the job well.

The *halo effect* refers to inappropriate generalizations from one aspect of a person's performance on the job to all aspects of a person's job performance. For example, a person who is outstanding on only one area of the job (e.g., inventory control) may be rated inaccurately as outstanding on all areas of the job (credit management, customer relations, community relations). Conversely, if a person is rated as deficient in one area of the job, that person may be rated incorrectly as doing poorly on all aspects of the job. The point here is that people have both strengths and weaknesses and each need to be evaluated independently.

Now consider a different rater error. Suppose that you could find the perfect person for the job in terms of background, aptitude, knowledge, and experience. Would you rate the person lower if that individual had twelve brothers and sisters, if the father drove a bus, and if the mother was a maid? Most people would give an emphatic no to this question. And if we persisted by asking whether such variables would influence their ratings in any way, they might wonder if we had lost our senses.

Managers who had several years of experience in conducting performance appraisals were given a detailed job description for a position in their unit. They then observed a videotape of a person who met all the requirements of the job. However, one group of predominantly middle class managers heard the applicant say that he had two brothers, a father with a Ph.D. in physics, and a mother with a Masters degree in social work. A second group of middle class managers received the exact same job description. They then saw the same videotape. The only difference was that the tape was spliced so that the managers heard the applicant say that he had 12 brothers and sisters, his father was a bus driver, and his mother was a maid. The first group rated the person a 9 on a 9-point scale indicating that he was outstanding. The second group gave this same person 5s and 6s.

The error these managers made is known as the *similar-to-me effect* (Rand & Wexley, 1975; Wexley & Nemeroff, 1974). This error is a tendency on the part of raters to judge more favorably those people whom they perceive as similar to themselves. That is, the more closely an employee resembles the rater in attitudes or background, the stronger the tendency of the rater to judge that individual favorably. Why does this effect occur? We all tend to like and to think more highly of others whom we perceive as like us rather than unlike us because it is flattering and reinforcing. This effect may be acceptable in social situations, but it is an error when making appraisals on the job because it can lead to charges of discrimination, not to mention the assignment of tasks to the wrong people.

Central tendency error is committed by the person who wants to play it safe. This error refers to people who consistently rate an employee on or close to the midpoint of a scale when the employee's performance clearly warrants a substantially higher or lower rating. If the manager rates the individual as average, and the individual subsequently does extremely well, the manager can say, "See, I told you the employee wasn't bad." On the other hand, if the employee does poorly, the manager can say, "What did you expect? I told you that individual wasn't all that good."

Negative and *positive leniency* errors are committed by the manager who is either too hard or too easy in rating employees. In the performance appraisal process, positive leniency may raise unwarranted expectations of the employee for raises, promotions, or challenging job assignments. With negative leniency or toughness, the employee may get tired of banging his or her head against the wall, because no matter how hard the individual tries, the boss cannot be satisfied. In both instances, the result can be the same: the employee stops working hard. It is interesting to note from anecdotal evidence that workers generally do not like supervisors who are tough unfairly, and they do not *respect* supervisors who are too lenient in their ratings. In the latter case it is demotivating to see someone who is lazy receive the same high rating as someone who is a hard worker.

TRAINING APPROACHES TO MINIMIZING RATER ERRORS

For years, psychologists have stressed the importance of providing training to improve objectivity and accuracy in evaluating an employee's performance. But, it is only recently that training programs for reducing rater errors have appeared.

Stockford & Bissell (1949) and Levine and Butler (1952) can be credited with some of the first known attempts at improving the rating practices of supervisors. Levine and Butler, for example, worked with 29 supervisors in a large manufacturing plant where it had been determined that the supervisors overrated those working in the higher job grades and underrated those in the lower grades. This evaluation was most unfair because the supervisors were obviously not rating the individual's performance as much as they were the job that individual held.

Consequently, these supervisors were randomly assigned to a control, a lecture, or a discussion group. Supervisors in the control condition were given no training or information. Supervisors in a second group were given a detailed lecture on the theory and technique of performance ratings. The lecturer explained to the supervisors the problem caused by their previous ratings, and what each supervisor needed to do to correct the problem. In the discussion group, the supervisors met together to discuss the nature of the problem and how it could be solved. The discussion leader merely acted as a moderator, avoiding interjection of his own opinions. After generating a number of ideas, the group arrived at one solution acceptable to all, namely, to focus solely on the extent to which the person is fulfilling the requirements of the job.

The results showed that the lecture method had practically no influence on changing the supervisor's method of rating. The same was true for the control group who had received no training. Only the group discussion method, in which the members participated in arriving at solutions to the problem, was successful in overcoming the rating errors.

Two limitations of this study were that it dealt with only one rating error, and the effects of the training were not assessed over time. Nevertheless, a major conclusion of this research was that *knowledge alone* (i.e., lecturing) *is not sufficient to change rating behavior.*

Similarly, in a university setting, Wexley, Sanders, and Yukl (1973) found that warning individuals to recognize

TABLE 1
Performance Criteria

Rater/	*Technical ability*	*Human relations skills*	*Organizational commitment*	*Safety*	*Overall*
1	5	6	5	5	5
2	5	3	6	3	4

and avoid contrast effects did not reduce this error. Only an intensive workshop resulted in a behavior change. The workshop was based on psychological principles of learning, namely, active participation, knowledge of results or feedback, and practice. Specifically, the workshop gave trainees a chance to practice observing and rating actual videotaped individuals. In addition, the trainees were given immediate feedback regarding the accuracy of their ratings.

A recent review of the literature by Spool (1978) indicated that the majority of the approaches to reducing rating errors suffer from one or more methodological problems. For example, many training programs do *not* provide trainees an opportunity to practice the skills learned, nor do they provide them feedback on how well they are performing (Bernardin, 1978; Bernardin & Walter, 1977). Other studies fail to include a control group (Borman, 1975), while others do not evaluate the effects of training at all (Burnaska, 1976).

What is worse, is that many training programs have taught trainees inappropriate behaviors. For example, in the training programs developed by Bernardin (1978) trainees are shown rating distributions such as those shown in Table 1.

He tells the trainees that the ratings provided by Rater 1 probably contain halo error while those provided by Rater 2 probably do not. Explicit in Bernardin's programs is that certain rating distributions are desirable. As another example, skewed distributions are said to be an indication of leniency error. Raters are encouraged to conform more closely to a normal distribution across ratees. This training is inappropriate because it teaches people to use the entire range of the scale when evaluating people, when the advice may be unwarranted; and, to give low rather than high ratings (Bernardin & Pence, 1980). It is therefore not surprising that rater reliability and accuracy (validity) does not improve as a result of this approach to training.

Bernardin and his colleagues (Bernardin & Buckley, 1979; Bernardin & Pence, 1980) concluded correctly that rater training programs, if they are to be effective, should concentrate on enhancing the accuracy of ratings through discussion of the multidimensionality of work performance, the importance of recording objectively what is seen, and the development of specific examples of effective and ineffective employees. This is an advantage of using BOS (behavioral observation scales). BOS specifies standards of what is meant by effective/ineffective performance for the observer. Finally, Bernardin (Bernardin & Buckley, 1979) concluded that only training programs similar to that used by Wexley, Sanders and Yukl (1973) are likely to be effective in improving rating accuracy.

On the basis of Wexley's work, Latham, Wexley and Pursell (1975) developed a performance training program to help people minimize rating errors when observing and evaluating others. In addition they developed a group discussion method similar to that used by Levine and Butler. Both methods were selected because each one had previously been effective in reducing at least one type of rating error. They have subsequently turned out to be the only two programs that have been shown to systematically reduce rating errors and increase rate accuracy in organizational settings. In fact, they have been described as "the most advanced rater training programs related to rating job performance." (Borman, 1979, p. 412).*

In a study to evaluate the effectiveness of this training program, sixty personnel people and line managers were randomly assigned to one of three conditions: a workshop, a group discussion, or a control group that was not to receive training until it was certain that at least one of the two training methods could attain the objectives for which it was designed, namely to reduce rating errors. The training required six to eight hours of instruction depending on the amount of discussion generated among the trainees. Note the marked contrast with previous training programs that lasted from five minutes to an hour (e.g., Bernardin, 1978; Bernardin & Walter, 1977) and did not bring about a lasting behavioral change.

WORKSHOP

The workshop consisted of videotapes of job candidates being evaluated. The trainees gave a rating on a 9-point scale according to how they thought the manager in the videotape rated the candidate; they also rated the candidate. Group discussions concerning the reasons for each trainee's rating of the job candidate followed. In this way, the trainees had an opportunity to *observe* other managers making errors, to *actively participate* in discovering the

*The results of the workshop approach have been successfully replicated by Bernardin and Pence (1980).

degree to which they were or were not prone to making the error, to receive *knowledge of results* regarding their own rating behavior, and to *practice* job-related tasks to reduce the errors that they were making. The relationship between the training content and the actual job was similar in principle so as to facilitate *transfer of learning* back to the job.

The first exercise focused on the similar-to-me effect. The trainees were given a job description and a list of the job requirements for a loan officer's position. They were then shown a videotape of an interview. The content of the interview revealed a strong attitudinal and biographical similarity betwen the manager and the applicant. Relatively little job-related information from this below average applicant was elicited by the manager. When the tape ended, the trainees were asked to give two ratings: (1) How would you rate the applicant? (2) How do you think the manager rated the applicant? Their ratings were then discussed in relation to the similar-to-me effect. Possible ways of minimizing this error in performance appraisal situations were discussed by the trainees. Typical of the many solutions brainstormed by the trainees for minimizing this error in performance appraisals are as follows:

1. Establish the standards of performance expected on all jobs before rating employees.
2. Make certain that all criteria on which employees are evaluated are clearly job related.
3. Rate employees solely in relation to the job responsibilities, not in terms of how similar they are to oneself.
4. Have employees evaluated by multiple raters with different backgrounds and attitudes from one another.

The second exercise focused on the halo effect. The trainees were again shown a videotaped situation and they rated how the manager and they themselves would rate an individual who was outstanding in only one area of the job.

As with the similar-to-me error, the trainees were asked to brainstorm solutions to halo error in performance evaluation settings. The solutions suggested most frequently by the workshop participants are as follows:

1. Do not listen to comments about a person until you have made your own evaluation.
2. When an individual is to be evaluated by multiple raters, be certain that the raters assign their ratings independently; group discussion about the employee should come after everyone has had an opportunity to observe and evaluate the individual. The discussion should not take place before the ratings are assigned.
3. Rate the individual solely on the behavioral items that define a given criterion (e.g., safety). Recognize that different performance measures are not always related. A person can do well on one criterion and perform poorly on another (e.g., a professor may be a good researcher and a poor teacher).

The third exercise dealt with contrast effects. The trainees were given a job description and a list of the job requirements for an accountant's job. Trainees were then given a resumé of a highly qualified applicant and were asked to make a rating. The procedure was repeated with a second highly qualified applicant and then with an average applicant. The fact that evaluations of job applicants can be affected by the suitability of immediately preceding applicants, and that subordinates are often evaluated in comparison to other subordinates rather than on established standards was discussed. The necessity of basing ratings on predetermined job standards was then emphasized.

Solutions to contrast effect are:

1. Appraise a large number of people at the same point in time; the error is more frequent when only a few individuals are interviewed or appraised.
2. Base your performance evaluations on specific *predetermined* job requirements or standards.
3. Do not rate people in any particular order (i.e., don't rate the best or the worst people first.)
4. Rate people on the extent to which they fulfill the requirements of the job; compare people after, rather than before, an evaluation. For example, Kim received an A in Algebra while Pat received a B. Kim's score was compared with Pat's after each test was graded in accordance with predefined standards, namely, the answer key. The two students were not rated on a curve.

The final exercise was a demonstration of the effects of *first impression*. The trainees were given a job description and a listing of the specific job requirements for an insurance rater. They were then shown a videotape of an interview. The interview began with the applicant presenting a poor impression by her answers, actions, and appearance. The remainder of the interview showed that the applicant was acceptable for the job; however, the interviewer continued to act according to the initial impressions. Again, the trainees gave two types of ratings: (1) How would you rate the applicant? and (2) How do you think the interviewer rated the applicant? The trainees discussed their individual ratings as well as ways to reduce the rating error in the performance appraisal. Among the solutions mentioned by the trainees were:

1. Reserve all judgments about an employee until the end of the time period for which the appraisal is scheduled.
2. Be a note taker rather than an evaluator during the interval between performance appraisals. Ideally, supervisors should record daily a subordinate's behavior that they observed lead to adequate or inadequate performance on job assignments. The incidents should be reviewed later by the manager when it is time to assign ratings. Read the incidents in an order

other than the recorded sequence. For example, first read the incidents that occurred during the middle of the appraisal period, then read those that occurred toward the beginning of the appraisal period. The recording of incidents should be done regardless of whether BOS or BES (behavioral expectation scale) are used. The advantage of using BOS is that where the incidents have not been recorded daily, the items on the BOS can facilitate recall of incidents.

The final exercise dealt with positive and negative leniency. Again, raters were trained to record exactly what they saw, and to compare what they recorded with critical job behaviors/standards required in a job description or contained in the appraisal instrument.

GROUP DISCUSSION

In the group discussion method each error was defined by the trainer. An example of each error was given in the context of a performance appraisal, a selection interview, and an off-the-job situation. This procedure was followed to insure that the trainees thoroughly understood the error. The trainees were then divided into groups to discuss personal examples that they had experienced in these three situations. Following this, the trainees generated solutions to the problem. These solutions were identical to those given in the workshop.

The advantage of the group discussion procedure over the workshop method was that it was less formal. Thus the trainees could be more relaxed. In addition, the expense of preparing the videotapes and the renting of equipment was not necessary.

The disadvantage of this method compared to the workshop was that the trainees did not have an opportunity to experience the errors or to practice solutions to the errors. Thus, they were able to obtain knowledge from the trainer and from each other about their understanding of the problem, but not about their own specific behavior with regard to the problem. Note that in neither the workshop nor the group discussion procedure were examples given of good/bad rating distributions or intercorrelations among ratings. Instead, training focused solely on the necessity for recording exactly what was said or done by the person on the videotape so as to be able to justify a given rating in terms of the job description/responsibilities the trainees received prior to viewing the videotape.

REFERENCES

- Bernardin, H.J. "Effects of rater training on leniency and halo errors in student ratings of instructors." *Journal of Applied Psychology,* 1978, *63,* 301–308.
- Bernardin, H.J. & Buckley, M.R. "A consideration of strategies in rater training." Unpublished manuscript, 1979.
- Bernardin, H.J. & Pence, E.G. "The effects of rater training: Creating new response sets and decreasing accuracy." *Journal of Applied Psychology,* 1980, *65,* 60–66.
- Bernardin, H.J. & Walter, C.S. "Effects of rater training and diary-keeping on psychometric error in ratings." *Journal of Applied Psychology,* 1977, *62,* 64–69.
- Blum, M.L. & Naylor, J.C. *Industrial Psychology: Its Theoretical and Social Foundations.* New York: Harper & Row, 1968.
- Borman, W.C. "Effects of instructions to avoid halo error on reliability and validity of performance evaluation ratings." *Journal of Applied Psychology,* 1975, *60,* 556–560.
- Burnaska, R.J. "The effects of behavior modeling training upon managers' behaviors and employees' perceptions." *Personnel Psychology,* 1976, *29,* 329–335.
- Feldman, J.M. "Beyond attribution theory: Cognitive processes in employee performance evaluations." Paper presented at the annual meeting of AIDS, New Orleans, 1979.
- Latham, G.P., Wexley, K.N., & Pursell, E.D. "Training managers to minimize rating errors in the observation of behavior." *Journal of Applied Psychology,* 1975, *60,* 550–555.
- Levine, J., & Butler, J. "Lecture versus group discussion in changing behavior." *Journal of Applied Psychology,* 1952, *36,* 29–33.
- Rand, T.M., & Wexley, K.N. "A demonstration of the Byrne similarity hypothesis in simulated employment interviews." *Psychological Reports,* 1975, *36,* 535–544.
- Spool, M. "Training programs for observers of behavior: A review." *Personnel Psychology,* 1978, *31,* 853–888.
- Stockford, L., & Bissell, H.W. "Factors involved in establishing a management-rating scale." *Personnel,* 1949, *26,* 94–116.
- Wexley, K.N., & Nemeroff, W.F. "Effects of racial prejudice, race of applicant, and biographical similarity on interviewer evaluations of job applicants." *Journal of Social and Behavioral Sciences,* 1974, *20,* 66–78.
- Wexley, K.N., Sanders, R.E., & Yukl, G.A. "Training interviewers to eliminate contrast effects in employment interviews." *Journal of Applied Psychology,* 1973, *57,* 233–236.
- Wexley, K.N., Singh, J.P., & Yukl, G.A. "Subordinate personality as a moderator of the effects of participation in three types of appraisal intervies." *Journal of Applied Psychology,* 1973, *58,* 54–59.
- Wexley, K.N., Yukl, G.A., Kovacs, S.Z., & Sanders, R.E. "Importance of contrast effects in employment interviews." *Journal of Applied Psychology,* 1972, *56,* 45–48.
- Yukl, G.A., Wexley, K.N., & Seymore, J.D. "Effectiveness of pay incentives under variable ratio and continuous reinforcement schedules." *Journal of Applied Psychology,* 1972, *56,* 19–23.

Discussion on Training Programs for Observers of Behaviors

by Mark D. Spool

With some exceptions the training programs reviewed were generally effective in increasing the accuracy of observation. This result occurred regardless of the training design. Since comparison of the degree of success of each training program was not feasible, one can only conclude that some training is better than none. Caution is in order in considering such an interpretation because close to half of the studies reviewed did not use a control group. An uncontrolled factor which may account for the general positive findings in such studies may be the different motivational levels elicited between trained and untrained observers. Similar to the concept of the Hawthorne effect, raters who are more involved and more interested in the task (because they were participants in a training program) will make more careful and more accurate ratings (Conrad, 1932).

Still to be answered, however, is the question posed earlier: What approach(es) to training has (have) been most effective in increasing accuracy in observation? While many studies reported that training improved observation and rating proficiency, few compared more than one type of training program. For those that did, it appears that some form of training beyond lecture or cognitive learning alone is necessary to significantly improve the accuracy of observations. For example, two of the most systematic research studies reviewed, Latham et al. (1975) and Wexley et al. (1973), found that a workshop, where (a) observers/raters viewed a videotape of different types of rating errors, (b) practiced rating and (c) discussed their ratings, was more effective than (a) only group discussion of rating errors, (b) warnings about rating errors, (c) use of anchoring stimuli on the rating scale, or (d) no training at all.

Nevertheless, it was unclear to Wexley et al. exactly what features of the workshop were responsible for its success. This limitation, unfortunately, exists with all of the studies reviewed as none of them examined the relative contribution of any of their training components toward overall effectiveness of the training program. If progress is to be made in the area of training observers of behavior, systematic investigation of which training components contribute what must be done.

The approach followed by the successful training programs is remarkably similar to the training model advocated by Goldstein and Sorcher (1974). In their applied learning approach (also called behavior modeling), the training design consists of four major activities which have been linked to conditions for effective learning (see Kraut, 1976): (a) *modeling,* in which trainees observe model persons (usually via videotape) behaving in appropriate or effective ways; (b) *practice,* where the trainees rehearse (e.g., through role playing) the effective behaviors demonstrated by the models; (c) *social reinforcement,* which is provided by the trainer and trainees in the form of constructive feedback, and (d) *transfer of training,* which is enhanced by continual use of the above three activities in increasingly more complex and realistic situations in addition to using general principles, identical elements and performance feedback. In the Wexley et al., (1973) study, for example, certain rating errors were reduced only by a fairly intensive workshop. Their training workshop gave subjects a chance to *practice* observing and rating actual videotaped applicants, provided subjects with immediate *feedback* concerning the accuracy of their ratings, and maintained the subjects' interest by using *realistic* stimuli and by encouraging informal group discussions.

Goldstein and Sorcher state that all four components must be present to have a successful training program. Unfortunately, there is no research which indicates the effect on a training program's overall success when certain of these components are lacking; that is, the relative contribution of each component to the effectiveness of a total training program.

Examination of some of the studies reviewed vis-à-vis the components recommended by Goldstein and Sorcher will now be discussed. First, there were no studies in which the *only* missing component of the Goldstein-Sorcher model was modeling. One study (Levine and Butler, 1952), which lacked practice, showed an elimination of only one rating error (halo). Another study which lacked feedback (Bernardin and Walter, 1977) produced fairly positive results with respect to halo error, leniency effect and interrater reliability, but revealed that the trained group did not discriminate across ratees any better than the untrained group. Finally, results of two studies which did not include a transfer of training component (Cline and Garrard, 1973; Weinrott, 1975), reflected such a deficit. Cline and Garrard obtained results in which the trainees, while being better in psychiatric symptom recognition and better at making psychiatric diagnoses, were not better than the control group at evaluating psychiatric patients *at the bedside.* Weinrott, who compared the results obtained in a

---

This is the discussion section from "Training Programs for Observers of Behavior: A Review." *Personnel Psychology,* 1978, *31,* 879–888. Reprinted with permission.

laboratory setting with that from a field setting, found no differences between trained and untrained groups.

Several studies lacked more than one applied-learning training component. One study had no practice and feedback in its training program (Schuh, 1971). It consisted of a lecture only; trainees had no opportunity to practice and receive feedback. Schuh concluded that this training was only partially effective in breaking up the halo error. Two other studies (Borman, 1975; Crow, 1957) lacked all the major components of the Goldstein-Sorcher training model—modeling, practice, feedback and transfer of training. Although Crow did provide trainees with the opportunity to interact with the patients before rating them, both studies relied solely on verbal/written instruction. Appropriately, both studies reported a loss of accuracy in rating (determined either by comparing trainees' ratings with other trainees' or with ratees' self-ratings).

In contrast to the above training programs, the one in the Latham et al. study included all four recommended training components. Their results were very clear—trainees committed no errors of similarity, first impressions, contrast effect or halo effect. The group which was limited to group discussion only (modeling of the rating errors but no practice or feedback) committed impression errors.

The conclusion one can draw from these comparisons is that each of the training components recommended by Goldstein and Sorcher (1974) appears to make a significant contribution to the overall success of the training program. In fact, when the results of the studies reviewed are analyzed in terms of Goldstein and Sorcher's training model, many of the results obtained (both positive and negative) become more understandable.

However, the fact that decrements in performance (accuracy) after training occurred have been observed (Borman, 1975; Bunney and Hamburg, 1963; Crow, 1957) is not explained by the model and is worth discussing. If one assumes that the training was conducted properly, one would expect that accuracy would increase. Cronbach (1955) advanced the following hypothesis, "There is an optimal degree of differentiation in making judgments.... The person who attempts to differentiate individuals on inadequate data introduces error even when the inferences have validity greater than chance" (p. 181). It follows from Cronbach's hypothesis that, if a subject increases the variability of his judgments (by being more responsive to individual differences) from one time to another and if his *ability* to make accurate judgments does not increase correspondingly, then he will make more errors the second time than the first.

Crow (1957) addressed this issue in light of typical training programs for observers of behavior:

> These results indicate that training programs devoted to increasing accuracy...run the risk of decreasing accuracy when they increase the trainees' responsiveness to individual differences. Since very little is known about how to train people to make more accurate judgments about others, training programs frequently utilize a procedure of 'exposure' and little else. The belief that placing the trainee in a position to observe others and to make judgments will produce desirable results is challenged by these findings. Such experience may lead the trainee to differentiate among people far beyond his capacity to do so accurately. In the absence of dependable measures of his accuracy, the trainee lacks knowledge of his errors and many continue inappropriate over-differentiation long after the training has ceased (p. 358).

Crow's cogent argument states that unless one develops a training program beyond the 'exposure' stage—one based upon some substance rather than common sense—similar negative results may be obtained. This point leads us to the second question posed earlier: What are the theoretical or empirical bases for the development of the successful training programs? Of the 27 studies reviewed in this paper, less than half included training programs which were based upon learning theory or past research. Only two articles (Cannell, 1953; Wexley, et al., 1973) mentioned specifically that their training programs were based upon principles of learning. Three other articles (Cline and Garrard, 1973; Rossan and Levine, 1974; Schlessinger et al., 1968) implied that their training programs were based upon theory (e.g., principles of learning). Only five training programs were developed on the basis of past research (Bernardin, 1978; Bernardin and Walter, 1977; Brown, 1975; Bunney and Hamburg, 1963; Latham et al., 1975).

The lack of a theoretical or research base is not too surprising; it merely reflects, unfortunately, the present state of the art in training (Campbell, 1971; Campbell, Dunnette, Lawler, and Weick, 1970; Hinrichs, 1976). Hinrichs (1976) succinctly described this condition when he stated, "Such [training] principles have been ignored by training practitioners with amazing regularity, except to the extent that they find their way into program design as a result of the administrator's 'common sense' about what works best" (p. 831).

SUMMARY AND CONCLUSIONS

This review covered the past 25 years of research literature on training observers of behavior, specifically in the areas of interviewing, reducing rater bias, interpersonal perception and observation as a research tool. In general, there seems to be a lack of concern regarding training programs for observers of behavior. This is exemplified by the fact that most of the training programs reviewed were based more upon common sense rather than upon theory or past research. Moreover, many studies placed greater emphasis on evaluation of their observation *method* (usually a coding system) than on evaluation of their training program. Finally, two-thirds of the studies did not compare more than one training program. Of those studies that did, none made reference to which aspects or components of the training program contributed most to its overall effectiveness. These findings reflect the current state of training evaluation described by Hinrichs, "Very little is known, for research evaluation has not revealed which techniques or combinations of techniques are most effective for achieving specific objectives" (1976, p. 842).

Many of the studies reviewed suffered from methodological problems such as lack of a control group or the use of inappropriate unit of analysis. Some studies did not even evaluate training at all. In contrast, the level of training evaluation did appear to be more promising. Behavioral measures, such as interrater reliability, observer agreement, and rating errors, were used in most of the studies. With regard to the outcomes of the studies reviewed, the findings were fairly consistent, even though the training designs used in the different studies varied. Almost all of the studies concluded that some training improved accuracy in observing behavior in others. Unfortunately, most studies stopped there. The few studies that compared more than one training program suggest that some form of training beyond lecture or cognitive learning alone is necessary to significantly improve accuracy in observation. Only indirect evidence exists which suggests that the Goldstein-Sorcher training model may be the most effective procedure for training observers of behavior. Until systematic research is conducted, however, this conclusion can only be tentative.

In conclusion, the state of the art in training observers of behavior appears to be in its infant stage. To date not much research has been conducted and of the research that does exist, most have serious methodological flaws, and extremely few are comparative or systematic in nature. As a result, very little is known about which training approach is most effective in increasing accuracy of observation and which components of the training design contribute most of the overall effectiveness of the training program.

REFERENCES

- Bernardin, H.J. Effects of rater training on leniency and halo errors in student ratings of instructors. *Journal of Applied Psychology,* 1978, *63,* 301–308.
- Bernardin, H.J. and Walter, C.S. Effects of rater training and diary-keeping on psychometric error in ratings. *Journal of Applied Psychology,* 1977, 62, 64–69.
- Borman, W.C. Effects of instructions to avoid halo error on reliability and validity of performance evaluation ratings. *Journal of Applied Psychology,* 1975, *60,* 556–560.
- Brown, E.M. Influence of training, method, and relationship on the halo effect. *Journal of Applied Psychology,* 1968, *52,* 195–199.
- Bunney, W.E. and Hamburg, D.A. Methods for reliable longitudinal observation of behavior. *Archives of General Psychiatry,* 1963, *9,* 280–294.
- Campbell, J.P. Personnel training and development. *Annual Review of Psychology,* 1971, *22,* 565–602.
- Campbell, J.P., Dunnette, M.D., Lawler, E.E., and Weich, K.E. *Managerial Behavior, Performance, and Effectiveness.* New York: McGraw-Hill, 1970.
- Cannell, C.F. "A study of the effects of interviewers' expectations upon interviewing results." Unpublished doctoral dissertation, Ohio State University, 1953.
- Cline, D.W. and Garrard, J.N. Evaluation of the SAID teaching program. *American Journal of Psychiatry,* 1973, *130,* 582–585.
- Conrad, H.S. The personal equation in ratings. I. An experimental determination. *Pedagogical Seminary and Journal of Genetic Psychology,* 1932, *41,* 267–292.
- Cronbach, L.J. Processes affecting scores on "understanding of others" and "assumed similarity." *Psychological Bulletin,* 1955, *52,* 177–193.
- Crow, W.J. The effect of training upon accuracy and variability in interpersonal perception. *Journal of Abnormal and Social Psychology.* 1957, *55,* 355–359.
- Goldstein, A.P. and Sorcher, M. *Changing Supervisor Behavior.* New York: Pergamon Press, 1974.
- Hinrichs, J.R. Personnel training. In M.D. Dunnette (ed.), *Handbook of Industrial and Organizational Psychology.* Chicago: Rand McNally, 1976, 829–860.
- Kraut, A.I. Developing managerial skills via modeling techniques: Some positive research findings—A symposium. *Personnel Psychology,* 1976, *29,* 325–328.
- Latham, G.P., Wexley, K.N., and Pursell, E.E. Training managers to minimize rating errors in the observation of behavior. *Journal of Applied Psychology,* 1975, *60,* 550–555.
- Levine, J. and Butler, J. Lecture versus group discussion in changing behavior. *Journal of Applied Psychology,* 1952, *36,* 29–33.
- Rossan, S. and Levine, N. Field methods: A course for teaching non-laboratory research methods. *Bulletin of the British Psychological Society,* 1974, *27,* 123–218.
- Schlessinger, N., Muslin, H.L., and Baittle, M. Teaching and learning psychiatric observational skills. *Archives of General Psychiatry,* 1968, *18,* 549–552.
- Schuh, A.J. "Effects of employment interviewing training on perceptions of a job applicant." (Doctoral dissertation, Ohio State University, 1971) *Dissertation Abstracts International,* A71, 32, 3051 B. (University Microfilms No. 71-27, 554).
- Weinrott, M.R. Observation training and practice: Effects on perception of behavior change. Unpublished doctoral dissertation, McGill University, 1975.
- Wexley, K.N., Sanders, R.E., and Yukl, G.A. Training interviewers to eliminate contrast effects in employment interviews. *Journal of Applied Psychology,* 1973, *50,* 233–236.

Documenting Employee Performance

by Michael Smith

- Supervisor to personnel manager: "I've had it with Harry; he isn't performing. I want to terminate him."
- Personnel manager: "Let me see your documentation. . . ."
- Supervisor: "What documentation?"

Could you be the supervisor in this conversation? It's common for personnel management to expect supervisors to know how to document performance. But, unless you have been exposed to a rather extensive appraisal process course, you probably have never learned how to keep track of performance.

Documentation is a skill needed by every supervising manager. Doing it well takes adherence to a reasonable standard and some practice. But once documenting performance becomes a habit, wasted time and some potentially uncomfortable situations can be avoided.

USES OF DOCUMENTATION

Documentation serves many purposes. One of its most important uses is to show the reasoning that led to necessary, though unpleasant, decisions to terminate or discipline employees. However, it is just as important to document *good* performance. Written documentation can be a memory jogger for performance reviews, justification for moves, promotions, raises, or rebuttal to EEO complaints involving work performance.

You should not seek to produce either positive or negative documentation. What you do is document performance. The employee's performance determines what you write. And once written, you are able to talk from *facts,* not from memory. You are preparing "silent feedback." That is, silent until you talk with the person you are writing about. It is useless as a means of producing behavior change unless you talk with the employee about his or her performance and work with the individual to try to improve it.

Both positive and negative feedback can help a supervisor motivate an employee to improved performance. When an employee hears that the work he or she is doing is appreciated, chances are good that the individual will work harder to achieve even better results. In the case of the poor performer, he or she may be unaware of the problem. Accurate and unbiased documentation can help a supervisor explain precisely what an employee is doing wrong, thus giving him or her a chance to change. By pointing out performance in specific incidents, a supervisor cannot be accused of prejudice or simply placing blame. This is one of the major benefits of documentation.

It is not enough to give your opinion, or to write statements like "Harry did a poor job on his last assignment." Instead, you should say *why* Harry did a poor job—and what he could have done to have succeeded. The following can be used as guidelines in preparing documentation:

1. Be accurate.
2. Document facts, not opinions.
3. Note direct performance observations of actions and results. Do not include hearsay in your documentation.
4. Do not rely on your memory. Write things down soon after they happen.
5. Do not include documentation that is not behavioral.
6. Be consistent.

The last two guidelines could use some clarification. By behavioral, we do not mean psychological. What we do mean is that the documentation should describe an employee's behavior, not his or her attitude. For instance, you might write in an employee's file that he is "lazy, introverted, and requires approval for anything he might accomplish." This does not constitute behavioral documentation. Instead, you should write, "Harry doesn't meet established deadlines, he doesn't make the phone calls necessary to get the job done unless he's prompted more than once, and lastly, he stops working until I personally review his work and tell him he's correct." By documenting his actions (or his lack of action), a third party reading your documentation will undoubtedly reach the same conclusions that you have, but the reader will have reached them by reading your observations of the employee in question, not your opinion.

The sixth guideline—be consistent—means that it is important to document the performance of all of your subordinates—not just those who are performing unsatisfactorily. It's worth repeating here also the dictum that both positive and negative performance be documented. This way you cannot be accused of inventing a case against your employee, something you must be particularly cautious of, especially when minority or women employees are involved.

Besides ensuring that the written record is accurate, behavioral, and consistent, some other things must be considered, too. One is congruence.

CONGRUENCE

Congruence is expected of supervisory documentation (written records of performance), communication (feedback, coaching, reviews, and so on) and action (ratings, recommendations for raises, promotions, and terminations). Whether the performance is good, poor, or outstanding should be evident in the documentation, the communication, and subsequent management action.

Managers often write about poor performance but talk with a poor performer only about the good aspects of his or her performance, or with a good performer only about the poor aspects of performance. Neither of these situations is very helpful in the long run. It is quite important for your own credibility that you document, talk, and act based on your observations of performance. Usually an individual's performance will be composed of both positive and negative elements. If the total picture is negative, serious thought should be given to what should be done to help the person improve. With ongoing documentation the need for improvement will become apparent before the yearly appraisal session, and the employee may be able to improve before his or her appraisal is affected. If the total picture is positive, you want to make sure your subordinate gets the appropriate message— "You're doing well and continued performance at or above what you've been doing will continue or even improve your rating."

HOW MUCH DOCUMENTATION?

How much documentation is enough? A useful "rule of thumb" would be to assume someone else at your level with appropriate experience was going to look at your documentation. He or she should be able to come to the same conclusion you did or should at least be able to say, "I can see how you concluded that." That's enough documentation.

Documentation, of course, can be overdone too. If you record page after page of minute details, you waste time and intimidate your subordinate. Only those aspects of performance that significantly contribute to or hamper the work effort are appropriate for documentation.

Try to use some discretion in deciding how much time to devote to documentation. If something unusual occurs, it is best to write it down as soon as possible, lest you forget. For everyday occurrences, a weekly or monthly summary of the employee's behavior should suffice.

TEST YOURSELF

Documentation requires time and effort, but the factual base for decisions, ratings, and discussions that it provides makes it all worthwhile.

To see if you can identify accurate, behavioral, and consistent documentation, read the ABC's of Documentation (Figure 1) and take the test on the facing page.

In the following test there are three columns labeled A, B, and C. The A column stands for accurate; the B, for behavioral; and the C, for consistent—representing the three basic requirements for proper documentation of employee performance. Read the sample documentation and mark "yes, no, or not applicable" under each column. When you are finished, check your answers to see how well you understand the principles of performance documentation.

FIGURE 1
ABC's of Documentation

Documentation should be:	*To document performance*
Accurate	Record *objective* facts concerning actual performance as they occur rather than from memory.
	Record only *job-related* behavior.
	Record *direct observations* rather than relying on "hearsay" reports from others.
Behavioral	Describe *specific behavior* rather than making evaluative statements or describing an individual's personality.
Consistent	Record both *positive and negative* behaviors rather than emphasizing either.
	Keep the same basic format and level of detail of documentation for *each* subordinate.
	Maintain documentation on all employees in a given work group. Periodically review the collective documentation to be sure that desired quantity, quality, and consistency are being maintained.

Test Yourself

Sample Documentation	*A*	*B*	*C*
	(yes, no, or not applicable)		
Documentation of a secretary's performance (the secretary serves three supervisors and five engineers):			
1. Secretary made only two errors on the report.	______	______	______
2. Secretary was able to compile revised client list while maintaining usual production.	______	______	______
3. The standard of 90 percent of all correspondence with no typos met last month.	______	______	______
4. I've heard that secretary wastes time when making copies.	______	______	______
5. During the year the secretary was too nasty for her own good.	______	______	______
Documentation of an engineer:			
6. Engineer prepared technical evaluation report on her own with little assistance. Report was concise, clear, and highlighted the impact of the new specification changes. Recommendations made were evaluated by the standards group, and most of them were implemented.	______	______	______
7. Engineer gave technical presentation to customer group, didn't control audience, visuals were poor, spoke in monotonous voice. Didn't answer questions well. Supervisor had to take over meeting to "salvage it."	______	______	______
8. Engineer met following objective: to create scheduling procedure for project XYZ that was usable by purchasing, contract administration, and field construction people. This was done two months after starting the project.	______	______	______
9. Engineer's "know-it-all" attitude interferes with her work.	______	______	______
For a training specialist:			
10. Seven of eight "students" have reported that trainer is abusive in class, cutting people off, not answering questions, and scolding students for being wrong.	______	______	______
For an accountant:			
11. Accountant didn't cross check "124" report figures with "388" report. This resulted in incorrect data being given to the general manager.	______	______	______
For a supervisor:			
12. Supervisor doesn't delegate properly.	______	______	______
13. Supervisor gives most assignments to one subordinate, thereby creating one overloaded subordinate and other subordinates with little to do.	______	______	______
14. Supervisor is an excellent leader.	______	______	______
15. Supervisor lacks proper knowledge of structural engineering to give guidance to engineers under his direction.	______	______	______
16. Supervisor documents performance of her subordinates following the ABC approach. She also conducts quarterly reviews of performance, and her subordinates "accept" her ratings.	______	______	______
17. Supervisor doesn't accept criticism well.	______	______	______

Test Yourself (answers)

The issue of consistency cannot be addressed on any of these statements because there is not enough data. Consistency is a matter of documenting positive and negative performance over time. It also requires keeping the same basic format and level of documentation for all subordinates.

Accurate	*Behavioral*	*Question*	*Rationale*
Yes	Yes	1, 2, 3	This is an objective, factual, specific-behavior record.
No	No	4	This is hearsay—someone else's opinion that time is being wasted.
No	No	5	Trusting memory for a year's observation is not accurate; it might be job-related but definitely not behavioral. This statement is based on a subjective judgment and is poor documentation.
Yes	Yes	6, 7, 8	This is a very clear, specific behavioral description of what was accomplished.
No	No	9	It might be accurate, but it is worthless feedback to the engineer. It is definitely a personality description rather than a job-related behavior. How does it interfere with work and just what is a know-it-all attitude, are questions it raises.
Yes	Yes	10	Although hearsay, the job of a trainer is such that frequent observation isn't always possible so hearsay is okay here. This documentation is best used when substantiated by at least one classroom observation.
Yes	Yes	11	This is an objective, factual, specific-behavior record.
Yes	No	12	This documentation might be accurate but is not specific enough.
Yes	Yes	13	This is an objective, factual, specific-behavior record.
Yes	No	14	This might be true, but what does the statement mean and does it relate to department results?
Yes	Yes	15	This is a judgment, yes, but it is specific, factual, and clear.
Yes	Yes	16	This is objective, factual, specific behavior.
No	No	17	This might be true but few of us do accept criticism well. Documentation of this behavior needs to be more specific, and job relevance must be shown.

Nonevaluative Approaches to Performance Appraisals

by Les Wallace

For the supervisor who deals predominantly with high-quality performers, the performance appraisal process is not a frightening one. But though every supervisor would prefer to work in this type of situation, most find themselves working with employees whose performance ranges from unacceptable to exceptional and therefore having to adjust their discussion appraisals to fit each employee. For the supervisor untrained in counseling on different kinds of performance problems, adjusting his or her approach to fit the needs of high-quality and lower-quality performers can be difficult—and in some cases, disturbing.

For example, during a conversation I had recently with one production supervisor, he bragged that he thoroughly enjoyed writing and discussing the performance evaluations of his 26 subordinates. But two weeks later this same supervisor was back on the phone, frantically asking for advice on how to handle a poor performer and complain-

Reprinted, by permission of the publisher, from *Supervisory Management,* March 1978, © 1978 by Amacom, a division of American Management Associates. All rights reserved.

ing that this difficult appraisal was taking all the fun out of the process.

So this is the most common appraisal situation for supervisors. They have employees at all levels of performance—good, poor and mediocre—and they have personnel forms and management strategies by the dozens to follow in carrying out the appraisals. But the biggest problem for supervisors is that employees react to the appraisal on a personal level, not on a professional one. And unfortunately many supervisors lack the communication skills to get the essential message of an appraisal across to the employee without causing bigger problems in the process. As Douglas McGregor pointed out some 20 years ago, problems with adequate performance appraisals revolve around "a normal dislike of criticizing a subordinate and perhaps having to argue about it and a lack of skill needed to handle the interview."

QUESTIONS FOR THE SUPERVISOR

Now that we have some idea of the problems supervisors face when they enter the appraisal arena, let us ask: What communicative approaches could a supervisor use to more clearly communicate to an employee what he or she must do to improve performance? At the same time, what approaches would help reduce employee hostility and defensiveness and also generate cooperation in working to improve performance?

Most suggestions that have been made for improving the appraisal process deal more with the theory of performance appraisal and the goals of a supportive exchange rather than with concrete skills and examples of how to achieve these goals. Whether one looks at the problem-solving interview, the participative approach to performance improvement, or the supportive-defensive climate contrasts, these are all theories suggesting a particular approach but omitting the specifics on how to put the approach into practice. As one personnel manager remarked to me recently, "Who could disagree with such ideas? I just want my supervisors to learn how to make these theories useful."

Consequently, I want to make some specific suggestions for the supervisors who have to face their subordinates eyeball-to-eyeball during performance appraisals. By utilizing such suggestions, a supervisor should be able to get much more mileage out of the performance interview and be able to approach counseling sessions with high, medium, or low performers with the same self-assured attitude.

EVALUATIVE VS. DESCRIPTIVE

First, what are the conditions in an interview that lead to employee defensiveness rather than to the more desired cooperation? Of course, we know that when a supervisor exhibits *evaluative*—that is, blame-putting—behavior, this will almost always elicit defensive behavior from an employee. But beyond this, the more personal, negative, and accusatory the evaluation by a supervisor is, the more hostile and defensive the employee will become.

The way to avoid evoking such defensive behavior is by using descriptive rather than evaluate approaches to the problem. By simply stating, in a nonpersonal way, that a problem exists and then describing that problem, the supervisor makes it possible for him and the employee to arrive at a joint decision—or even an employee-initiated decision—on how to resolve the problem. Some examples of both evaluative and descriptive comments that the supervisor might make in performance appraisals are as follows:

Evaluative	*Descriptive*
• "You simply can't keep making these stupid mistakes."	• "We're still having a problem reducing the number of scrap parts produced."
• "Bob, you're tactless and undiplomatic."	• "Some people interpret your candor as hostility."
• "You're too belligerent when dealing with co-workers."	• "Many employees perceive your attitude to be belligerent."
• "The accident was your fault. You ignored the safety regulations on that project."	• "This accident appears to involve some differences in interpreting the safety regulations."

Using descriptive, nonevaluative comments in the appraisal interview, the supervisor is signaling to the employee that he wants to analyze and discuss a problem, not look for an "easy out" or demean the employee. In such a way, the interview can then move on to the more constructive elements of the appraisal process.

THE THREAT OF CONTROL

Sometimes in a performance appraisal the supervisor will make the mistake of assuming a *control* communicative stance. The stance emphasizes the superior's power over the subordinate, and it reflects an error in the supervisor's thinking because, like most of us, employees don't like to feel dominated by another person and react defensively when they do.

Opposed to the control stance is *problem orientation,* which is a communicative approach designed to allay an employee's fear and increase his sense of personal control over whatever problems exist. Problem orientation conveys a respect for the employee's ability to work on a problem and to formulate meaningful answers to the problem.

Examples of these approaches that could be found in many performance appraisals are:

Control	*Problem Orientation*
• "John, I'd like to see you doing X, Y and Z over the next week."	• "John, what sort of things might we do here?"
• "I think the only answer is to move you over by Margaret on the line."	• "One possibility is to have you move over by Margaret on the line. Is that likely to help?"
• "I think my suggestions are clear, so why don't you get back to work?"	• "Let's think about these possibilities and get back together next week, after you've thought about them."
• "Arthur, you'd better tone down your criticism of co-workers."	• "Arthur, this sensitivity among co-workers requires us all to try for a bit more diplomacy."
• "You've got a problem here."	• "We've got a problem here."
• "I've decided what you must do to reduce mistakes."	• "Have you thought about what we might do to reduce mistakes?"

Problem-oriented communication will generate more options for solving the problem by encouraging the employee to make suggestions and inducing a mutual concern for controlling the problem, not the person. Furthermore, problem orientation can also improve the appraisal discussion by aiding both parties in truly listening to what the other is saying, by encouraging both parties to offer suggestions, and by fostering a more open climate in which disagreement is not only tolerated but invited.

NEUTRALITY AND EMPATHY

Just as inimical to the appraisal process as control is a supervisor's *neutrality,* which is usually interpreted by the subordinate to be disinterest about the outcome's impact on the employee. Like the rest of us, employees tend to be more guarded and less communicative when their superior lacks real concern over their welfare. Ironically, supervisors who display such unconcern often are very interested in their employees, but they don't realize that some of their actions are interpreted by subordinates to be indicative of a neutral attitude.

Showing *empathy,* on the other hand, signals a clear concern for the employee and his situation. But to get this message across unequivocally, the supervisor must make an overt communication attempt—one that the employee cannot help but notice. Some examples of neutral and empathetic approaches are:

Neutrality	*Empathy*
• "I really don't know what we can do about it."	• "At this point I can't think of anything, but I know where we might look for help."
• "Well, that's one way to look at it."	• "I get the feeling you don't feel confident with our original plan."
• "I didn't know that."	• "I wasn't aware of that. Let me make sure I understand."
• "Too bad, but we all go through that."	• "I think I know how you're feeling. I can remember one experience I had that was similar..."
• "You could have something there, but let's go back to the real problem."	• "I'm not certain I understand how that relates to this problem. Why don't you fill me in before we go on?"

Supervisors communicate empathy best when they listen well, when they follow up on suggestions, and when they inquire how employees feel about questions and solutions raised in the appraisal. Displaying a concerned sympathy about difficult problems will also signal an understanding attitude by the supervisor and encourage the employee's cooperation.

A NEED FOR EQUALITY

In any discussion between a superior and a subordinate—whether the distinction has been brought about by legal, financial, or emotional factors—if the superior uses communicative techniques that emphasize his superiority, this will correspondingly induce feelings of unworthiness in the subordinate. For example, the supervisor who keeps the subordinate at arm's length by stifling feedback and overtly rejecting his help only increases the employee's need to defend himself and prove his self-worth.

However, the supervisor who tries to reduce the distance between himself and his employees encourages the employees to feel they share a certain equality with the supervisor. This feeling can be aided by a supervisor showing concern for sharing information with the subordinates and gaining their input in solving problems. Some characteristic differences between superiority and equality-evoking comments can be seen in these examples:

Superiority	*Equality*
• "Bob, I've worked with this problem for 10 years and ought to know what will work."	• "This idea has worked before. Do you think it might work in this case?"

- "Well, I don't think I need to give you all the background. Why don't we just do it this way for now?"
- "Arthur, you might find some of the background information helpful, so let me fill you in a bit."
- "This supervisory staff thought this policy through pretty thoroughly."
- "We've only discussed this policy at the supervisor's meetings and I'm interested in your reactions and thoughts."
- "Oh, the rationale should be of no interest to you people on the line."
- "Let me go over the rationale with you. Some of you might find it helpful."
- "Look, I'm being paid to make these decisions, not you."
- "I'll have to make the final decision, Mary, but why don't you get your suggestions in to me right away?"

Of course, workers generally do not expect complete equality from their bosses, nor are they interested in sharing the supervisor's responsibility for decisions that are implemented. Instead, they appreciate a supervisor who shares information with them, seeks their feedback, and listens to their concerns. Such communicative approaches can easily be made part of the performance appraisal process, and the supervisor should see a more enthusiastic and less defensive attitude among employees as a result.

WHO HAS THE LAST WORD?

Supervisors who emphasize certainty tend to phrase everything they say as if the last word has been said and a decision could never be changed. Such a dogmatic stance makes the employee feel that there is no need to offer new ideas or different solutions to the approach already outlined by the supervisor. This in turn leads to loss of morale and a feeling of powerlessness among employees.

But a supervisor who shows *provisionalism* demonstrates that he is willing to have his own ideas be challenged in order to arrive at the best possible solution to a problem. Communication that encourages analysis and investigation can restore enthusiasm and provide a challenge for employees that might otherwise not be there. Examples of certainty and provisionalism are:

Certainty	*Provisionalism*
• "I know what the problem is, Tom. I don't think I need another opinion."	• "I have a view of the problem Tom, but I'd be interested in your perception."
• "This is the way we're going to do things. Period."	• "Let's try this for a couple of weeks, then we can reconsider, based on that experience."
• "I've thought these suggestions through thoroughly, Mary, so let's not waste time arguing."	• "I've tried to think these suggestions through pretty thoroughly, Mary. Can you see anything I may have left out?"

Let us add that a provisional approach does not deny the fact that decisions have to be made and policies adhered to. Instead, it suggests that decision making is an alterable process and that employee suggestions and creativity are important to and appreciated by management.

FROM APPRAISAL TO ANALYSIS

These examples of communicative approaches are all designed to help the supervisor reduce the defensiveness of employees, and as such they all share a common base: They emphasize a process of analysis, rather than appraisal, of employee problems. Of course, inherent in any analysis is some evaluation of past performance, but hopefully the employee will be led to approach this evaluation from a more participative and less defensive position. Instead of being told simply that he or she failed, the employee's help is enlisted to pinpoint problems and come up with answers to problems. An analytical process should emphasize the employee's personal worth and demonstrate the confidence that management has in the employee's ability to learn from and improve on past behavior.

Unfortunately, not all employees will be able to recognize and resolve their performance problems, no matter what supervisors do. But the supervisor who validates an employee's worth through supportive, nonevaluative communicative techniques will at least find that his suggestions to the employee on improving performance are received with less defensiveness and anger. Similarly, supervisors I have talked with report several other benefits that result from using nonevaluative communicative techniques including:

- Improved creativity in solving problems, due to greater employee input.
- Less supervisory reluctance to discuss employee performance problems.
- A clearer understanding by the employee of why and how he or she needs to change work behavior.
- The growth of a climate of cooperation, which increases individual and group motivation to achieve performance goals.
- Greater employee self-reliance, which improves the individual's ability to diagnose problems and react quickly with less supervisory assistance.

The supervisor who implements constructive, nonevaluative appraisal techniques becomes more of a leader and teacher to his or her employees and less of a disciplinarian. This also means that employees come to see the supervisor as more of a friend and helper who assists them when their own ideas and abilities run short and less a management representative looking for a scapegoat on whom to blame poor performances. Of course, implementing such techniques does not essentially change the performance appraisal; a supervisor's suggestions and high performance goals remain part of the process. But constructive communicative techniques, when correctly used, should make the process a little less painful and intimidating for all concerned.

Performance Interview Guidelines

by Walter Mahler

A performance interview is defined as a discussion between a superior and a subordinate about the latter's performance. It may be impromptu, it may be scheduled ahead of time. Usually, the initiative for the interview comes from the superior. It often occurs because of a dissatisfaction on the part of the superior with some aspect of the subordinate's performance.

As long as one is a manager one is faced with the challenge of conducting performance interviews. How can one's managerial effectiveness be increased by conducting performance interviews? One way is to analyze what you now do in an interview which is effective and what you now do which is ineffective. Interviewing is a skill. We learned long ago, with golf and other sports, that practice doesn't always make perfect. Practice is helpful only if you know what you are trying to master.

An analysis of many interviews, both good and bad, has led to the development of six suggestions. These six suggestions are guidelines. They will help you in assessing where you are effective and where you are ineffective in conducting performance interviews.

Let us mention the six suggestions. Then we will consider each one in turn. The six suggestions are:

1. Coach on results.
2. Get down to cases.
3. Determine causes.
4. Make it a two-way process.
5. Set up an action plan.
6. Provide motivation.

We will need to secure a complete understanding of each suggestion, so let's consider each one more thoroughly.

Reprinted from Walter Mahler, *How Effective Executives Interview* (Homewood Ill.: Dow Jones-Irwin, 1976), pp. 111–125. © 1976 by Walter Mahler, Mahler Associates.

COACH ON RESULTS

If I "attack" you, what will you do? Defend yourself, of course. The same reaction occurs when you "attack" a subordinate in a performance interview. Predictably, the subordinate will defend himself or herself. Let's consider some examples:

- A manager says: "You are a poor long-range planner." This manager is criticizing the person. Another manager says: "The long-range planning in your organization is poor." This manager is stressing the result desired, namely, good long-range planning.
- A manager says: "You are careless." Certainly, this is personal. Suppose instead the manager says: "The quality of work turned out by your organization has too many errors." Here, the manager is stressing results.

When you find it necessary to criticize, endeavor to criticize the result you are concerned about. Usually, there is a variance between what is necessary and what has been accomplished. You could express your concern, then "attack the variance, not the person."

Coaching on results doesn't mean you will avoid defensive or negative reactions altogether. It just reduces the likelihood of such reactions. This suggestion is consistent with the earlier stress on an atmosphere of approval. Coaching on results permits both superior and subordinate to jointly "attack the variance."

This suggestion reveals the critical value of having a subordinate define results he or she is going to achieve in advance. Suppose you had committed yourself to your superior to improving the long-range planning six months ago, or to improving the quality of the product. Certainly, it would be easier for the superior to talk about a variance between what you committed yourself to accomplish and what was accomplished. But whether targets have been set in advance or not, this suggestion is a very useful one to keep in mind.

It is particularly important to analyze your interviewing habits when you are under stress. A subordinate fails to get an important result for you. It embarrasses you with your superior. You may speak in anger. Often, at a time like this you "attack" the subordinate. Use this first suggestion as a guideline to access the effectiveness of your interviewing skill.

GET DOWN TO CASES

Subordinates frequently comment on the generalized nature of criticism provided by their superior. The superior "hints at something." The superior "beats around the bush." In surveys conducted by Mahler Associates of more than 5,000 managers, we get the same results year after year. About one half of those surveyed report their manager is very general in talking with them about their performance.

So suggestion Number 2 is "get down to cases." Be specific about the result. Identify the variance you are concerned about. Cite data. Provide examples. Use incidents which illustrate the result you want to see improved. Let's go back to the long-range planning illustration. The manager might well say:

> I've been concerned about the limited attention given to long-range planning in your organization. Just recently, you came to me with a rush request for equipment. You also asked for permission to work overtime. Under the emergency conditions I approved the action on both the equipment and overtime. However, as I see it, the need for the equipment could have been anticipated. If it had been, it is likely we wouldn't need to be working overtime. Hence, I feel the long-range planning in your organization has been inadequate.

With this explanation, the subordinate has a much better concept of just what the manager is really concerned about.

Let's consider the second illustration used above having to do with the "quality of reports." After the preliminary remarks, the manager might well use the questioning approach: "How satisfactory has the quality of our monthly reports been in the last few months?" The subordinate might well reply: "In general, I think they have been about the same as our previous months." The manager then comments: "As I look at the quality of our monthly reports, I'm not satisfied. True, the quality is about the same as previous months, but this level of quality is just not acceptable." Notice, the supervisor shifted from talking about "quality" in general to a specific quality problem with monthly reports.

So here is a second suggestion against which to assess your interviewing skill. You can check your implementation of this skill during the course of a performance interview. Just ask subordinates to define, in their own words, what result it is that you are concerned about. The closer they come to defining it the same as you do, the better. If they don't come close, double back and talk about more specifics.

DETERMINE CAUSES

Analysis of many interviews reveals that this suggestion is most often overlooked. A manager establishes the fact that a variance exists. A result is not forthcoming. A problem exists. So then the manager says: "What are we going to do about it?" This "what" question bypasses the concern about causes. You might well ask why should one get concerned about causes? For several reasons. Consideration of causes makes the entire process much more of a problem-solving process. It permits exploring the need for action by subordinate, by superior, and by others. To go from a variance directly to a question: "What are you going to do about it"? gets back to personalizing the problem. We are putting the monkey on the subordinate's back. Now maybe this is where the monkey belongs. But, let's not jump to that conclusion.

Time spent exploring why a variance exists helps identify possible actions which might be taken. It increases the likelihood that the action which is taken will really reduce the variance.

When exploring causes, urge the subordinate to identify three or four possible causes. Don't reject the first one mentioned, even if you think it is an alibi. Ask for other causes. Once you have several causes on "top of the table" you can, jointly, identify those which are more important to consider and endeavor to do something about it.

Again, let's consider the "long-range planning" example. The manager says: "Why do you feel our long-range planning, particularly on equipment and manpower, is not adequate?" The subordinate might well reply:

> I really haven't given it the attention it deserves. Equally important, I'm not sure just how to go about doing it. How far ahead should you try to plan? How farsighted can you be, actually? Certainly, if we are going to get serious about long-range planning I'll have to get some staff help, at least part-time assistance.
>
> Let me mention another possible cause. I can identify a need for new equipment or for more or different manpower, but if you or your superior are as conservative as you have been, we will still be talking about our long-range planning problem year after year.

Here, in short order, are four possible causes. Each suggests quite different actions. Notice that exploration of causes provides an opportunity for upward communication. It is difficult to get subordinates to share their thinking with their managers on ways the manager might change or improve. With encouragement, this type of input can be obtained during a discussion of causes. This suggestion deserves special attention because it is so often neglected.

Decision-making courses are popular today in many organizations. The big stress in rational decision making is on proper definition of the problem. This is then followed by exploring causes. Hence, the performance interview provides a rather specific opportunity for the application of rational decision making.

MAKE IT A TWO-WAY PROCESS

Stress was placed on the performance interview being a joint problem-solving process—the superior and subordinate versus the variance! To be a joint problem-solving process requires that it be a two-way process. Neither superior nor subordinate should dominate the discussion.

The performance interview is often thought of as a "telling" process. The superior calls subordinates in and tells them what is wrong, tells them why it is wrong, and tells them what to do about it.

This type of approach is not likely to be effective. It develops "puppets," not capable individuals. It develops resistance rather than enthusiasm for change.

Some managers find it quite natural to implement this suggestion. Some may find it quite difficult to do so. In fact, some managers may not ever recognize they are completely dominating the entire interview.

The key hint for implementing this suggestion is the judicious use of questions. In the very beginning you can ask subordinates if they see the "variance" in the same way you do. You can ask them for possible actions. Two-way also means that the manager comments on the questions when such expressions are needed to insure realism governs the interview.

How effective are you in making performance interviews a two-way, joint, problem-solving process? The more affirmative your answer to this question, the better.

SET UP AN ACTION PLAN

You can consider a performance interview effective if it leads to improved performance. To refer to a term used earlier, if the variance between the expected and the actual is reduced, the interview is effective. Here is where the fifth suggestion is so important. Setting up an action plan increases the likelihood that results will be forthcoming.

Deciding on appropriate action flows naturally from the consideration of causes. Once you have jointly identified the important cause or causes, you can begin to explore a variety of possible actions.

Implementation of this suggestion requires:

- Considering several possible actions to correct a given cause.
- Concentration on one or two specific actions.
- Being specific about the who, what, and when.
- Providing for follow-up or report back.
- Reducing the plan to writing.

Let us refer to the previous illustration of variance having to do with long-range planning. Four causes were identified:

1. The subordinate didn't give long-range planning sufficient attention.
2. The subordinate didn't know how to get started.
3. The subordinate hadn't made use of staff assistance.
4. The subordinate felt that asking for equipment and manpower would be rejected by higher management.

A variety of actions would grow out of these causes. Some commitment, some means of self-discipline is needed to insure adequate attention. A commitment to produce a specific long-range plan by a given date represents an effective approach. Getting advice or assistance from a staff man on technique or methodology of long-range planning also seems like a natural action to correct the second and third causes. The final cause might well be met by an agreement on the part of the supervisor to "go to bat" to get needed equipment and manpower once a well-documented Long-Range Plan has been prepared.

PROVIDE MOTIVATION

In this section, the practical application of motivational theory is discussed.

A change in behavior requires that an individual be motivated to change. You don't wait until the end of the interview to implement this suggestion. You implement it throughout the interview.

Stress the benefits to the subordinate in achieving the necessary results. The benefit has to be of consequence to the subordinate. It may be advancement, it may be an increase in compensation, it may be gaining additional responsibility or status, or it may be the sense of accomplishment gained from a job well done.

The manner in which the interview is conducted has an important impact upon the motivation of the subordinate. Much more motivation is secured if the subordinate sees it as a two-way problem-solving process. In contrast, little sustained motivation is secured from the nonconstructive, nonhelpful type of interview.

SUMMARY

We have considered six suggestions for conducting effective performance interviews. With these suggestions in mind, practice can make perfect! Well, if not perfect, at least, the suggestion will make for increased effectiveness in performance interviews.

Keep the suggestions in mind in preparing for an interview. Review them, in self-analytical manner, after a performance interview. A checklist for doing this follows.

Such actions should lead to both increased ability and increased confidence in conducting effective performance interviews.

Performance Interview Checklist

1. Coach on results:
   Were results stressed or were traits stressed?

If traits were stressed, were they related to end results?
Was criticism personal or job centered?

2. Get down to cases:
How specific were the reasons given for my opinions?
Were specific incidents used well?
How frank was I?
3. Determine causes:
Was an attempt made to get at causes?
Did we get at several causes?
Did we get at the real cause(s)?
4. Make interview a two-way process:
Was I dominant?
Who did the most talking?
Was there good give-and-take discussion?
Were questions used to stimulate thinking?
5. Set or reset goals or targets:
Were goals set against which subordinate could measure progress?
Were goals specific or general?
Were goals imposed or developed jointly?
6. Provide motivation:
Did I evidence concern about subordinate?
Did I use positive motivation?
Was the subordinate motivated to act differently in the future?

We will find it helpful to differentiate between four different types of performance interviews. We will then suggest a process specific to each type. The four types are:

1. Progress reviews against goals.
2. Annual accomplishment reviews against goals.
3. Performance interview in absence of goals.
4. Group review of progress against goals.

Let's consider processes appropriate to each type.

PROCESS FOR PROGRESS REVIEWS AGAINST GOALS

Progress reviews are done against a set of goals. It is desirable for the superior to set the frequency of reviews when goals have been approved. A quarterly review is practically a must. It is also desirable to decide on whether to review all goals or a selected list.

The process for the progress review involves the following steps:

- Subordinate reviews progress on all goals. During this step the discussion revolves around clarification questions and pushing for specificity. No attempt is made at getting at causes. A note can be made of any causes which are commented upon in this step.
- Superior comments on the overall results.
- The superior indicates the variances he or she is most concerned about.
- The top priority variance is considered. The question to be explored thoroughly is: What are the causes: Here's a hint. Get the subordinate to talk about three or four or even more causes. Don't argue about the first one or two. They are often delightful rationalizations.

  If the subordinate doesn't do so, suggest that either or both you and the subordinate may be a cause. Once you have a set of causes, sort out the causes you should both be most concerned about.
- Identify appropriate action to overcome the causes. You may want the action plans to be reflected in work plans.
- Repeat the above process for variance of second priority.
- Finally, if you haven't done so before, modify goals as necessary.

PROCESS FOR ANNUAL ACCOMPLISHMENT REVIEWS AGAINST GOALS

- The process followed in the progress review is quite appropriate for the annual accomplishment review.
- In addition, the superior can help the subordinate "wring a year's worth of learning" from a year of experience by asking the subordinate to:
- Comment on what he or she has learned over the last year.
- Contrast successful goal achievements with unsuccessful achievements.
- Discuss one's effectiveness as a manager and how one might improve. This can be converted to self-improvement goals for the next year.
- Attention needs to be given to any changes which need to be made in subordinate's—
- Responsibilities.
- Indicators.
- Goals.

PROCESS FOR PERFORMANCE INTERVIEW IN THE ABSENCE OF GOALS

There may be occasions when you feel the need to have a performance interview in the absence of goals. The following process is recommended:

- Advise the subordinate that you want to discuss a given result or condition or situation. Ask him or her to prepare for the discussion.
- Begin by describing or defining the result you are concerned about and the reasons for your concern.
- Discuss the present status and what would constitute a satisfactory result.
- Discuss the causes for the variance between present status and desired result.

- Set appropriate action plans to accomplish the improvement.

GROUP REVIEW OF PROGRESS AGAINST GOALS

The progress review can be conducted in a group session. The usual setup is for an executive to conduct such a session with direct reports. Occasionally, a manufacturing manager or a regional sales manager may want to set up this "tandem" review process. The top manager and the plant manager are in the meeting. Superintendents report their progress in front of both.

We have discovered that the following process makes for effective group reviews.

- Have direct reports give the status on goals for their No. 1 responsibility. If you are using a restricted list of goals, have the individuals report on their No. 1 goal. Each direct report does this.
- Repeat the process for the No. 2 and No. 3 responsibilities. Permit interruptions for clarification purposes only.
- Ask each direct report to give the status on any other goals which would be of interest to the others.

Caution: Do not get into a problem-solving process unless a given variance is of concern to a majority of the participants. Schedule needed problem-solving efforts restricted to those directly involved.

- Consider any suggestions, comments, and observations that individuals want to make to be helpful to others.
- Occasionally, a revision in a goal becomes necessary. Also a trade-off between two goals may be necessary.

Some managers conduct quarterly group sessions and hold individual sessions on an "as needed" basis.

The group process is a powerful one. It works best when there is a real need for team work.

SOURCES SECTION FIVE

EVALUATING PERFORMANCE APPRAISAL SYSTEMS

LEGAL REQUIREMENTS

Performance Appraisal: Legal Aspects

by J. Vernon Odom, revised by Keith J. Edwards

- Explains the legal requirements for performance appraisal.
- Presents ways employers can comply with the law.
- Lists characteristics a performance appraisal system must have to comply with the law.

MANAGERIAL REQUIREMENTS

Analyzing Performance Appraisals Systems: An Empirical Study

by William H. Holley, Hubert S. Feild, and Nona J. Barnett

- Presents procedures for analyzing a continuing performance appraisal system.
- Explains how the procedures were used in an organization.

Appraising Appraisal: Ten Lessons from Research for Practice

by Marshall Sashkin

- Develops guidelines for effective performance appraisal systems.

RESEARCH AND THEORETICAL REQUIREMENTS

Criteria of Appraisal Effectiveness

by Jeffrey S. Kane and Edward E. Lawler, III

- Lists and explains five criteria to use for evaluating appraisal effectiveness: validity, reliability, discriminability, freedom from bias, and relevance.

Performance Rating

by Frank J. Landy and James L. Farr

- Reviews research studies which investigate the roles, context, vehicle, process, and results of performance appraisal.
- Develops a theoretical model for understanding the performance appraisal process.

Performance Appraisal: Legal Aspects

by J. Vernon Odom (revised March 1979 by Keith J. Edwards)

ABSTRACT

The Center for Creative Leadership, as part of its review of the literature on performance appraisal, examined the legal aspects of performance appraisal. In a question and answer format, the major points of Title VII and the EEOC guidelines are presented. In a Comments to Employers section, suggestions are presented for compliance with the legal requirements of performance appraisal and for limiting their liability under Title VII.

ACKNOWLEDGEMENTS

I would like to express my thanks to the staff of the Center for Creative Leadership for its help and cooperation in preparing this report. Particular thanks are due to David DeVries and Morgan McCall for assigning me to this project. Michael Lombardo made a number of helpful editorial comments. Also, I wish to thank Dennis Boring for his help in showing a layman how to do a legal search. Without his offer of assistance, I would never have attempted the task.

PERFORMANCE APPRAISAL: LEGAL ASPECTS

The Center for Creative Leadership is interested in applying social science knowledge to organizational problems. Of major concern to psychologists are procedures for evaluating and predicting job-related performance. Combining this traditional interest of psychologists with the Center's goals has resulted in a number of research efforts on the process of performance appraisal.

The Civil Rights Act of 1964 (and as amended in 1972) has greatly transformed the context within which performance appraisal is conducted. The usual performance appraisal procedure, namely supervisory ratings, has been called into question by the courts (Edwards, 1976; Holley & Feild, 1975; Lazer, 1976). The law now requires scrupulous fairness in employment procedures (Equal Employment Opportunity Commission, 1970; Equal Employment Opportunity Coordinating Council, 1976; Equal Employment Opportunities, 1974) and demands valid procedures for appraising performance.

Given the intricate relationship of the law and performance appraisal, CCL's research division examined the legal aspects of performance appraisal as part of its larger review of performance appraisal. This paper presents our understanding of Title VII and the EEOC and EEOCC Federal Guidelines on Selection Procedures. It also includes suggestions to employers for aid in complying with the law.

On August 25, 1978, the Uniform Guidelines on Employee Selection Procedures were published in the *Federal Register* and adopted by the four major government agencies involved in civil rights enforcement (Equal Employment Opportunity Commission, Civil Service Commission, Department of Labor, and Department of Justice). The new guidelines supercede the EEOC guidelines of 1970. While the new guidelines are not substantially different from the 1970 version, they do present a shift in emphasis. The 1970 guidelines endorsed criterion-related validation as preferable over the techniques of content validation and construct validation. The 1978 Uniform Guidelines give all three methods equal status. This shift in emphasis is important for assessments of job performance used for decisions affecting salary, promotion, and terminations. The job-relatedness of "selection devices" such as performance appraisal is most appropriately demonstrated by the content validation strategy. Some of the requirements for content validation as defined in the Uniform Guidelines are explained later in this report.

What follows are some questions (and accompanying answers) critical to understanding the issue of performance appraisal and the law:

1. *What types of employment procedures are controlled by Title VII?* Any procedure, formal or informal, scored or unscored, which is used to make *any* personnel decision, including hiring, promotion, transfer, or dismissal, is covered by federal guidelines (Equal Employment Opportunity Commission, 1978). This includes performance appraisal and personnel interviews as well as standardized tests (Edwards, 1976; Holley & Feild, 1975).
2. *What is evidence of discrimination or unfair employment practices?* Under Title VII, it is not necessary to prove *intent to discriminate* in order to prove discrimination. The presence of disproportionate numbers of employees from either a majority or minority group is considered *prima facie* evidence of dis-

Reprinted by permission of the Center for Creative Leadership from Technical Report Number 3, copyright 1977.

[1] Edwards, K.J. Performance appraisal and the law: Legal requirements and practical guidelines. Paper presented at *Managerial feedback: Appraisals and alternatives.* Conference held at the Center for Creative Leadership, Greensboro, North Carolina, January 1976.

crimination. Any test or performance appraisal system leading to such differential hiring, promotion, or dismissal of groups of employees may be discriminatory. Differential employment practices are determined relative to the population of possible employees (Equal Employment Opportunity Commission, 1978); usually EEOC considers possible employees to be the population in a given geographical area. Employers may present evidence indicating that another definition of "possible employees" is more appropriate—for example, all of the people in a given area who hold a certain degree or who are interested in employment of a given type.

The Uniform Guidelines (EEOC, 1978) introduced a rule of thumb for judging adverse impact called the 4/5ths rule. The rule states that the selection ratio (e.g., number promoted/number eligible) for minorities must not be less than 4/5ths (80 percent) of the majority selection ratio. For example, if 50 percent of the majority eligibles were promoted, then promoting less than 40 percent of the minorities would be considered as evidence of adverse impact (50% × 4/5 = 40%). This ratio is used by the California State Guidelines and applies to every group, including Caucasians.

3. *What federal governmental agencies are responsible for insuring compliance with the law?* Equal Employment Opportunity Commission (Equal Employment Opportunities, 1974); Office of Federal Contract Compliance (Executive Order 11246 (1965); Executive Order 11375 (1967)); and Federal Courts, Department of Labor, Department of Justice (Equal Employment Opportunities, 1974).
4. *Who is protected by law?* Title VII states that one may not discriminate in employment on the basis of race, religion, sex, or national origin (Equal Employment Opportunities, 1974). Protection is granted to all American citizens. Because of past discrimination, the greatest enforcement efforts have been directed toward the protection of racial minorities and females.
5. *Would a procedure not used in employment decisions have to comply with federal guidelines?* No, only procedures used to make employment decisions need comply with the law (Equal Employment Opportunity Commission, 1978). However, most personnel procedures are used for employment decisions of one kind or another.
6. *Under what conditions is the presence of differential employment patterns insufficient evidence for a claim of discrimination?* The guidelines deal with this issue in the context of defining necessary properties of a "test"—with performance appraisal included in this category:

> . . . (a) a test has been validated and evidences a high degree of utility (in practical usefulness, as evidenced by predictiveness . . .) and (b) the person giving or acting upon the results of the particular test can demonstrate that alternative suitable hiring, transfer, or promotion procedures are unavailable for use. (Equal Employment Opportunity Commission, 1970, p. 12334)

Recent court causes have modified condition (b) above. The courts have maintained that it is the burden of the plaintiffs to prove the existence of an equally valid alternative selection procedure with less adverse impact. While the Uniform Guidelines (1978) still attempt to place this burden on the employers, the courts have not done so to date. Performance appraisal is not discriminatory even if there is an adverse impact on hiring, transfer, or promotion of minority groups or other groups protected by Title VII if the performance appraisal procedure has been validated (Edwards, 1976; Holley & Feild, 1975).

7. *Who is responsible for validating a test or performance appraisal system?* Employers have sole responsibility for validating the employment procedures they use. If the procedures are questioned, the employer must prove them valid. It is not necessary for the plaintiff to prove the tests invalid if evidence of discrimination exists (see Question 2). (Equal Employment Opportunity Commission, 1978)
8. *Does the employer have any option other than validation of the personnel procedures?* Employers' alternatives to validation have become limited. In the 1970 guidelines, the EEOC said that if employers were unwilling (or unable, for financial or other reasons) to validate their test procedures, they had the "option of adjusting employment procedures so as to eliminate the conditions suggestive of employment discrimination" (Equal Employment Opportunity Commission, 1970, p. 12336). In other words, employers may hire and promote employees using procedures (such as random selection) which insure a representative proportion of minorities and women in the relevant jobs. Implementation of the "adjustment" option sometimes entails making employment decisions on bases other than merit.

Such "adjustment" procedures have been challenged recently in the courts on constitutional grounds as "reverse discrimination." The *Bakke* decision is the first of many such cases to come down. The Uniform Guidelines point out that if an employer takes the route of trying to eliminate adverse impact, the alternative procedures chosen "should be lawful and as job related as possible." (EEOCC, 1978, Sec. 6A, p. 38299)

An employer may also use an unvalidated procedure on an interim basis provided "(1) the user has available substantial evidence of validity, and (2) the user has in progress, when technically feasible, a study which is designed to produce the additional evidence required by these guidelines in a reasonable time." (EEOC, 1978, Sec. 5J, p. 38298–38299) However, if the validity study fails, the employer is liable for any adverse impact during the interim use period.

9. *If employers opt to validate their current procedures, what evidence will be accepted as proof of the utility of an employment procedure?* Under the 1970 guidelines, empirical data were satisfactory evidence of a test's utility and validity. Validity cannot be assumed on the basis of a procedure's reputation (Equal Employment Opportunity Commission, 1978). In other words, the employer cannot assume a procedure is valid because it was recommended by a professional. In general, the employer must collect empirical data on the use of a procedure proving that it is valid for the purpose for which it is being used. Although the federal guidelines admit the possibility of accepting validation studies from other locations, companies, etc., employers must prove in these cases that the job to which the validation is being extended is truly comparable. Similarly, employers must demonstrate the utility of a procedure by the use of empirical data.

As noted earlier, the Uniform Guidelines (1978) give equal weight to the procedure of content validation. The following excerpts from the Uniform Guidelines define content validity more specifically:

> "A selection procedure may be supported by a content validity strategy to the extent that it is a representative sample of the content of the job." (Sec. 14.C.1, p. 38302)
>
> "A content validity strategy is not appropriate for demonstrating the validity of selection procedures which purport to measure traits or constructs such as intelligence, aptitude, personality, common sense, judgment, leadership, and spatial ability. Content validity is also not an appropriate strategy when the selection procedure involves knowledge, skills, or abilities which an employee will be expected to learn on the job." (Sec. 14.C.1)
>
> "There should be a job analysis which includes an analysis of the important work behaviors required for successful performance and their relative importance.... Any job analysis should focus on work behavior(s) and the tasks associated with them." (Sec. 14.C.2)
>
> "To demonstrate the content validity of a procedure, a user should show that the behaviors demonstrated in the selection procedure provide a representative sample of the work product of the job.... The closer the content and the context of the selection procedure are to work samples or work behaviors, the stronger is the basis for showing content validity." (Sec. 14.C.4)

The classic example of a content valid selection procedure is a typing test. Performance appraisals, in that they purport to be assessments of actual work behavior, are amenable to the content validity strategy. The care with which the appraisal system is developed, the objectivity of the content being rated, the training of raters, and the standardization of how the appraisals are used will all be relevant in judging the content validity of performance appraisals under the Uniform Guidelines.

10. *What standards must the validation procedures meet?* In general, they should meet American Psychological Association standards (1974). They should also meet certain minimal EEOC criteria: (1) the validation sample must be representative of *potential employees* as well as current employees; (b) *tests should be administered under standardized conditions,* and the results should not be available to those determining criterion ratings (to avoid contamination of the ratings); (c) the criterion variables, including ratings, must be work related and free "from factors which would unfairly depress scores" (Equal Employment Opportunity Commission, 1970, p. 12335) of groups protected under Title VII; (d) data should be analyzed and the system shown to be valid for subgroups, e.g., blacks and whites or males and females, as well as for the population as a whole; (e) the relationship between a performance measure and work performance must be shown to be both statistically and practically significant (Equal Employment Opportunity Commission, 1970).

Generally, the term "practically significant" means that the performance measure is related to profitability, production, or other specific organizational indices. Practical significance is affected by three factors: the number of job openings, the proportion of employees who do poorly on the test yet remain good employees, and the "economic and human risks involved in hiring an unqualified applicant" (Equal Employment Opportunity Commission, 1970, p. 12335).

11. *Are there any special problems with implementing a newly validated performance appraisal system?* Yes, it is not enough to simply validate a new PA system if its use perpetuates a past practice of discrimination. "No new test or other employee selection standard can be imposed upon a class of individuals protected by Title VII who, but for prior discrimination, would have been granted the opportunity to qualify under less stringent selection standards previously in force" (Equal Employment Opportunity Commission, 1970, p. 12336). Employers are liable for past discriminatory practices even if these practices have been discontinued. Employers who implement stringent criteria for promotion and apply those criteria to all employees may be said to be continuing a past discrimination if, when criteria for promotion were less stringent, they discriminated against some group. The employer's past discrimination may have limited the promotional opportunities under the present equitable system.

The current system, even though it does not discriminate, may perpetuate a pattern of past discrimination, and would be improper. For example, assume a company hired a number of people twenty years ago into entry level positions. In the intervening years most, if not all, of those people have been promoted. Until fifteen years ago, there was an unwritten rule not to promote women. About seven years ago new objective criteria were established for promotion. The new criteria are far more stringent than the past criteria. Currently, approximately the same proportion of males and females are promoted (on the basis of merit); nonetheless, the current fair, strict standards assure a continued underrepresentation of women at higher levels. The women hired twenty years ago were denied promotion during the succeeding five years; the current stringent criteria, although undeniably fair, prevent women who might have been promoted under the less stringent criteria (if they had not been discriminated against) from being promoted. The current procedures continue past discrimination.

12. *Is it necessary to validate a performance appraisal system for each job or location in which it is used?* Yes. Unless the employer can demonstrate that sufficient similarities exist to generalize from one location or job to another, the system must be validated for each job or location in which it is used (Equal Employment Opportunity Commission, 1978).

13. *Is it necessary to validate a performance appraisal system for each protected group in the employer's work force?* One provision of the 1970 guidelines that generated a great deal of debate and study was the requirement to differentially validate all selection procedures for each protected group. The concept is most easily understood in the context of a criterion-related validity study. The hypothesis is that tests which predict job performance for the majority group may not predict job performance for minorities. The Uniform Guidelines (1978) incorporate this concept under the rubric of "Test Fairness" (Sec. 14.B.8) articulated under the section which defines criterion-related validation. Test fairness is not discussed in relation to content validity. However, appraisal systems that are not well developed and not applied systematically and which have adverse impact are viewed by the courts as suspect in regard to the fairness issue. Care must be taken to insure as much objectivity as possible in performance appraisals. Since objectivity is dependent on the rater as well as the quality of the rating system, training of raters with monitoring and feedback as well as use of multiple raters wherever possible should be considered.

14. *To what degree are employees entitled to feedback on their performance, to appeal of employment decisions, and to confidentiality of information about them?* If prospective or current employees who have performed poorly can claim additional training or experience, they should have the opportunity to be reevaluated (Equal Employment Opportunity Commission, 1978). To make such a request, prospective or current employees must have some knowledge of the results of their evaluations. Recent laws governing rights to privacy and rights to information suggest that in the future employers may have to pay increased attention to the issues of privacy, feedback, and the right to information. There are no definitive court cases. The issue of privacy will be discussed further below.

15. *Do federal agencies differ with respect to the criteria they use for evaluating discrimination? Do the courts have different criteria for discrimination, depending on the type of case?* Prior to 1978 there were two sets of federal guidelines regarding discrimination, the Equal Employment Opportunity Commission (EEOC) and the Equal Employment Opportunity Coordinating Council (EEOCC). The EEOC guidelines rigidly favor predictive validation of selection procedures and have been discussed above. They, in general, have been the criteria used by courts in evaluating Title VII cases. The EEOCC guidelines were accepted by all of the federal agencies dealing with discrimination cases on August 25, 1978 (Equal Employment Opportunity Coordinating Council, 1976).

The criteria for *prima facie* evidence of discrimination vary depending on whether the case is a Title VII case or a constitutional case. As indicated earlier, in Title VII cases the fact that a disproportionate number of a group have been hired, promoted, etc., is *prima facie* evidence of discrimination. In a constitutional case brought under the Fourteenth Amendment, the plaintiff must also show that the defendent *intended* to discriminate. In other words, if employers promote disproportionate numbers of persons from one group on the basis of performance appraisal, but have no *intent* to discriminate against the groups which were not promoted, a plaintiff would probably have a *prima facie* case under Title VII, but not a *prima facie* case on constitutional grounds (Robertson, 1977; Scharf, 1976).

The courts tend to vary their criteria for discrimination with the degree of adverse impact. The greater the adverse impact, the greater their concern and doubt regarding validation of selection procedures (Edwards, 1976; Holley & Feild, 1975).

With the issuance of the Uniform Guidelines (1978) all agencies are endorsing one set of criteria. A helpful set of questions and answers clarifying the requirements of the new guidelines have been published in the Federal Register (EEOC, 1979).

COMMENTS TO EMPLOYERS

In the process of our review, we have found several suggestions which may help employers comply with the law.

These are listed below, along with several problem areas in which clear-cut suggestions cannot be made because definitive court cases have not appeared.

1. Employers should have records of job applicants, new employees, and promoted and demoted employees categorized by race, sex, national origin, and religion. Information on job applicants is particularly important. In many cases, the degree of employers' liability under the law is determined by the relative proportions of Title VII protected groups in the population of possible employees (see Question 2) versus the relative proportions of protected groups currently employed. Frequently, the proportions of applicants are considerably different from those in the population of the city or region at large. Federal compliance agencies tend to use the census figures of the municipality or region in which an employer is located. Therefore, keeping records of applicants may provide employers with a means of limiting their liability under the law, if not actually proving their compliance. In general, the severity of court requirements for validation increases with the magnitude of differential hiring practices (Edwards, 1976). Occasional local manpower surveys may also serve this purpose.
2. Employers should have a formal appraisal system. There is no way to validate an informal system; therefore, in any lawsuit where *prima facie* evidence of discrimination exists, employers without a formal system would be found liable (Stanton, 1976). Remember, if differential employment patterns exist, it is the employers' responsibility to demonstrate that their employment practices are based on *job-related criteria* and not on any prejudicial intent (Equal Employment Opportunities, 1974). Only a formal appraisal system can provide that evidence.

   As noted previously (see Question 10), practical significance is of great importance in determining the appropriateness of an employment procedure. Even if a performance appraisal method reflects or predicts differences in performance, one must ask the question "Is the prediction great enough and reliable enough in the specific context?" Major contextual factors considered in the past have been the "cost" (monetary and human risk) for poor job performance and the number of jobs openings versus the number of applicants (selection ratios) (Edwards, 1976; Gilbreath, 1977; Higgins, 1976).

   With the shift in emphasis in the Uniform Guidelines to content validity as a viable option, practical significance becomes harder to define. Where performance appraisals are concerned, the courts have tended to acknowledge the employer's right to evaluate employees' on-the-job performance. The statistically oriented definitions of practical significance are difficult to apply to performance appraisals built on the content validity approach.

   The thrust of the guidelines is to prevent the development and use of appraisal systems that are poorly conceived, contain ill-defined rating criteria, and are applied in a superficial and haphazard way on the job.
3. When conducting criterion-related validation studies, one should use measure of actual job performance whenever possible. Supervisory ratings of job performance are second best. Enforcement agencies frequently argue that rater bias causes protected groups to do more poorly, and at least one lower court has stated that supervisors' ratings are not a fair measure for promotion purposes (Burton & Pathak, 1976; Edwards, 1976; Holley & Feild, 1975; Holley, Feild, & Barnett, 1976; Lazer, 1976).
4. Given the expense of validation studies, how can small companies afford to comply with the law?

   It seems likely that in the future smaller companies will either have to abandon all differential employment practices or have to pool resources for hiring consultants to do their validation. One means of accomplishing this end might be through trade organizations.
5. To meet the qualifications of recent court cases, a performance appraisal system should have at least six characteristics:
   - The performance ratings should be job related.
   - The variables rated should be developed through job analysis.
   - Raters must be able to observe the performance they are to rate.
   - Ratings should not be based on raters' evaluations of vague, subjective factors.
   - Care should be taken through the choice of measures, through training, etc., to insure that ratings are not biased by prejudice regarding race, sex, or religion.
   - Ratings should be collected and scored under standardized circumstances (Edwards, 1976; Holley & Feild, 1975; Holley, Feild, & Barnett, 1976).
6. Caveats. Several unresolved problems exist for employers. Three such problems are employee right to privacy, reverse discrimination, and fair practices which continue past discrimination. The demands of each may seem opposed to the demands of Title VII. Each of these issues is explored in greater depth below.

RIGHT TO PRIVACY

Currently, the State of California protects, by statute, employees' access to their files. Proposals have been made for national legislation to protect employees' right to privacy. No such federal legislation has been passed, however. Nonetheless, it seems reasonable to conclude that, in the future, employees' right to privacy will increase in importance and that the bounds of the concept of privacy will be expanded in accord with other recent privacy legislation. Recent federal privacy legislation has been based on ten principles:

- *Mutuality.* All parties must have an interest in the proper use of records.
- *Consent.* The person on whom data are collected has the right to participate in deciding the content, use, and disclosure of that data.
- *Relevance.* Recorded data should include only necessary and relevant information.
- *Fiduciary Duty.* The person collecting data is responsible for the security of data.
- *Notice.* No secret personal data systems may exist; the person on whom data are collected must be notified of the existence of such data.
- *Access.* The person on whom data are collected must have access to such data and must have the opportunity to challenge and correct data.
- *Confidentiality.* Dissemination of data should be monitored so that only parties who need the information should receive it.
- *Warranty.* Information should be collected for specific purposes and used only for those purposes.
- *Accuracy.* Records should be checked for accuracy and relevance; obsolete, unnecessary, or inaccurate information should be reclassified, sealed, deleted, or destroyed.
- *Remedy.* An individual's right to privacy should be protected by legislation so that individuals might protect their rights through legal action. Enforcement agencies should exist to insure compliance with the law (Kellogg, 1964; Mironi, 1974; Mossman, 1975).

If companies voluntarily attempt to comply with these principles, several unresolved issues remain:

1. What information is "personal"? What types of information are confidential to the company?
2. Who should have access to what information? How does one decide?
3. What constitutes consent? Must employees be informed each time data pertaining to them are used for any personnel decision?
4. How does one deal with unanticipated consequences?
5. Does the right to access include access to subjective information about employees?
6. How does one resolve the superficial conflict of Title VII and right to privacy? The fewer data collected, the easier it is to protect privacy; protection against charges of discrimination requires the collection of considerable data (Schein, 1976).

AFFIRMATIVE ACTION

Reverse discrimination refers to the "decision to hire," transfer, or promote persons because they belong to a minority group. In other words, it is the preferred treatment of certain Title VII protected classes. When such practices occur, it is frequently because an organization is trying to comply with what it perceives as the requirements of Title VII. It is argued that reverse discrimination is necessary (1) to counteract past discrimination against racial minorities and females and (b) to comply with the requirements of affirmative action and equal employment opportunity.

The only Supreme Court case to date on the issue is the *Bakke* decision which involved a medical school applicant who was white. The University of California at Davis had a system which explicitly designated a fixed number of slots in the entering class for minorities before consideration of the qualifications of the available applicants. This race-conscious system was held unconstitutional. The general principle that derives from the court's decision in the *Bakke* case is that preferential treatment of minorities is legal only when the employer has been found guilty of discrimination and the court has ordered race-conscious remedies. Voluntary preferential treatment schemes fostered under the guise of affirmative action are illegal. Now, more than ever, it is imperative that employers have job related (validated) selection procedures. Other cases are currently pending that will affect the course of affirmative actions in the future. Up-to-date assessment from legal counsel is the best source of information for the employer.

Title VII has contradictory provisions about reverse discrimination. It alternately forbids any discrimination and provides special exemptions for other groups (Civil Rights Act, 1964, compare sections 703(a), (j), (g)). Some governmental agencies, while stating that reverse discrimination should not occur, recommend it if all other means have failed to increase very low levels of minority employees (Seligman, 1973). The U.S. Supreme Court has maintained that Title VII does not require that less qualified employees be favored over more qualified; rather than qualifications and not race, sex, or religion should be the factor which controls employment decisions (Supreme Court, 1971).

In the case of reverse discrimination, the only guideline one can offer is that of common sense. The purpose of the constitutional amendments and the law is to provide every individual with equal protection and rights. Organizations should seek that end. To accomplish that end, corporations should appraise individuals' performance on job-related criteria and not on the basis of race, religion, or sex.

In general, systems of preferential treatment that have been ordered by courts only *after* a finding of illegal discrimination have been upheld (e.g., quotas—"race conscious evils require race conscious remedies"). Preferential treatment in affirmative action, even under a consent decree, may be illegal.

PAST DISCRIMINATION

The major problem for employers who make an honest effort not to discriminate is the problem created by changes of practices which continue past discrimination. The most difficult practice to deal with is the seniority system. Seniority systems are one of the most widely used practices in industry. They are common in both union and nonunion industries. Seniority systems generally fall into one of two types: seniority for time in position or plant-wide (company-wide) seniority. As long as a seniority system is universally applied, it is not discriminatory.

Title VII specifically excludes *bona fide* seniority systems from classification as discriminatory (Civil Rights Act, 1964, Section 703(h)). *Bona fide* is undefined. The courts have, in general, interpreted *bona fide* to mean a currently fair system which does not continue past discrimination. The courts have held discriminatory seniority systems, generally, to be those systems based on position or job seniority, or which are based on mergers of such systems, so that jobs previously having separate seniority systems are arranged hierarchically with predominantly minority filled jobs at the bottom. The implementation of any new personnel practice, especially one which tightens the criteria for promotion, salary increase, etc., should be examined to see if it will continue a past discrimination (Blumrosen, 1971; Cooper & Sober, 1969; Friedman, 1976).

SUMMARY

One may view the present concerns as temporary. The intent of the law is to insure that merit rather than race, sex, religion, or national origin is the basis of employment decisions. Many of the present problems, such as reverse discrimination or seniority system fairness, derive from a past history of using criteria other than merit in employment decisions. The longer the period during which merit has demonstrably been the basis of employment practices, the fewer the problems posed by these factors (Affirmative action: Some notes, 1975; Testing and equal opportunity, 1975).

REFERENCES

- Affirmative action: Some notes. *Civil Rights Digest,* 1975, *7*(3), 52–54.
- American Psychological Association. *Standards for Educational and Psychological Tests.* Washington, D.C.: APA, 1200 SW 17th Street, 1974.
- Blumrosen, A.N. *Black employment and the law.* New Brunswick, N.J.: Rutgers University Press, 1971.
- Burton, G., & Pathak, D.S. 101 ways to discriminate against equal employment opportunity. *S.A.M. Advanced Management Journal,* 1976, *41*(4), 23–30.
- Cooper, G., & Sober, R.B. Seniority and testing under fair employment laws: A general approach to objective criteria of hiring and promotion. *Harvard Law Review,* 1969, *82,* 1603.
- Equal employment opportunities. Title 42, Chapter 21, Section 2000e. *United States Code,* 1974 revision.
- Equal Employment Opportunity Commission, Guidelines on employee selection procedures. *Federal Register,* 1970, *35*(249), 12333–12336.
- Equal Employment Opportunity Commission. Uniform Guidelines on Employee Selection. *Federal Register,* 1978, *43*(166), 38290–38309.
- Equal Employment Opportunity Commission. Adoption of questions and answers to clarify and provide a common interpretation of the Uniform Guidelines on Employee Selection Procedures. *Federal Register,* 1979, *44*(43), 11996–12009.
- Equal Employment Opportunity Coordinating Council. Employee selection procedures: Uniform guidelines. *Federal Register,* 1976, *41*(136), 29016–29022.
- Friedman, B.A. Seniority systems and the law. *Personnel Journal,* 1976, *55,* 334–339.
- Gilbreath, J.D. Sex discrimination and Title VII of the Civil Rights Act. *Personnel Journal,* 1977, *56,* 23–26.
- Higgins, J.M. A manager's guide to the equal employment opportunity laws. *Personnel Journal,* 1976, *55,* 406–412.
- Holley, W.H., & Feild, H.S. Performance appraisal and the law. *Labor Law Journal,* 1975, *26,* 423–430.
- Holley, W.H., Feild, H.S., & Barnett, N.J. Analyzing performance appraisal systems. *Personnel Journal,* 1976, *55,* 457–463.
- Kellogg, M.K. The ethics of employee appraisal. *Personnel,* 1965, *42*(4), 33–39.
- Lazer, R.I. The "discrimination" danger in performance appraisal. *The Conference Board Record,* 1976, *13*(3), 60–64.
- Mironi, M. The confidentiality of personnel records: A legal and ethical view. *Labor Law Journal,* 1974, *25,* 270–292.
- Mossman, K. A new dimension of privacy. *American Bar Association Journal,* 1975, *61,* 829–833.
- Robertson, D.E. Update on testing and equal opportunity. *Personnel Journal,* 1977, *56,* 144–147.
- Schein, V.E. Privacy and personnel: A time for action. *Personnel Journal,* 1976, *55,* 604–615.
- Seligman, D. How equal opportunity turned into employment quotas. *Fortune,* 1973, *87*(3), 160–168.
- Sharf, J.C. Washington v. Davis decided by Supreme Court. *The Industrial-Organizational Psychologist,* 1976, *13*(4), 13–15.
- Stanton, E.S. The discharged employee and the EEO laws. *Personnel Journal,* 1976, *55,* 128–129; 133.
- Testing and equal opportunity. *Civil Rights Digest,* 1975, *7*(3), 42–51.

- U.S. Congress. Civil Rights Act of 1964 (Public Law 88–352, July 2, 1964). *United States Statutes at Large,* 1964, *78,* 240.
- U.S. President. Executive Order 11246. Reassignment of civil rights functions. *Weekly Compilation of Presidential Documents,* 1965, *1,* 305–309.
- U.S. President. Executive Order 11375. Equal opportunity for women in federal employment and employment by federal contractors. *Weekly Compilation of Presidential Documents,* 1967, *3,* 1437–1438.

Analyzing Performance Appraisal Systems: An Empirical Study

by William H. Holley, Hubert S. Feild, and Nona J. Barnett

The subject of performance appraisal is now receiving considerable attention in many organizational settings. This attention has emerged from new demands for performance accountability brought about by "belt-tightening" campaigns and reduced revenues during an economic recession even though expectations of high performance have continued. Equally important are recent EEOC and court decisions that have alarmed employers to possible discriminatory effects of their perfomance appraisal systems.[1] As a result, emphasis is now being directed toward examining performance appraisal systems to determine the degree to which objectives of the appraisal systems are being met and to determine whether or not any discriminatory effects are present. Since previous studies[2] have shown that performance appraisal systems are quite common in organizations, this article will have special significance to any organization that is currently considering an analysis of its present performance appraisal system or that believes it may do so in the near future.

Organizations today do not have a choice of whether or not to examine their present performance appraisal system; the choice actually is between the alternatives available to them. Those organizations which possess adequate financial resources may choose to employ external researchers who specialize in analyzing performance appraisal systems in order to gain greater objectivity and expert guidance. On the other hand, some organizations not so fortunate in resources, but still possessing similar problems, must analyze their appraisal system internally using their own personnel.[3] The internal approach has considerable merit because the organization will be developing internal resourcefulness in a key management area, and those persons who conduct the analysis will remain on the staff thereby retaining knowledge of and experience with the particular performance appraisal system.

An approach will be presented in which an organization may analyze its present system and develop the basis for revising its system. This approach is based on an analysis of a performance appraisal system which has been in effect in an organization for nearly 15 years. In this system employees are rated annually by their immediate supervisor on the basis of work traits (e.g., quality of work, quantity of work, cooperation, etc.) and care of equipment. Points are given for each rating factor and totaled to determine the overall evaluation. The rating results are reviewed by the supervisor of the rater and whether or not the ratee is informed of the rating results is left to the discretion of the rater. Upon completion, the ratings are filed with other employee records so they can be retrieved for decisions regarding salary increases, promotions, layoffs, reemployment, transfers and demotions.

ANALYSIS OF THE APPRAISAL SYSTEM

Since analysis of an existing performance appraisal system sets the stage for any future activities (e.g., designing a new system, revising the present system, objectives of the present system, the degree to which these objectives are accom-

Reprinted with permission of *Personnel Journal,* Costa-Mesa, California. Copyright September, 1976.

[1]William H. Holley and Hubert S. Feild, "Performance Appraisal and the Law," *Labor Law Journal,* Vol. 26, No. 7, July 1975, pp. 423–430.

[2]Hubert S. Feild and William H. Holley, "Performance Appraisal—An Analysis of State-Wide Practices," *Public Personnel Management,* Vol. 4, No. 3, May–June, 1975, pp. 145–160 and Bureau of National Affairs, Inc., *Managerial Performance Appraisal Programs,* Washington, D.C., 1974.

[3]The choices are not actually between selecting a consultant and no consultant. Other choices are available such as receiving guidance from an expert but conducting the study internally.

plished) rater tendencies in evaluations, rater error and legal considerations must be analyzed. To do this in the present analysis, five primary sources of information were used: (a) interviews with organizational employees, (b) employee records, (c) external data from appraisal systems in comparable settings, (d) questionnaires completed by managerial personnel, and (e) court and EEOC cases regarding performance appraisal.

Interviews

Initially, interview were conducted with 17 key managers from various departments throughout the organization. These interviews were structured in such a way that the responses could be analyzed objectively. Subjects covered in the interviews were:

1. Strengths and weaknesses of the present system and
2. Recommendations for: (a) eliminating the weaknesses, (b) how the system should work and (c) criteria for evaluating different kinds of employees.

Data from the interviews were content-analyzed. Results proved to be useful not only in further analysis of the present system, but also in developing alternatives to be considered in modifying the existing system.

Analysis of Employee Records

Because the organization employed over 20,000 employees, a random sample of 1,961 employees was selected. Every tenth employee file was retrieved and data were obtained from the employee records and from the performance appraisal forms. Because one of the purposes of this analysis was to determine possible discriminatory effects, data on race, sex, and age were collected in addition to such variables as: rating scores, job titles, departments and job tenure. The performance ratings were analyzed for rater errors, e.g., central tendency, leniency and halo error, to help determine whether or not the form needed revision, raters needed training, etc.

Rating errors. The problem of central tendency (when raters do not use the extremes of the rating continuum but tend to give average ratings to employees) was determined by analyzing frequency distributions, means and standard deviations of the ratings given to the rating factors. Figure 1 shows the lack of central tendency by the raters since less than half of the employees were classified in the two middle categories and approximately six out of 10 were rated in one of the two extreme categories.

Another rating error, leniency (when raters tend to give a disproportionate number of favorable ratings to employees), was also investigated. This error was flagrant in the organization studied. Figure 1 shows that over 50% of the employees were rated in the most favorable category. Excellent. Whereas the average rating would be expected to be 1.5, the mean rating for employees in this organization was above 2.5, thereby reflecting a substantial leniency error.

The possibility of halo error (when raters tend to let their overall assessment of ratees be unduly influenced by their evaluation of one factor) was also investigated. To examine this error, simple correlations were computed between each of the rating factors. From the data presented in Figure 2, one might conclude that the halo effect seems to be substantial, but high correlations do not necessarily mean a rating error has taken place. A halo error is suspected, but high correlations could possibly indicate that the rating factors are not completely independent and should in fact be highly correlated. On the other hand, the halo effect may be due to the problem of generality of the factors rated and more specific factors may be needed. Further examination of the data suggested that a halo error did exist and that specific behavioral definitions of each rating factor were needed.

Relationships between ratee characteristics and ratings given. Additional analyses of the system included an examination of the characteristics of the ratee

FIGURE 1
Distributions of Ratings Given Employees

	Unsatisfactory		*Fair*		*Good*		*Excellent*		*Total*		
Rating factors	*N*	*%*	*N*	*%*	*N*	*%*	*N*	*%*	*N*	*M*	*SD*
1. Quality of work	3	0.2	38	1.9	826	42.1	1,094	55.8	1,961	2.54	.55
2. Quantity of work	6	0.3	49	2.5	826	42.1	1,080	55.1	1,961	2.52	.56
3. Cooperation	2	0.1	45	2.3	577	29.5	1,334	68.1	1,958	2.65	.53
4. Initiative	3	0.2	63	3.2	832	42.5	1,060	54.1	1,958	2.51	.57
5. Care of equipment	0	0.0	11	0.8	567	43.2	734	56.0	1,312	2.44	.51

Note: Unsatisfactory = 0; Excellent = 3.

FIGURE 2
Intercorrelations Among Rating Factors

Rating factors	*1*	*2*	*3*	*4*	*5*	*N*	*M*	*SD*
1. Quality of work	—	.57	.45	.53	.47	1,961	2.54	.55
2. Quantity of work	—	—	.47	.56	.53	1,961	2.52	.56
3. Cooperation			—	.46	.52	1,958	2.65	.53
4. Initiative				—	.45	1,958	2.51	.57
5. Care of equipment					—	1,312	2.55	.51

Note: Unsatisfactory = 0; Excellent = 3.

and the rating situations. These analyses involved correlations between the overall assessment of each ratee (mean ratings) and several variables: (a) job tenure, (b) age, (c) race, (d) sex, (e) hours of training, (f) whether results of the ratings were discussed with the ratee and (g) whether work covered under the rating form was discussed with the ratee anytime during the year. (Note: To guarantee anonymity of the organization because of the sensitive nature of the data, the actual findings are not presented in this section. However, a hypothetical case is shown to demonstrate how the analysis was conducted.)

Figure 3 demonstrates the correlations between the mean rating points and the variables above. The hypothetical data shown in Figure 3 demonstrate significant, but very weak, correlations between a number of personal characteristics of the ratee as well as the rating situation and ratings given the ratee. These correlations indicate that as job tenure, age and hours of training increased, the mean ratings of employees were likely to increase. Further, the hypothetical data depict the possibility of a discrimination problem in that male and white employees received higher rating than female and black employees. With results such as these showing the potential of discriminatory employment practices, the organization would have the burden of proving that the results were not discriminatory in the event that any EEOC or court case emerged from personnel decisions based on the rating results. With regard to the characteristics of the rating situation, negative correlations with the ratings are shown. These negative correlations suggest that when supervisors discussed the performance ratings with the employees, they tended to feed back higher ratings. Such actions by supervisors may have been taken to avoid possible defensive behaviors from employees resulting from feedback of low ratings.

FIGURE 3
Correlations Between The Rating Points and Characteristics Of The Ratee and Rating Situation*

Characteristics of the ratee:	*r*
1. Job tenure	.32
2. Age	.24
3. Race (1 = white, 2 = black)	−.22
4. Sex (1 = male, 2 = female)	−.22
5. Hours of training	.25
Characteristics of rating situation:	
6. Results of rating discussed with the employee (1 = yes, 2 = no)	−.25
7. Work covered by rating (1 = yes, 2 = no)	−.12

*These correlations are based upon hypothetical data.

Analysis of Systems in Comparable Settings

An important source of data for this analysis came from existing systems in comparable settings. After comparable settings were identified according to type of organization, objectives, and types of employees, performance rating forms, policy manuals and handbooks were obtained from 39 organizations. These materials were subsequently analyzed with respect to the following areas: (a) purposes for which ratings were used, (b) rating techniques which were employed, (c) types of factors evaluated, and (d) variables most frequently used in the rating forms. Figure 4 summarized the most significant results from this analysis.

Identifying Rating Factors

Analysis of performance appraisal systems in comparable settings provided useful information for this study. However, any new performance appraisal system must be tailored to the specific needs and objectives of a particular organization's idiosyncrasies and organizational climate. Moreover, if the ratings are to be used as a basis for personnel decision making, EEOC regulations require a thorough job analysis, specification of job-related rating factors, standardized administration and non-discriminatory results. Thus, any new performance appraisal system must incorporate many factors which cannot be obtained from comparable organization, but must be designed for the specific organization. To obtain this data, a study of manager perceptions of the relative importance of behaviors and traits was conducted. In order to examine these perceptions,

FIGURE 4
Results from Analyzing Comparable Performance Appraisal Systems

Components analyzed		*Percent of organization (N = 39)*
Purposes of performance appraisal		
1. Promotions, demotions, and/or layoffs		58
2. Manpower planning and utilization		46
3. Salary adjustments		39
4. Communications between supervisors and subordinates		39
5. Determination of management development needs		38
Performance appraisal techniques used		
1. Numerical rating scale		62
2. Essay evaluation		13
3. Essay evaluation and numerical rating scale		13
Types of factors evaluated		
1. Personal traits		82
2. Job behaviors		80
3. Managerial skills		74
4. Achievement of previously established goals		26
Frequency of variables used on appraisal forms		
	Supervisory personnel	*Non-supervisory personnel*
1. Quality of work	59	67
2. Quantity of work	49	56
3. Initiative	44	49
4. Human relations	41	33
5. Judgement	36	28
6. Job knowledge	33	39
7. Work habits	33	33
8. Dependability	31	41

FIGURE 5
Mean Rating of the Importance of Selected Traits in Performance Appraisal

	Types of employees							
	All managers (N = 1,117)		*Clerical administrative (N = 188)*		*Technical-professional (N = 115)*		*Unskilled labor (N = 134)*	
Rating factors	*Mean*	*Rank*	*Mean*	*Rank*	*Mean*	*Rank*	*Mean*	*Rank*
Dependability	6.45	1	6.41	2	6.59	1	6.37	1
Quality of work	6.35	2	6.46	1	6.58	2	6.12	5
Cooperation	6.27	3	6.27	4	6.28	5	6.33	2
Communication ability	6.20	4	6.26	5	6.47	3	5.86	12
Favorable job attitude	6.06	5	5.94	9	6.17	6	6.07	8
Accuracy of work	6.02	6	6.34	3	6.00	10	5.57	20
Relations with public	5.99	7	5.93	10	5.98	12	5.62	18
Relations with others	5.96	8	5.92	11	5.86	15	6.07	7
Willingness to learn	5.95	9	5.85	13	6.08	8	6.09	6
Use of work time	5.93	10	5.97	8	6.10	7	5.90	10

*Includes managers only supervising employees in a respective managerial group.

a questionnaire, the Trait Rating Questionnaire (TRQ), which asked supervisory personnel to assess the importance of a variety of traits in their employees' job success was developed and administered to 2,000 supervisors. Because of the variability of responses to the TRQ by 1,117 managers (see Figure 5), it was concluded that one form would not be sufficient to meet the essential requirements for the new system. Although there were several common factors identified for clerical-administrative, technical-professional and unskilled employees, one form with the same factors could not satisfy the requirement of job specificity.

Legal Considerations

Because performance ratings are often used as a basis for personnel decisions, they are receiving considerable attention from the EEOC and courts. Since an organization has the burden of proving validity of a performance rating instrument after a *prima facie* case of employment discrimination has been established, it is essential that organizations be cognizant of EEOC and court rulings regarding the use of performance ratings.

Analysis of recent court decisions has revealed that inappropriate use of performance ratings may occur for any one or more of the following reasons:

1. The performance rating method has not been shown to be job-related;
2. The content of the performance rating method has not been developed from thorough job analysis;
3. Raters have not been able to consistently observe the performance of the ratee;
4. Ratings have been used on rater's evaluations of subjective or vague factors;
5. Racial, sexual or other biases of raters may have influenced the ratings given to the ratees; and
6. Ratings have not been collected and scored under standardized conditions.[4]

To assure non-discrimination, these factors must be taken into consideration in analyzing any existing performance appraisal system. Further, they must also be considered in the design of any new system.

DESIGN OF THE NEW PERFORMANCE APPRAISAL SYSTEM

Based on the internal research conducted, analyses of performance appraisal systems in comparable settings, survey of manager perceptions, legal considerations and published research on performance appraisal, it was decided that the present system needed revision. Three different performance rating forms were designed: two for non-managerial employees and one for managerial and professional personnel. The structure of the form for the non-managerial employees was basically the same, except that two of the seven rating factors used were different. To meet the requirement of job-relatedness, the rater was asked to give weights to each of the rating factors in accordance to their relevance to a specific job. To achieve objectivity, rating factors were given five degrees and each degree was specifically defined in behavioral terms.

For managerial and professional personnel, a MBO-oriented Performance Planning and Review (PPR) was designed. This program required the ratee to set individual performance goals for his or her job with the counsel and approval of the supervisor. Performance would then be compared to the established goals to determine the evaluation results. Using accomplishments and experiences in the first period as the basis, goals for the next period would then be established and performance evaluation again would be based on a comparison of goals and accomplishments.

Upon introduction of the new performance appraisal system, the organization should immediately establish a means for assessing the effectiveness of the new system. The approach used in this study with its accompanying statistical analyses should provide guidance for any future analyses and efforts in other settings.

[4]William H. Holley and Hubert S. Feild, "Performance Appraisal and the Law," *Labor Law Journal*, Vol. 26, No. 7, July 1975, pp. 423–430.

Appraising Appraisal: Ten Lessons from Research for Practice

by Marshall Sashkin

Performance appraisal is, or should be, a major concern of all middle- and upper-level managers. This may sound like a homily that is valid but of no more intrinsic merit than "A stitch in time saves nine," or "Do unto others...." But two factors make performance appraisal an especially relevant topic of concern today. First, the Civil Service Reform Act (CSRA) mandates that new performance appraisal systems that meet CSRA guidelines be in place and operational by October 1, 1981. Thus *all* federal administrators will have to become aware of performance appraisal—perhaps painfully. Second, federal courts are beginning to hear business and industry cases in which plaintiffs argue, on behalf of management, that Equal Employment Opportunity Commission (EEOC) and other agency guidelines have actually contributed to unfair and illegal employment practices. The alleged unfair practices include promotions, demotions, transfers, and dismissals on the basis of performance appraisals. In such cases, courts are finding with some consistency that performance appraisals are psychological employment tests and, as such, are subject to Uniform Selection Guidelines and court rulings. Thus most private sector managers will soon wish they knew more about what constitutes legal performance appraisal.

ROUGH APPRAISAL OF THE SYSTEM

Before reading further, you may want to fill out the brief six-item questionnaire in Figure 1. It is designed to elicit a rough picture of an organization's appraisal system. The scoring will be discussed after we review some defined purposes of performance appraisal systems.

This brief overview of performance appraisal is intended to aid public and private sector managers in assessing their own performance appraisal system and practices, with a view toward identifying good and poor aspects of the systems and practices. It is much easier to evaluate a particular appraisal instrument (such as a graphic rating scale) or a technique or practice (such as an interview) than to assess an organization's entire system that's set up to reach specific performance appraisal objectives. Although these objectives can be broken down into fine detail, Douglas McGregor's classic article gives a breakdown that adequately covers the basic aims:

1. Performance appraisal systems should generate information needed for short- and long-range administrative actions, such as salary decisions, promotions, and transfers (all short-range) or human resources planning and managerial succession (long-range).
2. Appraisal systems should let subordinates know where they stand, how well they are doing, and what changes in their behavior the superior wants.
3. Appraisal systems should provide a means for coaching and counseling subordinates in order to train and develop them to their full potential.

The simple "OPAQUE" questionnaire in Figure 1 was designed to get a rough assessment of an organization's appraisal system using McGregor's purposes. The first two items, summed to yield score A, relate to the aim of *developing subordinates.* The second two, whose sum is score B, are concerned with the aim of *letting people know where they stand.* The final two items, summed to yield score C, indicate how well the system *provides information for administrative actions.*

For each aim, the score may range from 2 to 10. Scores of 9 or 10 suggest that the aim is being well-met; scores of 4 to 8 indicate average success in attaining that aim; and scores of 2 or 3 suggest that this aim is not being met at all well. It is also possible to determine whether problems stem from superiors or subordinates. If both items making up score A, B, or C are weak, the problem may be characteristic of the system as a whole.

The sum of scores A, B, and C gives a rough overall rating for the organization's appraisal system, ranging from a possible low of 6 to a potential high of 30. Scores of 26 to 30 suggest that the organization's appraisal system is doing an excellent job of meeting McGregor's objectives. Scores of 11 to 25 would be average, 21 to 25 good, and 11 to 15 fair. Scores of 6 to 10 indicate that the system is doing quite poorly.

It would, of course, be foolish to place too much importance on a six-item questionnaire. These items and scores can best be used as thought-provokers—that is, to start one thinking about performance appraisal aims and how well these aims are being attained.

OVERVIEW OF THE SYSTEM

The purpose of this overview is to explore, in detail, those appraisal system characteristics that are more specifically diagnostic—that is, those that signify whether performance

From *Organizational Dynamics,* Winter, 1981, Vol. 9, Number 3, 37–50.

appraisal systems are effective or ineffective. I don't plan to weigh the strengths and weaknesses of current appraisal techniques—there are many good techniques available today. Of course, a technique must be properly developed and correctly used if accurate assessments are to be made. However, a generally good technique, such as behaviorally anchored rating scales (BARS), may be undermined by a poor system. For example, the BARS format might be used in conjunction with a combined feedback and salary review meeting to justify an already-made salary decision that was based on comparison among all rated workers at the same level. Such an approach goes against several heuristics developed by various writers and researchers.

Another example is detailed by Robert Lazar and Walter Wikstrom in their recent review of performance appraisal systems in organizations throughout the United States. They describe an RCA Corporation system that uses explicit peer comparison ratings based on percentile scores on graphic rating scales. The nature of the system, however, makes up for the deficiencies of this focus on peer comparisons (which will be discussed later). The company uses a multiple rating system—that is, several independent raters evaluate each individual, who receives anonymous detailed feedback including an anonymous rating by his or her superior. This system seems to make it easier for the appraiser (the superior) to give the appraisee coaching and developmental help.

These examples show that specific guidelines for using certain techniques (such as, "Use BARS to get maximum personnel involvement in evaluation form development and to minimize rater halo and leniency.") may be negated by poor systems, while specific "rules of thumb" or heuristics advising one to avoid some techniques (such as, "Avoid direct peer comparisons.") may be less important when the system is particularly innovative and well-designed. Despite these limitations, which apply to any heuristic guidelines, we can identify a set of heuristics that may, overall, compensate for the occasional inapplicability of one or another specific bit of advice.

I must emphasize that I do not intend to deal with the psychometric aspect of performance appraisal, nor do I intend to explicitly view the legal aspects of appraisal or the economic utility of effective performance appraisal. Important as these aspects of performance appraisal are, the intent of this article is to integrate a variety of research-based opinions that are relevant to the operation of an organization's performance appraisal program as an effective *human resources management* system. Therefore, a relevant question is, "How can an organization (rather than a lone supervisor) improve on what currently exists?" In the following guidelines, I try to tell the reader what to look for and indicate generally what needs to be done.

HEURISTIC GUIDELINES

The following ten "rules of thumb" or heuristic guidelines present characteristics of effective performance appraisals. They will help you assess your current system and suggest possible changes.

Heuristic #1: Are managers rewarded for developing their subordinates? Like their subordinates, managers respond to rewards and punishments from their own superiors. The time and effort invested by the manager in subordinate development may not only go unrewarded, but, sometimes, such efforts are actually punished—perhaps not intentionally, but punished nonetheless. (Note: In all examples, the names of persons and organizations have been altered and circumstances disguised, unless otherwise noted.)

An example of punishment for exceptional effort occurred in the District Contractor's Supply Company where Mike Nolan was manager of a 27-person department with three assistant managers, each of whom supervised a group of 7 to 12 people. I say "was" because six months ago Mike took a similar (but slightly better-paying) job with a rival firm. During his exit interview, Mike was candid about the lack of advancement he perceived at DCSC. He was accurate, too. Several of his former subordinates—Mike had been with DCSC for 11 years—had bypassed him and moved into higher management positions, some with DCSC and some with other firms. Whether Mike's experience was typical of many firms or not (and I fear it was), it is a good illustration of how developers may lose out on promotion because they invest time and effort helping subordinates while managers who spend more time on concrete production output are considered more promotable.

Being a good developer can be unrewarding in other ways. The manager of one store in a chain of ten retail office supply stores is known throughout the organization for his skill at training new employees. Thus when employees with potential are hired in any division, they are typically assigned to his store first. One consequence is high turnover in his unit; another is the need for this manager to devote an unusually large proportion of his time to new-employee training. Moreover, he has to take on certain responsibilities himself that might be delegated if he had more long-term employees. In spite of these circumstances, he receives no special allowances in terms of sales quotas or operating budget.

In such situations, most rational managers would minimize their developmental activities. Despite the fact that practically all appraisal systems incorporate subordinate improvement as an explicit goal, the organization's reward system may actually negate any efforts toward meeting this goal. And even when subordinate development is not actually punished, it isn't a real managerial goal unless there's "something in it"—that is, a positive reward—for the manager. For an effective performance appraisal system to exist for any length of time, the organizational reward system must clearly tie subordinate development to positive outcomes for managers. One immediate clue, therefore, on which to assess the system is the presence or absence

FIGURE 1
Organizational Performance Appraisal Questionnaire Evaluation (OPAQUE)*

Instructions
Respond to the following six statements by indicating the extent to which you agree (or disagree) that the statements accurately describe performance appraisal in your organization. Some statements refer to your experiences in appraising your subordinates' performance; others refer to your experiences in being appraised yourself. Try to reflect as accurately as you can the current conditions in your organization based on your experiences.

SA = Strongly Agree A = Agree ? = Neither Agree nor Disagree D = Disagree SD = Strongly Disagree

Statement					
1. I have found my boss's appraisals to be very helpful in guiding my own career development progress.	SA	A	?	D	SD
2. The appraisal system we have here is of no use to me in my efforts toward developing my subordinates to the fullest extent of their capabilities.	SA	A	?	D	SD
3. Our performance appraisal system generally leaves me even more uncertain about where I stand after my appraisal than beforehand.	SA	A	?	D	SD
4. The appraisal system we use is very useful in helping me to clearly communicate to my subordinates exactly where they stand.	SA	A	?	D	SD
5. When higher levels of management around here are making major decisions about management positions and promotions, they have access to and make use of performance appraisal records.	SA	A	?	D	SD
6. In making pay, promotion, transfer, and other administrative personnel decisions, I am not able to obtain past performance appraisal records that could help me to make good decisions.	SA	A	?	D	SD

of subordinate development as one appraisal criterion used to evaluate manager's job performances.

Heuristic #2: Do managers receive skill training and assistance in using the system and, specifically, in being helpers or counselors? Research during the past decade has repeatedly demonstrated the value and importance of training managers in the effective use of appraisal forms. Walter Borman (and many investigators since) found that even brief lecture discussions can reduce rater errors based on the "halo" effect and that the training needed to reduce other rater errors (for example, leniency, harshness, avoidance of extremes) is not extremely extensive or expensive. In a very recent report, however, John Bernardin and Patricia Smith observe that behaviorally anchored rating scales (BARS), which are particularly costly to develop, are frequently used incorrectly simply because raters are not trained in how to use them.

Even when the rating format is less innovative and more familiar to users than BARS, some training is necessary. One division of a service firm experienced interdepartment conflicts. Intergroup conflict resolution based on organization development efforts led to the discovery that one source of these long-standing conflicts was the variation among department heads in the harshness or leniency with which they rated subordinates. The large number of departments and complex schedule of appraisals had masked this issue, but it turned out that some managers rated similar levels of performance better (or worse) than others. The upshot was that groups of subordinates felt unfairly treated—not by individual managers, who were typically seen as consistent and fair toward them as individuals, but as members of a group compared with other groups in the organization. Of course, they were right. While this was only one aspect of the intergroup problems this firm had, it illustrates the systemic, organizationwide impact that individual rater training—or its absence—can have.

Scoring

Use the following grid to determine point scores for each item by transferring your responses onto the grid. Place the number in the box at the bottom of each column, then add pairs of columns as indicated.

		Statement Number					
		1	2	3	4	5	6
Response	SA	5	1	1	5	5	1
	A	4	2	2	4	4	2
	?	3	3	3	3	3	3
	D	2	4	4	2	2	4
	SD	1	5	5	1	1	5

+   +   +

A   B   C

A + B + C =

A contrasting example is evident in the Chevrolet Sales Division of General Motors. When that division developed a new appraisal system, one key aspect was a trainer/coach who was assigned to assist managers in making more accurate ratings. The coach was simply a manager who had been trained in the methods. The coaching duties were rotated among middle-level managers after they were trained. Perhaps this example is unusual because of the extent of training and coaching assistance given raters, but it shows that such training and assistance is not impossible even when the organization is geographically dispersed.

When individuals are hired or promoted into managerial positions, it is often assumed that they have the managerial skills needed to function effectively. Very often, however, new managers are hired or promoted on the basis of technical skills, and they lack any formal training in managerial skills, including performance appraisal. It is a waste of resources to develop excellent assessment tools that are misused or abused when training methods are relatively simple and widely available. It is also important that training not be a "one shot" effort, but that it be repeated or reviewed regularly and frequently.

Everyone knows of appraisal interviews that didn't go as well as they should have and of problem interviews which culminated in an employee's being fired or, worse, being turned off. Even when the rater is trained in psychometric error, a performance appraisal system is likely to be ineffective unless managers possess the more complex skills needed to conduct effective performance appraisal interviews. In particular, the nondirective counseling skill first developed by Carl Rogers and often called active reflective, or empathic listening, is an invaluable asset in appraisal interviews. However, this skill is rarely part of a manager's behavioral repertoire even though Herbet H. Meyer and his associates at General Electric showed how important this skill is for effective performance appraisal more than fifteen years ago. The best-known report of that research (which generated most of the practical knowledge about performance appraisal systems in the 1960s) refers to splitting the role of the appraiser into "counselor" and "judge," a topic we will discuss later. What gets relatively little attention in that report, however, is the nature of training needed by managers to prepare them to operate as counselors or the method of designing and implementing such training and developing the necessary skills. While such skills are more complex and difficult to learn than those needed to avoid rating errors, there are now, fortunately, a number of available training tools targeted to develop just such skills. To be effective, a performance appraisal system should incorporate manager training in the skills for rating *and* conducting appraisal interviews.

Heuristic #3: Are job descriptions or specific job goal documents based on behavioral or job-relevant performance standards? Recent court decisions have called the appraisal system a selection test when it is used as a criterion for promotions and transfers; this makes the system subject to the federal Uniform Selection Guidelines. In one recent court case, an employer was ordered to rehire a worker who had been terminated after several unacceptable performance ratings. The worker argued that he had never been told exactly what was unacceptable about his performance or what he would have to do to improve his ratings. Since he had been given no written or documentable job performance standards, and the employer could not show that the employee had been told how to correct his performance or what an acceptable level of performance was, his argument was upheld; the court ordered the company to reinstate him with back pay (for all the lengthy time his case was being adjudicated). An interesting aspect of this case: The employer was the federal Equal Employment Opportunity Commission! A look at the performance appraisal instrument that EEOC used at the time this case developed helps explain why the problem arose. The appraisal format included such traits as industriousness, resourcefulness, and judgment as graphic rating scales (no behavioral description required). This ironic situation rather vividly demonstrates the importance of having, and using, specific job descriptions and clear performance standards—basic elements necessary for compliance with federal Uniform Selection Guidelines. The closer an organization conforms to a reasonable interpretation of the guidelines, the less likely that management will be faced with legal actions that are, at best, costly and time-consuming and, at worst, economically disastrous. Aside from these legal implications, when behavioral standards exist, it is much more likely they will be attained. Extensive research on goal setting has repeatedly shown that indefinite "do your best" goals result in inferior performance when compared with specific, measurable goals, regardless of whether the goals are assigned or determined by both employees and supervisors.

Goal-setting based or management by objectives (MBO) systems do not automatically solve this issue of standards. Several years ago a medium-size business firm installed an MBO system. There were problems, but managers were willing to try it, and employees felt positive and supported the new system because they had been deeply involved in developing the job objectives. The system did work, and when managers rated their subordinates at the end of the first "cycle," most found that subordinates substantially exceeded their objectives. The summary ratings tended to be quite high. The executive vice-president, who reviewed the ratings, was quite displeased. He didn't feel the written evaluations and descriptions of objectives achieved supported the high overall ratings. He changed a number of these ratings without giving any reason, although the reason was clear: He felt improper standards had been applied. Needless to say, his actions thoroughly undermined employee confidence in the new system and effectively killed it.

While this case may be extreme, the basic issue of superior-subordinate communication about, and understanding of, the subordinate's job is a very common problem. Appraisal cannot be accurate when the appraiser and appraisee are seeing different things. A good appraisal system must incorporate clear job goals or performance standards as the basis for appraisal.

Heuristic #4: Are employees actively involved in the appraisal process? Several years ago Larry Cummings conducted a field study. He got people—subordinates as well as managers—from one division of a company involved in designing a new appraisal system. He then compared it with the old management-designed system that was still being used in another comparable division of the company. The new system worked better and was more readily accepted by employees at all levels than the old system. Objectively, the new system was probably a bit better, but the differences in functioning seemed to be as much a result of people's involvement in the design process as the quality of the new system. Clearly, an appraisal system in which employees participate actively is perceived by subordinates as superior to a management-developed system.

The problem is how to get employees involved. It isn't necessary to set up entire new systems very often, but there is a relatively constant need for system refinement—for example, the development or refinement of job descriptions or performance criteria or measures. Employees can be actively involved in goal setting, problem solving, and helping/counseling interactions; employees' increased participation in these functions is usually associated with improved performance. Formal goal-setting approaches, MBO in particular, offer extensive opportunities for involvement. But even at the very basic level of developing the appraisal form, employee participation can result in important benefits entirely aside from the increased quality of the form. The more employees are involved in all phases of the appraisal process, the better the system is likely to be.

Heuristic #5: Does mutual goal setting take place? Some years ago when MBO was new and faddish, Harry Levinson asked, sardonically, "Management by *whose* objectives?" His point was that mutuality in goal setting is especially difficult when one of the parties is "more equal" than the other. More recent research on MBO and on goal setting in general has shown that goal setting is beneficial even when the goals are imposed rather than participative. However, while it may be difficult to ensure the true "mutuality" of goal setting, such participation is especially valuable because mutually set goals are likely to be higher than those the supervisor assigns—unilaterally—and the higher the goals, the better the actual performance is likely to be.

To elaborate: Research indicates that goal setting is usually associated with performance improvement. When the process works poorly, it is usually because goals have been imposed on a subordinate who doesn't know how to achieve them, or who lacks the knowledge, skills, experience, and so forth needed to develop operationally effective paths to the goals. Or subordinates may be "turned off" by sham participative goal setting.

Both problems are present in a state educational service agency where goals, in terms of client cases served and closed, are set for one year. Even though feasible goals should reflect a wide range of partly known and controllable factors at the operational level, actual goals are set by administrators several levels removed from day-to-day operations. For both superiors and subordinates in field offices, this exercise in goal setting is an annual ritual, carried out in disgust. The goals, if they have any effect at all, may act to demotivate workers (who know that they are faced with unreasonable or impossible expectations), while the process itself is certainly demoralizing.

By contrast, if there's real participation in mutual goal setting, the organizational climate associated with increased satisfaction and productivity that's espoused by Rensis Likert evolves. Joint superior-subordinate goal setting is an important element of an effective performance appraisal system.

Heuristic #6: Do appraisal sessions have a problem-solving focus? Even a little problem solving is better than none. Citing faults and attaching blame does little to correct performance deficiencies when the causes of the problems remain unknown. Criticism rarely has any positive results because it generates defensiveness in the person being criticized. The terms "constructive" and "criticism" are simply incompatible, much as we might like to believe otherwise. Appraisal interviews have traditionally been based on the delusion that people will respond to being told what they are doing wrong by doing right in the future. Appraisers, of course, quickly learn the truth: People do not want to hear what is wrong; they will evade unpleasant truths, deny them, excuse them, rationalize them, and do almost anything but admit error and vow to correct it. Frequently the appraisee will simply reinterpret or deny the appraiser's information or evaluation in order to maintain his or her self-image. Appraisers, therefore, choose from a variety of anti-avoidance strategies: They hide criticism in between clumps of praise; they attenuate criticism (often to the point that it is not recognizable as such), or they capitulate to the appraisee's needs and simply avoid the appraisal interview. None of this does anyone much good. In fact, research has demonstrated that the more criticism the subordinate receives, the *worse* his or her future performance will be.

Ever since Douglas McGregor took "an uneasy look at performance appraisal" in 1957, writers and practitioners have echoed his call for greater attention to solving problems and developing subordinates and for less focus on errors, flaws, and so forth. Even so, this aim, a focus on problem solving and development, seems to be particularly elusive; the reason may be because this important characteristic of the system emerges only in actual appraisal interviews. It may be that a problem-solving focus is nothing more than the application of helping and counseling skills.

A problem-solving focus calls for a supportive organizational climate that fosters a problem-oriented approach to a wide variety of issues, including but not limited to performance issues. Such a supportive climate may manifest itself as part of the systemwide climate characteristics defined by Rensis Likert in his now-classic works on systems of management. Likert's ideal or "System 4" climate involves trying to make all superior-subordinate interactions as supportive to the subordinate as possible. However, to accomplish this on an organizational level may require the company to make major organizational development changes. Although this may be desirable, a more limited training approach may be more practical.

Over twenty years ago, Norman Maier took a performance appraisal case based on an actual situation and made it into a role-play case. A umber of people then acted out the case and were tape recorded. He found three basic approaches, one of which was problem solving (which Michael Beer describes in detail in his article in this issue of *Organizational Dynamics*). Maier later adapted these tapes and developed a training program for problem-solving appraisal interviewing. Of course, there are many other forms of training aimed at developing a problem-solving approach. For example: At one small firm in which managers sit in on appraisal interviews conducted by their subordinates, the managers then provide detailed observational feedback and work with subordinates to develop new and more successful appraisal interview behaviors to facilitate problem solving.

When individuals receive no training in the skills needed to conduct problem-solving appraisal interviews, the system cannot be expected to have a problem-solving focus. Furthermore, even when people do have these skills, it doesn't necessarily mean the skills are effectively used. To evaluate an appraisal system, one ought to observe and analyze actual appraisal interviews looking for a problem-solving orientation as well as the other characteristics we have discussed.

Heuristic #7: Is the judge role clearly separated from the helper/counselor role? McGregor's intuitive insight into the basic conflict between being a helper and being a judge has proved to be correct. Norman Maier was among the first to support McGregor's views that were based solidly on the work of Carl Rogers and Abraham Maslow. The extensive research program conducted in the General Electric Company in the early 1960s by Maier's student, Herbert H. Meyer, and his associates resulted in empirical research evidence that demonstrated beyond doubt that a clear separation of the incongruent judge and helper (or coach/counselor) roles led to a more effective appraisal system in terms of employee satisfaction and performance improvement. The functions of rewarding/punishing and of helping seem to be so incompatible that the surest way to ruin an otherwise good appraisal system is to require the supervisor to perform both roles in one appraisal session. Again, Beer's article elaborates on this point.

Implementing "split roles," however, is not simple. On an organizational level, at least three major shifts in organizational policies and actions are needed. The first requires that meetings dealing with salary actions be separated from performance counseling sessions. This does not mean that performance and results aren't used to determine pay and rewards; it only means that evaluation and reward sessions be separated in concept and in act from problem-centered performance counseling sessions. Second, frequent work counseling (or "work progress review") sessions must be fostered. The third shift requires that managers be trained to conduct counseling reviews so they avoid criticism and use a problem-centered approach.

Heuristic #8: Does the paperwork and technical assistance required by the appraisal system place an unreasonable workload on managers? Some appraisal techniques require more skill than others; some seem to require more "paper pushing" than others, and some simply involve more effort than others. For example, the development and use of a BARS involves more effort than the creation of a graphic rating scale that's equally good technically. MBO is known for its tendency to overwhelm users with forms. Integrative essays on subordinates and coaching interviews require more skill than checking off simple scales on a one-page form and handing the subordinate a copy to look at. All performance appraisal techniques have their good and bad points in terms of work and effort required to use them.

The MBO forms used by the state educational services agency mentioned earlier require lengthy narratives about staff relations, EEO requirements, supervision training needs, and plans for crisis situations (among other issues). Actual performance reviews with supervisors, however, are perfunctory and deal only with percent of goal attainment (recall that agency goals are set by upper-level administrators). Not even salary or promotion feedback is given, because these issues are decided, again, at higher levels after all goal attainment data are available for comparison. Both superior and subordinate are, nonetheless, expected to complete the forms annually. Unsurprisingly, the forms are filled out once (often without any useful detail) and the numbers and dates are changed annually. It isn't clear if the system fails because there's no realistic goal setting, because problem issues are ignored or covered up superficially, because there's no managerial training, because the obviously troublesome forms are used, or because of all these factors. We do know that these factors create an administrative nightmare with no practical use.

All of the technical and role requirements placed on the appraiser must be examined to see if the function has become unreasonably demanding. If it has, managers will quickly find a way to appear to be carrying out their performance appraisal duties while actually minimizing their efforts to work effectively with the appraisal system.

Heuristic #9: Are peer comparisons a central feature of the appraisal process? As I was gathering information about one organization's appraisal system, a technical professional (nonsupervisory) employee told me, "I am appraised by direct comparison with the other thirty-four people in my department even though there isn't anyone in this entire organization who performs tasks similar to mine. I sometimes wonder on just what basis I'm being compared." This comment illustrates one of several problems with using peer comparison as a basic approach to performance appraisal—that is, one may be comparing incomparable items.

A related problem concerns the usefulness of peer comparisons. One of the least useful types of feedback is the knowledge that one is in the "n^{th}" percentile of all employees in work quality rating. Such data tell the employee that his or her work is relatively good or bad in comparison with others', but it does not tell *how* good or bad or the real quality of the work. If most people are rated "above average" (a common practice) then an "average" percentile rating may be a signal of serious work quality problems. On the other hand, if a normal bell-shaped distribution is used, as sometimes happens, half of the workers are told they are below average; thus half the workforce is alienated, perhaps even insulted. What is more, a normal distribution may not really apply. Some departments do have members who are all exceptionally good—or poor. It is foolish to impose an artificially and inaccurately normal distribution on a group of people who were selected very carefully to perform exceptionally well.

A third major issue regarding peer comparisons has to do with legality. In the landmark *Moody v. Albemarle Paper Company* case, a peer comparison performance rating was used to validate a selection test. The court found this to be illegal because there were no performance evaluation guidelines; supervisors simply compared people rather than performances. In another similar case, *Watkins v. Scott Paper Co.,* a similar ruling was made. Thus an apparently simple way to avoid legal requirements for validating selection instruments is, actually, illegal. In a lower federal court case, *Brito v. Zia Company,* the court found that the company had violated Title VII of the Civil Rights Act of 1964 when it laid off certain Spanish-surnamed workers on the basis of peer comparison ratings that it couldn't prove were based on objective performance criteria.

Other cases are still proceeding through the courts but one lesson is already clear: Peer comparison is not a way around guidelines for implementation of Title VII. (It remains to be seen whether MBO systems will be found illegal on similar grounds—that is, that inequitable peer comparison judgments are being made when no equivalent performance standards exist for the appraisees.)

In some ways organizations are ultimately "zero sum" systems. For example, all organizations have limited resources for reward. Thus distribution of many rewards—promotions, pay increases, and so forth—must be zero-sum; that is, to the extent that some people get these rewards, others do not. For such purposes, one must obviously make peer comparisons. However, such comparisons need not involve everyone in the organization—not everyone is considered for promotion slots or merit pay. More important, such comparison decisions should be based on performance criteia, not on simple overall person-to-person comparison ratings.

Not all rewards are limited. Recognition for achievement, feelings of satisfaction due to the nature of the work, and many individually designed rewards (such as time off, special projects, working with friends, and so forth) are not limited. Neither is performance, and to think of performance as basically zero-sum has distinct negative consequences. Phillip Thompson and Gene Dalton, in particular, argue against the use of any technique or policy that forces one to compare workers on some absolute scale. This may be an extreme position (recall, for example, the RCA Corporation case mentioned earlier that used peer comparison in the context of an innovative development-oriented system). However, it is probably wise to avoid peer comparisons. An appraisal system that is substantially based on and emphasizes such techniques is not likely to be a good—or legal—system.

Heuristic #10: Is information that is needed for administrative actions accessible and effectively used? Our discussion has focused on appraisal activities—rating, interviewing, making reward decisions, counseling and coaching, and so forth. Remember, though, that one of the three basic appraisal system objectives is providing accurate organizational information to be used for administrative actions. Thus, we can consider the system seriously flawed if such information is not readily accessible or if there are no procedures for its use or input into relevant decision processes.

In one innovative system, appraisal information was entered into the organization's computer, but edited and coded so that individuals could not be identified without the code. This information could be accessed by any employee, with hard (printed) copy available. Administrative action notices—promotions, pay increases, terminations, transfers, and so forth—were accompanied by examples of the dat on which they were based. Anonymity was maintained by including more than one individual case in any example used. This process graphically showed how appraisal data were actually used for administrative actions, and it also let employees know what kinds of performance behaviors were being rewarded or punished.

The longer-range issue of human resources planning is frequently considered as quite separate from performance appraisal, but the type of data yielded by an effective appraisal system can be extremely useful for long-range planning. Both the RCA and Chevrolet Sales Division cases mentioned earlier involved the generation and storage of information about individuals' special strengths, training needs, and development potentials for long-range human resources planning purposes. Unfortunately, there are little hard data about how widespread such systems are today. Given our current level of computer technology, it is relatively easy to design and implement complex human resources information storage and retrieval systems. It is much more difficult to develop operational decision-making systems that make effective use of such information for long- or short-range administrative purposes.

However, with most organizations faced with increasingly "turbulent" environments, it is not enough that an appraisal system operates effectively in terms of the feedback and development functions. Administrative action issues, such as managerial succession and human resources planning, must be considered to avoid potentially disastrous problems. An appraisal system can operate effectively only when it is designed to gather relevant data, locate them in an accessible place, and feed these data into organizational decision processes as regular, expected inputs.

CONCLUSION

These ten heuristic "rule of thumb" guidelines for evaluating a performance appraisal system do not exhaust all possible important criteria. Nor are they listed in the order of their relative importance. I find it encouraging, however, that many of the specific issues and recommendations discussed here are consistent with the guidelines given by Gary Lubben, Duane Thompson, and Charles Klasson in their review of the legal aspects of performance appraisal in the May-June 1980 issue of *Personnel.*

In attempting to evaluate a specific appraisal system, it would be inappropriate to praise or condemn the system simply on the basis of these guidelines. Rather, my intent has been to lead the reader to take the long view by examining the overall picture and trying to characterize the system as a whole. One may then focus on correcting problems, redesigning the system, or changing one's own personal appraisal behaviors or procedures. Then ten guidelines should be useful for any or all of these aims.

SELECTED BIBLIOGRAPHY

The literature on performance appraisal is not voluminous, which is both a blessing and a shortcoming. It means that we can identify classic or critical works fairly easily, but it also means that there are serious gaps in our knowledge. Certainly the single best-known classic article is Douglas McGregor's "An Uneasy Look at Performance Appraisal," first published in the *Harvard Business Review* (May-June 1957). Perhaps the best currently available overview can be found in Robert I. Lazar and Walter S. Wikstrom's report, *Appraising Managerial Performance* (The Conference Board, 1977). Richard Henderson's recent textbook, *Performance Appraisal* (Reston, 1980) is less comprehensive and pragmatic but does focus on the MBO-style appraisal systems favored by the U.S. Office of Personnel Management in applying the Civil Service Reform Act of 1978 as it relates to performance appraisal in federal agencies. The best academic overview is Frank Landy and James Farr's "Performance Ratings" (*Psychological Bulletin,* January 1980).

For information on skill training, see a research paper by Gary Latham, Kenneth Wexley, and E. D. Pursell, "Training Managers to Minimize Rating Errors," in the *Journal of Applied Psychology* (October 1975). One good training program is that by Dennis Kinlaw, *Helping Skills for Human Resource Development* (University Associates, 1981).

A classic study analyzing the agreement between superiors and subordinates on the nature and definition of the subordinates' jobs is that by Norman R. F. Maier, L. Richard Hoffman, John J. Hooven, and William H. Read, *Superior-Subordinate Communication in Management* (American Management Associations, 1961, Research Study 52).

The study on involvement by L. L. Cummings, "A Field Experimental Study of the Effects of Two Performance Appraisal Systems," can be found in *Personnel Psychology* (Winter 1973). The review of goal setting by Gary Latham and Gary Yukl, "A Review of the Research on the Application of Goal Setting in Organizations," (*Academy of Management Journal,* issue No. 4, 1975) is comprehensive, while Harry Levinson's pragmatic, entertaining "Management by *Whose* Objectives?" is in the *Harvard Business Review* (July-August 1970).

Norman R. F. Maier's 1958 book on problem-solving appraisal interviews was updated in 1976. His book, *The Appraisal Interview* (University Associates, 1976), and a training package, *Appraising Performance* (both available from University Associates in San Diego) are classics. Herbert H. Meyer's work at General Electric is best known through the *Harvard Business Review* article, "Split Roles in Performance Appraisal," co-authored with Emanuel Kay and John R. P. French, Jr. (Jan/Feb. 1965). A great many technical and practice-oriented reports were published on the work at GE; the earliest is Edgar Huse and Emanuel Kay's "Improving Employee Productivity Through Work Planning" In J. W. Blood's book, *The Personnel Job in a Changing World* (American Management Associations, 1964). An excellent overview article on appraisal interviewing is Ronald Burke and D. S. Wilcox's "Characteristics of Effective Employee Performance Review and Development Meetings" (*Personnel Psychology,* Autumn 1969).

Phillip Thompson and Gene Dalton's vehement critique of peer comparison, "Performance Appraisal: Managers Beware," appeared in the *Harvard Business Review* (January-February 1970). The two key court cases I discussed are referenced as *Brito et al. v. Zia Company,* 478 F. 2d 1200, and *Moody v. Albemarle Paper Co.,* 474 F. 2d 134. (The latter decision was upheld by the Supreme Court on June 25, 1975.) A current and practice-oriented legal update can be found in a *Personnel* (May-June 1980) article by Gary Lubben, Duane Thompson, and Charles Klasson.

Two books by Elmer Burack and Nicholas Mathys, *Human Resource Planning,* (Brace-Park Press, 1980) and *Career Management in Organizations* (Brace-Park Press, 1980) do a good job of showing how appraisal information can and should fit into administrative long- and short-range planning systems.

Criteria of Appraisal Effectiveness

by Jeffrey S. Kane and Edward E. Lawler, III

Five criteria are important to consider in evaluating appraisal effectiveness: validity, reliability, discriminability, freedom from bias, and relevance. Throughout our discussion of these criteria, we shall refer to the raters or appraisers as *sources,* to the ratees or appraisees as *objects,* and to the aspects of performance on which people are being appraised as *performance dimensions* or *PDs.* In our discussion of the five effectiveness criteria, we shall lean heavily on the concept of multitrait-multimethod (MT-MM) data (Campbell and Fiske, 1959). Such data consist of ratings by two or more sources for two or more PDs on the same set of objects. By considering sources, PDs, and objects as separate factors in a three-way analysis of variance, many aspects of appraisal effectiveness can be tested for significance. Much of the discussion to follow in this section will focus on how to use the results of this kind of ANOVA to draw conclusions about appraisal effectiveness. Those desiring more background on MT-MM data and the use of ANOVA to evaluate it are referred to Campbell and Fiske (1959), Stanley (1961), Boruch et al. (1970), and Kavanagh et al. (1971).

VALIDITY

Validity is at the top of nearly everyone's list of what constitutes an effective appraisal (see e.g., Campbell et al., 1970). There also seems to be a consensus that construct validity is the only relevant type of validity to consider, since the other major type—criterion-related validity—requires the availability of a more nearly ultimate measure of job success. If the latter were available, there would be no need for an appraisal, except perhaps to identify specific performance characteristics for developmental purposes.

The conceptualization of construct validity was revolutionized by Campbell and Fiske's (1959) exposition of the multitrait-multimethod (MT-MM) matrix and subsequent methodological developments regarding its analysis (Stanley, 1961; Boruch et al., 1970; Kavanagh et al., 1971). Evidence of the construct validity of an appraisal system can be derived from an analysis of appraisal score variance attributable to source, object, and performance dimension factors, and their interaction. The needed mean square terms for this ANOVA can be obtained either by conducting a standard ANOVA of the raw data by analyzing the variance-covariance matrix in the manner shown by Stanley (1961), or by combining terms in the (MT-MM) correlation matrix.[1]

Once the mean squares have been computed for all main, interaction, and total effects, we arrive at the question of how to analyze them to assess convergent and discriminant validity. In the case of convergent validity, we encounter some serious problems with the methods that have been proposed for using ANOVA to assess it that have not been addressed in any published sources we know of. In order to establish the nature of these problems, let's first establish how the concept of convergent validity applies to performance appraisals.

Campbell and Fiske (1959) proposed the term convergent validity to refer to the extent to which multiple methods agree in their measurements of the same traits. The degree of convergent validity is reflected by the size of the monotrait-heteromethod correlations, also called the validity diagonals, of the MT-MM matrix. In our terms, each of these coefficients reflects the correlation between sources in the ratings they assign to a set of objects on a PD. The average size of these correlations is inversely proportional to the strength of the source × object interaction and directly proportional to the strength of the object main effect in the analysis of variance of the MT-MM data (Stanley, 1961; Boruch et al., 1970).

At this point a question arises as to whether convergent validity should be viewed from the standpoint of the degree to which it is present or the degree to which it is

From Performance Appraisal Effectiveness: Its Assessment and Determinants, *Research in Organizational Behavior:* Vol. 1 (Greenwich, Connecticut: JAI Press, Inc., 1979).

[1]It should be noted that there may be a problem with the latter approach. The derivations of the formulas expressing the sums of squares components in terms of the MT-MM correlations have been credited to Wolins (Boruch, et al., 1970; Kavanagh, et al., 1971), but as far as we can tell neither he nor anyone else has ever published them. Unfortunately, the first publication of the products of these derivations (Boruch, et al., 1970, p. 830) contained a serious typographical error, which resulted in the formulas for two sums of squares components being presented as identical. This error was corrected (although not with reference to the error) in an article by Kavanagh et al. that presented further underived formulas for obtaining variance components directly from the MT-MM correlations. All of these formulas have apparently been used by subsequent researchers without comment or effort to replicate the derivations. While the formulas may very well be accurate, the publication and verification of the derivations is long overdue, since they are being used rather frequently.

The standard ANOVA procedure applied to raw data can be used to obtain the needed sums of squares terms until such a time when the Wolins formulas have been properly verified. This approach should not present any problems, since computer programs (e.g., SAS-GLM, BMDSV, SPSS) that will handle any number of objects likely to be encountered are widely available.

absent. Kavanagh et al. (1971) advocate evaluating whether it is present to a significant degree, as revealed by a significant object main effect. The problems with this approach are twofold. First, the object main effect could reach significance at useless levels of convergence between sources, especially when the object sample is large. Second, the strength of the object main effect's evidence for the presence of convergent validity may be less or not significantly greater than the strength of the evidence against convergent validity provided by the source × object interaction effect. Thus, the danger exists that one may conclude that convergent validity is present when the evidence for its absence is stronger than the evidence for its presence.

Adopting a disconfirmatory approach to assessing convergent validity by testing whether the null hypothesis of no source × object interaction effect can be rejected is better than the confirmatory approach because it is more conservative. However, it too has some drawbacks. These include its excessive conservatism in larger samples and the fact that it offers no basis for concluding that convergent validity is in fact present.

A way out of this bind is to conceptualize the confirmation of convergent validity as a function of the extent to which evidence for its presence outweights evidence for its absence. This conceptualization suggests a comparison between the object main and source × object interaction effects to determine whether the former is significantly stronger than the latter. This comparison can be made by computing the ratio of the object to the source × object mean squares, which is distributed as the *F* distribution under the most typically applicable ANOVA model (PDs fixed, sources and objects random) and can be adjusted to meet *F* distribution assumptions under other models by forming quasi *F* ratios. This approach will only conclude that convergent validity is present when the confirmatory evidence is significantly greater than the disconfirmatory evidence rather than significantly greater than zero. This guarantees that at least a majority of the total variance relevant to convergent validity (i.e., the sum of the object and source × object mean squares) is due to convergence rather than to nonconvergence if the presence of convergent validity is confirmed. Thus, negligible correlations between sources in their ratings of objects would never be interpreted as indicating convergent validity, regardless of the levels of significance that they reach.

Discriminant validity is revealed by the strength of the object × PD interaction effect, which reflects the degree to which objects are ordered differently on each PD. To the extent that this effect is significant, discriminant validity is present. The *practical* significance of discriminant validity can be assessed by examining the ratio of the object × PD variance component to the total variance (i.e., the omega squared index). This ratio expresses the percent of total variance due to the tendency for objects to be ordered differently on different PDs and has the advantage of being capable of direct comparison with the same ratio obtained in other studies. Previous writers (e.g., Boruch et al., 1970; Kavanagh et al., 1971) have also proposed that the intraclass correlation of the object × PD effect constitutes an expression of the level of discriminant validity. However, this index focuses more on the consistency with which PDs are differentiated than on the differences between PDs, and therefore seems more useful as a reliability estimate than as a discriminant validity index.[2,3]

RELIABILITY

There are three basic forms of reliability: consistency between occasions, consistency between methods, and consistency between items from the same domain. Each of these has relevance to the effectiveness of appraisals under certain conditions, but only the latter two seem to be generally relevant. Consistency between occasions, known generally as test-retest reliability or stability, requires that the source, object, and context of appraisal remain stable across replications. This condition is difficult to create in the laboratory and rarely occurs in real world settings. Stability should therefore be viewed as a generally inappropriate index of appraisal reliability.

To some extent the conception of reliability as consistency between methods, generally known as inter-rater reliability, shares a drawback similar to that of stability when applied to appraisals. It is an entirely appropriate index when used in the laboratory, where the acquaintance of a number of sources with the object can be controlled. However, the assumption of identical acquaintance among sources with members of an object group is unlikely to be met in real world situations, as Borman (1974) and Klimoski and London (1974) have shown. Care should therefore be taken to ascertain that sources are comparable in their acquaintance with objects' previous performance on the PD to be rated before any importance is attached to inter-rater reliability. When this condition prevails, the MT-MM data can be used to obtain an estimate of inter-rater re-

---

[2]A word of caution should be mentioned in regard to the use of MT-MM analysis to assess convergent and discriminant validity. The technique relies on the assumption that the multiple sources employed as the method factor are equally capable of assessing each object on each PD, and that there is no dependency between the judgments of different sources. If these assumptions are seriously violated, the technique cannot be used in the form presented above. The assumption most likely to be violated in organizational settings is that sources are equally capable of assessing each object. A possible way of circumventing this problem is to substitute alternate rating techniques for sources as the method factor. The resulting dependency between methods in this case (stemming from the same sources being employed for each method) could be accounted for by adjusting the ANOVA effects through the analysis of covariance, using sources as the (dummy-coded) covariate.

[3]Appendix A contains the formulas for constructing various components under the ANOVA model appropriate for the typical appraisal research or evaluation situation (i.e., PDs fixed, sources and objects random).

liability. This estimate is provided by the intraclass correlation for the object effect, which reveals the extent to which there is more similarity in ratings within objects than between objects. Note that it is usually the average agreement of a single source with other sources that is indicative of inter-rater reliability. However, if appraisals are to consist of the collective judgments of multiple sources, the Spearman-Brown prophecy formula should be used to adjust the intraclass correlation accordingly (Winer, 1971, Tinsley and Weiss, 1975).

The final possibility conceives of reliability as consistency between items from the same domain and is generally known as internal consistency reliability. It is closely related to discriminant validity. Whereas discriminant validity addresses the issue of whether there are sufficient differences between PDs to justify considering them as distinct constructs, internal consistency focuses on whether a single construct is being measured by a purported measure of that construct. Clearly, if the distinctions between PDs are no greater than the error of measurement, no PD measure can be considered to be measuring one PD construct any more than it is measuring any other PD construct. The appraisal, therefore, must be viewed as an unreliable measure of the PDs it purports to measure. It is consequently asserted that the intraclass correlation of the object × PD ANOVA effect constitutes an estimate of the average internal consistency reliability of the ratings of the PDs comprising an appraisal system. This approach makes use of the discriminant validity ANOVA component to express the degree of purity of the constructs that were discriminated. This form of reliability and the method for measuring it holds an advantage over the previous two forms in that it is not as sensitive to differences in source acquaintance with the objects. It holds the disadvantage that if only one construct is reliably measured by several PD measures, it would ascribe zero reliability to the measurement of all PDs. However, a system that purports to measure multiple PDs but actually measures only one cannot be considered effective anyway, regardless of how reliably that one PD is measured.

DISCRIMINABILITY

The degree to which an appraisal device succeeds in differentiating among objects and thereby imparts variability to the resulting distribution of scores constitutes its discriminability. According to Garner (1960), this is the most fundamental quality that must be possessed by rating methods. Discriminability has two aspects: structural and operational.

Structural Discriminability

Structural discriminability refers to the capacity of the appraisal system itself to express the degree of differentiation existing in the object population. This is jointly determined by three characteristics of the system used to elicit and record source judgments (hereafter referred to as the response scale): its score ratio, uncertainty, and profile differentiation. The score ratio of a response scale refers to the number of response alternatives it offers relative to the number of distinct levels of the construct that are actually present in the object population. For example, suppose overall performance was being appraised on a 7-point scale, and the object population was sufficiently large so that twenty-five distinct levels of overall performance existed. In this case seven possible response alternatives are provided by the response scale relative to twenty-five distinguishable levels of performance, yielding a score ratio of 7/25, or 28 percent. Clearly, an appraisal system cannot fully reflect the degree of differentiation in an object population unless its distinguishable levels of the construct being appraised. Thus, appraisal system response scales must be characterized by score ratios of at least 100 percent if maximum discriminability is to emerge.

The uncertainty of a response scale refers to a response scale's capacity to impart information. Specifically, uncertainty is the extent to which the number of response alternatives in each region of a scale continuum varies directly with the proportion of a given object population whose performance falls within the respective region. Uncertainty reaches its highest point when the expected proportion of the object population that will be assigned each scale alternative equals $1/K$, where $K=$ the number of alternatives on the response scale. High uncertainty is a desirable characteristic of response scales, because it permits objects to be differentiated in the regions of scales where they tend to cluster. The failure to observe the uncertainty principle in the construction of appraisal rating scales is widespread. For example, the complaint is often heard that 80 percent or more of manager populations are rated at the highest one or two levels of performance. The uncertainty principle indicates that 80 percent of the response alternatives should occur in the region of highest performance in order to maximize discriminability, rather than the 15 to 40 percent typically found.[4]

---

[4]The uncertainty of a response scale is computed by the following formula:

$$U = \sum_{i=1}^{n} p(xi) \log_2 p(xi)$$

where $p(xi) =$ the probability of response alternative i being selected

The higher the value of U, the more information a scale is able to convey, and hence the more discriminating it is. Thus, the number of alternatives placed in a region of a response scale should be in direct proportion to the region's probability of being selected, up to the limit of the number of discriminable levels in the region. The use of truncated range response scales in attitude surveys reveals an implicit recognition of this principle. However, little or no such recognition of it exists in the area of appraisal; its explicit recognition as a relevant standard by which to evaluate appraisal systems is long overdue.

The third and perhaps the most important aspect of response scales is profile differentiation. Most existing methods of appraisal require sources to characterize each object's performance in terms of a single point on a continuum of goodness (i.e., satisfactoriness). The only appraisal methods that do not fit this description include ranking, forced distribution, and other methods that focus directly on each object's standing in a group. In order to select a single goodness level to represent an object's performance in a PD, the source must make a summary judgment about all the times that the object performed in the PD during the appraisal period. For some PDs this might, of course, involve hundreds of performance instances. These instances of exhibiting a PD can be represented in terms of the proportion of the total number of instances that occurred at each of the levels comprising the goodness continuum. This way of representing the instances of exhibiting a PD will be called a *performance distribution.* The source's task in most rating systems can therefore be conceived as one of attempting to select a single goodness level to represent an entire performance distribution.

Like any other distribution, a performance distribution has a variety of parameters on which its distinguishing features are manifested. These include the distribution's mean, median, mode, variance, kurtosis, skewness, and its definitional equation. Despite this multiplicity of available parameters, the research of human judgment suggests that when forced to characterize a series of events in terms of a single point on an evaluative continuum, people tend to select what they consider to be the average or expected value of the series. Discounting the other features of the frequency distribution of the events in the series is in fact optimal behavior from a statistical perspective: When a distribution is to be represented by a single point on the continuum over which it extends, the error in such a representation is minimized by the use of the mean. Any tendency sources may have to moderate their judgments by considering other features of the object's distribution such as the variability of performance is actually suppressed by anchoring the intervals of the goodness continuum in behavioral terms. Such behavioral anchoring prevents consideration of the overall goodness of the distribution of performance and focuses the source's attention more directly on the object's typical way or outcome of performing.

Ignoring all of the distinctions between people's performance distributions except for their average or expected values can only be rationalized by taking the view that performance is completely determined by stable intra-individual characteristics (i.e., traits). Under such a view, the average of a performance distribution represents an object's true level on the relevant underlying trait. All instances of the object's exhibiting higher or lower goodness levels are ascribed to measurement error, and any deviation of the performance distribution from normality is ascribed to sampling error. However, this view of performance ignores the massive accumulation of evidence that performance, and human behavior generally, is determined at least as much by variable intra- and extra-individual factors as by traits. For example, the effect of variable motivational states is commonly seen in the tendency for periods of high achievement to often be followed by slacking-off periods; and conversely, for periods of "coasting alone" to be followed by compensatory flurries of achievement. Differences in the extent to which people were successful in overcoming the adverse influences of variations in such internal and external factors can therefore be seen as leading to more and less desirable patterns of performance. These differences in the patterns of performance exhibited over a period are reflected in all of the parameters of performance distributions, not just in their means. It follows that differences on the other parameters cannot be viewed as random error but must instead be considered to reflect meaningful distinctions between the ways that people performed—distinctions that are being ignored by virtually all existing appraisal systems.

The way to ensure that appraisals reflect all the distinguishing features of each performance distribution is to elicit ratings in terms of the rates at which each object exhibited the given PD at a series of benchmark goodness levels. The representation of an object's performance distribution that results from this rating process then has to be scored in a way that meaningfully expresses the combined goodness of the distribution on all of its parameters. These specifications can be met through a scoring system that uses profile similarity measures to express the proximity of obtained and ideal distributions along the three parameters of profile variability: elevation, shape, and scatter. This approach to eliciting and scoring ratings of performance over a series of trials will be called *distributional measurement,* and represents what we feel is a new paradigm for the appraisal of performance.

The use of an appraisal method that requires sources to evaluate performance in terms of a single point on a goodness continuum, and that thereby ignores most of the distinguishing features of performance distributions, may not raise serious problems when only gross discriminations are to be made for purposes such as allocating merit pay increases. However, the inadequacy of such methods does raise serious problems when appraisals are used as the bases for promotions and as criteria in the validation of selection and training programs. Range restriction in performance and criterion validity are usually the principal problems to be overcome in such applications of appraisal, and the needed increases in variance and validity can only be achieved through a distributional measurement method that can accurately express all the distinctions among performances.

This extended discussion has been necessary in order to make apparent the important implications of the third aspect of structural discriminability—profile differentiation. This aspect refers to the extent to which a response scale yields measurements that can be scored in distributional measurement terms that express all differences between performance distributions. Nothing approaching maximum discriminability can be achieved unless the response scale can be scored to express more of the differences between performance distributions than merely those between their means.

Operational Discriminability

Operational discriminability refers to the extent to which the actual use of an appraisal system succeeds in distinguishing members of a population. The index of this form of discriminability is derived from MT-MM data. It is simply the significance of the object main effect relative to residual error. The magnitude of this effect can be expressed in terms of the omega squared of its variance component, which is useful for comparisons across studies. Note that this third use of the object main effect is different from the previous two. Its use in assessing convergent validity involved comparing it to the source × object interaction instead of to residual error. Its use in assessing inter-rater reliability focused on expressing the percent of total object variance that was true variance.

FREEDOM FROM BIAS

Bias is the systematic tendency for sources to make assessments without regard to actual differences between objects (people), constructs (i.e., performance dimensions), or both. This definition implies three basic forms of bias, each of which can be conceptualized in terms of MT-MM ANOVA effects. Object bias refers to the tendency for some sources to rank certain objects consistently higher or lower than do other sources across all PDs. As such, it is a disregard of actual differences among objects and a bias for or against certain objects. Guilford (1954) referred to this bias as relative halo, and pointed out that its presence is revealed by a significant source × object interaction effect. In light of our previous discussion of this ANOVA component, we can also view this bias as a major cause of decrements in convergent validity.

Construct bias refers to the tendency for some sources to rank certain performance constructs higher or lower than do other sources. It may therefore be viewed as a disregard of actual differences between PDs in service of a preconceived notion about the relationships between PDs. This bias, which is reflected by a significant source × PD interaction effect, seems to express the influence of different *implicit theories of performance* held by the sources. Such implicit theories about the interrelationships of many other human characteristics have been well-established as having an influence on judgments of such characteristics (e.g., Mulaik, 1964; Passini and Norman, 1966; Rosenberg and Sedlak, 1972). However, the existence of implicit theories of performance has yet to be explored with respect to whether appraisals are reflections of external reality or of the internal belief systems of sources.

Finally, source bias refers to the tendency of some sources to give higher or lower ratings regardless of the object or PD being assessed. When such a condition prevails, the ANOVA will reveal a significant source main effect. This bias has been variously referred to elsewhere as a leniency or severity bias.

RELEVANCE

This final criterion of appraisal effectiveness refers to the extent to which the entire domain of performance, and no extraneous domains, is accurately represented by the PDs on which an appraisal system assesses objects. Brogden and Taylor (1950) posited three dimensions of relevance that have stood the test of time. Slightly changed to orient them toward the primary purpose of appraisal—discrimination between objects—they are as follows:

1. *Deficiency:* The extent to which an appraisal system *fails* to include all of the performance dimensions for which the organization holds recognized standards for satisfactory levels of performance.
2. *Contamination:* The extent to which an appraisal system includes performance dimensions for which an organization holds no recognized standards for satisfactory levels of performance.
3. *Distortion:* The extent to which prevailing standards on the relevant value criterion call for different weights than: a) those being used to differentiate the goodness of the various ways or outcomes of performing on each dimension, b) those being used to differentiate the influence of *scores* on different performance dimensions on composite scores, or c) both *a* and *b*.

The deficiency dimension of relevance can be assessed through evaluation of the process through which a system was developed. If the process considered for inclusion all performance dimensions on which any party with a formal interest in how well a job is performed recognizes standards, and if it selected PDs for inclusion on the basis of a rigorous assessment of the degree to which standards on them were generally recognized by sources and objects (i.e., the definitiveness of standards), confidence in the system's freedom from deficiency can be high. To the extent that such a course was not followed, the resulting system must be considered deficient until proven otherwise. Post hoc evaluation of a system is possible and requires an assessment of whether the interested parties perceive that any PDs on which they recognize definitive standards were excluded from the system.

Contamination can be quantitatively assessed by collecting data from the salient source and object populations on their perceptions of the standards for satisfactory and unsatisfactory performance on each PD. If the standards for all PDs included in the system are found to be significantly definitive, the system can be considered free from contamination.

Finally, assessing freedom from distortion in the weights attached to the ways or outcomes of performing within each performance dimension, or to the performance dimensions themselves, requires the comparison of the actual weights to consensus weights derived from surveys of formally interested parties. Care should be taken to use effective rather than nominal weights (i.e.g, the weights nominally assigned), as the actual weights is the case of performance dimensions. Each performance dimension's effective weight is computed as the product of its variance and the square of its nominal weight.

REFERENCES

- Borman, W.C. (1974) "The Rating of Individuals in Organizations: An Alternate Approach," *Organizational Behavior and Human Performance 12:* 105–124.
- Boruch, R.F., J.D. Larkin, L. Wolins, and A.C. MacKinney (1970) "Alternate Methods of Analysis: Multitrait-Multimethod Data." *Educational and Psychological Measurement 30:* 833–853.
- Brogden, H.E., and E.K. Taylor (1952) "The Theory and Classification of Criterion Bias," *Educational and Psychological Measurement 10:* 159–186.
- Campbell, D.T., and D.W. Fiske (1959) "Convergent and Discriminant Validation by the Multitrait-Multimethod Matrix," *Psychological Bulletin 56:* 81–105.
- Campbell, J.P., M.D. Dunnette, E.E. Lawler and K.E. Weick (1970) *Managerial Behavior, Performance, and Effectiveness,* New York: McGraw-Hill.
- Garner, W.R. (1960) "Rating Scales, Discriminability, and Information Transmission." *Psychological Review 67:* 343–356.
- Guilford, J.P. (1954) *Psychometric Methods, (2nd edition),* New York: McGraw-Hill.
- Kavanagh, M.J., A.C. MacKinney, and L. Wolins (1971) "Issues in Managerial Performance: Multitrait-Multimethod Analyses of Ratings." *Psychological Bulletin 75:* 34–49.
- Klimoski, R.J., and M. London (1974) "Role of the Rater in Performance Appraisal." *Journal of Applied Psychology 59:* 445–451.
- Malaik, S.A. (1964) "Are Personality Factors Raters' Conceptual Factors?" *Journal of Consulting Psychology:* 506–511.
- Passini, F.T. and W. Norman (1966) "A Universal Conception of Personality Structure?," *Journal of Personality and Social Psychology 4:* 44–49.
- Rosenberg, S. and A. Sedlak (1972) "Structural Representations of Implicit Personality Theory," in L. Berkowitz (ed.). *Advances in Experimental Social Psychology,* Volume 6, New York: Academic Press, Inc.
- Stanley, J.C. (1961) "Analysis of Unreplicated Three-way Classifications with Applications to Rater Bias and Trait Independence." *Psychometrika 26:* 205–219.
- Tinsley, H.A. and D.J. Weiss (1975) "Interrater Reliability and Agreement of Subjective Judgments." *Journal of Counseling Psychology 22:* 353–376.
- Winer, B.J. (1971) *Statistical Principles in Experimental Design (2nd ed.).* New York: McGraw-Hill.

Performance Rating

by Frank J. Landy and James L. Farr

The measurement of performance in industrial settings has occupied the attention of psychologists for 50 years. Performance description and prediction plays an important role in all personnel decisions. Criteria are necessary for validation studies and training evaluation; indices of effectiveness or relative worth are necessary for feedback and employee counseling; there is even some indication that the process of performance evaluation may function as a reward and be capable of inducing feelings of satisfaction in some employees (Landy, Barnes, & Murphy, 1978).

Unfortunately, realizing the importance of performance measurement and actually measuring performance accurately are two different matters. In some ideal sense, complete performance measurement would include the combination of objective, personnel, and judgmental indices (Landy & Trumbo, in press). Unfortunately, it is difficult to obtain objective indices of performance for many job titles. In addition, personnel information is applicable to a small portion of the employee population in any organization (e.g., 5¢ of the employees may have 100% of the accidents, less than 8% of the employees may have more than one unexcused absence per year, tardiness records are not well kept, etc.).

Consequently, most individuals concerned with performance measurement depend on judgmental indices of

From *Psychological Bulletin, 87*(1), 1980, 72–107.

We are indebted to Janet Barnes for help with the literature review.

one type or another. Guion (1965) reported that 81% of the published studies in the *Journal of Applied Psychology* and *Personnel Psychology* between 1950 and 1955 used ratings as criteria. Blum and Naylor (1968) sampled articles from the *Journal of Applied Psychology* for the period from 1960 to 1965 and found that of those using criterion measurement, 46% measured performance via judgmental indices. Landy and Farr (1976) reported that 89% of 196 police departments in major metropolitan areas used supervisory ratings as the primary form of performance measurement. Finally, Landy and Trumbo (in press) reported that a literature review of validation studies in the *Journal of Applied Psychology* between 1965 and 1975 revealed that ratings were used as the primary criterion in 72% of the cases. By any standard, judgmental measurements of performance are widely used.

In spite of the widespread use of judgmental indices of performance, there has been a constant dissatisfaction with these measures on the part of both researcher and practitioner. The source of this dissatisfaction has been the vulnerability of these measures to both intentional and inadvertent bias. As a consequence, an enormous amount of research has been conducted in an attempt to improve the validity of judgmental indices of performance. These studies have covered a wide variety of issues, such as rater and ratee individual differences, types of formats, conditions surrounding the judgmental process, and so forth. In this article, we review the outcomes of this research.

We limit the scope of this review to a consideration of one particular form of performance judgment—the performance rating. We choose to concentrate on this method for three reasons: (a) As indicated in earlier reviews (Guion, 1965; Landy & Farr, 1976; Landy & Trumbo, in press), the rating is by far the most ubiquitous form of performance judgment; (b) research on various aspects of rating is more common than research on any other judgmental index of performance, and (c) other judgmental methods, such as ranking, pair comparison estimation, and other forms of worker-to-worker comparison, imply a qualitatively different discrimination process. Thus, the review deals primarily with a consideration of rating methods. In addition, since Wherry (Note 1) completed an exhaustive review of performance rating research prior to 1950, we deal predominantly with the literature appearing subsequent to that review. Other reviews have appeared since 1950 (e.g., Barrett, 1966b; J. P. Campbell, Dunnette, Lawler, & Weick, 1970; Lopez, 1968; Miner, 1972; Smith, 1976) but these have generally been more narrowly focused than is the present review.

We exclude detailed consideration of several broader issues in the measurement of job performance. These include such issues as the dynamic nature of criteria (B. M. Bass, 1962; Ghiselli & Haire, 1960; Prien, 1966), the composite criterion versus multiple criteria controversy (Dunnette, 1963; Guion, 1961; Schmidt & Kaplan, 1971) and the relationship of ratings to more general theories or models of human performance (James, 1973). These are excluded because they deal with all forms of criterion measures, not just ratings of performance. Their inclusion would necessitate extensive space that is not available, and their discussion would not be appropriate here. The relationships between performance rating and broader organizational questions of selection, training, counseling, and job satisfaction are generally not addressed. Works by Barrett (1966b), Lopez (1968), and Miner (1972), among others, address many of these relationships.

The literature in the area of performance rating is fragmented. Some do research on different rating formats, whereas others examine characteristics of raters and ratees. This insularity has tended to obscure the fact that performance rating is best thought of as a system comprising many different classes of variables. The rating instrument and the characteristics of raters and ratees are only parts of that larger system. At a general level, that system might include the following classes of variables: (a) the roles (rater and ratee), (b) the vehicle (the rating instrument), (c) the rating context (the type of organization, the purpose for rating, etc.), (d) the rating process (administrative constraints, individual rater strategies, etc.), and (e) the results of the rating (raw and transformed performance information, actions based on that information, etc.). Our review deals with research results bearing on those major classes of variables. Figure 1 is a graphic representation of how those components might interact. Although Figure 1 might be heuristically helpful in structuring the body of the review, it is not particularly illuminating with respect to the specific influences affecting the judgment that one person makes of another's performance. Consequently, after reviewing the available research evidence, we present a more elaborate model of the performance rating process that should be more theoretically useful than Figure 1.

There are some unique constraints on the performance rating literature. Consider the phenomenon in question. Typically, a supervisor is asked to consider the past performance of one or more subordinates. The period of past performance is typically 1 year. During that period of time, the supervisor and the subordinate have interacted frequently and probably know each other reasonably well. Most research on the topic of performance rating has considered the adequacy of rating in this type of context. For that reason, we have excluded from consideration studies dealing with the evaluation of applicants in interview situations. This literature has been well covered elsewhere and is not directly relevant to traditional performance rating. We conceive of the prototypic performance rating as a retrospective synthesis by one individual of the efforts or performance of another. Thus, we are dealing with an appraisal

[1]Wherry, R.J. *Control of bias in rating: Survey of the literature* (Tech. Rep. DA-49-0853 OSA 69). Washington, D.C.: Department of the Army, Personnel Research Section, September 1950.

of a long string of actions rather than a single one; in addition, we are dealing with a constellation of activities rather than with single physical or mental operations in isolation.[1] We have included in the review studies of simulated work settings that have experimentally manipulated variables of interest to performance rating, if the behaviors of the ratees were observable rather than represented only by a pencil-and-paper task.

Since the research on performance appraisal is predominantly in the form of field studies, we are unable to make comparisons from one study to another to make comparisons from one study to another with respect to the dimensions of performance examined. Each organization has a different idea of what may be important in assessing their people; consequently, each rating instrument is ultimately unique. This is unfortunate, since there is every reason to believe that different types of performance may be evaluated more or less accurately than others. For example, interpersonal skills might be more accurately evaluated than creativity. However, this is a source of variation over which we have no control as reviewers. These are the structural boundaries of the review.

FIGURE 1
Component Model of Performance Rating

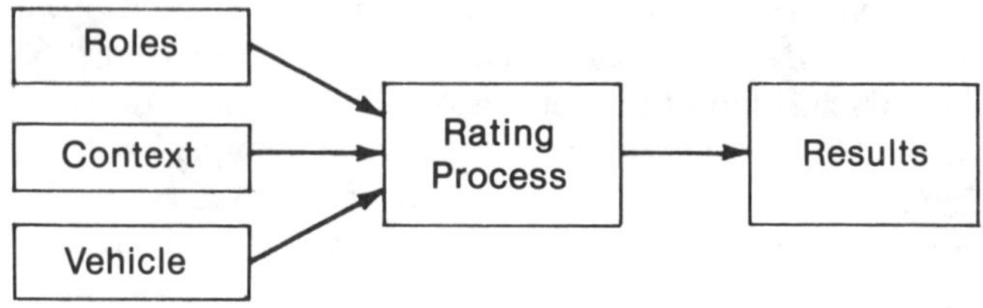

ROLES

Rater Characteristics

A great deal of research has examined the relationship between characteristics of the rater and various criteria of rating effectiveness. These studies are grouped into three classes: personal characteristics of the rater, type of rater vis-à-vis the ratee, and rater knowledge of the ratee and the job.

Personal characteristics. Among the personal characteristics of the rater that have been investigated as possible sources of rating variation are demographic variables, psychological variables, and job-related variables.

The most popular demographic variable has been the sex of the rater. These studies have all been published since 1970. In the majority of these studies, there has been no consistent effect of rater sex on ratings obtained in various contexts, including instructional settings (Elmore & LaPointe, 1974, 1975; Centra & Linn, Note 2), simulated work settings (Rosen & Jerdee, 1973), and laboratory research settings (Jacobson & Effertz, 1974; Mischel, 1974). Lee and Alvares (1977) found that rater sex affected the description of supervisory behavior but not the evaluation of such behavior. In a simulated work setting, London and Poplawski (1976), studying college students' evaluations in simulated appraisal and interview situations, found that female subjects gave higher ratings on some dimensions but not on overall performance. Hamner, Kim, Baird, and Bigoness (1974) found that females gave higher ratings than did males when evaluating performance in a simulated work setting, especially for high levels of performance.

Several studies have examined the effect of the race of the rater on ratings. Research conducted by the Educational Testing Service in conjunction with the U.S. Civil Service Commission (Crooks, Note 3) found that in a majority of cases, supervisory raters gave higher ratings to subordinates of their own race than to subordinates of a different race. Hamner et al. (1974) found results similar to those reported in Crooks, but the effect accounted for only 2% of the rating variance. DeJung and Kaplan (1962) and Cox and Krumboltz (1958) obtained results comparable to those of Crooks, with stronger effects for black raters. Schmidt and Johnson (1973), examining peer ratings in an industrial setting, found no race of rater effect. The work setting in which this research took place was highly integrated with subjects who had been exposed to human relations training. The ratings were gathered for research purposes only and required a prescribed distribution. It is likely that some or all of these factors influenced the results of this study.

Mandell (1956) and Klores (1966) have examined the effects of rater age on performance ratings. Mandell found that younger supervisors were less lenient in their ratings of subordinates, whereas Klores found no effect of supervisor age in his study of forced-distribution ratings.

The education level of raters was examined by Cascio and Valenzi (1977). They found a significant effect of rater education on supervisory ratings of the job performance of police officers, but the effect accounted for such a small percentage of total rating variance that Cascio and Valenzi concluded that rater education was of no practical importance in their study.

A large number of psychological variables have been studied as possible influences on performance ratings. Un-

[1] We are grateful to an anonymous reviewer for helping us to elaborate this position.

[2] Centra, J. A., & Linn, R. L. *Student points of view in ratings of college instruction* (ETS RB 73-60). Princeton, N.J.: Educational testing Service, 1973.

[3] Crooks, L. A. (Ed.). *An investigation of sources of bias in the prediction of job performance: A six-year study.* Princeton, N.J.: Educational Testing Service, 1972.

fortunately, in most instances, there has been only a single study investigating any one variable. Thus, general conclusions are difficult, if not impossible, to make about their effects.

Mandell (1956) found that raters who were low in self-confidence were less lenient in their ratings of subordinates than raters high in self-confidence. Lewis and Taylor (1955) reported that individuals high in anxiety tended to use more extreme response categories than those lower in anxiety. Rothaus, Morton, and Hanson (1965) found that increased psychological distance of the rater tended to result in ratings that were more critical and negative.

In a study of rater policy using regression and cluster analytic methodology, Zedeck and Kafry (1977) investigated whether several psychological variables would be related to how a rater used performance information to form overall ratings of performance. Their results indicated that interest measures, social insight, and intelligence measures (verbal or nonverbal) were not significantly related to the rating strategies of the subjects.

Schneier (1977) found that the cognitive complexity of raters had an effect on ratings. Cognitive complex raters were less lenient and demonstrated less restrictions of range with behaviorally anchored scales than did cognitively simple raters. The cognitively complex raters also exhibited less halo in their ratings than did the simple raters, with both behavioral scales and a simpler form of rating scale. Cognitively complex raters also preferred the behaviorally anchored scale to the simple format.

Among the personal characteristics of the rater that can be thought of as job-related variables are the rater's job experience, performance level, and leadership style. The results of studies that examined the rater's length of job experience are mixed. Jurgensen (1950) found that more experienced raters had more reliable ratings, and Mandrell (1956) noted that raters with more than 4 years of experience as supervisors tended to be more lenient in their ratings than were raters with less experience. Klores (1966) obtained no significant effect of rater experience. Cascio and Valenzi (1977) found a significant effect of rater experience but noted that it accounted for only a small percentage of total rating variance.

Several studies have found that the performance level of the rater affects the nature of the ratings assigned to others by that rater. D. E. Schneider and Bayroff (1953) and Bayroff, Haggerty, and Rundquist (1954) reported that peers who received high aptitude test scores and were rated positively during training gave ratings of their fellow trainees that were more valid in predicting subsequent job performance. Mandell (1956) found no difference in central tendency between good and poor job performers but did find that those raters who were poor performers tended to disagree more with consensus ratings of subordinates than did the more favorable performers. Kirchner and Reisberg (1962) found that the ratings given to subordinates by supervisors high in job performance were characterized by greater range, less central tendency, and by more emphasis being placed on the independent action of subordinates as the basis for ratings. In a related study Mullins and Force (1962) obtained evidence for a generalized ability to rate others accurately. Peer raters who were more accurate in judging one skill of their coworkers also were accurate in judging another performance dimension. (Accuracy was assessed by comparing the ratings with scores on pencil-and-paper tests.)

The effects of the rater's leadership style on the ratings have been examined by E. K. Taylor, Parker, Martens, and Ford (1959). They found that production-oriented supervisors gave lower ratings to subordinates. Klores (1966) reported that raters who were high in consideration were more lenient in their ratings of subordinates than were raters who were high in initiation of structure. Those raters high in initiation of structure exhibited more range in their ratings and gave more weight to the planning and organization function when evaluating their subordinates' overall job performance. Zedeck and Kafry (1977) found that leadership style was not correlated with rater strategies, as identified by regression and cluster analytic techniques.

Type of rater. The studies reviewed in this section are concerned with rating differences obtained with raters who differed in the type of relationship they held in regard to the ratee (e.g., supervisor, peer, self, or subordinate). Studies that focused on only one type of rater are generally not reviewed here. Discussions of investigators that deal with the various single types of raters are available elsewhere (e.g., Guion, 1965; Kane & Lawler, 1978; Lewin & Zwany, 1976).

The most frequent rater type comparison has been that of supervisory rating versus peer rating. These studies have generally demonstrated differences between the two rater types. Springer (1953), Rothaus et al. (1965), and Zedeck, Imparato, Krausz, and Oleno (1974) found that supervisors were less lenient in their ratings than were the peers of the ratees. Klieger and Mosel (1953) and Springer both found that there was more interrater agreement with supervisory ratings than with peer ratings, but L. V. Gordon and Medland (1965) reported greater reliability for peer ratings of leadership than for similar supervisory ratings.

Although Booker and Miller (1966) obtained general agreement between peers' and instructors' ratings of Reserve Officers' Training Corps students, Springer (1953) and Borman (1974) reported less supervisor-peer agreement than was found within either type of rater group. Data reported by Borman (1974) and Zedeck et al. (1974) suggest that supervisor-peer rating differences may be expected and do not necessarily suggest that either type of rating is invalid or unreliable. Borman (1974), as well as Landy, Farr, Saal, and Freytag (1976), found that the dimensions of job performance resulting from the development of behavior-anchored scales for use by peers and supervisors differed. Zedeck et al. obtained similar dimensions of performance for the two rater types, when developing behavior-anchored scales but did find that the specific examples of job behaviors used to anchor the dimensions differed between the two rater types. Thus, supervisory and peer ratings may represent two distinct views of a common individual's job performance and may be equally valid, even though they are not highly correlated.

Supervisory ratings have also been compared with the ratees' self-ratings. Parker, Taylor, Barrett, and Martens (1959) and Kirchner (1965) found that self-ratings were more lenient than supervisory ratings, but Heneman (1974) found less leniency with self-ratings than with supervisory ratings. Heneman's data were gathered for research purposes via a mailed questionnaire that was returned to the researcher. These factors may have affected his results. Kirchner and Heneman reported more halo in supervisory ratings than in self-ratings, whereas Parker et al. found no differences in halo. Both Kirchner and Parker et al. reported only moderate agreement between supervisory ratings and self-ratings.

Lawler (1967) and Klimoski and London (1974) examined self-, supervisory, and peer ratings of performance. Lawler found that supervisory and peer ratings exhibited greater convergent and discriminant validity than did self-ratings. Klimoski and London reported that each rater type was distinct, with regard to use of information, and that supervisory and peer rating strategies were more similar than self-ratings. Supervisory ratings demonstrated a strong correlation between effort and performance ratings, whereas peer ratings and self-ratings differentiated between effort and performance.

A few studies have compared peer ratings to other nonsupervisory ratings. Bartlett (1959) reported that whereas peer ratings on a forced-choice scale of leadership were useful for both evaluative and diagnostic purposes, self-ratings on a similar scale were adequate only for diagnostic purposes. Centra (Note 4) compared peer and student ratings of college instructors. Peer ratings were found to be more lenient and to have lower interrater agreement than the student ratings.

Freeberg (1969), Fiske and Cox (1960), and Rothaus et al. (1965) compared peer ratings with observer ratings in various role-playing and group activities. Fiske and Cox and Rothaus et al. found that peer ratings were more lenient than observer ratings. Freeberg reported that when peers and observers had similar relevant contact with the ratee, peer ratings were more valid predictors of cognitive skills than were the observer ratings. Kraut (1975) also found that peer ratings in a month-long management training program were more predictive of promotion and future performance appraisals than were ratings by the training staff.

Rater knowledge of ratee and job. Although some minimum rater knowledge of the ratee's job performance and of the job in question is certainly necessary before valid ratings can be obtained, the extent of knowledge that is necessary has been a focus of much research. Several studies have found only low to moderate agreement among the ratings made by supervisors at differing organizational levels, relative to the ratee (Berry, Nelson, & McNally, 1966; Borman & Dunnette, 1975; J. P. Campbell, Dunnette, Arvey, & Hellervik, 1973). Whitla and Tirrell (1953) found that first-level supervisors' ratings more accurately predicted job knowledge test scores of subordinates than did the ratings of second- or third-level supervisors. Zedeck and Baker (1972) reported better construct validity for ratings by first-level supervisors than for those by second-level supervisors. Individuals with more knowledge of the requirements of the particular job have been found to be less influenced by serial position (Wagner & Hoover, 1974) and to more validly predict future performance (Amir, Kovarsky, & Sharan, 1970) than individuals with less knowledge of the job requirements.

The amount and type of contact between the rater and ratee has also been of concern to performance appraisal researchers. Although Ferguson (1949) reported that reliability of ratings increased as the amount of rater-reported acquaintance with the ratee increased, more recent research has not generally supported this finding. Klieger and Mosel (1953) found no effect of rater-reported opportunity to observe the rater on rating reliability. Fiske and Cox (1960), L. V. Gordon and Medland (1965), and Klores (1966) found no effect of length of rater acquaintance with ratee. Hollander (1957, 1965) found no differences in peer rating reliability or validity for ratees who had been acquainted for 3, 6, or 12 weeks. Brown (1968) found that peer raters were not influenced by degree of acquaintance but that untrained peer raters' ratings were characterized by increased halo for less well-known ratees. Waters and Waters (1970), Amir et al. (1970), and Suci, Vallance, and Glickman (1956) reported little or no effect on the validity or reliability of ratings, when the rater's friendship with the ratee was considered. Finally, Freeberg (1969) reported that the relevance of the rater-ratee acquaintance was important in terms of the validity of the ratings. Raters who interacted with the ratees in a situation relevant to the dimension being rated were more valid in their evaluations than were raters who interacted with the ratees in a nonrelevant situation. Similarly, Landy and Guion (1970) reported that raters with daily but peripheral contact with ratees had a median interrater reliability of .24, in contrast to a median reliability of .62 for those raters with more relevant contacts with the ratees. Thus, relevancy rather than frequency of contact appears to be the critical factor.

Summary

The research on rater characteristics provides relatively few general conclusions. Since most studies examine only one

[4] Centra, J. A. *Colleagues as raters of classroom instruction* (ETS RB 74-18). Princeton, N.J.: Educational Testing Service, 1974.

or a few characteristics, it is likely that unmeasured or unreported variables have had some effect on the results of any single study. This results in a chaotic pattern of findings in many instances. Nevertheless, some generally consistent effects can be described. Sex of the rater does not generally affect ratings, although female raters may be more lenient. Raters usually give higher ratings to same-race ratees, although this may be moderated by the degree of contact that members of each race have with each other. Rater age and education have been studied too infrequently to make general statements about their effects.

Psychological characteristics of raters have not been systematically researched, but it appears (and has been empirically demonstrated to some extent) that cognitive complexity may be an important variable to examine. There is a large body of research in other content areas which suggests that cognitive complexity affects information processing and evaluation.

Rater experience appears to positively affect the quality of performance ratings, but the mechanism or mechanisms responsible (e.g., more training or experience with the rating form, better observation skills, better knowledge of the job requirements, etc.) is not known. The general job performance of the rater is related to rating quality, with better performers also providing higher quality ratings. Production-oriented (as opposed to interaction-oriented) raters seem to be less lenient and to pay more attention to planning activities.

Comparisons of different types of raters suggest that in general, one should expect only low to moderate correlations among raters of different types (e.g., peer, supervisory, self, etc.). It cannot be stated that any one type of rater is more valid than any other, although peer ratings appear to be especially useful for predicting promotions. Peer ratings appear to be more lenient than supervisory ratings. As Borman (1974) and others have suggested, the best conclusion may be that different types of raters have different perspectives on performance that influence their ratings. Lawler (1967) and Blood (1974) have noted that these differences may provide valuable information for the diagnosis of organizational problems.

Raters require knowledge of the individual ratee and of the requirements of the ratee's job to adequately evaluate job performance. The relevance of the rater-ratee interaction is apparently more important than simply the amount of interaction.

Ratee Characteristics

The research on the effects of the ratee characteristics on performance ratings is divided into two broad categories: personal characteristics and job-related variables.

Personal characteristics of the ratee. The two ratee characteristics that have been examined most frequently in recent research have been sex and race. Much of the research concerned with ratee sex supports the hypothesis that the sex stereotype of the occupation (i.e., whether a particular job is typically perceived as masculine or feminine) interacts with the sex of the ratee. Studies in which the occupation would be likely to be perceived as masculine (e.g., managerial positions) have found that females received less favorable evaluations than did males (Schmitt & Hill, 1977). In addition, Terborg and Ilgen (1975) found in an in-basket exercise that whereas female ratees received ratings similar to those of males, females received lower salaries and less challenging job assignments. Rosen and Jerdee (1973) and Bartol and Butterfield (1976) reported in simulation studies that the sex of the supervisor influenced the rater's perceptions of the appropriate behavior of the supervisor in a sex stereotypic fashion. Elmore and LaPointe (1974, 1975) found that students gave essentially equal ratings to male and female college instructors, an occupation perhaps perceived as less sex specific than management jobs. Lee and Alvares (1977) obtained no effect of ratee sex on evaluations of interviewers. Once again, perhaps the job of interviewer is considered to be neither masculine nor feminine. Bigoness (1976) and Hamner et al. (1974) examined ratee sex effects in semiskilled and low-skilled tasks. Bigoness and Hamner et al. both found that females received higher ratings than did males in a simulation study in which objective performance was controlled. Again, since sex stereotypes were not measured, it is difficult to determine if these studies support the interaction hypothesis. Jacobson and Effertz (1974) obtained results opposite to those predicted by the sex role stereotype hypthesis. They found that male leaders were evaluated more negatively than were female leaders but that male followers received higher ratings than did female followers. It should be noted that many of the studies that examined the effects of ratee sex on evaluations were simulations. Relatively few studies (Elmore & LaPointe, 1974, 1975; Schmitt & Hill, 1977) have been conducted in which real-world performance of the ratee was being rated.

The effect of the race of the ratee has been examined in several studies. Most of these investigations have used ratings of the real-world performance of ratees as the behavior of interest, whereas some have used simulation methodology. Ratees have been found to receive higher ratings from same-race raters by Crooks (Note 3), DeJung and Kaplan (1962), and Hamner et al. (1974), whereas Schmidt and Johnson (1973) found no such effect with peer ratings that were obtained in a highly integrated setting. Landy and Farr (1976) reported that supervisors (the large majority of whom were white) rated the performance of white police officers more favorably than that of black officers on four of eight rating dimensions.

Other studies have demonstrated an interaction between ratee race and ratee performance level. Bigoness (1976) and Hamner et al. (1974), both using videotaped task performance controlled for level, found interactions of race and objective performance levels. Bigoness reported that among low performers, blacks were rated more favorably than were whites, whereas there were no racial differences for the high performers. Hamner et al. found that raters significantly differentiated between high and low white performers but did not for black ratees.

Huck and Bray (1976) and Schmitt and Hill (1977) both examined ratings gathered in assessment center settings. Huck and Bray found that black female assessees received lower ratings than did white female assessees. The validities of those ratings for predicting future job performance were about equal for blacks and whites. The black women also received lower criterion ratings than the white women. Schmitt and Hill reported that black female assessees tended to receive lower ratings when their assessment center group was composed principally of white males than when the group was better integrated in terms of race and sex.

Several studies that were primarily interested in the validity of selection devices for black and white workers have reported data for performance ratings for the racial subgroups. Farr, O'Leary, and Bartlett (1971) found that white employees received higher performance ratings than blacks in 13 of 22 comparisons. The other 9 comparisons revealed no differences in the rating means for the two groups. Greenhaus and Gavin (1972) reported that white employees were rated higher than blacks on all three supervisory ratings used in their study. Toole, Gavin, Murdy, and Sells (1972) split their workers into younger and older subgroups, the cutoff being age 35. There were no racial differences on a rating measure for the older workers, but white workers received higher ratings than did blacks in the younger group. Kirkpatrick, Ewen, Barrett, and Katzell (1968) found only one significant difference among 8 possible comparisons of rating means for black and white workers. In that one case the white workers received a higher rating than black workers. Crooks (Note 3) reported that white employees were rated more favorably than were black employees but that white employees also received a higher mean score on an objective test of job knowledge. Fox and Lefkowitz (1974) found no mean racial difference for a supervisory rating measure.

A. R. Bass and Turner (1973) found no significant mean differences for black and white raters, when age and job tenure were held constant for full-time employees, and they found small but statistically significant racial differences (with white ratees evaluated more favorably) for part-time workers. However, ratings of black and white employees were differentially related to more objective criterion measures. The ratings of black employees were more strongly related to attendance and error data than were those of white employees. Crooks (Note 3) reported that black ratees received more valid ratings from black and white raters. Validity of the ratings was measured by their relationship to scores on a job knowledge test. These results suggest that the meaning of performance ratings may differ for members of different racial groups. Further research is needed on this issue.

Several other characteristics of ratees have been investigated, each in a small number of studies. Ratee age was found to have no relationship to performance ratings by Klores (1966). No ratee age effect for part-time workers was reported by A. R. Bass and Turner (1973), who did not find significant positive relationships between age and supervisory ratings for white full-time workers on one half of the dimensions being evaluated. No significant correlations between age and ratings were found for black full-time employees. Cascio and Valenzi (1977) found no effect of ratee education on supervisory ratings of police officers.

Personality factors have been investigated in a few studies. Graham and Calendo (1969) found no relationship between supervisory ratings of job performance and the ratees' personality as measured by eight scales from various personality tests. Elmore and LaPointe (1975) reported that student ratings of college instructors' effectiveness were positively correlated with student ratings of instructor warmth.

Job-related variables. A small number of recent experimental studies have examined the effects of the performance level of the ratee on ratings of that performance. Bigoness (1976) found that actual performance had the largest effect on performance ratings. Task performance was experimentally manipulated and videotaped to standardize the stimuli for the subjects. Leventhal, Perry, and Abrami (1977) manipulated lecture quality in addition to other variables and found that student ratings of the instructor were consistently affected by the lecture quality level. Hamner et al. (1974) also found that actual performance accounted for the largest percentage of variance in performance ratings (30%), although the sex and race of the raters and ratees accounted for an additional 23% of the rating variance.

M. E. Gordon (1970, 1972) has identified what he has termed the *differential accuracy phenomenon.* He has reported that ratings were more accurate when the behavior in question was favorable rather than unfavorable. Baker and Schuck (1975) reanalyzed Gordon's data from the framework of signal detection theory and noted that the differential accuracy phenomenon appeared to be limited to only some rating dimensions and not others. The reason the effect was observed for some but not all performance dimensions was unclear, but it deserves more research attention. In a related finding Kaufman and Johnson (1974) found that negative peer nominations add little to the predictiveness of positive peer ratings. This finding is compatible with the differential accuracy phenomenon. The effect may be explainable in terms of base rates of information. Negative performance information is probably less frequent than positive information. Lay, Burron, and Jackson (1973) found that low base-rate information led to more certainty of judgment than high base-rate information. These findings, combined with those of Gordon, suggest that unfavorable information may be less accurately perceived but given more weight in the judgment process.

The effects of variability of the level of ratee performance were examined in an interesting study conducted by Scott and Hamner (1975). They manipulated the variability of subordinate performance as well as changes in the average level of performance. Variability of performance resulted in more favorable ratings of ability of task motivation but had no effect on ratings of overall task performance. A descending order of performance level led to less favorable rating of task motivation but did not affect the other two ratings. In a related study that specifically focused on the decision-making process of human judges, Brehmer (1972) found that an inconsistent cue (as variable performance could be considered) received less weight than its actual validity in a prediction task.

In a correlational field study of supervisory ratings of the performance of clerical workers, Grey and Kipnis (1976) found that the proportion of complaint and noncomplaint members of a work group affected the performance ratings. A compliant worker was defined as one who had no basic job weaknesses related to lack of ability or to an inappropriate work attitude. Ratings tended to be higher for compliant members in work groups with a large proportion of noncompliant workers than in work groups with few or no noncompliant workers. Also, ratings of noncompliant workers tended to be lower in work groups in which there were many compliant workers than in work groups with few compliant workers. The data of Grey and Kipnis, as well as those of Willingham (1958), suggest that more attention be paid to ratee group composition in research on performance rating.

Organizational and job tenure have been investigated as possible influences on performance ratings. Jay and Copes (1957) reviewed the results of 47 studies, with a total sample size of 2,462, and found that the average correlation between measures of tenure and evaluations of job performance was .17. There was a stronger relationship between tenure and performance ratings as the skill level and organizational level of the job increased. Much of the recent research in this area has supported the general findings of Jay and Copes. A. R. Bass and Turner (1973), and Cascio and Valenzi (1977), and Zedeck and Baker (1972) found positive but low correlations between tenure measures and performance ratings. Leventhal et al. (1977) manipulated the level of perceived task experience of the ratee and found that ratings of performance were higher in the condition of higher perceived experience. Some research has obtained contradictory results. Klores (1966) found no relationship between organization tenure and performance rating, although a significant positive relationship between skill level within a job family and ratings was found. Svetlik, Prien, and Barrett (1964) found a negative relationship between supervisory ratings and the job tenure of the ratee. Rothe (1949) noted that the relationship between tenure and performance ratings appeared to be affected by such factors as the organizational reward system, the intended use of the ratings, the raters' acceptance of the rating system, and the rating system's application to organizational problems. This suggestion has not been explicitly investigated to date.

Summary

The research on the effects of ratee characteristics on performance ratings offers some general conclusions. It appears that the sex stereotype of an occupation interacts with the sex of the ratee, such that males receive more favorable evaluations than do females in traditionally masculine occupations but that no differences or smaller differences in favor of females occur in traditionally feminine occupations. Ratees tend to receive higher ratings from raters of their same race, although this may not occur in highly integrated situations. Race and performance level of the ratee appeared to interact in complex ways. Further research is needed to determine if performance ratings have the same meaning for ratees of different races. Other personal characteristics of ratees have been studied too infrequently to yield conclusions about their general effects.

Experimental studies of the effect of the performance level of the ratee on performance ratings generally support the validity of the ratings. Performance level and ability have been found to have the strongest effect on ratings in these studies, although other ratee variables also significantly affect ratings. Raters may evaluate favorable performance more accurately than unfavorable, but not for all performance dimensions. Performance variability also appears to influence rating accuracy and reliability. Contrast effects may be important in performance ratings and need further investigation. Tenure and performance ratings are generally positively but weakly correlated, although situational variables may moderate this relationship.

Interaction of Rater and Ratee Characteristics

The preceding two sections have been concerned primarily with main effects of rater and ratee characteristics. This section examines the research literature that has investigated whether certain combinations of rater and ratee characteristics have effects on performance ratings.

A number of studies have been reported in which the interaction of the sex of the rater and the sex of the ratee was of interest. These studies found no interaction effect of rater sex and ratee sex on ratings (Bartol & Butterfield, 1976; Elmore & LaPointe, 1974, 1975; Hamner et al., 1974; Jacobson & Effertz, 1974; Lee & Alvares, 1977; Rosen & Jerdee, 1973). It should be noted that the majority of these studies have involved laboratory tasks. No studies of the effects of a rater sex and ratee sex interaction on performance ratings have been reported in which both rater and ratee were actual employees of an organization. Elmore and LaPointe did investigate the ratings of college instructors by students.

The lack of rater-ratee sex interaction suggests that if the sex role stereotype hypothesis described in the Ratee Characteristics section of this article is correct, it holds for both male and female raters. Schein (1973, 1975) has reported data consistent with this interpretation. She found that both male and female managers perceived that successful middle-level managers possessed traits more commonly ascribed to men in general than to women in general. Thus, men and women seem to share common sex role stereotypes about work-related variables and could be expected to evaluate male and female ratees with common biases.

The interaction of rater race and ratee race has been investigated in several studies. The results of these studies are mixed. Schmidt and Johnson (1973) found no interaction effect of race on peer ratings in a study conducted in a highly integrated setting with individuals who had completed a human relations training program. Crooks (Note 3), DeJung and Kaplan (1962), and Hamner et al. (1974) found that raters tended to give ratees of their same race higher ratings than they gave to ratees of a different race. Crooks also found that the validity of ratings, as measured by a job knowledge test, was affected by the rater-ratee race interaction, but the results were complex. For black raters there were more valid ratings for black ratees, but for white raters nonwhite ratees received more valid ratings.

One recent study examined the hypothesis that the similarity (biographical, attitudinal, etc.) of judges and ratees affects evaluations. Frank and Hackman (1975) examined similarity effects in actual college admission interviews conducted by three college officials. They found considerable individual variation in the effect of rater-ratee similarity. One interviewer showed no similarity effects, one showed positive but weak effects, and one showed strong, positive effects of similarity. The similarity hypothesis has not been directly examined in a performance rating setting, although the data on racial similarity effects fit into this conceptual framework. Research on the similarity effect and its individual correlates appears to be a fruitful area for performance rating work.

Barrett (1966a) found that supervisor–subordinate agreement on the requirements of the subordinate's job had no effect on the mean rating or reliability of the supervisor's rating of the job performance of the ratee.

Summary

Rater sex and ratee sex do not appear to interact in their effects on evaluative judgments. Research in actual work settings is needed, however. Both male and female raters may have common sex role stereotypes that affect judgments. Raters often give more favorable ratings to same-race ratees, although situational factors may moderate this effect. It was suggested that the similarity of rater and ratee on background and attitudinal factors may affect ratings, although no direct results are available that bear on this question.

VEHICLE

An enormous amount of effort has been spent exploring the potential effects of various rating formats over the years. The hypothesis has been that the vehicle that is used to elicit information has an effect on the accuracy and utility of that information. In our examination of the literature bearing on this hypothesis, we deal with methods of direct rating (in which the rater actually assigns a number to a ratee representing some level of performance), methods of derived rating (in which the rater makes a series of discrete judgments about the ratee, from which a performance rating can be derived), and technical issues, such as response categories and rating scale anchors.

Direct Rating

Graphic scales. Paterson introduced the graphic rating scale to the general psychological community in 1922. In his opinion, this new method was characterized by two things: (a) The rater was freed from quantitative judgments, and (b) the rater was able to make as fine a discrimination as desired. The scales consisted of trait labels, brief definitions of those labels, and unbroken lines with varying types and number of adjectives below. Little research was conducted on this basic format until the latter years of World War II and the postwar period. There was a growing disenchantment (Ryan, 1958) with the subjective and arbitrary nature of the graphic system. Symptoms such as leniency and halo often eliminated any potential usefulness of performance ratings. Basic research related to the properties of graphic scales was carried out by Wherry (Note 5) with armed forces personnel, but it was not widely known. In 1958, Barrett, Taylor, Parker, and Martens tested the adequacy of four different formats, varying in degree of structure. Format 1 consisted of a 10-inch (25.4 cm) line with 15 divisions and a trait name; there were no trait definitions or anchors on the scale. Format II consisted of the same segmented line, but trait definitions were added to the trait names. In Format III, the segmented line was defined by behavioral anchors; there were trait labels but no definitions. Format IV consisted of the segmented line defined by the behavioral anchors and trait definitions but had no

[5]Wherry, R. J. *The control of bias in rating: A theory of rating* (Personnel Research Board Rep. 922). Washington, D.C.: Department of the Army, Personnel Research Section, February 1952.

trait labels. Format III showed higher reliability, lower leniency, and lower halo.

Madden and Bourdon (1964) compared several other variations of rating scale format. They varied the position of the high end of the scale, spatial orientation of the scale (horizontal vs. vertical), segmentation of the scale (segmented vs. unbroken), and numbering of scale levels (1 to 9 vs. −4 to +4). The results showed a significant main effect for the experimental manipulations taken as a whole, although the effect was small.

In a later study by Blumberg, DeSoto, and Kuethe (1966), spatial orientation of the scales was examined once again. They found no significant differences as a result of the location of the "good" end of the scale (top, bottom, left, or right). They concluded that raters might have preferences for various formats but that these preferences have little or no effect on the actual rating behavior.

The literature on logic and development of graphic scales is meager. As is demonstrated, real progress was made as a result of the introduction of alternative methods and comparisons of these methods to the traditional graphic system.

Behaviorally anchored scales.[2] In 1963, Smith and Kendall introduced a new method for rating scale development and use called *behavioral expectation scaling*. This type of scale has become alternatively known as the Behaviorally Anchored Rating Scale (BARS). Physically, it differs from traditional graphic scales in that the anchors that appear at different intervals on the scale are examples of actual behavior rather than adjectives modifying trait labels or simply numbers. More is said about the anchoring procedure in a later section. The present section deals with the use of the completed scales.

Smith and Kendall (1963) demonstrated that the scales could be used effectively for describing nursing performance. Maas (1965) demonstrated the effectiveness of the scales for measuring interview performance. Landy and Guion (1970) demonstrated the utility of the technique for ratings of work motivation. In the last 8 years, this type of rating scale has been used in a sufficient number of settings to warrant the characterization of widespread use.

In terms of direct methods of performance rating, the BARS system currently commands most attention. Nevertheless, in the course of research on this type of scale, some negative findings have emerged. There is a continuing problem with identifying anchors for the central portions of the scales (Harari & Zedeck, 1973; Landy & Guion, 1970; Smith & Kendall, 1963). There is some dispute concerning the generalizability of scales from one setting to another. Borman and Vallon (1974) contended that the scales may be limited to use in the settings in which they were developed. Goodale and Burke (1975) and Landy et al. (1976) demonstrated generalizability beyond developmental settings. A similar type of scale was suggested for improving judgments in clinical settings (J. B. Taylor, Haeffele, Thompson, & O'Donoghue, 1970). Although there have been some tentative extensions of the basic BARS format (Latham & Wexley, 1977; Schwartz, 1977), the physical nature of the rating format has remained relatively constant across studies.

Almost all researchers in the area agree that a BARS is expensive to produce. The generally accepted developmental practice requires independent groups of judges (normally, samples of the population of raters who will eventually use the scales) to develop the dimensions to be rated and the definitions of these dimensions, to develop and subgroup behavioral examples of various levels of these dimensions, and finally, to assign scale values to these examples as part of the scale anchoring process. The effectiveness of the scales is assumed to be based, at least in part, on the independence of the groups engaged in each of the developmental phases. Thus, it can be seen that the investment of time is considerable. The major objection to the BARS currently is whether the ratings that these scales produce are so error free that they justify the cost of scale development. In the next section, we examine empirical comparisons of the BARS with other direct rating methods.

Comparison of graphic scales to BARS. There has been a good deal of careful work attempting to assess the relative effectiveness of the BARS in relation to traditional graphic methods of rating. J. P. Campbell et al. (1973) compared the BARS method to summated ratings and concluded that the BARS format yielded less method variance, less halo, and less leniency in ratings.

Borman and Vallon (1974) found that the BARS technique yielded ratings that were superior in reliability and rater confidence in ratings but that simpler numerical formats resulted in less leniency and better discrimination among ratees.

Burnaska and Hollmann (1974) compared three different formats. The first format was the standard behaviorally anchored scale. The second format consisted of the same dimensions and definitions, but adjectival anchors were substituted for behavioral ones. The third format was a traditional graphic rating format with a priori dimensions. Although leniency and composite halo were present in all three formats, the BARS method reduced leniency and increased the amount of variance attributable to ratee differences. Nevertheless, Burnaska and Hollmann concluded that improvements in some aspects of rating, when the BARS method was used, was accompanied by problems in other areas: "Innovations in rating, although plentiful, are likely to result in robbint Peter to pay Paul" (p. 307). Each format seemed to have its own unique problems.

Keaveny and McGann (1975) compared the student ratings of college professors on behaviorally anchored and

[2]There are several good reviews of the research in the area of developing and using behaviorally anchored scales (J. P. Campbell et al., 1973; Schwab, Heneman, & DeCotiis, 1975).

graphic rating scales. Behaviorally anchored scales resulted in less halo, but they did not differ from graphic scales in terms of leniency. Their general conclusion was that neither format could be judged superior to the other.

Borman and Dunnette (1975) compared the standard BARS format to rating scales that had identical dimension labels and definitions but numerical anchors, and with traditional graphic rating scales that had trait labels and numerical anchors. They concluded that in spite of the fact that the standard BARS format was psychometrically superior (in terms of halo, leniency, and reliability), format differences accounted for trivial amounts of rating variance (approximately 5%).

Bernardin, Alvares, and Cranny (1976) compared summated ratings with BARS ratings. They concluded that summated ratings were characterized by less leniency and greater interrater agreement than were BARS ratings. They hypothesized that the rigor of scale development was a crucial issue in the resistance to rating errors, regardless of the format of the scales. In a follow-up study Bernardin (1977) demonstrated that when item analysis procedures are used for choosing anchors in the BARS method, there is no difference between BARS ratings and summated ratings.

Finally, Friedman and Cornelius (1976) compared ratings from three groups: (a) a group who participated in developing BARS, (b) a group who participated in developing graphic rating scales, and (c) a group who did not participate in scale development. There was no difference in rating errors between Groups 1 and 2. The ratings of Group 3 were characterized by significantly higher levels of rating error (halo) than were the ratings of either of the other two groups.

In general, the comparisons of the BARS method with alternative graphic methods make it difficult to justify the increased time investment in the BARS development procedure. In addition, the work of both Bernardin (Bernardin, 1977; Bernardin, Alvares, & Cranny, 1976) and Friedman and Cornelius (1976) suggests that superior scales are a result of psychometric rigor in development and of some level of participation of individuals representative of those who will eventually use the scales to make ratings rather than of some characteristic unique to behavior anchors per se. More is said about the nature of anchors in a later section. In general, one must conclude that although enthusiasm greeted its introduction, the BARS method has not been supported empirically.

Derived Rating Systems

Forced-choice rating. By far the most popular alternative to direct rating schemes has been the method of forced-choice rating. In this system, the rater is required to choose from among a set of alternative descriptors (normally four items) some subset that is most characteristic of the ratee; variations of this method require the rater to choose both most and least characteristic descriptors. These descriptors function in a manner similar to that of anchors in direct rating. In direct rating schemes, the rater uses anchors to place an individual on a continuum; in a forced-choice system, the choice of descriptors by the rater allows a rating to be derived, since the descriptors have been assigned a priori scale values through some scaling process. In addition, the descriptors have usually been equated or balanced for social desirability. A review by Zavala (1965) gives a good perspective of the range of occupations and situations in which the forced-choice format has been used.

One of the assumed advantages of forced-choice rating was its resistance to leniency. This was due to the fact that the rater did not know the preference and discrimination indices of the various descriptors. Lovell and Haner (1955) found that even when students were specifically instructed to make instructors look good or bad, there was little positive or negative leniency present in the resulting ratings of their teachers. Isard (1956) found that ambiguous descriptors were more reliable and valid than either positive or negative statements and were also less prone to intentional bias. The value of neutral statements was recently confirmed in a study by Obradovic (1970) of blue-collar and white-collar performance. An attempt to use critical incidents (Flanagan, 1954) as descriptors in a forced-choice format yielded ratings with low reliabilities (Kay, 1959).

Comparison of forced-choice with other formats. As was the case with research on graphic formats, more is learned from the comparison of the forced-choice format with other formats than from an examination of variations within the forced-choice format. Staugas and McQuitty (1950) compared the forced-choice technique to both graphic ratings and peer rankings. Since the correlations between forced-choice ratings and the other two performance measures were higher than similar indices for the other two methods, it was concluded that forced-choice methodology was superior. Were they to rewrite the discussion section today, the authors would undoubtedly use the term *convergent validity* to describe advantages of the method. A number of other studies used similar logic for supporting the superiority of the forced-choice format. Berkshire and Highland (1953) demonstrated that forced-choice ratings had higher correlations with overall ranking than did graphic ratings. E. K. Taylor, Schneider, and Clay (1954) found the correlations between forced-choice ratings and graphic ratings to be high, but forced-choice ratings showed less leniency bias. Cotton and Stoltz (1960) showed less range restriction on forced-choice ratings than on graphic ratings. It seems that these studies point to one major advantage of forced-choice ratings—they seem to maximize interindividual variance, although little is known about their effects on intraindividual variance. Since forced-choice scales were introduced primarily in an attempt to control positive bias or leniency, little attention was paid to the problem of halo error. Nevertheless, there is some peripheral evidence available. Sharon and Bartlett (1969) examined the relative resistance of forced-choice and graphic ratings to leniency bias under four conditions: (a) rater anonymous, research purposes only; (b) rater anonymous, feedback to instructor; (c) rater identified, research purposes only; and (d) rater identified, follow-up discussion with ratee. The ratings represented student evaluations of college instructors. Although the results showed significant leniency for all graphic rating conditions, the forced-choice ratings were uniformly resistant to leniency bias.

In one of the few comparative studies dealing with reliability, Lepkowski (1963) found that graphic ratings and forced-choice ratings yielded equal reliability, when scales were developed from critical incidents; from the earlier studies of descriptors reported previously, it might be concluded that these descriptors worked to the disadvantage of the forced-choice format.

E. K. Taylor and Wherry (1951) compared forced-choice and graphic rating systems in a military setting. In one condition, they told raters that the ratings were for experimental purposes; in a second condition, they implied that the ratings would be used to make administrative decisions. They found an increase in the mean ratings for both formats under the "for keeps" condition. Nevertheless, the impact seemed to be greater on the graphic ratings. In addition, there was poorer discrimination among ratees at the top of the scale in the graphic, for keeps condition. They suggested that graphic rating scales that followed forced-choice scales might be less biased.

In 1959, Cozan reviewed the studies that addressed the validity of the forced-choice format and concluded that unless a new system was clearly superior to an existing system, the costs of organizational change argued in favor of the old system. Since the studies to that date had not presented any compelling reason for choosing forced-choice formats over alternative formats, he suggested that traditional graphic rating schemes be retained. The argument is similar to that made against the increased cost of developing BARS formats. Nevertheless, there does seem to be evidence that the forced-choice format reduces range restriction. Unfortunately, sufficient data are not available to determine what price is paid for this psychometric advantage.

Recently, a variation of the derived rating format has appeared. Blanz and Ghiselli (1972) suggest a method in which the rater is required to indicate if the ratee is better than, equal to, or worse than the behavior presented. Since these behaviors have been previously scaled in terms of the level of performance that they represent, it is possible to derive a rating from these judgments. Since behaviors from many different dimensions are randomly arranged, it is difficult for the rater to determine order of merit values for the various statements or to determine which dimensions are being measured. This is thought to protect against intentional bias. Although it is much too early to draw any firm conclusions about this technique, some early results (Saal & Landy, 1977) have been disappointing. Although halo errors are lower in this format than in graphic or BARS formats, reliabilities seem to be exceptionally low. In addition, there are some serious problems with the scoring formats suggested in the original presentation of the method. Arvey and Hoyle (1974) found that scales developed by Guttman scaling techniques (the methodological foundation of the mixed standard scale) demonstrated good convergent and discriminant validity but that attempts to use the technique to identify poor raters were not successful. There was only slight evidence to suggest that raters who made rating errors on one job dimension also rated poorly on other dimensions or that raters who made errors in rating one individual also made errors when rating other individuals. The Guttman-based scales also exhibited higher rating intercorrelations than more traditional behavioral-based scales.

Rating Dimensions

The nature of what dimensions are to be rated has created some controversy. Kavanagh (1971) argued that the empirical literature does not allow one to choose unequivocally the type of content of rating scales (i.e., performance results vs. observable job behaviors vs. personal traits of the incumbent). Brumback (1972) has called for the elimination of personal traits as rating dimensions in preference to performance factors. Kavanagh (1973) rejoined that the question of appropriate rating dimensions can only be answered by a consideration of the nature of the job requirements, the relevance of personal and performance factors for that job, and the empirical defensibility of each content type in terms of reliability, resistance to rating errors, and construct validity.

Several authors (e.g., J. P. Campbell et al., 1970; James, 1973; Ronan & Prien, 1966; Smith, 1976) have argued that global ratings of job performance are more likely than more specific ratings to be affected by extraneous sources of variance and to omit important relevant sources of variance.

Number of Response Categories

A series of careful studies by Bendig (1952a, 1952b, 1953, 1954a, 1954b) provide firm evidence concerning the most efficient number of response categories for rating formats. Considering both scale reliability and rater reliability, there is no gain in efficiency when the number of categories increases from 5 to 9; reliability drops with 3 categories or less and with 11 categories or more. Finn (1972) studied the effect of number of categories on reliability of rating and found that reliability dropped with less than 3 or more than 7 response categories. Lissitz and Green (1975), in a Monte Carlo study of the effect of response categories on scale reliability, concluded that there was little increase in reliability when there were more than 5 scale points or response categories. Bernardin, LaShells, Smith, and Alvares (1976) compared a continuous to noncontinuous 7-point response format and found no differences in rating errors. Finally, Jenkins and Taber (1977), in another Monte Carlo study of factors affecting scale reliability, agreed with Lissitz and Green that there is little utility in adding scale categories beyond 5.

Since several studies have found that an excessive number of categories can have negative effects on scale reliability, the studies on number of response categories seem to have serious implications for scales that allow the rater to define the number of categories of response. Specifically, the format should require the individual to use one of a limited number of response categories, probably less than nine. In spite of the fact that the Bernardin, LaShells, Smith, and Alvares (1976) results do not support the generalization, the weight of evidence suggests that individuals have limited capacities for dealing with simultaneous categories of heterogeneous information. This was suggested long ago by Miller (1956) in his now-famous seven, plus or minus two dictum and appears to generalize to rating behavior.

Anchors

Type. Rating scales typically have one of three types of anchors: numerical, adjectival, or behavioral. There have been several studies directed toward determining the relative effectiveness of these alternative anchoring systems. This, of course, begs the question of whether there should be any anchors at all. Several studies have demonstrated the positive effect of increasing the degree of scale anchoring. Bendig (1952a, 1952b, 1953) found that scale reliability improved with increased anchoring. Barrett et al. (1958) demonstrated the increased effectiveness of anchored scales compared to unanchored ones. D. T. Campbell, Hunt, and Lewis (1958) examined the effect of shifting context on ratings of cognitive organization that are present in responses of schizophrenics. They found that a nine-point scale with detailed anchors was less susceptible to distortion than a similar scale with a minimum of descriptive anchoring.

A number of studies have suggested the relative effectiveness of behavioral anchors as compared with simple numerical or adjectival anchors (Barrett et al., 1958; Bendig, 1952a, 1952b; Maas, 1965; Peters & McCormick, 1966; Smith & Kendall, 1963). Since the BARS format has relied heavily on the behavioral nature of the scale anchors, almost all studies positive toward the BARS format might also be thought of as positive toward behavioral rather than adjectival or numerical anchors. Nevertheless, there have been some studies that have cast some doubt on the nature of elaborate anchors. Finn (1972) found no difference in means or reliabilities of ratings as a function of the manner of defining scale levels. It did not seem to matter if the anchors were numerical or descriptive. Kay (1959) found that using critical incidents to anchor rating scales depressed reliability values. He suggested that critical incidents were too specific and context bound for use as anchors.

The importance of the type and number of anchors probably covaries with the adequacy of the dimension definition. In the absence of adequate definitions of the dimensions to be rated, the rater must depend on the anchors to supply the meaning of the scale. In the Barrett et al. (1958) study, it was found that scales with good behavioral anchors and no dimension definitions (only trait labels) had higher reliability, less halo, and less leniency than either scales with definitions and anchors or scales with definitions but no anchors. In general, it seems that anchors are important, and there is some evidence to suggest that behavioral anchors are better than numerical or adjectival ones.

Scaling. Traditionally, one of the weaker procedures in the development of rating scales has been the process of assigning scale values to anchors. Although there have been some attempts at modifying scale intervals with numerical and adjectival anchors (Bendig, 1952a, 1952b), for the most part there has been little research on the nature of the psychological scale of measurement implied by traditional graphic rating scales.

In the forced-choice format, indices of discrimination and favorability are determined for each item to be used. The discrimination index is the degree to which the particular item or phrase discriminates between high and low performers; the preference value is the degree to which the trait or behavior represented by the item is valued by the typical rater. Both Isard (1956) and Obradovic (1970) found that neutral items were superior to positive or negative items in terms of psychometric characteristics of the resulting ratings. By implication, one might conclude that items with intermediate scale values on the preference dimension were more useful than high- or low-preference items.

Smith and Kendall (1963) used item analysis to determine the ability of particular behavioral anchors to discriminate good from poor nurses. Unfortunately, few studies that followed the Smith and Kendall lead were rigorous in terms of either selection or placement. The most common technique for anchoring in the BARS method is the use of judges to estimate how much of a particular dimension a behavioral example represents. This is usually accomplished with graphic ratings on adjectivally or numerically anchored graphic rating scales. These items have been previously judged for content. The final selection of anchors is based on the resulting mean value of the item and on its standard deviation. The decision rule is frequently arbitrary. (Choose items that represent as many points along the continuum as possible, and have standard deviations less than a specified value.) Bernardin (Bernardin, 1977; Bernardin, Alvares, & Cranny, 1976) demonstrated that the resistance of rating scales to traditional rating errors depends, to some degree, on the rigor of scale development and anchoring. He suggests that this rigor can be introduced through standard item analysis procedures. Barnes (Note 6) demonstrated that a Thurstone solution of a pair comparison scaling of behavioral anchors produces anchor scale values that are significantly different from those produced by the graphic rating method common to BARS development. It may very well be that the reason for the relatively disappointing showing of the BARS format compared with other formats has been due to a lack of rigor in the selection and scaling of anchors. This has been suggested by Schwab, Heneman, and DeCotiis (1975), Bernardin (1977), and Landy (Note 7).

There are some data which suggest that the anchoring process itself is susceptible to the same kinds of biases that new rating formats, such as BARS, are attempting to eliminate. Thus, the situation becomes one of infinite regress; the anchoring procedure introduces the very type of error variance that the format attempts to eliminate. Wells and Smith (1960), Rotter and Tinkleman (1970), Landy and Guion (1970), and Barnes (Note 6) have all demonstrated that anchoring procedures affect ultimate item scale values and standard deviations. These data suggest that anchoring be accomplished by means of some method based on firm psychometric theory (such as Thurstone's law of comparative judgment).

Summary

After more than 30 years of serious research, it seems that little progress has been made in developing an efficient and psychometrically sound alternative to the traditional graphic rating scale. Nevertheless, we have learned some things about rating formats in general. In spite of the fact that people may have preferences for various physical arrangements of high and low anchors, of graphic numbering systems, and so forth, these preferences seem to have little effect on actual rating behavior. The number of response categories available to the rater should not exceed nine. If a continuous rather than discrete response continuum is contemplated, it would be wise to conduct some pilot studies to determine how many response categories are perceived by the potential raters. There is some advantage to using behavioral anchors rather than simple numerical or adjectival anchors. This advantage is probably increased in the absence of good dimension definitions. Finally, it is important that rigorous item selection and anchoring procedures be used in the development of rating scales, regardless of the particular format being considered. It may be that new techniques, such as the BARS or the mixed standard, will show improvements over more traditional methods, if more rigorous developmental procedures are used.

CONTEXT

Included in this section are studies that have examined the effects of factors that are not explicitly related to the nature of the rater, ratee, or rating instrument but that may be considered as part of the context in which the rating occurs.

A number of studies have investigated the effect of the intended use of the ratings on various psychometric properties of the ratings. Several studies have shown that ratings are more lenient under conditions of administrative use than under conditions of research use (Borresen, 1967; Heron, 1956; E. K. Taylor & Wherry, 1951; Centra, Note 4), whereas Sharon (1970) and Sharon and Bartlett (1969) found a similar effect for graphic rating scales but not for a forced-choice scale. Bernardin (1978) found that leniency decreased in conditions in which the importance of the ratings was stressed. Kirkpatrick et al. (1968) reported that whereas rating on three scales intended for research purposes only did not differ for black and white ratees, ratings for the same sample of ratees on a scale intended for administrative use were more favorable for the white employees. Hollander (1957, 1965) found no difference between administrative and research conditions in terms of the reliability or validity of ratings.

A few investigations of the effect of position or job characteristics on performance ratings have been conducted. Much of this literature has been concerned with the sex role stereotype hypothesis discussed in previous sections of this review. In general, the data suggest that ratings are influenced by the interaction of the sex of the ratee and the sex role stereotype of the job or task, although not all studies support this general conclusion (e.g., Jacobson & Effertz, 1974).

In other research that examined position characteristics, Svetlik et al. (1964) found that job difficulty, as measured by a job evaluation point system, was weakly but positively related to a supervisory rating of job competence, although not to a rating of overall effectiveness. Klores (1966) reported that performance ratings were positively correlated with skill levels within a job classification. Myers (1965) partialed job level from rating intercorrelations and found a reduction of halo effects in the correlation matrix and a more meaningful factor structure.

Several other contextual effects on ratings have been reported. Cascio and Valenzi (1977) hypothesized that the

---

[6]Barnes, J. L. *Scaling assumptions in behaviorally anchored scale construction.* Paper presented at the meeting of the American Psychological Association, Toronto, August 1978.

[7]Landy, F. J. Discussion. In S. Zedeck (Chair), *A closer look at performance appraisal through behavioral expectation scales.* Symposium presented at the meeting of the American Psychological Association, San Francisco, August 1977.

expectation of favorable performance because the ratees had passed selection and training hurdles might cause raters to be lenient in their judgments. Rosen and Jerdee (1973) found that observer ratings of the effectiveness of supervisors' leadership styles were affected by the sex of the supervisor and the sex of the subordinates. In general, ratings were more favorable when the leadership style of the supervisor was appropriate for traditional sex role stereotypes. Rothe (1949) found that the nature of the incentive system could affect ratings. When the ratees were given pay increases based on performance ratings, and the pay for each job had a ceiling, supervisors gave more favorable ratings to less senior subordinats who had not yet reached the pay maximum.

Summary

Ratings for administrative purposes will be more lenient than those for research purposes. Unfortunately, since most of the published research was done in the resarch purposes context, too little information is currently available to draw firm conclusions about impact of purpose for rating. Although it does not appear that the variances of the ratings are affected by the purpose component, more definitive tests of this relationship are needed.

RATING PROCESS VARIABLES

Another class of variables affecting performance ratings are those factors related to the process by which ratings are obtained, exclusive of the rating instrument itself. Included here are such variables as rater training, rater anonymity, and sequence of traits and ratees.

A large number of primarily recent studies have examined the effect of rater training on rating errors and validity, following the suggestions for such research from Borman and Dunnette (1975), Moore and Lee (1974), and Schneier (1977), among others. Most investigations have found that training raters reduces rating errors, although some data suggest no differences between trained and untrained raters (J. B. Taylor et al., 1970; Vance, Kuhnert, & Farr, 1978) or only shortterm effects (Bernardin, 1978). Wexley, Sanders, and Yukl (1973) found that only extensive training was effective in reducing rating errors, a finding corroborated by Brown (1968), Latham, Wexley, and Pursell (1975), and Bernardin and Walter (1977). Borman (1975) reported decreased halo, with no reduction in the validity of ratings, with only a brief training program.

Although rater training programs have concentrated on the avoidance of the typical rating errors such as halo and leniency, only Bernardin (1978) has demonstrated a correlation between knowledge of such errors, as measured by a test, and a reduction of the errors in actual ratings. Data from a few other studies suggest that the nature of rater training programs should include instruction in more than rating errors. M. E. Gordon (1970) found that greater experience with a particular rating instrument improved rater accuracy, and Friedman and Cornelius (1976) found that rater participation in rating scale development resulted in decreased rating errors, regardless of scale format. These studies can be interpreted as pointing to the inclusion of detailed instruction in the use of whatever scale format has been selected. Klieger and Mosel (1953) noted that better interrater agreement among supervisory raters, when compared to peer raters, might be the result of supervisory training that gave raters a common frame of reference for the evaluation of performance. Rater training should also stress performance requirements of the job as well as instruction in observation techniques.

Bayroff et al. (1954), Sharon and Bartlett (1969), and Stone, Rabinowitz, and Spool (1977) found no difference in rating errors or validity between identified and anonymous raters. Creswell (1963) reported no effect on leniency of ratings but did find more variance with confidential ratings as opposed to ratings that were to be shown to the ratees or to the rater's superior.

A suggestion for the reduction of halo error by Guilford (1954), among others, was to rate all ratees on a given trait or dimension, then to rate all ratees on the next trait, and so forth. This was predicted to result in less halo error than the process of rating a given ratee on all traits, then rating the next ratee on all traits, and so forth. However, studies that have compared these two rating processes have found no differences (Blumberg et al., 1966; Brown, 1968; Johnson, 1963; E. K. Taylor & Hastman, 1956). Johnson (1963) is a reanalysis of Johnson and Vidulich (1956), using more appropriate statistical techniques that resulted in the conclusion by Johnson (1963) of no effect.

Several studies have reported data concerning the question of whether position of the ratee in a sequence affects the rating of the ratee. Bayroff et al. (1954) found that ratings early in a sequence were more valid than those later in the sequence. Wagner and Hoover (1974) reported that raters who were not especially knowledgeable about the technical aspects of the task performance being evaluated tended to be more favorable to ratees early in the sequence. Finally, Willingham (1958) found that ratings tended to be biased in the direction of the previous rating and that this tendency increased as the number of response categories increased.

In an isolated study of a rating process variable, Wright (1974) found that when faced with less time to reach a judgment, individuals tended to use fewer sources of information and to weigh unfavorable information more heavily in making evaluations.

Summary

Rater training has generally been shown to be effective in reducing rating errors, especially if the training is extensive and allows for rater practice. Questions still remain about the longitudinal effects of such training, about the effect of rater training on the validity of ratings, and about the optimal content of such training programs.

Identified raters, as opposed to anonymous raters, appear to give equivalent ratings. There appears to be no reduction in halo error when all ratees are evaluated on one trait, then all ratees are evaluated on the next trait, and so forth. Serial position appears to have some effect on ratings, but no general pattern has emerged from the research to date.

RESULTS OF RATING

After one gathers ratings of performance, decisions must still be made concerning the manner in which these data might be analyzed to produce accurate and reliable performance descriptions. It is possible that various analytic techniques are more successful at reducing or eliminating rating errors than other techniques. In this section, we review the research that addresses this issue.

Dimension Reduction

Traditionally, the performance of individuals is considered with respect to a number of presumably independent dimensions. We use the term *presumably* because, in spite of the attempt by the research to identify and define independent aspects of performance, the intercorelations among ratings on these dimensions are often high; this problem is usually introduced as one of halo error. A number of studies have examined the effect of combining ratings across dimensions into some smaller number of homogeneous subsets. The process of combination is assumed to produce new, derived performance scores that are more reliable and that better describe important aspects of work-related performance, allowing the construction of more efficient selection and training programs.

The most common technique for data reduction and combination in the area of performance ratings has been factor analysis. Factor scores have been computed and used as the criteria for various administrative, counseling, and research purposes. Grant (1955) suggested that factor analysis was a useful device in determining the degree of halo present in ratings, as well as the degree to which discriminations might be made among individuals on performance dimensions. Guilford, Christenson, Taaffe, and Wilson (1962) proposed that certain marker tests and variables be included in a factor analysis of performance ratings to better understand exactly what was being rated. Schultz and Siegel (1964) gathered estimates of judged similarity among performance dimensions from raters and used those judgments as the basis for identifying more basic performance dimensions through multidimensional scaling procedures. Dickinson and Tice (1977) used factor analytic techniques to improve the discriminant validity in performance ratings. They suggested that factor analysis could be used to eliminate complex anchors (anchors loading on more than one dimension) and thus reduce trait intercorrelations. Kane and Lawler (1978) suggested that performance ratings be factor analyzed and that the first unrotated factor score be used as a measure of overall performance for administrative purposes.

Unfortunately, there have been no rigorous tests of the hypothesis that reduced scores tell us more about the performance of the ratee than do raw scores. As a matter of fact, there are several studies that have implied that a factor analysis of ratings tells us more about the cognitive structure of the raters than about the behavior patterns of the ratees. Grant (1955) suggested that factor analysis might tell us how the raters interpreted the items on the rating scale. Norman and Goldberg (1966) instructed raters to evaluate individuals with whom they had little familiarity and individuals with whom they were quite familiar. The factor structures derived from a factor of the two data sets independently were similar. They concluded that the similarity among these dimensions was more a property of the raters' views of performance than of the ratees' actual behaviors. This has serious implications for the use of factor analytic results for developing selection or training programs. Kavanagh, MacKinney, and Wolins (1971) demonstrated the difficulties in determining the number of performance dimensions represented in managerial ratings. Using multitrait–multimethod procedures (D. T. Campbell & Fiske, 1959), they had serious difficulties in identifying independent aspects of managerial performance. They were able to identify "personality dimensions" suitable for rating. They imply that for the first time, a procedure was available for identifying and measuring personality-based performance aspects in managers. This begs the question of the existence of these dimensions in the behavior patterns of the ratees. It may be that they exist in the cognitive framework of the raters and have little or no reality with respect to ratees.

In general, this particular area of research raises many more questions than it answers. The identification of behavioral patterns in ratees is an extremely complex issue. Data reduction techniques such as factor analysis and cluster analysis of ratings seriously confound dimensions of rater cognitive structure with ratee behavior. More is said about this problem in a later section on implicit personality theory.

Weighting and Grouping Methods

Factor analysis might be thought of as one technique for assigning weights to performance dimensions; these weights would represent relative importance and could be calculated on the basis of variance accounted for by a particular component or factor. Jurgensen (1955) suggested that statistical weights might help improve the relationship between performance ratings on specific dimensions and overall performance. He found that statistical weights were no better than arbitrarily assigned weights. In light of the recent research of Dawes and Corrigan (1974), this finding might be extended to include unit weights. Naylor and Wherry (1965; Wherry & Naylor, 1966) were able to describe distinctly different rater "policies" in rating behavior. Each of these different policies could be described by a unique set of relative weights. Consequently, if different raters have different policies, it is likely that computing statistical weights on a group basis will not be effective in weighting specific dimensions—some initial subgrouping is required. Passini and Norman (1969) suggested a complicated weighting scheme for improving the reliability of peer nominations and rankings that might be extended to cover ratings as well. They suggest that indices of agreement be computed within and across ratees; dimensions with greater agreement across raters would receive heavier weights, and dimensions that have highest interobserver agreement within rates would also receive heavier weights.

The Passini and Norman (1969) procedure assumes that two or more raters are available for each ratee. Several researchers have suggested that multiple ratings are desirable. Carter (1952) suggested that multiple ratings would improve criterion reliability. Windle and Dingman (1960) found that perceptions shared by two raters were more predictive of an independent criterion than were perceptions unique to each judge. This study was in response to an earlier study by Buckner (1959) that proposed that unique views of individual judges were ultimately more valuable than common views of a ratee. Overall (1965) suggested an optimal weighting scheme based on the reliability and variance of individual raters. He was concerned with methods for combining ratings from multiple judges. He developed a scheme for weighting judgments by factors that represented the reliability and variance of individual raters. Einhorn (1972) proposed combining components of expert judgment to take advantage of differential validity of individual judges. All of these suggestions assume the existence of multiple ratings on a single ratee. This is seldom the case in applied settings. Nevertheless, even if it were possible to accumulate multiple ratings, the results of Naylor and Wherry (1965; Wherry & Naylor, 1966) and Passini and Norman (1969) imply that there are significant differences among raters in rating policies. This, in turn, implies that gains produced by collapsing ratings across judges may be illusory.

There have been some suggestions that scoring schemes might be developed for improving various types of rating data. Meyer (1951) suggested a binary scoring scheme based on the absolute number of items checked in a checklist type rating scale. He found no differences between this simple technique and more complicated ones. B. M. Bass (1956) suggested a binary scoring system that was based on the relative distribution of superior and inferior performers on a five-point scale. The simple binary recording system reduced leniency without significantly reducing internal consistency. There have been some recent studies in scoring procedures, but they have been confounded with scale format and instructions (Bernardin, LaShells, Smith, & Alvares, 1976; Blanz & Ghiselli, 1972; Zedeck, Kafry, & Jacobs, 1976), and the results do not easily generalize to weighting and grouping principles.

Other Techniques of Statistical Control

Myers (1965) attempted to remove halo from the ratings of job factors in a job analysis study of 82 different jobs on 17 dimensions. He partialed out the effect of organizational leel on these ratings and substantially reduced dimension intercorrelations. As a result, he suggested that researchers look for demographic factors that correlate highly with ratings and that remove the influence of those factors statistically, thereby reducing unwanted halo.

Ritti (1964) substantially reduced halo in supervisory ratings by standardizing both the rows and the columns of the rating matrix. He was able to demonstrate through factor analytic results that the simple structure was improved, that the within-factor correlations remained high, and that the between-factors correlations were substantially reduced.

Landy and Vance (Note 8) partialed out an overall rating from ratings on 15 specific performance dimensions and found a substantial reduction in factor correlation, a reduction in variance accounted for by the first unrotated factor (a possible measure of method variance) and an improved simple-structure factor solution.

Summary

The research on dimensional combination strategies resulting from data reduction algorithms has been equivocal. A substantial amount of research still must be done before it will be possible to specify what those performance factors represent—behavioral patterns of ratees or cognitive constructs of raters. The research on the combination of multiple ratings is also equivocal. If distinct patterns of rating exist among raters (i.e., policies), the presumed gains in reliability may represent a hollow victory. On a practical basis, it seems unlikely that techniques based on multiple ratings will prove useful in applied settings, although they may be of value in cataloging sources of error. The research by Myers (1965), Ritti (1964), and Landy

[8]Landy, F. J., & Vance, R. J. *Statistical control of halo.* Unpublished manuscript, 1978. (Available from Frank J. Landy, Department of Psychology, Pennsylvania State University, University Park, Penn. 16802.)

and Vance (Note 8) suggests a possible avenue for continued research in data analysis procedures.

PROCESS MODEL OF PERFORMANCE RATING

Many researchers in the area of performance rating have concluded that a model of some sort is necessary before any significant advances can be made in understanding judgmental performance measures (DeCotiis, 1977; Jenkins & Taber, 1977; Kane & Lawler, 1978; Schwab et al., 1975; Zedeck, Jacobs, & Kafry, 1976). Figure 1 was presented earlier as a first or promitive representation of the rating process. On the basis of our review, as well as on some theoretical influences that are described below, we propose that Figure 2 is a more refined, coherent, and catholic representation of the system of performance rating. In Figure 2, we have tried to be more specific about the subsystems that form the larger rating system. Thus, the context component of Figure 1 has been broken into three components: position characteristics, organization characteristics, and the purpose for rating. Similarly, the rating process component now comprises two subsystems: the cognitive process of the rater (observation, storage, recall, and judgment) and the administrative rating process of the organization. With this general evolution in mind, we now discuss specific components of the model.

The model assumes that there are certain characteristics brought to the rating task that are properties of the rater and ratee, respectively. For example, the rater brings to the task "sets" or biases that may be related to age, sex, race, leadership style, personal relationship to ratee, and so forth. In addition, the ratee possesses certain characteristics, in addition to level of performance on the dimension

FIGURE 2
Process Model of Performance Rating

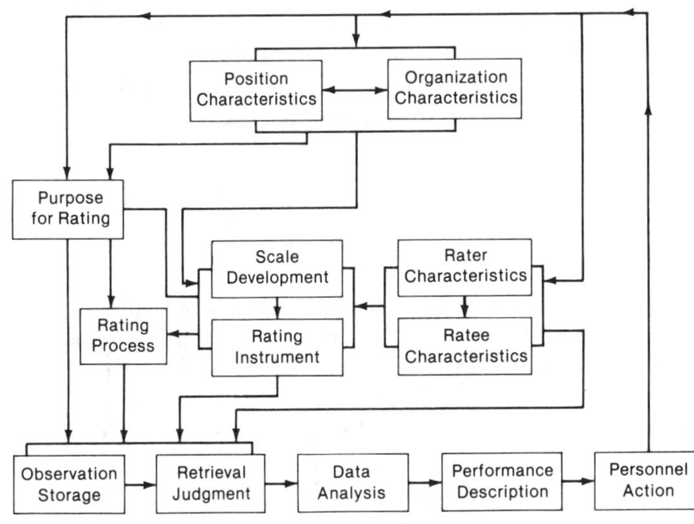

under consideration, that may influence the judgment. In addition to the main effects that these respective rater and ratee characteristics represent, there are undoubtedly interactions of rater and ratee characteristics. Thus, in addition to the fact that black ratees may receive lower ratings than white ratees and in addition to the fact that black raters may be harsher in rating than white raters, there is also the possibility of an interaction of the race of the rater and the race of the ratee in performance judgment. The same would be true of other rater–ratee characteristics. The model also implies that the characteristics of the rater and ratee have an influence on the selection and/or development of the rating instrument. These characteristics might include education, previous experience with performance rating, and tenure in the organization.

The most immediate context in which rating occurs is defined by the particular organization and the particular position under consideration. Organizational size moderates such critical variables as span of control, seasonal variation in work force, levels of turnover, part-time to full-time employee ratio, and so forth. It has also been proposed that organizations differ with respect to the climate that is perceived by their members. In addition to differences among organizations, there are distinct differences among positions within those organizations. Positions differ with respect to level within the organizational hierarchy; they also differ with respect to line versus staff and blue collar versus white collar designations. We propose that position and organizational characteristics jointly affect both the choice and/or development of a rating instrument and the purpose for which rating is done. It is not uncommon to see ratings used to make administrative decisions at one level in an organization but used for counseling at another level. In addition, supportive organizations often use ratings for employee development, whereas punitive organizations might use the same information for employee terminations. It is appalling to note how little systematic research has addressed the impact of position and organizational characteristics on performance rating.

The purpose component of the model is of central importance.[3] Employee counseling usually requires an instrument different from that to be used simply for administrative purposes. In addition, the purpose for the rating also affects the rating process. As an example, employees are often permitted to examine supervisory comments in development or training contexts, but they are usually not permitted similar access in the context of salary decisions. Finally, the purpose for ratings is assumed to have a substantial effect on the cognitive process of the rater. As indicated in the earlier review, ratings done for research purposes differ substantially from those done for administrative purposes.

[3]We are grateful to Shelly Zedeck for suggesting that this is an explicit component of the model rather than a derivative component.

A conceptually independent variable in the system is the vehicle or instrument actually used to gather the performance information. Through a process of scale development or selection, an instrument is identified that presumably is capable of helping raters make distinctions among ratees with respect to various categories of behavior. The scale development may involve developmental groups, as in the case of the BARS methodology, or item analysis derived from a study of current employees, as in the case of summated ratings or forced-choice inventories. Regardless of the method of development, an instrument will be selected or constructed to produce judgments about performance. This instrument will have certain phenotypic characteristic—type and number of anchors, number of response categories, spatial orientation, and so forth. As indicated previously, these characteristics will be directly influenced by the rating context (including position characteristics, organizational characteristics, and purpose for rating) and the characteristics of the rater and ratee. The final instrument will have a major impact on the cognitive operations of the rater.

The component labeled rating process refers to the constraints placed on the rater by requests or demands. For example, ratings gathered once a year will have different characteristics than those gathered twice a year; ratings gathered on the same day for all ratees will have different characteristics than those gathered on the anniversary of the date of hire for each ratee; ratings done in a noisy, public, distracting environment will have different characteristics than those done in a quiet, private, distraction-free environment; ratings that will eventually be seen by the ratee will have different characteristics than those that will not be seen by the ratee; rating sessions preceded by brief training modules will yield ratings that have different characteristics than those produced "cold," and so forth. As indicated earlier, the rating process is not developed in isolation. It will inevitably be influenced by the purpose for rating and the instrument used for the rating.

The cognitive operations of the rater are thought to fall into two temporal categories. In the first category we find observation and storage. Usually, the rater is asked to retrieve and use that information at some later time. These cognitive operations are influenced by a multitude of variables: the purpose for the rating, the administration rating process, the instrument used, and interacting rater–ratee characteristics.

After performance judgments are made by the rater, a decision must be made concerning how to treat that information. As we have seen in the literature review, these decisions may have substantial effects on error variance estimates. One might use influences identified in previously discussed rater, ratee, position, or organizational components as covariates or moderators. The way in which the data are treated must be considered as a potential source of variance in the resulting performance description. The long-standing argument regarding composite versus multiple criteria is evidence of the importance of this component in a general performance measurement system (Landy & Trumbo, in press). If information is improperly combined and inaccurately fed into the personnel decision system, it will inevitably have negative effects on that system.

The component labeled performance description implies that the data analytic procedure yields a result that is fed back to appropriate sources. These sources might be personnel departments engaged in validation studies or training evaluation studies. They might include administrative officers engaged in salary or work force planning for the coming year. They might include ratees who receive performance feedback interviews from supervisors. In a sense, each of these sources engages in a personnel action either actively or by default—selection systems are maintained or changed, salaries or work force levels are maintained or changed, employees are told of strengths and weakness or ignored. These actions, or lack thereof, influence the characteristics of both raters and ratees. If layoffs resulting from rating data, both raters and ratees will be changed by virtue of that action. Rater biases or sets and ratee behavior will most likely both change. Presumably, accurate performance data fed back in a nonpunishing manner will help individuals eliminate weakness and maintain strengths.

The feedback loop from personnel action to purpose for rating has an important implication. It implies that we must consider how the purpose for rating is perceived by the rater; it is the resulting personnel action that will clearly inform the rater of the purpose for rating rather than the organization's stated purpose, if the two are at odds.

As can be seen from the descriptions of the model in Figure 2, there is a good deal of research still to be done if we are to understand the nature of performance ratings in any nontrivial way. The model is strongly process oriented and must be eventually supported by more substantive propositions concerning where rater biases come from, why certain rating processes minimize rating error, whereas other procedures exaggerate those errors, and so forth. Two substantive approaches that may be useful to use in conjunction with the process model previously described are implicit personality theory and Wherry's (Note 5) psychometric theory of rating. We now describe how these approaches complement and support our process model.

IMPLICIT PERSONALITY THEORY

For a substantive theoretical framework to be of value in understanding a behavioral phenomenon, such as rating of performance, it should be able to unify the various manifestations of the phenomenon; it should have the capacity to explain conflicting results, to bring order to disorder. The major theme in the research that has been conducted in the area of performance rating has been that variables of major importance can be found in the rating scales themselves. Individual differences in raters were only occasionally investigated. Even when these differences were examined, they tended to be second-level or demographic differences, such as sex or experience, rather than first-level direct influences, such as cognitive operations or feelings toward the stimulus object.

It is our feeling that implicit personality theory research is rich with implications for understanding rating behavior. Bruner and Tagiuri (1954) considered implicit personality theory to be assumed relationships among traits. This is close to the definition of halo in performance rating that one might infer from reading the literature that we have reviewed in the earlier sections of this article. Cronbach (1955) expanded this definition to include not only the covariation among traits but also the means and variances of the traits, implying some relationship between implicit personality theory and leniency and central tendency errors.

In some senses, performance ratings may represent specific instances of implicit personality theories of raters—assumed values on performance dimensions that are independent of actual behavior of the ratee on those dimensions. The work of Passini and Norman (1969) and Norman and Goldberg (1966) is interesting in that respect. They were able to demonstrate that the correlation among traits could be accounted for through constructs of the rater rather than through co-occurrences of behavior patterns in ratees.

An earlier study by Koltuv (1962) demonstrated that implicit personality theories were most likely to operate in situations in which there was low familiarity of rater with ratee. Thus, one might reasonably conclude that the means, variances, and covariances of performance ratings will depend to a certain extent on the degree of familiarity of rater with ratee. This will not come as a surprise to anyone who has conducted research in the performance rating area; nevertheless, it represents a more general phenomenon, since it has been found in settings other than that of performance ratings. In addition, the finding takes on more cognitive overtones when it is embedded in other findings in the implicit personality theory research. For example, implicit personality theories seem to operate more often in trait evaluations than in behavioral evaluations (D. J. Schneider, 1973). Particularly, trait labels seem to lead more often to implicit assumptions. Together, these findings suggest that rating scales should be behaviorally anchored with no trait labels at all. It may be that the labels that introduce the scales create response sets that the definitions and anchors are unable to eliminate. It would be easy enough to test this hypothesis by examining the intercorrelations of ratings made with labels and without labels; although the presence or absence of definitions has been examined, and the presence or absence of behavioral anchors has been examined, little attention has been paid to dimension labels, which invariably read as trait names.

There has been also the suggestion in implicit personality theory research that we seek less information about persons we dislike or about individuals from different strata. This is similar to the Differential Accuracy Phenomenon (DAP) described by M. E. Gordon (1970, 1972) that led him to conclude that low performers are described less accurately than high performers; in addition, the number of levels in the organization that separate the rater and ratee seem to affect the accuracy of the performance judgment (Whitla & Tirrell, 1953; Zedeck & Baker, 1972).

The interesting aspect of implicit personality theory as a heuristic device for examining performance ratings is that it brings a new outlook to some old and vexing questions. It requires us to view rating errors in a new light. These errors become behavioral phenomena governed by individual differences. Landy et al. (1976) suggested that rating errors are not simply properties of scales or instruments. Errors are governed by many parameters, and some of these parameters may be cognitive differences among raters. One might apply Kelly's (1955) notions of personal constructs to performance rating and come to the same conclusion. As another example, Tajfel and Wilkes (1963) found that subjects made more extreme judgments on dimensions that they provided themselves rather than on those given to them. What would happen if we were to allow raters to choose a subset of dimensions from a larger number of dimensions? Would halo be reduced? Would central tendency be reduced? Would new errors appear? The point we are trying to make is that we have a substantive body of research more clearly tied to interpersonal evaluation than currently exists in the performance evaluation literature. This body of research appears under the rubric of implicit personality theory. We feel that advances can be made in understanding rating behavior, if we view rating as a specific instance of the more general phenomenon of person perception.

PSYCHOMETRIC THEORY OF RATING

Wherry (Note 5) in 1952 proposed a theory of the rating process that has received little attention. He noted that rating accuracy is dependent on (a) the performance of the ratee, (b) the observation or perception of the ratee's performance by the rater, and (c) the recall of the observation of performance by the rater. Each of these three components of a rating may be broken into subcomponents. Drawing on classical mental test theory (e.g., Gulliksen, 1950), Wherry assumed that each component of the rating process had a systematic part and a random part. The systematic part can be further partitioned into a true aspect and a bias aspect, where bias is systematic.

In particular, the actual job performance of the ratee at a given time is equal to the sum of the true level of the ratee's job performance, environmental influences on the ratee's performance (bias), and random error. Each of these three subcomponents is weighted in proportion to its importance in a given situation, with the constraint that the sum of the squared weights is unity.

The perception or observation of the actual performance of the ratee can be similarly partitioned into several aspects. The perception of one instance of job performance can be considered to be the sum of actual performance of the ratee in that instance, the bias of perception of the performance, and random error. The bias aspect can be further partitioned into three elements that are related to (a) the expected performance of the ratee, based on the true behavior component; (b) the residual effect (called areal bias) of all previous error and nonrelevant experiences that the rater has had with the ratee in situations identical or similar to the current one; and (c) an overall bias representing the residual effect of all possible areal bias effects. Each of these subcomponents of the perception of the actual performance is weighted in proportion to its importance as an effect on rating accuracy on a given occasion, with the constraint that the sum of the squared weights is unity.

The final stage of the rating process is the recall and reporting of previously perceived job performances. This recall is composed of the sum of the previous perceptions of performance, a systematic bias of recall, and random error of recall. The bias factor of recall may be considered to be composed of three elements analogous to those related to perception: true, areal bias, and overall bias. Again, each element of the recall component is weighted with regard to the magnitude of its effect on the rating, such that the sum of squared weights equals unity.

If it is assumed that the true performance level of a given ratee is constant, that a rater uses the same weights for the various components in all performance situations, that the areal bias of recall is equal to the areal bias of perception, and that the overall bias of recall is equal to the overall bias of perception, then the Wherry (Note 5) model of the rating process may be written in standard score units as

$$z_{X_R} = W_T \tilde{z}_T + W_{BRA} \tilde{z}_{BRA} + W_{BRO} \tilde{z}_{BRO} + W_I \tilde{z}_I + W_{EA} \tilde{z}_{EA} + W_{EP} \tilde{z}_{EP} + W_{ER} \tilde{z}_{ER}, \quad (1)$$

where z_{X_R} = recall of previous performance, z_T = true performance, z_{BRA} = areal bias of recall, z_{BRO} = overall bias of recall, z_I = environmental influences on performance, $\tilde{z}_{EA}$ = random error of performance, $\tilde{z}_{EP}$ = random error of perception, $\tilde{z}_{ER}$ = random error of recall, and the *W*s represent the weights assigned to the components, such that

$$W_T^2 + W_{BRA}^2 + W_{BRO}^2 + W_I^2 + W_{EA}^2 + W_{EP}^2 + W_{ER}^2 = 1.00.$$

From Equation 1 Wherry (Note 5) derived a total of 46 theorems and 24 corollaries concerning rating validity and reliability. Although we cannot describe in detail all of these theorems and corollaries, it is instructive to examine a few to better understand the substantive nature of the theory. For example, Wherry hypothesized that tasks in which the performance is maximally controlled by the ratee rather than by the work situation are more likely to result in accurate ratings because the z_I component will receive a relatively small weight. In addition, it was hypothesized that raters would be accurate in their ratings, if they had had much relevant contact with the ratee, consistent with later research by Freeberg (1969).

In other derivations from Equation 1, Wherry (Note 5) predicted that ratings gathered under research conditions would be more accurate than ratings gathered under administrative conditions and that increasing the number of observations, judgments, or raters will tend to reduce error. In particular, obtaining ratings about different areas of performance tends to reduce areal bias but has no effect on overall bias. Multiple raters may reduce both areal and overall bias, depending on the degree of correlation among irrelevant portions of rater–ratee contact.

An important theorem derived by Wherry (Note 5) stated that the reliability of a rating scale conveys little information about its validity, since the reliability of the measurement may be due to bias rather than to true performance. Since a frequent criterion of the value of a rating scale is its reliability, this theorem suggests that much rating research has been misdirected toward reliability rather than the important issues of validity and accuracy. More recently, several authors have stressed the necessity of using rating accuracy as the prime criterion in rating research (e.g., Borman, 1978; Vance et al., 1978).

The Wherry (Note 5) model also suggests several areas of research that have received only little attention to date. It is hypothesized that rating scales that refer to tasks that are operator paced will result in more accurate ratings than scales that refer to tasks that are environmentally controlled. Wherry also states that rater training should include instruction in observational techniques and in the keeping of written performance observations between rating periods. He also suggests that the requirement that ratings be seen by both the ratee and the rater's superior will tend to cancel out the effects of showing the ratings to only one or the other. Although many rating forms currently in use follow this suggestion, it has not been empirically tested.

From this brief exposure to the psychometric rating theory of Wherry (Note 5), it is evident that this approach has much to offer performance rating research. However, only a small number of studies concerned with performance ratings have cited Wherry (e.g., Barrett, 1966; Borman, 1978; Freeberg, 1969; Ross, 1966; Sharon & Bartlett, 1969; Centra, Note 9). This low citation level is probably due to the fact

[9] Centra, J. A. *The influence of different directions on student ratings of instruction* (ETS RB 75-28). Princeton, N.J.: Educational Testing Service, 1975.

that the theory has never been published in the generally available literature. The theory should be carefully examined by performance rating researchers and tested empirically to a much greater extent than has already occurred.

The Wherry model has influenced the process model presented in Figure 2 principally in the consideration of the components of the cognitive element. The partitioning of the rating into variance components also has heuristic value. The identification of factors that influence ratings is simplified, when one considers that observation, storage, recall, and judgment constitute the rater's task rather than trying to deal with a unitary phenomenon of rating. Wherry also began a consideration of position characteristics, process variables, and so forth, that are more fully developed in the process model. In many ways, Figure 2 is a graphic representation of the variables discussed by Wherry. Figure 2 extends Wherry by considering the interactions among variables and the explicit cyclical nature of the total rating system. The process model developed above also suggests more clearly the many factors impinging on the cognitive element.

UNIFIED APPROACH TO PERFORMANCE RATING

As indicated earlier, many researchers in the field of performance rating have recognized the need for models or frameworks to apply to the rating context. These models should integrate the various potential influences on performance descriptions into a single system. The process model that we propose in Figure 2 might be thought of as a superstructure of rating behavior. As such, it is primarily taxonomic in nature. Nevertheless, taxonomies represent a significant step in theory building. By identifying major components of the system, hypothesis generation and testing is facilitated. Through the application of substantive models related to the process in question, higher level theories emerge. We feel that such is the case with the combination of our process model, implicit personality theory research, and Wherry's deductive propositions regarding variance components in ratings.

It is clear from even a cursory examination of the rating process that all information must ultimately pass through a cognitive filter represented by the rater. Multiple raters simply imply multiple filters that combine in some particular manner. Thus, one must understand the way in which environmental changes or constancies affect this cognitive operation called judgment. Organismic characteristics such as the sex, race, or age of the rater are peripheral. The more important questions relate to how cognitive operations are affected by group membership. The phenotypic characteristics of a rating format are theoretically less important than the interaction of these characteristics with cognitive operations that are involved in recording judgments concerning the behavior of others. Even data analytic procedures, such as factor analysis of multiple rating dimensions, presume that rater observations and the resulting ratings are veridical.

There are, of course, considerations beyond theory building. For the purposes of application and administration, it is useful to know the effect of contextual factors on ratings. Forewarned of certain systematic interactions between rater and ratee characteristics, practitioners are better able to develop equitable decision systems. The administrative implications of Wherry's model of rating variance are important. His propositions make it possible to determine what price is being paid for decreases in particular types of rating error (Wherry, Note 5). For example, the use of a rating scale with multiple items to be rated for each performance dimension increases the reliability of the performance rating for that dimension (due to random error reduction) but does not increase the relative proportion of true score to bias. Also, the addition of multiple raters, each evaluating the ratee on several performance dimensions, will reduce overall and areal bias in the composite rating only if the raters' irrelevant contacts with the ratee are at least somewhat different. If these contacts are the same, then there will be no reduction in bias. In addition to the administrative implications, Wherry clearly emphasized the importance of the cognitive operations of the rater, an emphasis only recently appearing in the applied literature on rating.

There is an enormous amount of work to be done, both inductive and deductive, in tying the propositions of person perception to the components of the process model. The propositions of Wherry regarding variance partitioning represent a procedure for accomplishing the initial steps of this integration.

Future Research Needs

The literature review suggests some global conclusions that can be drawn on the basis of available evidence. In one sense, rater and ratee characteristics are fixed—they cannot be changed as easily as can the format of a rating scale. Since little is known concerning the dynamics by which demographic characteristics, such as race and sex, affect ratings, it is difficult to imagine training programs that would eliminate specific biases peculiar to group membership. On the other hand, there is some indication that training in the use of a particular rating format is of value in reducing common rating errors. We must learn much more about the way in which potential raters observe, encode, store, retrieve, and record performance information, if we hope to increase the validity of ratings.

Given the superficiality of our knowledge of the cognitive processes of raters, we probably have gone as far as we can in improving rating formats. We know that the rater should have a clear understanding of the rating task, that the number of response categories should be limited, that the anchors on the scale should be rigorously developed, and that those anchors should be more than simple descriptive labels, such as poor, average, outstanding, and so forth. Nevertheless, even when all of these suggestions are taken into account, evidence suggests that their effect may be minimal. Data reviewed earlier indicate that about 4%–8% of the variance in ratings can be explained on the basis of format. When one considers that the designs that yielded these estimates were seldom sensitive enough to identify true levels of performance, even this effect may be an overestimate. Thus, at least for the time being, we suggest a moratorium on format-related research.

Research in the area of statistical control of common rating errors has been sparse but encouraging. There are two distinct lines of research that might be fruitful. The first is the development of schemes for deriving residual performance scores—scores with rater–ratee context factors partialed out. Although this is a mechanical solution that implies no increase in the understanding of the rating process, it offers the possibility of simultaneously providing the practitioner with better numbers and the researcher with hypotheses. A second research line suggested by data analytic procedures is using ratings or judgments to derive cognitive maps or sets of raters. This would require some sophisticated designs directed toward understanding how individual raters construe their reality (Kelly, 1955).

Finally, our process model implies that the rater's experience with ratings affects the validity of those ratings. We know little or nothing about the effects that decisions based on current ratings have on future ratings. It is reasonable to assume that there are such effects. We can demonstrate that ratings for research purposes have different properties than ratings for administrative purposes. This implies that there is a feedback loop of some sort. Research in this area is long overdue. It is time to stop looking at the symptoms of bias in rating and begin examining potential causes.

REFERENCES

- Amir, Y., Kovarsky, Y., & Sharon, S. Peer nominations as a predictor of multistage promotions in a ramified organization. *Journal of Applied Psychology,* 1970, *54,* 462–469.
- Arvey, R. D., & Hoyle, J. C. A Guttman approach to the development of behaviorally based rating scales for systems analysts and programmer/analysts. *Journal of Applied Psychology,* 1974, *59,* 61–68.
- Baker, E. M., & Schuck, J. R. Theoretical note: Use of signal detection theory to clarify problems of evaluating performance in industry. *Organizational Behavior and Human Performance,* 1975, *13,* 307–317.
- Barrett, R. S. Influence of supervisor's requirements on ratings. *Personnel Psychology,* 1966, *19,* 375–387. (a)
- Barrett, R. S. *Performance rating.* Chicago: Science Research Associates, 1966. (b)
- Barrett, R. S., Taylor, E. K., Parker, J. W., & Martens, L. Rating scale content: I. Scale information and supervisory ratings. *Personnel Psychology,* 1958, *11,* 333–346.
- Bartlett, C. J. The relationship between self-ratings and peer ratings on a leadership behavior scale. *Personnel Psychology,* 1959, *12,* 237–246.
- Bartol, K. M., & Butterfield, D. A. Sex effects in evaluating leaders. *Journal of Applied Psychology,* 1976, *61,* 446–454.
- Bass, A. R., & Turner, J. N. Ethnic group differences in relationships among criteria of job performance. *Journal of Applied Psychology,* 1973, *57,* 101–109.
- Bass, B. M. Reducing leniency in merit ratings. *Personnel Psychology,* 1956, *9,* 359–369.
- Bass, B. M. Further evidence on the dynamic nature of criteria. *Personnel Psychology,* 1962, *15,* 93–97.
- Bayroff, A. G., Haggerty, H. R., & Rundquist, E. A. Validity of ratings as related to rating techniques and conditions. *Personnel Psychology,* 1954, *7,* 93–114.
- Bendig, A. W. A statistical report on a revision of the Miami instructor rating sheet. *Journal of Educational Psychology,* 1952, *43,* 423–429. (a)
- Bendig, A. W. The use of student rating scales in the evaluation of instructors in introductory psychology. *Journal of Educational Psychology,* 1952, *43,* 167–175. (b)
- Bendig, A. W. The reliability of self-ratings as a function of the amount of verbal anchoring and of the number of categories on the scale. *Journal of Applied Psychology,* 1953, *37,* 38–41.
- Bendig, A. W. Reliability and number of rating scale categories. *Journal of Applied Psychology,* 1954, *38,* 38–40. (a)
- Bendig, A. W. Reliability of short rating scales and the heterogeneity of the rated stimuli. *Journal of Applied Psychology,* 1954, *38,* 167–170. (b)
- Berkshire, J. R., & Highland, R. W. Forced-choice performance rating—A methodological study. *Personnel Psychology,* 1953, *6,* 355–378.
- Bernardin, H. J. Behavioral expectation scales versus summated scales: A fairer comparison. *Journal of Applied Psychology,* 1977, *62,* 422–427.
- Bernardin, H. J. Effects of rater training on leniency and halo errors in student ratings of instructors. *Journal of Applied Psychology,* 1978, *63,* 301–308.
- Bernardin, H. J., Alvares, K. M., & Cranny, C. J. A recomparison of behavioral expectation scales to summated scales. *Journal of Applied Psychology,* 1976, *61,* 564–570.
- Bernardin, H. J., LaShells, M. B., Smith, P. C., & Alvares, K. M. Behavioral expectation scales: Effects of developmental procedures and formats. *Journal of Applied Psychology,* 1976, *61,* 75–79.
- Bernardin, H. J., & Walter, C. S. Effects of rater training and diary-keeping on psychometric error in ratings. *Journal of Applied Psychology,* 1977, *62,* 64–69.
- Berry, N. H., Nelson, P. D., & McNally, M. S. A note on supervisor ratings. *Personnel Psychology,* 1966, *19,* 423–426.
- Bigoness, N. J. Effect of applicant's sex, race, and performance on employers' performance ratings: Some additional findings. *Journal of Applied Psychology,* 1976, *61,* 80–84.
- Blanz, F., & Ghiselli, E. E. The mixed standard scale: A new rating system. *Personnel Psychology,* 1972, *25,* 185–199.
- Blood, M. R. Spin-offs from behavioral expectation scale procedures. *Journal of Applied Psychology,* 1974, *59,* 513–515.
- Blum, M. L., & Naylor, J. C. *Industrial psychology.* New York: Harper & Row, 1968.

- Blumberg, H. H., DeSoto, C. B., & Kuethe, J. L. Evaluations of rating scale formats. *Personnel Psychology,* 1966, *19,* 243–259.
- Booker, G. S., & Miller, R. W. A closer look at peer ratings. *Personnel,* 1966, *43(1),* 42–47.
- Borman, W. C. The rating of individuals in organizations: An alternate approach. *Organizational Behavior and Human Performance,* 1974, *12,* 105–124.
- Borman, W. C. Effects of instructions to avoid halo error on reliability and validity of performance evaluation ratings. *Journal of Applied Psychology,* 1975, *60,* 556–560.
- Borman, W. C. Exploring upper limits of reliability and validity in performance ratings. *Journal of Applied Psychology,* 1978, *63,* 135–144.
- Borman, W. C., & Dunnette, M. D. Behavior-based versus trait-oriented performance ratings: An empirical study. *Journal of Applied Psychology,* 1975, *60,* 561–565.
- Borman, W. C., & Vallon, W. R. A view of what can happen when behavioral expectation scales are developed in one setting and used in another. *Journal of Applied Psychology,* 1974, *59,* 197–201.
- Borresen, H. A. The effects of instructions and item content on three types of ratings. *Educational and Psychological Measurement,* 1967, *27,* 855–862.
- Brehmer, B. Cue utilization and cue consistency in multiple-cue probability learning. *Organizational Behavior and Human Performance,* 1972, *8,* 286–296.
- Brown, E. M. Influence of training, method, and relationship on the halo effect. *Journal of Applied Psychology,* 1968, *52,* 195–199.
- Brumback, G. A reply to Kavanagh. *Personnel Psychology,* 1972, *25,* 567–572.
- Bruner, J. S., & Tagiuri, R. The perception of people. In G. Lindzey (Ed.), *Handbook of social psychology* (Vol. 2). Reading, Mass.: Addison-Wesley, 1954.
- Buckner, D. N. The predictability of ratings as a function of interrater agreement. *Journal of Applied Psychology,* 1959, *43,* 60–64.
- Burnaska, R. F., & Hollmann, T. D. An empirical comparison of the relative effects of rater response biases on three rating scale formats. *Journal of Applied Psychology,* 1974, *59,* 307–312.
- Campbell, D. T., & Fiske, D. W. Convergent and discriminant validation by the multitrait-multimethod matrix. *Psychological Bulletin,* 1959, *56,* 81–105.
- Campbell, D. T., Hunt, W. A., & Lewis, N. A. The relative susceptability of two rating scales to disturbances resulting from shifts in stimulus context. *Journal of Applied Psychology,* 1958, *42,* 213–217.
- Campbell, J. P., Dunnette, M. D., Arvey, R. D., & Hellervik, L. V. The development and evaluation of behaviorally based rating scales. *Journal of Applied Psychology,* 1973, *57,* 15–22.
- Campbell, J. P., Dunnette, M. D., Lawler, E. E., III, & Weick, K. E. *Managerial behavior, performance, and effectiveness.* New York: McGraw-Hill, 1970.
- Carter, G. C. Measurement of supervisory ability. *Journal of Applied Psychology,* 1952, *36,* 393–395.
- Cascio, W. F., & Valenzi, E. R. Behaviorally anchored rating scores: Effects of education and job experience of raters and ratees. *Journal of Applied Psychology,* 1977, *62,* 278–282.
- Cotton, J., & Stoltz, R. E. The general applicability of a scale for rating research productivity. *Journal of Applied Psychology,* 1960, *44,* 276–277.
- Cox, J. A., & Krumboltz, J. D. Racial bias in peer ratings of basic airmen. *Sociometry,* 1958, *21,* 292–299.
- Cozan, L. W. Forced choice: Better than other rating methods? *Personnel Psychology,* 1959, *36,* 80–83.
- Creswell, M. B. Effects of confidentiality on performance ratings of professional personnel. *Personnel Psychology,* 1963, *16,* 385–393.
- Cronbach, L. J. Processes affecting scores on understanding of others and assuming "similarity." *Psychological Bulletin,* 1955, *52,* 177–193.
- Dawes, R., & Corrigan, B. Linear models in decision making. *Psychological Bulletin,* 1974, *81,* 95–106.
- DeCotiis, T. A. An analysis of the external validity and applied relevance of three rating formats. *Organizational Behavior and Human Performance,* 1977, *19,* 247–266.
- DeJung, J. E., & Kaplan, H. Some differential effects of race of rater and combat attitude. *Journal of Applied Psychology,* 1962, *46,* 370–374.
- Dickinson, T. L., & Tice, T. E. The discriminant validity of scales developed by retranslation. *Personnel Psychology,* 1977, *30,* 217–228.
- Dunnette, M. D. A note on *the* criterion. *Journal of Applied Psychology,* 1963, *47,* 251–254.
- Einhorn, H. J. Expert measurement and mechanical combination. *Organizational Behavior and Human Performance,* 1972, *7,* 86–106.
- Elmore, P. B., & LaPointe, K. Effects of teacher sex and student sex on the evaluation of college instructors. *Journal of Educational Psychology,* 1974, *66,* 386–389.
- Elmore, P. B., & LaPointe, K. A. Effect of teacher sex, student sex, and teacher warmth on the evaluation of college instructors. *Journal of Educational Psychology,* 1975, *67,* 368–374.
- Farr, J. L., O'Leary, B. S., & Bartlett, C. J. Ethnic group membership as a moderator of the prediction of job performance. *Personnel Psychology,* 1971, *24,* 609–636.
- Ferguson, L. W. The value of acquaintance ratings in criteria research. *Personnel Psychology,* 1949, *2,* 93–102.
- Finn, R. H. Effects of some variations in rating scale characteristics on the means and reliabilities of ratings. *Educational and Psychological Measurement,* 1972, *32,* 255–265.
- Fiske, D. W., & Cox, J. A., Jr. The consistency of ratings by peers. *Journal of Applied Psychology,* 1960, *44,* 11–17.
- Flanagan, J. C. The critical incident technique. *Psychological Bulletin,* 1954, *51,* 327–358.
- Fox, H., & Lefkowitz, J. Differential validity: Ethnic group as a moderator in predicting job performance. *Personnel Psychology,* 1974, *27,* 209–223.
- Frank, L. L., & Hackman, J. R. Effects of interviewer-interviewee similarity on interviewer objectivity in college admissions interviews. *Journal of Applied Psychology,* 1975, *60,* 356–360.
- Freeberg, N. E. Relevance of rater-ratee acquaintance in the validity and reliability of ratings. *Journal of Applied Psychology,* 1969, *53,* 518–524.
- Friedman, B. A.,& Cornelius, E. T., III. Effect of rater participation in scale construction on the psychometric charac-

teristics of two rating scale formats. *Journal of Applied Psychology,* 1976, *61,* 210–216.

- Ghiselli, E. E., & Haire, M. The validation of selection tests in light of the dynamic character of criteria. *Personnel Psychology,* 1960, *13,* 225–231.
- Goodale, J. G., & Burke, R. J. Behaviorally based rating scales need not be job specific. *Journal of Applied Psychology,* 1975, *60,* 389–391.
- Gordon, L. V., & Medland, F. F. The cross-group stability of peer ratings of leadership potential. *Personnel Psychology,* 1965, *18,* 173–177.
- Gordon, M. E. The effect of the correctness of the behavior observed on the accuracy of ratings. *Organizational Behavior and Human Performance,* 1970, *5,* 366–377.
- Gordon, M. E. An examination of the relationship between the accuracy and favorability of ratings. *Journal of Applied Psychology,* 1972, *56,* 49–53.
- Graham, W. K., & Calendo, J. T. Personality correlates of supervisory ratings. *Personnel Psychology,* 1969, *22,* 483–487.
- Grant, D. L. A factor analysis of managers' ratings. *Journal of Applied Psychology,* 1955, *39,* 283–286.
- Greenhaus, J. H., & Gavin, J. F. The relationship between expectancies and job behavior for white and black employees. *Personnel Psychology,* 1972, *25,* 449–455.
- Grey, J., & Kipnis, D. Untangling the performance appraisal dilemma: The influence of perceived organizational context on evaluative processes. *Journal of Applied Psychology,* 1976, *61,* 329–335.
- Guilford, J. P. *Psychometric methods* (2nd ed.). New York: McGraw-Hill, 1954.
- Guilford, J. P., Christenson, R. R., Taaffe, G., & Wilson, R. C. Ratings should be scrutinized. *Educational and Psychological Measurement,* 1962, *22,* 439–447.
- Guion, R. M. Criterion measurement and personnel judgments. *Personnel Psychology,* 1961, *14,* 141–149.
- Guion, R. M. *Personnel testing.* New York: McGraw-Hill, 1965.
- Gulliksen, H. *Theory of mental tests.* New York: Wiley, 1950.
- Hamner, W. C., Kim, J. S., Baird, L., & Bigoness, N. J. Race and sex as determinants of ratings by potential employers in a simulated work sampling task. *Journal of Applied Psychology,* 1974, *59,* 705–711.
- Harari, O., & Zedeck, S. Development of behaviorally anchored scales for the evaluation of faculty teaching. *Journal of Applied Psychology,* 1973, *58,* 261–265.
- Heneman, H. G., III. Comparisons of self- and superior ratings of managerial performance. *Journal of Applied Psychology,* 1974, *59,* 638–642.
- Heron, A. The effects of real-life motivation on questionnaire response. *Journal of Applied Psychology,* 1956, *40,* 65–68.
- Hollander, E. P. The reliability of peer nominations under various conditions of administration. *Journal of Applied Psychology,* 1957, *41,* 85–90.
- Hollander, E. P. Validity of peer nominations in predicting a distant performance criterion. *Journal of Applied Psychology,* 1965, *49,* 434–438.
- Huck, J. R., & Bray, D. W. Management assessment center evaluations and subsequent job performance of white and black females. *Personnel Psychology,* 1976, *29,* 13–30.
- Isard, E. S. The relationship between item ambiguity and discriminating power in a forced-choice scale. *Journal of Applied Psychology,* 1956, *40,* 266–268.
- Jacobson, M. B., & Effertz, J. Sex roles and leadership: Perceptions of the leaders and the led. *Organizational Behavior and Human Performance,* 1974, *12,* 383–396.
- James, L. R. Criterion models and construct validity for criteria. *Psychological Bulletin,* 1973, *80,* 75–83.
- Jay, R., & Copes, J. Seniority and criterion measures of job proficiency. *Journal of Applied Psychology,* 1957, *41,* 58–60.
- Jenkins, G. D., & Taber, T. A Monte Carlo study of factors affecting three indices of composite scale reliability. *Journal of Applied Psychology,* 1977, *62,* 392–398.
- Johnson, D. M. Reanalysis of experimental halo effects. *Journal of Applied Psychology,* 1963, *47,* 46–47.
- Johnson, D. M., & Vidulich, R. N. Experimental manipulation of the halo effect. *Journal of Applied Psychology,* 1956, *40,* 130–131.
- Jurgensen, C. E. Intercorrelations in merit rating traits. *Journal of Applied Psychology,* 1950, *34,* 240–243.
- Jurgensen, C. E. Item weights in employee rating scales. *Journal of Applied Psychology,* 1955, *39,* 305–307.
- Kane, J. S., & Lawler, E. E., III. Methods of peer assessment. *Psychological Bulletin,* 1978, *85,* 555–586.
- Kaufman, G. G., & Johnson, J. C. Scaling peer ratings: An examination of the differential validities of positive and negative nominations. *Journal of Applied Psychology,* 1974, *59,* 302–306.
- Kavanagh, M. J. The content issue in performance appraisal: A review. *Personnel Psychology,* 1971, *24,* 653–668.
- Kavanagh, M. J. Rejoinder to Brumback "The content issue in performance appraisal: A review." *Personnel Psychology,* 1973, *26,* 163–166.
- Kavanagh, M. J., MacKinney, A. C., & Wolins, L. Issues in managerial performance: Multitrait-multimethod analysis of ratings. *Psychological Bulletin,* 1971, *75,* 34–49.
- Kay, B. R. The use of critical incidents in a forced-choice scale. *Journal of Applied Psychology,* 1959, *43,* 269–270.
- Keaveny, T. J., & McGann, A. F. A comparison of behavioral expectation scales and graphic rating scales. *Journal of Applied Psychology,* 1975, *60,* 695–703.
- Kelly, G. A. *The psychology of personal constructs.* New York: Norton, 1955.
- Kirchner, W. K. Relationships between supervisory and subordinate ratings for technical personnel. *Journal of Industrial Psychology,* 1965, *3,* 57–60.
- Kirchner, W. K., & Reisberg, D. J. Differences between better and less effective supervisors in appraisal of subordinates. *Personnel Psychology,* 1962, *15,* 295–302.
- Kirkpatrick, J. J., Ewen, R. B., Barrett, R. S., & Katzell, R. A. *Testing and fair employment.* New York: New York University Press, 1968.
- Klieger, W. A., & Mosel, J. N. The effect of opportunity to observe and rater status on the reliability of performance ratings. *Personnel Psychology,* 1953, *6,* 57–64.
- Klimoski, R. J., & London, M. Role of the rater in performance appraisal. *Journal of Applied Psychology,* 1974, *59,* 445–451.
- Klores, M. S. Rater bias in forced-distribution ratings. *Personnel Psychology,* 1966, *19,* 411–421.
- Koltuv, B. Some characteristics of intrajudge trait intercorrelations. *Psychological Monographs,* 1962, *76*(33, Whole No. 552).
- Kraut, A. J. Prediction of managerial success by peer and

training-staff ratings. *Journal of Applied Psychology,* 1975, *60,* 14–19.

- Landy, F. J., Barnes, J., & Murphy, K. Correlates of perceived fairness and accuracy in performance appraisal. *Journal of Applied Psychology,* 1978, *63,* 751–754.
- Landy, F. J., & Farr, J. L. Police performance appraisal. JSAS *Catalog of Selected Documents in Psychology,* 1976, *6,* 83. (Ms. No. 1315)
- Landy, F. J., Farr, J. L., Saal, F. G., & Freytag, W. R. Behaviorally anchored scales for rating the performance of police officers. *Journal of Applied Psychology,* 1976, *61,* 752–758.
- Landy, F. J., & Guion, R. M. Development of scales for the measurement of work motivation. *Organizational Behavior and Human Performance,* 1970, *5,* 93–103.
- Landy, F. J., & Trumbo, D. A. *The psychology of work behavior* (Rev. ed.). Homewood, Ill.: Dorsey Press, in press.
- Latham, G. P., & Wexley, K. N. Behavioral observation scales for performance appraisal purposes. *Personnel Psychology,* 1977, *30,* 255–268.
- Latham, G. P., Wexley, K. N., & Pursell, E. D. Training managers to minimize rating errors in the observation. *Journal of Applied Psychology,* 1975, *60,* 550–555.
- Lawler, E. E., III. The multitrait-multirater approach to measuring managerial job performance. *Journal of Applied Psychology,* 1967, *51,* 369–381.
- Lay, C. H., Burron, B. F., & Jackson, D. N. Base rates and informational value in impression formation. *Journal of Personality and Social Psychology,* 1973, *28,* 390–395.
- Lee, D., & Alvares, K. Effect of sex on descriptions and evaluations of supervisory behavior in a simulated industrial setting. *Journal of Applied Psychology,* 1977, *62,* 405–410.
- Lepkowski, J. R. Development of a forced-choice rating scale for engineer evaluation. *Journal of Applied Psychology,* 1963, *47,* 87–88.
- Leventhal, L., Perry, R. P., & Abrami, P. C. Effect of lecturer quality and student perception of lecturer's experience on teacher ratings. *Journal of Educational Psychology,* 1977, *69,* 360–374.
- Lewin, A. Y., & Zwany, A. Peer nominations: A model, literature critique and a paradigm for research. *Personnel Psychology,* 1976, *29,* 423–447.
- Lewis, N. A., & Taylor, J. A. Anxiety and extreme response preferences. *Educational and Psychological Measurement,* 1955, *15,* 111–116.
- Lissitz, R. W., & Green, S. B. Effect of the number of scale points on reliability: A Monte Carlo approach. *Journal of Applied Psychology,* 1975, *60,* 10–13.
- London, M., & Poplawski, J. R. Effects of information on stereotype development in performance appraisal and interview context. *Journal of Applied Psychology,* 1976, *61,* 199–205.
- Lopez, F. M. *Evaluating employee performance.* Chicago: Public Personnel Association, 1968.
- Lovell, G. D., & Haner, C. F. Forced-choice applied to college faculty rating. *Educational and Psychological Measurement,* 1955, *15,* 291–304.
- Maas, J. B. Patterned scaled expectation interview: Reliability studies on a new technique. *Journal of Applied Psychology,* 1965, *59,* 431–433.
- Madden, J. M., & Bourdon, R. D. Effects of variations in rating scale format on judgment. *Journal of Applied Psychology,* 1964, *48.* 147–151.
- Mandell, M. M. Supervisory characteristics and ratings: A summary of recent research. *Personnel Psychology,* 1956, *32,* 435–440.
- Meyer, H. H. Methods for scoring a check-list type rating scale. *Journal of Applied Psychology,* 1951, *35,* 46–49.
- Miller, G. A. The magical number seven, plus or minus two: Some limits on our capacity for processing information. *Psychological Review,* 1956, *63,* 81–97.
- Miner, J. B. Management appraisal: A review of procedures and practices. In H. L. Tosi, R. J. House, & M. D. Dunnette (Eds.), *Managerial motivation and compensation.* East Lansing, Mich.: Michigan State University, Graduate School of Business Administration, 1972.
- Mischel, H. N. Sex bias in the evaluation of professional achievements. *Journal of Educational Psychology,* 1974, *66,* 157–166.
- Moore, L. F., & Lee, A. J. Comparability of interviewer, group, and individual interview ratings. *Journal of Applied Psychology,* 1974, *59,* 163–167.
- Mullins, C. J., & Force, R. C. Rater accuracy as a generalized ability. *Journal of Applied Psychology,* 1962, *46,* 191–193.
- Myers, J. H. Removing halo from job evaluation factor structure. *Journal of Applied Psychology,* 1965, *49,* 217–221.
- Naylor, J. C., & Wherry, R. J., Sr. The use of simulated stimuli and the "JAN" technique to capture and cluster the policies of raters. *Educational and Psychological Measurement,* 1965, *25,* 969–986.
- Norman, W. T., & Goldberg, L. R. Rater, ratees, and randomness in personality structure. *Journal of Personality and Social Psychology,* 1966, *4,* 681–691.
- Obradovic, J. Modification of the forced-choice method as a criterion of job proficiency. *Journal of Applied Psychology,* 1970, *54,* 228–233.
- Overall, J. E. Reliability of composite ratings. *Educational and Psychological Measurement,* 1965, *25,* 1011–1022.
- Parker, J. W., Taylor, E. K., Barrett, R. S., & Martens, L. Rating scale content: 3. Relationship between supervisory and self-ratings. *Personnel Psychology,* 1959, *12,* 49–63.
- Passini, F. T., & Norman, W. T. Ratee relevance in peer nominations. *Journal of Applied Psychology,* 1969, *53,* 185–187.
- Paterson, D. G. The Scott Company graphic rating scale. *Journal of Personnel Research,* 1922, *1,* 361–376.
- Peters, D. L., & McCormick, E. J. Comparative reliability of numerically anchored versus job-task anchored rating scales. *Journal of Applied Psychology,* 1966, *50,* 92–96.
- Prien, E. P. Dynamic character of criteria: Organizational change. *Journal of Applied Psychology,* 1966, *50,* 501–504.
- Ritti, R. R. Control of "halo" in factor analysis of a supervisory behavior inventory. *Personnel Psychology,* 1964, *17,* 305–318.
- Ronan, W. W., & Prien, E. P. *Toward a criterion theory: A review and analysis of research and opinion.* Greensboro, N.C.: Creativity Institute of the Richardson Foundation, 1966.
- Rosen, B., & Jerdee, T. H. The influence of sex role stereotypes on evaluations of male and female supervisory behavior. *Journal of Applied Psychology,* 1973, *57,* 44–48.
- Ross, P. F. Reference groups in man-to-man job performance rating. *Personnel Psychology,* 1966, *19,* 115–142.

- Rothaus, P., Morton, R. B., & Hanson, P. G. Performance appraisal and psychological distance. *Journal of Applied Psychology,* 1965, *49,* 48–54.
- Rothe, H. F. The relation of merit ratings to length of service. *Personnel Psychology,* 1949, *2,* 237–242.
- Rotter, G. S., & Tinkleman, V. Anchor effects in the development of behavior rating scales. *Educational and Psychological Measurement,* 1970, *30,* 311–318.
- Ryan, F. J. Trait ratings of high school students by teachers. *Journal of Educational Psychology,* 1958, *49,* 124–128.
- Saal, F. E., & Landy, F. J. The mixed standard rating scale. An evaluation. *Organizational Behavior and Human Performance,* 1977, *18,* 19–35.
- Schein, V. E. The relationship between sex role stereotypes and requisite management characteristics. *Journal of Applied Psychology,* 1973, *57,* 95–100.
- Schein, V. E. Relationships between sex role stereotypes and requisite management characteristics among female managers. *Journal of Applied Psychology,* 1975, *60,* 340–344.
- Schmidt, F. L., & Johnson, R. H. Effect of race on peer ratings in an industrial setting. *Journal of Applied Psychology,* 1973, *57,* 237–241.
- Schmidt, F. L., & Kaplan, L. B. Composite vs. multiple criteria: A review and resolution of the controversy. *Personnel Psychology,* 1971, *24,* 419–434.
- Schmitt, N., & Hill, T. Sex and race composition of assessment center groups as a determinant of peer and assessor ratings. *Journal of Applied Psychology,* 1977, *62,* 261–264.
- Schneider, D. E., & Bayroff, A. G. The relationship between rater characteristics and validity of ratings. *Journal of Applied Psychology,* 1953, *37,* 278–280.
- Schneider, D. J. Implicit personality theory. *Psychological Bulletin,* 1973, *79,* 294–309.
- Schneier, C. E. Operational utility and psychometric characteristics of behavioral expectation scales: A cognitive reinterpretation. *Journal of Applied Psychology,* 1977, *62,* 541–548.
- Schultz, D. G., & Siegel, A. I. The analysis of job performance by multi-dimensional scaling techniques. *Journal of Applied Psychology,* 1964, *48,* 329–335.
- Schwab, D. P., Heneman, H. G., III, & DeCotiis, T. Behaviorally anchored rating scales: A review of the literature. *Personnel Psychology,* 1975, *28,* 549–562.
- Schwartz, D. J. A job sampling approach to merit system examining. *Personnel Psychology,* 1977, *30,* 175–185.
- Scott, W. E., Jr., & Hamner, W. C. The influence of variations in performance profiles on the performance evaluation process: An examination of the validity of the criterion. *Organizational Behavior and Human Performance,* 1975, *14,* 360–370.
- Sharon, A. T. Eliminating bias from student ratings of college instructors. *Journal of Applied Psychology,* 1970, *54,* 278–281.
- Sharon, A. T., & Bartlett, C. J. Effect of instructional conditions in producing leniency on two types of rating scales. *Personnel Psychology,* 1969, *22,* 251–263.
- Smith, P. C. Behaviors, results, and organizational effectiveness: The problem of criteria. In M. D. Dunnette (Ed.), *Handbook of industrial and organizational psychology.* Chicago: Rand McNally, 1976.
- Smith, P. C., & Kendall, L. M. Retranslation of expectations: An approach to the construction of unambiguous anchors for rating scales. *Journal of Applied Psychology,* 1963, *47,* 149–155.
- Springer, D. Ratings of candidates for promotion by coworkers and supervisors. *Journal of Applied Psychology,* 1953, *37,* 347–351.
- Staugas, L., & McQuitty, L. L. A new application of forced-choice ratings. *Personnel Psychology,* 1950, *3,* 413–424.
- Stone, E., Rabinowitz, S., & Spool, M. D. Effect of anonymity on student evaluations of faculty performance. *Journal of Educational Psychology,* 1977, *69,* 274–280.
- Suci, G. J., Vallance, T. R., & Glickman, A. S. A study of the effects of "likingness" and level of objectivity on peer rating reliabilities. *Educational and Psychological Measurement,* 1956, *16,* 147–152.
- Svetlik, B., Prien, E., & Barrett, G. Relationships between job difficulty, employee's attitude toward his job, and supervisory ratings of the employee effectiveness. *Journal of Applied Psychology,* 1964, *48,* 320–324.
- Tajfel, H., & Wilkes, A. L. Salience of attributes and commitment to extreme judgments in perception of people. *British Journal of Social and Clinical Psychology,* 1963, *2,* 40–49.
- Taylor, E. K., & Hastman, R. Relation of format and administration to the characteristics of graphic scales. *Personnel Psychology,* 1956, *9,* 181–206.
- Taylor, E. K., Parker, J. W., Martens, L., & Ford, G. L. Supervisory climate and performance ratings, an exploratory study. *Personnel Psychology,* 1959, *12,* 453–468.
- Taylor, E. K., Schneider, D. E., & Clay, H. C. Short forced-choice ratings work. *Personnel Psychology,* 1954, *7,* 245–252.
- Taylor, E. K., & Wherry, R. J. A study of leniency in two rating systems. *Personnel Psychology,* 1951, *4,* 39–47.
- Taylor, J. B., Haeffele, E., Thompson, P., & O'Donoghue, C. Rating scales as measures of clinical judgment: 2. The reliability of example-anchored scales under conditions of rater heterogeneity and divergent behavior sampling. *Educational and Psychological Measurement,* 1970, *30,* 301–310.
- Terborg, J. R., & Ilgen, D. R. A theoretical approach to sex discrimination in traditionally masculine occupations. *Organizational Behavior and Human Performance,* 1975, *13,* 352–376.
- Toole, D. L., Gavin, J. F., Murdy, L. B., & Sells, S. B. The differential validity of personality, personal history, and aptitude data for minority and nonminority employees. *Personnel Psychology,* 1972, *25,* 661–672.
- Vance, R. J., Kuhnert, K. W., & Farr, J. L. Interview judgments: Using external criteria to compare behavioral and graphic scale ratings. *Organizational Behavior and Human Performance,* 1978, *22,* 279–294.
- Wagner, E. E., & Hoover, T. O. The influence of technical knowledge on position error in ranking. *Journal of Applied Psychology,* 1974, *59,* 406–407.
- Waters, L. K., & Waters, C. W. Peer nominations as predictors of short-term sales performance. *Journal of Applied Psychology,* 1970, *54,* 42–44.
- Wells, W. D., & Smith, G. Four semantic rating scales compared. *Journal of Applied Psychology,* 1960, *44,* 393–397.
- Wexley, K. N., Sanders, R. E., & Yukl, G. A. Training interviewers to eliminate contrast effects in employment interviews. *Journal of Applied Psychology,* 1973, *57,* 233–236.
- Wherry, R. J., & Naylor, J. C. Comparison of two approaches—

JAN and PROF—for capturing rater strategies. *Educational and Psychological Measurement,* 1966, *26,* 267–286.

- Whitla, D. K., & Tirrell, J. E. The validity of ratings of several levels of supervisors. *Personnel Psychology,* 1953, *6,* 461–466.
- Willingham, W. W. Interdependence of successive absolute judgments. *Journal of Applied Psychology,* 1958, *42,* 416–418.
- Windle, C. D., & Dingman, H. F. Interrater agreement and predictive validity. *Journal of Applied Psychology,* 1960, *44,* 203–204.
- Wright, P. The harassed decision maker: Time pressures, distractions, and the use of evidence. *Journal of Applied Psychology,* 1974, *59,* 555–561.
- Zavala, A. Development of the forced-choice rating scale technique. *Psychological Bulletin,* 1965, *63,* 117–124.
- Zedeck, S., & Baker, H. T. Nursing performance as measured by behavioral expectation scales: A multitrait-multirater analysis. *Organizational Behavior and Human Performance,* 1972, *7,* 457–466.
- Zedeck, S., Imparato, N., Krausz, M., & Oleno, T. Development of behaviorally anchored rating scales as a function of organizational level. *Journal of Applied Psychology,* 1974, *59,* 249–252.
- Zedeck, S., Jacobs, R., & Kafry, D. Behavioral expectations: Development of parallel forms and analysis of scale assumptions. *Journal of Applied Psychology,* 1976, *61,* 112–115.
- Zedeck, S., & Kafry, D. Capturing rater policies for processing evaluation data. *Organizational Behavior and Human Performance,* 1977, *18,* 269–294.
- Zedeck, S., Kafry, D., & Jacobs, R. Format and scoring variations in behavioral expectation evaluations. *Organizational Behavior and Human Performance,* 1976, *17,* 171–184.

SOURCES SECTION SIX

USING APPRAISAL FOR HUMAN RESOURCE MANAGEMENT

CARAREER PLANNING

Developing Life Plans

by Gordon Lippitt

- Explains how a career planning workshop should be run.
- Discusses how organizational performance requirements can be integrated with personal career plans.
- Presents a method for self-appraisal which can be the basis of career planning.

Human Performance Problems and their Solutions

by Geary A. Rummler

Few people would argue with the statement that managers are more successful in solving machine and system problems than in solving problems involving human performance. Part of this lack of success can be attributed to the complexity, unpredictability, and general "uniqueness" of human beings. A major part of our failure at solving people-centered or people-related performance problems, however, is our failure to analyze these problems completely before we try to solve them. If we were more effective at analyzing people problems completely before we try to solve them. If we were more effective at analyzing people problems, we could significantly reduce the number of such problems.

There are several factors that contribute to our lack of success in analyzing human-performance problems. First, when people are involved, we react to our biases or assumptions about human nature. Second, we are led by all the training courses and programs available, and by the staff people who support them, to separate human-performance problems from the job—from the complex environment in which they occur. We apparently assume the cause and solution of the problem are completely wrapped up within the individual—that the problem or the individual is in no way influenced by the unclear standards, the inconsistent interpretation of those standards by supervision, or the built-in conflicts surrounding most jobs in most organizations. Why else would we conclude that a manager "can't handle people" and send him off to a general course in "human relations" or "communications"?

Finally, there is really no useful, operational way for the manager to analyze performance problems, though there are some interesting theories about what makes people "tick." Perhaps, for example, it makes a manager more comfortable to hypothesize a problem-performer's "hierarchy of needs"—but it doesn't help him solve the problem. Such theories may be useful to corporate staffs, who can design policies and procedures sensitive to what are supposedly "satisfiers" and "dissatisfiers," but understanding people at some abstract level is a long way from solving performance problems, as most managers know.

The lack of any effective way of analyzing performance problems is reflected in the labels used by managers in describing "problems"—poor performance is the result of "poor motivation" and "poor attitude." These terms are not useful; they don't say anything, they don't lead us to any real solutions. Frequently, the result is that the performer who has the vaguely stated performance problem is exposed to a training program with an equally vague title, again, such as "communications" or "human relations."

This article is concerned with a viewpoint for analyzing human performance problems. It provides managers with a framework for examining performance problems—a framework that cuts through the level of generalities we are used to and in so doing identifies specific, workable, non-magic solutions to problems. An integral part of this approach is to examine the performer in his environment. The approach in fact concentrates on the dynamics of the relationship between the performer and his environment.

Moreover, the approach has the potential of overcoming our personal bias about people by ignoring it. Concentrating on the performance desired, and those factors in the environment that influence it, makes bias and assumptions about human nature less relevant. If not totally irrelevant (thereby deemphasizing the need for the currently popular training in awareness, prejudice, and sensitivity).

COULD HE DO IT IF HIS LIFE DEPENDED ON IT?

For the most part, human performance deficiencies can be classified as deficiencies of knowledge, which result from an employee's not knowing what to do, how to do it, or when to do it; or as deficiencies of execution, which result from an employee's failing to perform because of factors in the work environment: or as some combination of the two.

Distinguishing between deficiencies of knowledge and execution is a critical step in analyzing people-centered performance problems. A frequent result of failure to make this distinction accurately is that extended and expensive training is conducted in a foredoomed attempt to solve a supposed knowledge problem that is in fact an execution problem—a nontraining problem. In addition to being a waste of money, such training tends to reduce the credibility of the organization with the employee being trained, and frequently leaves management with the dangerous illusion that the performance problem in question is being solved.

Reprinted from *Human Resource Management* Vol. 19, No. 3, Winter, 1972, pp. 2–10. Graduate School of Business Administration, University of Michigan, Ann Arbor, Mich. 48109.

This critical distinction between a deficiency of execution (D/e) and a deficiency of knowledge (D/k) can usually be made by getting the answers to these questions:

1. What is the desired performance (job outcome)?
   What are the job standards?
   Says who?
   Does everybody agree on those standards?
   Does everybody (anybody) know whether these standards are now being met?
2. What are the specific performance differences between actual and expected performance?
   Has anyone ever performed as required?
   Who?
   When?
3. Could employees perform properly if their lives depended on it?
   Did employees perform properly when they first came on the job?
4. Do employees whose performance is deficient know:
   What is expected of them?
   That they are not performing correctly and how far they are from expected performance?
   How to perform correctly?
   When to perform?
5. What positive/negative consequences of performing correctly/incorrectly can employees expect:
   From their bosses?
   From their subordinates?
   From their peers?

As an example of what can happen if these questions are not asked, consider the case of the personnel function of a large bank that was about to launch an extensive three day program for all managers on "employee appraisal," in order to revitalize the current three-year-old appraisal program. A day was to be spent exhorting the executives on the importance of accurate employee appraisal and two days were to be spent in skill-training for conducting appraisal interviews, complete with videotape feedback on interview performance. Fortunately, before this program got off the ground and valuable management time and training-development money were expected, someone asked these questions:

1. *What exactly was the problem? How did "poor attitude" toward the existing appraisal system manifest itself?* The problem indicators included the fact that the annual review forms were returned to the personnel office weeks and sometimes months later. More important, a recent review of the evaluations showed that of the possible ratings of "outstanding," "excellent," "good," "fair," and "poor" for each item, the rating "good" was checked for nearly all items. (The items being evaluated were personality-oriented—e.g., initiative, ability to get along with others, thoroughness, integrity.) What had alarmed the personnel department was that the appraisal system did not discriminate among good and poor employees and was useless as a guide for manpower-planning and promotion. The conclusion was that managers didn't know how to evaluate performance properly.
2. *Has anyone ever performed as required? When?* Yes. When the program first began three years ago, the managers did a good job, as reflected in the evaluations, which showed a distribution of employees along the scale "outstanding" to "poor." Even now, a new manager will occasionally conduct an "accurate" appraisal when he first comes on the job.
3. *What are the consequences to a manager of performing correctly and incorrectly—i.e., of accurately recording a subordinate's performance versus "going down the middle" with "goods"?* The answers to this question were not easily articulated by the organization. Through observation and informal discussions with individual managers, it was learned that these consequences were frequently forthcoming.

- Predictably, subordinates did not like being told they were below "good." Their reactions to such a rating were unpleasant, to put it mildly. The nature of the personality items on the form left considerable room for judgment and frequently made the review session with a subordinate more of a negotiating session.
- Over time, it became apparent that employees whose overall performance was considered excellent or outstanding were promoted out of the department and that any employee whose overall performance was fair or poor attracted attention from Personnel and resulted in time-consuming explanations and commitments to develop the substandard performer.
- Finally, Personnel came to use the appraisal as a cross-check on the raises recommended by managers. The theory was that an outstanding performer should get a larger raise than a fair performer. The reality facing the manager was that he had to respond to better job offers from other organizations and the need to attract and keep new people. By rating everyone approximately the same (no large deviations), he had more flexibility in awarding raises.

In short, managers received basically positive consequences for their "poor" performance in appraising employees and fairly negative consequences for performing as desired by Personnel. Performance had deteriorated over the three years, not because managers forgot—but because they learned. All the refresher training in appraisal interviewing in the world would not help. Instead, the appraisal system underwent a major overhaul, the first step being to provide for appraisal along dimensions other than the vagaries of personality.

The managers in this example would have been able to perform properly "if their lives depended on it"—as could most problem-performers. In fact, performance problems caused by deficiencies of knowledge are by far the smaller category. It is a safe bet to say that of those problems initially identified as "training" problems, only 15 to 20% can in any way be solved through some form of training, formal or informal. The big problem area, and the area in which we are the least effective, is the deficiency of execution.

ANALYZING DEFICIENCIES OF EXECUTION

Part of our ineffectiveness in solving deficiencies of execution is that we have few useful models for looking at performance. As a result, we conclude that people don't care, aren't motivated, have lousy attitudes, and so on. Although such conclusions may be true to a certain extent, a majority of problems initially diagnosed as attributable to such causes can be solved by using a more refined model.

Deficiencies of execution, or the failure to exhibit learned behavior on the job, can further be classified as resulting from (see Figure 1):

- Lack of feedback. This problem arises when the person either does not know that the behavior is important or does not know that he is failing to perform to standard. The solution to this problem is to design and implement an adequate feedback system.
- Task interference. Here, the person cannot perform as desired because he lacks the tools or because the layout or organization of the job is such as to interfere with proper performance. The solution to this problem is job engineering.
- Punishment or unfavorable consequences. In this case, the person has no incentive for performing as desired; frequently, even it is against his own best short-term interests to do so. The solution to this problem is to *change the consequences* attendant on the job so as to encourage proper performance.

Another example will help illustrate this further classification of D/e's: A major manufacturer and distributor of typewriters was lamenting the poor motivation of its repair service men because of their lack of enthusiasm for a program by which they were to report sales leads to salesmen in their district offices. The program had begun with great fanfare a year ago and had netted a sizeable number of sales leads the first several months, but had slacked off to nothing. The procedure seemed simple enough. When a repairman identified a potential sale, he was to complete a card requesting several lines of basic information and drop the card in a box at the office next time he was in. Management was frustrated at the lack of performance and was considering quietly dropping the program altogether or "upping the ante" by providing a bonus for leads or a commission on ultimate sales.

FIGURE 1
Performance Symptoms: Classification and General Solutions

Symptoms	*General class of solutions*
Tasks are not being done up to the desired standard. Desired performance gradually deteriorates over time. Employees don't believe it is necessary to perform as desired.	IMPROVE (or INITIATE) FEEDBACK
Work is seldom done on time. There is a backlog of work to be done. Work is done, but seldom well. Tasks are not being done at all.	JOB ENGINEERING
Employees do the task correctly when first on the job, but their performance deteriorates after a short time. Employees do the job correctly only when a supervisor or other authority figure is present. Employees appear to be "lazy" or "not motivated."	CHANGE THE CONSEQUENCES

A quick analysis showed the following:

- No feedback to the repairmen. The cards were picked up from the box by a clerk and were supposedly distributed to the salesmen—without any word to the repairmen. Sometimes cards were discarded because the information was incomplete. In such cases, the repairmen were never notified of the incompleteness in the data supplied.
- No positive consequences to the repairmen for completing and turning in the cards. The consequences necessary were not extravagant. One repairman said: "At least he could acknowledge that he got them." Another observed, "The cheap guy didn't even buy me a bottle at Christmas." There were, however, some negative consequences in the form of salesman rebuffs, such as, "Thanks for nothing. I chased clear across the country to follow up on that 'lead' and found they were going out of business. Don't do me any more favors." It took only a couple of remarks like this to bring a repairman up short.

This "motivation" problem becomes something else when you look at it more closely. There is no feedback on the results of the desired behavior, there are no particular positive consequences for doing as desired, and in fact there is a risk of mild "punishment" for doing as desired.

Perhaps the anté does have to be upped now to get and maintain the desired behavior. But this could have been maintained initially at little cost by providing feedback to the repairmen—in the form of as simple a thing as returning the card with a salesman's notation: "Made sale on 11/2/71. Customer appreciated your suggestion. Thanks."

This feedback/task-interference/consequence framework is extremely powerful. It can be used to analyze existing problems, predict problems before a job or system change is made, or solve problems. It provides an alternative to using labels such as "motivation," "communication," and "attitude" to describe problems. Now let's look more closely at each of the three causes of D/e's.

Feedback Problems

The individual performer is guided by the feedback he receives about his performance. In most cases where an individual agrees with the work goals, he will improve if he knows: 1) He is off target. 2) How to correct or get on target. If an individual fails to get feedback on his performance, he will begin to develop his own explanations of good and bad performance, of cause and effect—and he will inevitably develop superstitious behavior (i.e., he will erroneously attribute effects to certain causes).

The critical characteristics of effective feedback include:

- Frequency. Generally, the more frequent the feedback, the better.
- Immediacy. There should be little delay between the performance error and the feedback concerning it.
- Specificity. The feedback must in essence be "constructive criticism," in that it should differentiate the effects of various dimensions of performance.
- Understandability. The units used in stating the amount by which performance falls short should be clear to the person receiving the feedback.
- Positive orientation. The feedback should stress attainable performance subgoals, rather than punitive consequences—that is, reinforcement, rather than enforcement.

Most organizations abound with examples of poor feedback—computer printouts on last month's performance received three weeks into the next month (too infrequent, too late); production figures that lump all shifts together and memos to field noting "... a drop in overall performance which must be corrected" (not specific), and top management comment only when there is a negative exception, which means, "no news is good news."

Frequently, performance can be dramatically improved by improving feedback. Usually this requires collecting no new data, but simply redistributing existing data in a more useful format. Witness the following case. A vice president of an international freight company was concerned with the infrequency of container use by dockmen. Containerizing shipments represented a possible $20 saving in shipping costs for each container used. At one location, however, only 10 out of a possible 30 containers were being used on an average day. The 20 containers not used each day represented a $400 per-day lost saving. Multiplying by 260 working days yields a possible $104,000 annual saving through containerization that the company was failing to capitalize on. After observing freight handlers' performance at one location, the vice president concluded that workers were sufficiently familiar with the criteria for using containers. He found, however, that the freight handlers were unaware of the cost-benefits of containerization and had no specific standards against which to measure their performance.

The vice president's remedy was amazingly simple. He established 95% as the standard for containerizating shipments. (He maintained that no task can be done perfectly 100% of the time.) He made workers aware of the standard through their supervisors. The feedback system centered on a chart posted conspicuously in the freight terminal. On a typical day it read: OUT OF A POSSIBLE 30 CONTAINERS WE USED 25 TODAY. In this way, freight handlers knew exactly how well they had performed in relation to standard.

The results? One week after the feedback system was implemented, performance soared from 30% to 86% of standard and it's been improving ever since. When examining a performance problem that might be caused in part by lack of feedback, the following checklist of possible actions should point to effective corrective action.

Can Performance Be Improved by

1. Setting standards?
2. Stating existing standards in a shorter time frame (e.g., units per hour rather than per day)?
3. Providing feedback on:
   a. Fewer dimensions of performance?
   b. Different dimensions?
   c. Additional dimensions?
4. Designing the job so the performer can tell whether he is not performing properly (and if not, why not)?
5. Making the feedback message:
   a. More specific (e.g., by foreman rather than shift)?
   b. Less full of "noise" (e.g., on a single sheet, not as two inches of computer printout)?
6. Having the message delivered by a more objective and positive source?
7. Changing the format to show:
   a. Cumulative performance record (a history)?
   b. Composite of various performance indicators (for comparison)?
8. Increasing frequency?
9. Providing permanent storage for comparison by performer (a memory system)?

Consequence Problems

A person's performance is strongly influenced by the consequences he suffers or enjoys as a result of that performance. The consequences of performance may be positive, negative, or, for all practical purposes, nonexistent. They may also be immediate or long-term, and real or potential. Finally, they come simultaneously from a number of sources, including the work itself, subordinates, peers, bosses, and the organizational establishment. The result is that a person's "performance system" is a dynamic, multidimensional set of factors that significantly influence his behavior.

It follows that proper management of consequences is critical in maintaining desired performance. This is particularly true in organizational settings where a complex environment of people, equipment, and events continuously metes out consequences. The frequent, random, and arbitrary consequences that naturally occur in the organization must be brought under management's control, balanced, and managed in a way to support the desired performance.

Poor performance can frequently be traced to the fact that the organization (system, situations, procedures) inadvertently provides negative consequences for—that is, "punishes"—the desired behavior. Earlier, we reviewed the appraisal-interviewing case, where managers received negative consequences for accurately recording the performance of subordinates. We realize that "good" managers and employees should rise about this adversity and do what is correct. And most try to for a while, but are worn down over time or by the unrelenting nature of the negative consequences.

The long-term results of these inadvertent punishers are usually extremely costly. For example, the negative consequences of having more than 4% when he was 7%—and to do extreme things to "bury" that remaining 3% scrap. The result to the company will be excessive metal costs, an inventory shortage, scheduling headaches, and overtime to meet the inventory shortage.

A more subtle but frequent problem is exemplified by the airline manager who sought training in "decision-making" for his airport-terminal ticket-counter supervisors. When pressed for an example of poor decision-making, he was able to cite only the failure to add additional staff to the counter when the passenger lines extended beyond a certain point. The training analyst asked the counter supervisors why they didn't add staff under these circumstances. One replied that he had done so once, but got "burned" because it caused an overrun in the overtime budget. Now when he sees a need for additional staff, he calls his supervisor and asks him to decide. Not surprisingly, the supervisor's supervisor said much the same thing. Now he asks the manager, rather than run the risk of all that "heat." There are several costs that result from this set of negative consequences. One is the loss of service to customers and the possible loss of revenues. The other—the more insidious one—is that the manager is now bogged down making all manner of decisions that should be made two levels below him.

Sensitivity to the power of consequences will not only help analyze problems, but also will help predict problems. For example, the marketing function of a bank decided that it would launch a major training program for tellers in all its branches. The objective was to have tellers "sell" additional bank services, with particular emphasis on personal loans. Although the marketing staff was convincing in its argument that personal loans were extremely profitable, the program was doomed to failure because of the existing structure of consequences in the branches. First, there were immediate negative consequences to the tellers for errors in handling money. Failure to balance out at the end of the day and taking bad checks. This, coupled with long lines, kept the tellers' mind on the essentials: no fancy stuff. Second, there was no support from branch management for the personal-loan emphasis. The positive consequences for the branch manager (attracting attention downtown) were for building up a sizeable loan portfolio—which could be done quicker and at less cost by making a $1,000,000 loan to a small corporation. It takes a lot of $3,000 personal loans (and considerable expense per loan) to equal $1,000,000.

Given these two sets of consequences, thirty weeks of training in "selling services" would have negligible effect on personal loans as long as the balance of consequences itself was unchanged.

The following principles are basic to analyzing the balance of positive and negative consequences to performers.

- A consequence may be positive, neutral, or negative, depending on the individual, the time, and the circumstances.
- If a behavior continues, the balance of consequences is positive.
- If there are positive consequences for two mutually exclusive behaviors, the one with the greater positive consequence will occur.
- The further removed in time a consequence is from a behavior, the less effect that consequence will have on the behavior.
- The consequences that control the behavior are those that have value to the individual.

These principles can be restated as the following guidelines for analyzing the consequences of an act to a person:

1. Frequently, people don't just not do something; they do something else instead. There is value, therefore, in looking at the consequences of both what is desired and what is currently happening (i.e., undesired).
2. Do not mistake company policy and platitudes (e.g., "You will get promoted") for real consequences to the

individual (e.g., missing lunch with the fellas, having to do extra paperwork).

3. Separate immediate consequences (e.g., a sale today, holding up the car pool) from long-term consequences (e.g., week-end scrap report, monthly budget statement).
4. Consider the certainty of the consequence. We will often elect to engage in behavior with a high probability of immediate results (e.g., taking an extra 10 minutes for lunch, padding the call report) and low probability of negative consequences—i.e., getting caught.
5. Finally, remember that what one man considers a positive consequence, another man may consider very negative. Some people will bust their backs to get a chance to give a group presentation; others in the same office will go to extreme lengths to avoid such an "opportunity."

When trying to identify consequences and assess their power, you must be careful not to impose your value system on the analysis. You must look at what in fact is happening in the way of consequences and infer from your observations whether the consequences are positive or negative to the individual.

Task Interference

A number of very common causes of poor performance can be classified as "task inference"—that is, something interfering with the person's making the proper response in the desired situation. For a salesman, forms of task interference range from having to use a large, poorly laid-out parts or price manual to having more customers to call on than can possibly be done well in the time available.

In a manufacturing plant, task interference may range from a shortage of hand tools to an inadequate inventory-control system. Task interference describes those factors that make it either difficult or impossible to perform as desired. In addition to poor physical layout of a job, the major source of task interference is the lack of adequate resources—of time, tools or support equipment, or personnel.

Such problems can be identified by asking:

1. Is there enough time to perform the task?
2. Is there enough equipment to perform the task?
3. Are there enough support people and services to perform the task?
4. Are there competing tasks?
5. Are there things that distract the employee from the task?

Task-interference problems constantly creep into jobs as procedures are modified, assignments subtly change in scope, and systems slowly evolve. The problems can usually be solved by some form of job engineering. Although these kinds of problems are relatively straight forward and the solutions are far from profound, it is important that a manager identify and correct these problems. An employee may be slow to admit that such a problem exists or quick to work around it, assuming that it is "just one of those things." (In fact, human beings are generally so adaptive that they will be up to their ears in "just one of those things" unless someone keeps clearing them out of the way.) It is important that a manager identify task-interference problems and get the interference removed, or at least help a subordinate figure out the optimal way to get around the interference.

"TROUBLESHOOTING" PERFORMANCE PROBLEMS

We have presented a framework for looking at performance problems and some guidelines for analyzing them. A number of questions can be added that will make this framework into a troubleshooting guide for managers. First, we must determine whether there is in fact a real problem (e.g., is the symptom of "can't make decisions" in fact backed up by a performance discrepancy such as not enough ticket agents at the counter?) and whether the problem is in fact worth solving (e.g., what is the impact, economic or other, on customer wait time extending beyond X minutes?) Obviously, these are preliminary steps to forestall spending too much energy on solving a performance problem that either is no problem at all or is not worth solving. The second addition to the framework is the following very specific list of questions for probing a performance problem. The result is a troubleshooting guide for human-performance problems.

A Guide for Troubleshooting Performance Problems

A. IS THERE A PROBLEM? ____________________

What do you observe that indicates there is a problem?

1. How long has this been a problem?
2. How general a problem is it?
   - Where does it occur?
   - When does it occur?
   - How frequently does it occur?
   - Does it ever not occur in some locations or at some times?
3. How will you know when the problem is solved?
   - How will things look different?
   - What numbers will increase or decrease?

B. WHAT IS THE PROBLEM? ____________________

1. Who is the performer in question?
2. What is the desired action?
3. What specifically does he perform incorrectly?
4. Does he ever perform correctly?
   If yes: When?
   If no: Has anyone ever performed correctly?
   When?
   Where?

C. IS THE PROBLEM IMPORTANT? ____________________

What impact does the incorrect performance have on:

1. The product or service?
   Quality Cost Quantity
2. The company?
   Procedures Image
3. The performer or his department?
   Safety Ease of work
4. Other workers or departments?
   Safety Ease of work

D. WHERE HAS THE PERFORMANCE SYSTEM BROKEN DOWN? ____________________

Questions		*Action*
Does the performer:		
1. Know he is supposed to take the desired action? ● How do you know?	If no:	Instruct him.
2. Know what the desired action is? ● How do you know?	If no:	Instruct him.
3. Know when to take the desired action? ● How do you know?	If no:	Instruct him.
4. Know how to take the desired action? ● How do you know?	If no:	Instruct him.
5. Know the standard or level of performance expected? ● Are there standards? ● Does everybody agree on them? ● Is anyone meeting them now?	If no standards: If standards:	Set them. Instruct in them.
6. Know whether he is taking the desired action or not? ● How can he tell whether he is doing correctly?	If no:	Redesign job. Instruct in observing. Provide feedback.
7. Have adequate resources (e.g., time, equipment) to take the desired action?	If no:	Provide resources.
8. Receive negative consequences for taking the desired action? ● Consider such sources of consequences as superiors, peers, subordinates, and the system.	If yes:	Remove negative consequences.
9. Receive no consequences for taking the desired action?	If yes:	Provide positive consequences.
10. Receive immediate, positive consequences for doing something other than the desired action? ● Do "good" things happen to him if he doesn't do it?	If yes:	Remove positive consequences.
11. Receive no information on the consequences of taking the desired action? ● Does he know it makes a difference to do it right?	If no:	Provide feedback.
12. Receive wrong information on the consequences of his actions? ● Does information lead him to conclude he's doing okay when he is not?	If yes:	Correct feedback.

Questions		*Action*
13. Receive information on consequences that is not sufficient for him to correct his performance (i.e., not clear, not specific, too late, too infrequent)? • Does he receive enough information to know how to correct?	If yes:	Provide better feedback.
14. Know how to interpret information in order to correct his performance? • Given good information, can he figure out how to change?		Instruct on how to interpret data.

SUMMARY

As we have indicated, this D/k-D/e framework can be used to analyze existing problems and to predict problems that might occur if changes in procedures or changes in emphasis on some performance variable are being considered. The value of this framework or template for viewing people-related performance problems is that:

1. It makes possible (in fact requires) a closer look at the problem. It forces us to get off the "communication" and "doesn't care" level of abstraction and to get down to specifying what exactly is desired and how what is desired is different from what we are currently getting. In so doing, we then examine systematically the variables that influence performance—the consequences, the feedback, and the barriers to performance.
2. It provides real and specific solutions. The solutions are not grand abstractions such as "Change his attitude" or "Motivate him," nor are they vague preambles to training-course titles such as "He needs some training in 'communication'" or "Train him in 'human relations.' He can't handle men." The solutions that result from looking at performance problems from this viewpoint are specific ("He needs to have information on X and Y and in Z form" or "He will not do X as long as his supervisor persists in making him do Y every time he does"), and their implementation is frequently well within the domain and authority of management. There is little need to lateral the problem to staff—unless, of course, management doesn't want to face the problem, or really doesn't want it solved.

The value of this approach is considerable. Organizations and managers who have systematically applied it have accumulated an impressive list of results. It is a useful tool for the individual manager, but it is all the more powerful when used as the common approach by all the management of an organization.

How to Ruin Motivation with Pay

by W. Clay Hamner

Merit pay, or pay for performance, is so widely accepted by compensation managers and academic researchers that it seems foolhardy to criticize it. It is based on the "law of effect," which states simply that behavior that appears to lead to a positive consequence tends to be repeated. Most behavioral scientists believe in this principle, and it is followed by most large organizations that have a merit pay system for their management team.

Despite the soundness of the principle on which it is based, many academic researchers have criticized the merit system. They regard merit pay as detrimental to motivation rather than an enhancement, as it was designed to be.

One group of researchers contends that the merit system fails to increase motivation because managers mismanage merit programs and/or lack understanding of them.

Reprinted by permission of the publisher, from *Compensation Review*, 3rd Quarter,

These critics, therefore recommend that managers examine ways to improve the introduction of merit plans.

A second, though smaller, group criticizes the use of merit pay on grounds that it utilizes externally mediated rewards rather than focusing on a system in which individuals can be motivated by their jobs. They contend that employees who enjoy their jobs (that is, who are intrinsically motivated) will lose interest when a merit pay plan is introduced because they regard job satisfaction as their primary goal. These researchers, therefore, believe compensation managers should deemphasize merit pay and concentrate instead on improving other aspects of the job.

The research behind both of these positions deserves examination. And the review that follows concludes with recommendations designed to help managers utilize a "pay for performance" plan as a method of improving both quality and quantity of output.

WHY MERIT PAY SYSTEMS FAIL

As indicated above, some researchers have concluded that when merit plans fail, it is not due to a weakness in the law of effect. Rather, they blame weakness in the implementation of merit pay systems by compensation managers and line managers involved. For example:

- After reviewing pay research from General Electric and other companies, industrial psychologist Herbert H. Meyer concluded that despite the apparent soundness of the merit pay principle, experience tells us that it does not work with the elegance of its seeming simplicity. Instead, managers typically seem to be inclined to make relatively small discriminations in salary treatment among individuals in the same job regardless of perceived differences in performance. As a matter of fact, Meyer notes, when discriminations are made, they are likely to be based on factors other than performance, such as length of service, future potential, or perceived need for "catch up," where one employee's pay seems low in relation to others in the group.
- Michael Beer, director of organizational development at Corning Glass, observes that pay systems evolve over time. And in the process, he says, administrative considerations and tradition often override the more important considerations of behavioral outcomes in determining the shape of the merit pay system and its administration.

If, as both of these analysts seem to believe, it is not the merit pay theory itself that is defective, it is important to look at the specific shortcomings that Meyer, Beer, and other researchers say cause low motivation to result from merit pay.

1. *Pay is not perceived as being related to job performance.* Edward E. Lawler III, a leading researcher on pay and performance, has noted that managers often are unhappy with their wage system because they do not perceive the relationship between how hard they work (productivity) and how much they earn.

   In a survey of 600 middle and lower level managers, Lawler found virtually no relationship between their pay and their rated performance. Those who were most highly motivated to perform their jobs effectively were characterized by two attitudes: They said their pay was important to them, and they felt that good job performance would lead to higher pay for them.

Why don't managers perceive their pay as related to performance even when the company claims to have a merit pay plan? There are several reasons.

- Many rewards (for example, stock options) are *deferred payments,* and the time horizon is so long that the employee loses sight of its relationship to performance.
- The *goals* of the organization on which performance appraisals are based are unclear, unrealistic, or unrelated to pay. W. H. Mobley found that only 36 percent of the managers surveyed at a company using an MBO program saw goal attainment as having considerable bearing on their merit increase; at the same time, 83 percent of their bosses claimed that they used the goal attainments to determine their pay increase recommendations.
- The *secrecy* that so often surrounds annual merit pay increases may lead managers to conclude that their recommended pay increase is not related in any direct way to their past year's performance.

R. L. Opsahl and M.D. Dunnette claimed that secrecy is due in part to a fear of salary administrators that they would have a difficult time mustering convincing arguments in favor of many of their practices.

Lawler summarized his extensive research on secrecy of pay by stating that managers did not have an accurate picture of what other managers were earning. He found a general tendency among managers to overstate the pay of managers at their own level (thereby reducing their own pay, relatively speaking) and at one level below them (again reducing their own pay, relatively speaking); they also tended to underestimate the pay of managers one level above them (thus reducing the value of future promotions).

2. *Performance ratings are seen as biased.* While many managers working under a merit program believe that the program is a good one, they are dissatisfied with the evaluation of their performance by their imme-

diate superior. A merit plan is based on the assumption that managers can make objective (valid) distinctions between good and poor performance. Unfortunately, most evaluations of performance are subjective in nature and consist of a "summary score" from a general, and sometimes dated, performance evaluation form.

The supervisor's key role in determining pay creates a problem in that it reminds the employee very clearly that he or she is dependent on the supervisor for rewards. Therefore, the merit plan should, whenever possible, be based on objective measures (such as group sales, cost reduction per unit, and goal attainment) rather than subjective measures (such as cooperation, attitude, and future potential).

Even if subjective performance appraisals are not biased, Lawler believes that the complaints of managers and employees about the subjective nature of their performance evaluation may be a sign of poor leadership. "Many plans seem to fail," says Lawler, "not because they are mechanically defective, but because they were ineffectively introduced, there is a lack of trust between superiors and subordinates, or the quality of the supervisor is too low. No plan can succeed in the face of low trust and poor supervision, no matter how valid it may be from the point of view of mechanics." L. W. Gruenfield and P. Weissenberg support this poor leadership theory in their findings that good managers are much more amenable to the idea of basing pay on performance than are poor managers.

3. *Rewards are not viewed as rewards.* Management often has difficulty communicating accurately to employees the message intended to be conveyed through the pay raise. A raise can tell the employee "You're loved a lot," but at the same time it can also suggest: "I'm only average," "I'm not appreciated around here," or "I'd better get busy." Management often believes it is communicating a positive message when in fact the employee receives a negative signal, an interpretation that can have a detrimental effect on the employee's future potential. Therefore, the relationship between performance and attainment of the pay incentive must be explicit.

Management and employees' interpretations of reward messages can differ for several reasons. For example, conflicting reward schedules may be operating, a problem of inequity among employees is perceived to exist, or the merit increase may appear as threatening to the self-esteem of the employee.

Each of these problems centers on the fact that pay increases are generally kept secret, causing employees to draw erroneous conclusions, or that there is little or no communication in the form of coaching or counseling by supervisors during the year or following the performance appraisal. Instead, the employee is "expected to know" what the supervisor thinks about his or her performance.

Research has shown that the more frequent the formal and informal reviews of performance and the more the individual is told about the reasons for an increase, the greater his preference for a merit increase system and the lower his preference for a seniority system.

Conflicting reward schedules result from defects in the merit plan itself. For example, individual rewards (such as giving the best manager a free trip to Hawaii) are often set up in such a way that cooperation with other managers is discouraged; a cost reduction program may be introduced at the expense of production; or one department (sales) suffers while another department (manufacturing) benefits in the short run.

Some compensation managers stress that pay plans must change constantly because of general business conditions, shifts in management philosophy, competitive pressures, participant feedback, and modification in the structure and objectives of the organization. These changes, however, should be designed in such a way that the negative side effect of reduced cooperation does not result. For this reason, many companies use a companywide merit plan (such as the Scanlon Plan) that offers a financial incentive to everyone in the organization based on the performance of the total organization.

The question of inequity in pay arises when the employee perceives the merit increase to be unfair relative to his own past year's performance. The employee may be dissatisfied with the performance evaluation, or he may view the performance evaluation as fair but believes his supervisor failed to reward him in a manner consistent with the rating.

A more common problem is one that occurs when an employee who is satisfied with the dollar amount of his pay perceives that others performing at levels below him are receiving increases equal to his; or else he believes those who are performing at the same level are receiving higher raises. For example, an employee who was rated as above average receives an 8 percent pay increase but perceives this to be low since he believes that the average increase was 9 percent when in fact it was only 6.5 percent.

To avoid this type of problem—which will contribute to dissatisfaction with pay and possible lower job performance—Lawler recommends that, as a minimum requirement, managers explain to their employees how the salary raises were derived (for example, 50 percent based on cost of living and 50 percent on merit) and tell them the range and mean of raises given in the organization for people at their job level. Says Lawler: "There is no reason why organizations cannot make salaries public information."

Employee self-esteem can be undermined by merit pay because employees so often rate themselves as above average in performance and are disappointed when the merit raise doesn't jibe with the self-evaluation. Meyer, for example, concluded on the basis of his research that 90 percent of the managers at General Electric rated themselves above average. According to Meyer:

> The fact that almost everyone thinks he is an above average performer probably causes most of our problems with merit pay plans. Since the salary increases most people get do not reflect superior performance (as determined by interpersonal comparisons, or as defined in the guide book for the pay plan), the effects of the actual pay increases on motivation are likely to be more negative than positive. The majority of the people feel discriminated against because, obviously, management does not recognize their true worth.

4. *Managers of merit increases are more concerned with satisfaction with pay than job performance.* Most studies of managers' satisfaction with their pay have shown high levels of dissatisfaction—the rate has run as high as 80 percent in some surveys. But Beer points out that too often dissatisfaction with pay is assumed to mean dissatisfaction with amount. Beer's research suggests, however, that a change to a merit system with no increase in amount paid out by the company will increase satisfaction if the reasons for the increases are explained.

In contrast to the volume of research on satisfaction with pay, data in the area of the relationship between pay and job performance is less solid than any other field. Because of this failure to deal with the role of pay, Lawler notes that many managers have come to the erroneous conclusion that the experts in "human relations" have shown that pay is a relatively unimportant incentive.

In fact, Cherrington, Reitz, and Scott found that the magnitude of the relationship between satisfaction and performance depends primarily upon the performance-reinforcer contingencies that have been arranged—that is, people who were appropriately reinforced were satisfied with their pay, while those who were dissatisfied with their pay were those who were inappropriately rewarded. Likewise, Hamner and Foster found that the best performers working under a contingent (piece-rate) pay plan were more satisfied than the poorer performers, but that there was no relationship between satisfaction and performance for those paid under a noncontingent (across-the-board) pay plan.

Managers need to be concerned with two questions: *Is the merit raise based on performance,* and *who is doing the complaining?*

Numerous studies show that pay is not closely related to performance in many organizations that claim to have merit ranges. Typically, these studies show that pay is much more closely related to job level and seniority than performance. In fact, Belcher reports that low, zero, and even negative relationships between pay and supervisory ratings of performance occur even among managers where the relationship would be expected to be high.

Donald Finn, compensation manager at J. C. Penney, has said executives are often "hung up" as managers about the satisfaction of employees with pay recommendations. "So who is complaining and why?" asks Finn. "If low producers are low earners, the pay plan is working—but there will be complaints. If a company wants an incentive plan in which rewards are commensurate with risk, it must be willing to accept a relatively broad range of earnings and corresponding degrees of manager satisfaction."

5. *Trust and openness about merit increases is low.* A merit system will not be accepted and may not have the intended motivational effects if managers do not actively administer a performance appraisal system, practice good human relations, explain the reasons for the increases, and ensure that employees are not forgotten when eligibility dates come and go. The organization must provide an open climate with respect to pay and an environment where work and effort are valued.

The Xerox Corporation recognized the problem of trust and openness in a compensation planning model report that states this philosophy: "If pay and satisfaction are to be high, pay rates must vary according to job demands in such a way that each perceived increment in a job demand factor will lead to increased pay." The same document notes that organizations expect extremely high trust levels on the part of their employees, in that:

- Only 72 percent of 184 employing organizations in the study had a written statement of the firm's basic compensation policy covering such matters as paying competitive salaries, timing of wage and salary increases, and how raises are determined.
- Only 51 percent of these same organizations communicate their general compensation policies directly to all employees, while 21 percent communicate the policy only to managers.
- Contrarily, 69 percent of the firms do not provide their employees with wage and salary schedules or progression plans that apply to their own categories, thus indicating a low trust level toward employees.
- Over 50 percent of the firms do not tell their employees where this information is available.
- In only 48 percent of the firms do managers have access to salary schedules applying to their own level in the organization, and in only 18 percent of the companies do managers have knowledge of the salaries of other managers at their own level or higher levels.

6. *Some organizations view money as the primary motivator, ignoring the importance of the job itself.* The shortcomings discussed above deal with the criticism of researchers that the failure of the merit plan is due to poor implementation and not due to a weakness in

the theory of the "law of effect." The deficiency noted here centers on the criticism voiced by those who believe that employees who have interesting jobs will lose interest in the job when a merit pay plan is introduced.

An intrinsically motivating job can be defined as one that is so interesting and creative that certain pleasure or rewards are derived from completing the task itself. Until recently, most theories dealing with worker motivation have assumed that the effects of intrinsic and extrinsic reinforcement (such as merit pay) are addictive—that is, a worker will be more motivated to complete a task that combines both kinds of rewards than a task where only one kind of reward is present.

E. L. Deci, among others, criticizes behavioral scientists who advocate a system of employee motivation that utilizes externally mediated rewards—such as money—administered by someone other than the employee himself. In so doing, according to Deci, management is attempting to control the employee's behavior so he will do what he is told. The limitation of this method of worker motivation, for Deci, is that it satisfies only man's "lower order" needs.

Deci recommends that we move away from a method of external control toward a system in which individuals can be motivated by the job itself. He believes that this approach will allow managers to focus on higher-order needs in activities for which the rewards are mediated by the person himself (intrinsically motivated).

To motivate employees intrinsically, Deci believes tasks should be designed to make them interesting and creative. He also says workers should have some say in decisions that concern them "so they will feel like causal agents in the activities in which they engage."

Deci has introduced research data that suggests that a person's intrinsic motivation to perform an activity decreases when he receives contingent monetary payment for performing an interesting task. From these findings he concludes that:

> ...it seems clear that the effects of intrinsic motivation and extrinsic motivation are not additive. While extrinsic rewards such as money can certainly motivate behavior, they appear to be doing so at the expense of intrinsic motivation. As a result, contingent payment systems do not appear to be compatible with participative management systems.

Deci brings out an important point: Managers should not use pay to offset a boring or negative task. However, like Herzberg before him, his results don't appear to completely support his conclusion about the effect of money as a motivator. Research by Hamner and Foster has shown that the effect of intrinsic and extrinsic monetary rewards are additive and that even Deci's results themselves on close examination support this more traditional argument. In addition, I am not sure that merit pay plans are incompatible with a participative management system.

On both of these last two arguments, B. F. Skinner recommends that the organization should design feedback and incentive systems in such a way that the dual objective of getting things done and making work enjoyable are met. He says:

> It is important to remember that an incentive system isn't the only factor to take into account. How pleasant work conditions are, how easy or awkward a job is, how good or bad tools are—many things of that sort make an enormous difference in what a worker will do for what he receives. One problem of the production-line worker is that he seldom sees any of the ultimate consequences of his work. He puts on left front wheels day in and day out and he may never see the finished car....

MAKING A MERIT PAY SYSTEM WORK

In my discussion of the shortcomings of merit pay plans, various suggestions for overcoming these deficiencies were implied. More detailed recommendations on how to improve the quality and quantity of performance under merit pay are given below.

1. *Openness and trust should be stressed by the compensation manager.* As a minimum, employees should know the formula for devising the merit increases and should be told the range and mean of the pay increases for people at their job level. This alone should reduce some of the feeling of low self-esteem and inequity present in many organizations today.

Unfortunately, however, most companies cannot specify the formula for giving merit increases because there is no formula. Performance appraisals don't distinguish managers from each other since most managers are rated above average or higher. Line managers in most companies aren't told what the formula is, and they distribute the merit pay based on their own individual rule, which varies department by department and manager by manager.

The point is that most firms may have a merit plan in principle but do not have a merit program in fact. As a test, ask yourself these questions:

- Could I lay off managers based on their last merit increases—that is, if I had to reduce my managerial staff by 10 percent, could I identify these people by their last performance appraisal and merit increase?
- Would my line managers trust their own performance appraisals enough to have no other say in the merit increase—that is, could the compensation manager apply your company's formula by using the performance appraisal data only with no other consultation with the supervisor? If not, I would venture that

the reason lies in our failure to examine our merit plans to see why we do what we do and what impact it has on performance. Lack of knowledge about our own system is probably the main reason we don't have openness about our merit system.

2. *Supervisors should be trained in rating and feedback techniques.* Personnel managers should help design and carry out training programs that emphasize the necessity for consistency between performance ratings, other forms of feedback, and pay increases. In addition, managers should be trained to emphasize objective instead of subjective areas of job performance. Skinner in a recent interview in *Organizational Dynamics* states that poor training of managers is one of the greatest weaknesses in the motivation of workers through reinforcement principles. Stressing the need for effective training programs for managers, he predicted that "in the not too distant future, a new breed of industrial managers may be able to apply the principles of operant conditioning effectively."
3. *Components of the annual pay increase should be clearly and openly specified.* Organizations should allocate a certain percentage for both a cost-of-living increase (not to cover the total cost of living, however) and a percentage for merit. The percentage for merit should be an average and not a maximum, and the manager should be able to distribute this percentage in steps or degrees. In other words, it should not be an either-or situation where the worker either gets the full amount of the merit increase or none at all.

Any pay increase due to an adjustment for past inequities and pay increases due to promotions should come out of the payroll increase first, but it should not be included in the stated average pay increase. For example, if the organization can afford a 10 percent increase in wages and benefits, it might take 2 percent of this amount to use for the adjustments mentioned above and then allocate an 8 percent average increase to cost of living (say, 4 percent) and merit (not including adjustments). Along these lines, I feel it is important to give the increases in percentages and not dollar amounts since managers have a tendency to "cheat" long-term good performers (high-pay managers) when a dollar amount is used.

While I oppose having an absolute upper limit placed on a job range, many companies have this type of system. Where they do, it is important that managers and staff people in this job classification system know about the upper limit so that they are not surprised when they reach it.

Along this same line, many companies, in an attempt to avoid reaching the upper limit, give managers merit increases every 29 or 36 months rather than once a year. This is too long a period between merit increases. I therefore suggest that less money be allocated to annual cost-of-living increments, with the larger remaining amount going into the merit fund, and the increases awarded at least every 18 months.

Another related issue should be noted: In departments with a large number of senior employees who are eligible for only the minimum raise (due to an upper limit classification system), the full 8 percent should not be allocated for the pay increases. If it is, the department manager is tempted to overcompensate the less senior department members in order to spend the money he is allocated.

4. *Each organization should custom tailor its pay plan to the needs of the organization and individuals therein—with participation a key factor in the merit pay plan design.* One of the reasons the Scanlon plan (a group incentive plan) has been so successful is that it combines participation with the company's ability to afford a merit increase. Workers understand how they get their increases and how the amounts are set. In addition, each company using a Scanlon approach has a unique pay plan designed especially for that organization by the members of the organization.

In an example of a creative merit system, the Bendix Corporation decided to distribute its 1974 Christmas bonus to middle and lower middle managers based on merit. An average bonus of $1,500 per manager was distributed, but some managers received little or nothing whereas others received a healthy share. When combined with the regular merit increase, this feedback should have great informational value to the manager, especially in these economically depressed times when even managers themselves fear indefinite layoffs.

5. *Don't overlook other rewards.* Compensation managers should work with other staff people in the organization to improve the organizational climate, task design, and other forms of reward to insure that an employee has as much change of success as possible.

ETHICAL IMPLICATIONS

No discussion of effective uses of merit pay plans would be complete without a discussion of managers' ethical responsibilities in using pay as a motivator. There is no doubt that poorly designed reward structures can interfere with the development of spontaneity and creativity. Deceptive reinforcement systems and manipulation insult the integrity of man. The employee should be a willing party to the influence attempt, with both parties benefiting from the relationship.

The ethical responsibility of managers in the area of compensation is clear. The first step in the ethical use of monetary control in organizations is the understanding by managers of the determination of behavior. Since reinforcement is the single most important concept in the learning process, managers must learn how to design effective reinforcement programs that will encourage productive and creative employees.

Designing Appraisal Systems for Information Yield

by L. L. Cummings and Donald P. Schwab

The practice of performance appraisal suffers from a multitude of dilemmas. For example:

"Shouldn't all employees be told where they stand?"
"Yes, but experience indicates that poor performers usually don't improve when told they are in trouble!"
"Shouldn't feedback about performance be given as frequently as possible?"
"Yes, but some routine jobs allow for little variation in performance and most experienced employees believe that they know how they are doing without being bugged by the boss!"
"Shouldn't appraisal techniques and feedback methods be tailored to fit each individual and each situation?"
"Yes, but that would cost most organizations a fortune in time and money!"

The continued but generally unsatisfactory resolution of such stressful decisions has led to performance appraisals being both widely used and widely abused.

Much controversy surrounds their use. Concern continues to be expressed regarding their contribution to organizational and individual effectiveness and even their relevance.[1] Our purposes in this article are to suggest that the typical dilemmas and problems in applying appraisals derive from conflicting goals and inadequate attention devoted to the context of appraisal; propose conditioning factors that should influence the diagnosis and specification of appropriate goals for appraisal; and describe three systems of appraisal that are tailored to fit the differing purposes and contexts of effective performance evaluation.

Consider the following conversation between two second-level line managers of a major pharmaceutical manufacturer. Each has been reminded recently by the divisional personnel manager that their appraisals of their subordinates are due within the week.

"You know, Jimmy, these damn appraisals are a pain in the neck. Doing the damn things not only takes time away from the job but at least half of my people resent my talking with them about how they are doing. Take those gals working on the capsule machines. Most of them are over forty, married, and have been with the company for at least a dozen years. They want a steady job and friendly people to work with. They're not after promotions, status, development, and all that crap. They know damn well that the only reason for appraisal is to bug the gals who are not carrying their share of the load. Once in a while I can get a little bigger pay increase for one but I have to really build a big case for the old man."

"Jerry, you miss the point of why Personnel wants us to do these appraisals every year. The aim is to discover who has the track record and the capability of handling a bigger job. Without this appraisal process, some of our best people would be overlooked and forgotten when bigger, better jobs are open in the company. Besides, it's important to emphasize to our people that their development on the job is an important thing around here. Without that, a helluva lot of people wouldn't find this place very attractive. What's more, with the company's promotion-from-within policy, it's part of our job to be on the lookout for comers. When we do that, people react favorably to opportunities for feedback and suggestions for improvement."

This incident illustrates the difference between an essentially *evaluative* and a *developmental* use of appraisal systems and techniques. Evaluative uses of appraisal focus on providing information for making administrative decisions about employees. Examples of such decisions would be compensation changes, promotions, demotions, or transfers and even termination decisions. As developmental tools, appraisals are aimed at improving both performance and the potential for performance by identifying areas for growth and personal development. The essential differences between these two approaches are depicted in Table 1.

Historically, the predominant use of performance appraisals has been for evaluation of past and current performances of employees. This use of appraisal as an evaluative tool has been consistent with the use of the major techniques of the personnel profession. The responsibility for definition of organizational goals, the description and analysis of tasks to be completed, and the evaluation of

---

 Reprinted from *California Management Review,* Vol. 20, No. 4, pp. 18–25, by permission of the Regents.

[1]David L. DeVries (chairman), "Performance Appraisal and Feedback: Flies in the Ointment," Symposium presented at the 84th Annual Convention of the American Psychological Association, Washington, D.C., 1976.

TABLE 1
Appraisals for Evaluation and Development

	Evaluative role of appraisal	*Developmental role of appraisal*
Focus	On past performance	On improvement in future
Objective	Improve performance by more effective personnal and reward administration	Improve performance through self-learning and growth
Method	Variety of rating and ranking procedures	Series of developmental steps as reflected, for example, in management by objectives
Role of superior	To judge, to evaluate	To counsel, help, or guide
Role of subordinate	Passive or reactive, frequently to defend himself/herself	Active involvement in learning

Adapted from L. L. Cummings and Donald P. Schwab, *Performance in Organizations* (Glenview, Ill.: Scott, Foresman and Company, 1973), p. 5.

employee performance rested on management's shoulders. The employee was viewed as largely constrained in his or her responsibility to carry out the activities contained within the job descriptions developed by managerial and staff personnel. This distinction between managerial and subordinate responsibilities became epitomized in the separation of the planning and controlling (appraising) versus the doing of work. Systems of work simplification, applied industrial engineering, and scientific management were developed to implement this distinction in the pursuit of employee efficiency.

TRENDS TOWARD DEVELOPMENT

Events and trends in managerial thinking during the past fifteen years have transformed this predominantly evaluative philosophy. Several of these nudges toward a broader conception of appraisal are noteworthy.

First, there is increasing awareness that traditional performance appraisal techniques have failed to record the full variance or range of an individual's performance. This is partially because evaluators commit systematic errors when rating their subordinates. For example, tendencies toward unrealistically favorable (or unfavorable) evaluations are well documented. Appraisers also may tend to avoid spreading out their evaluations to the extent warranted by the actual performance differences among people. These, and other, errors in evaluating are well known and have generated considerable skepticism concerning traditional rating procedures and formats.[2]

Second, it has become increasingly apparent that most jobs are not solely and completely defined by the organization through the process of job analysis and job description. Incumbents of jobs enact and change the nature of their jobs over time. The nuances and subtleties of performing for many jobs provide ample opportunities for individuals to express their preferences and skills in actually carrying out the formal requirements of the task. In addition, the requirements of a task change over time as the performer learns the fundamentals of a job and begins to see opportunities for innovation and constructive change. Typically, these differences among individual performers in their perceptions of a job and the dynamic nature of tasks are not captured in static appraisal systems and procedures.

Third, evaluative appraisal became a favorite straw man of a number of advocates of work and organization humanization. McGregor, Argyris, and Drucker[3] each attacked the traditional evaluative systems of appraisal as mechanical, hierarchically centered and controlled, and demotivating artifacts of the bureaucratic system. The pebble of truth in these assertions was just large enough to cause a ripple of popular attack and pessimism concerning appraisals for evaluative purposes. These largely philosophic and normative confrontations appeared to be supported by the early results of an empirical study of reactions to appraisals among General Electric employees.[4] It was observed that bosses typically resisted conducting appraisals and providing feedback and subordinates typically did not change their behavior as a consequence of receiving evaluations. At worst, employees were reported to react hostilely and defensively to attempts to improve their performance through evaluation and feedback. Thus, the essentially speculative arguments of the 1950s and 1960s and some empirical evidence suggested that appraisals for evaluation

[2] L.L. Cummings and Donald P. Schwab, *Performance in Organizations* (Glenview, Ill.: Scott, Foresman and Company, 1973), chapters 6 and 7.

[3] Douglas McGregor, *The Human Side of Enterprise* (New York: McGraw-Hill, 1960), chapter 6; Chris Argyris, *Personality and Organization: The Conflict Between The System and The Individual* (New York: Harper & Bros., 1957), and *Integrating the Individual and the Organization* (New York: John Wiley & Sons, 1964), chapter 12; and Peter F. Drucker, *The Practice of Management* (New York: Harper & Bros., 1954).

[4] Herbert Meyer, Emanuel Kay, and John R.F. French, Jr., "Split Roles in Performance Appraisal," *Harvard Business Review* (1965), p. 123ff.

were of limited value. Despite the need to assess performance and make decisions based on those assessments, the hue and cry was heard for abandoning the evaluative tone and for focusing primarily on the developmental purpose and rationale of appraisal.

As a consequence of these types of events specific strategies and techniques for implementing development-oriented performance assessment systems evolved during the 1960s. These systems have been variously labeled management by objectives (MBO), management by results, goal-oriented management, and purposive management. Labels and specific techniques aside, however, these programs shared an emphasis on performance improvement rather than on performance evaluation.

Yet systems aimed at improving performance do not vitiate the need for personnel decisions that, in turn, require evaluative appraisals. Thus it is now common for appraisal systems to have both development *and* evaluative objectives. Thus, the desires of the organizational humanists have not been completely fulfilled. The fundamental purpose of performance appraisal has not changed. Rather, a new objective has been added to the old. Organizations now expect managers to both evaluate performance for institutional reward and punishment purposes, and to use the appraisal process to improve employee performance levels. Herein lies one of the dilemmas perplexing appraisal systems. The techniques and modes of thinking appropriate for development of performance are different from and may even be inconsistent with those appropriate for evaluating performance.

The potential problem has been rather widely recognized. Moreover, it is frequently recommended that the two objectives be procedurally separated insofar as possible. Recently, for example, Beer and Ruh described a three-stage appraisal system developed at Corning Glass Works.[5] A principal purpose of the three stages is the separation of developmental and evaluative aspects of the appraisal process. Nevertheless, it is surely naive to suppose that employees completely compartmentalize the two objectives no matter what the organization does in attempting to do so.

An alternative approach would involve a much more selective use of developmental appraisals than is recommended by the current conventional wisdom. Such selectivity is warranted primarily because of conditioning factors which limit the circumstances when the developmental use of appraisals is likely to be valuable. These conditioning factors have to do with assumptions about the behavioral processes underlying developmental appraisals and assumptions about characteristics of organizations and individuals that are necessary for the successful utilization of appraisals for developmental purposes.

[5]Michael Beer and Robert Ruh, "Employee Growth Through Performance Management," *Harvard Business Review* (1976), pp. 59–66.

CONDITIONING FACTORS

Characteristics of Goals

A critical behavioral assumption underlies most attempts to use developmental appraisals. It is assumed that *goal setting,* either by the manager or by the performer, will increase performance. Several characteristics of the goal setting process and of the resulting goals are known to impact the effectiveness of attempts to use goals as developmental tools.[6] To exert maximum performance impact, the development process should produce goals that are: (1) specifically stated with magnitude of achievement and time frame for accomplishment clearly spelled out; (2) perceived as attainable by the performer but yet difficult enough to stretch the performer incrementally beyond previous performance levels; and (3) accepted as meaningful and legitimate by the performer. Acceptance must be sought on two dimensions: the magnitude or level of the goal and the social or personal relevance of the goal.

Systems of performance improvement that do not include these components are not likely to yield positive results.[7] Additionally, there is a common problem associated with the implementation of the goal setting process not specified above. This problem can be seen in the following example from a national distributor of industrial chemicals.

At the 1975 national sales meeting, each regional manager of sales was asked to set cost-reduction goals for each of his regions. Goals were to be set in terms of percentage cost reductions for each quarter of the forthcoming year. The vice president for sales also emphasized that it was important for each manager to focus on improving the morale of his salespersons to keep turnover to a minimum. One year later, at the 1976 national meeting, it was disclosed that seven of ten managers had met their cost-reduction goals, but that no progress had been made on reducing salesperson turnover. Why?

One of the major reasons, recognized by the managers themselves, was that the specificity of the cost-reduction goal (expressed in quantified terms) had focused their attention on that goal. The ambiguous, unspecified nature of the morale and turnover goals somehow communicated that these were less important and that performance was less likely to be measured against these general objectives.

While the problem of differential goal specificity can be resolved with planning, others are not so easily overcome. Indeed, a bit of reflection will suggest that the goal-setting requirements specified above are not applicable to some jobs and to some persons.

[6]Richard M. Steers and Lyman W. Porter, "The Role of Task-Goal Attributes in Employee Performance," *Psychological Bulletin* (1974), pp. 434–452.

[7]E.A. Locke, N. Cartledge, and C.S. Knerr, "Studies of the Relationship Between Satisfaction, Goal-Setting and Performance," *Organizational Behavior and Human Performance* (1970), pp. 135–158.

The Nature of the Job

A major problem for developmental appraisal and meaningful goal setting has to do with the nature of the job performed. Realistically, many jobs are designed so that it would be nearly impossible to provide developmental potential through the job. This frequently arises because of a technologically constrained or defined job definition coupled with a work specialization and standardization system. The control over the *quality of work,* at least above a minimally acceptable level, depends heavily on the quality of materials available to the performer and on the proper care and maintenance of the equipment (or other technology) available to the performer. On routine tasks these factors are often out of the employee's control. Essentially the same realities apply when examining the *pace* at which the performer operates. In many cases, jobs and work flows are designed such that the schedule and rapidity of work are essentially beyond the performer's control. The only opportunity to influence pace may well be in a negative direction.

In these circumstances, successful developmental efforts would be possible only if jobs were redesigned to provide individuals with greater performance discretion. Such redesign may be worth considering in some instances. Clearly, however, many jobs cannot be meaningfully altered given the capital expenditures which would be required. Moreover, there is little evidence that job redesign consistently influences performance positively.[8]

Performer Characteristics

Another problem with developmental appraisals has to do with the *characteristics of people performing on jobs.* There is a substantial body of literature identifying individual differences in ability to perform and in actual performance. More recently it is becoming evident that persons differ substantially in their preferences for various types of work outcomes. Clearly, some seek task-related outcomes such as opportunity for growth and achievement, the type of outcomes successful developmental programs are built on. Others, however, seek more extrinsically oriented outcomes such as pay and pleasant working conditions. These people are less likely to be attracted to and motivated by a developmental orientation.

Also, it must be noted that people's behaviors and attitudes are more stable over time than change-focused managerial techniques typically assume. The best predictor of future behavior and preferences are the behaviors and preferences of the past. Someone with a record of poor performance in the past cannot reasonably be expected to evolve into a "hotshot" performer as a consequence of a developmental program. Indeed, it typically would be a waste of organizational resources to try to do so.

It is true that certain characteristics of developmental systems are attractive to employees. For example, there is reason to believe that it is satisfying to participate in the implementation of an appraisal system.[9] Moreover, opportunities to provide self-feedback in the form of appraising one's own performance also leads to satisfaction.[10]

At the same time, however, we know that self-feedback results in overstatements of performance relative to supervisory evaluations when rewards are attached to the results.[11]. Thus, if a low performer is allowed to provide self feedback, as is typical of developmental appraisal programs, the corrective features usually attributed to feedback are not likely to take place. Unfortunately, this undesirable consequence is most likely to occur among the persons who need most development, namely the low performers.

THREE SYSTEMS OF APPRAISAL

To review, the conditioning factors discussed above indicate that appraisals have developmental potential where meaningful and challenging goals can be established and accomplished. Characteristics of jobs, however, often prohibit significant performance variation making the idea of goal setting and performance enhancement of limited value. Moreover, employees are associated with a history of abilities, needs, and performance. This history imposes greater constraints on change than the typical developmental appraisal system acknowledges.

While we have no hard data, it is reasonable to suppose that no more than half the jobs in a typical organization allow for the variability in performance and flexibility in goal setting required by developmental appraisal. In addition, given some reasonable assumptions about organizational staffing, training, and reward policies and practices, we can expect that relatively very few high and very low performers are employed. Eighty percent or more are likely to be average performers. These assumptions suggest the need to assume a *contingency* posture toward designing, implementing, and evaluating employee appraisals. The following three systems are presented as a movement in this direction and are outlined in Table 2.[12]

---

[8]Jon L. Pierce and Randall B. Dunham, "Task Design: A Literature Review," *Academy of Management Review* (1976), pp. 83–97.

[9]L.L. Cummings, "A Field Experimental Study of the Effects of Two Performance Appraisal Systems," *Personnel Psychology* (1973), pp. 489–502.

[10]M.M. Greller and D.M. Herold, "Sources of Feedback: A Preliminary Investigation," *Organizational Behavior and Human Performance* (1975), pp. 244–256.

[11]M.M. Greller, "Employee Reactions to Performance Feedback," *Working Paper, Graduate School of Business,* New York University, 1976.

[12]These systems are developed in greater detail in Cummings and Schwab, *Performance in Organizations.*

TABLE 2
Three Appraisal Systems

DAP = Development Action Program:
Focused on proven high performer with upward potential.

MAP = Maintenance Action Program:
Focused on acceptable performer with limited upward potential.

RAP = Remedial Action Program:
Focused on substandard performer who requires close attention or who should be prepared for termination.

Developmental Action Program

A developmental action program (DAP) is applicable for the relatively small number of employees with a history of high performance. Such employees are found on jobs where goal setting and performance enhancement can take place. They are, therefore, ideally suited to benefit from developmental appraisal systems. Although specifics of such systems may vary, they will include: (1) participation by the subordinate in the establishment of goals; (2) subordinate and superior agreement on methods for measuring performance or additional skills and resources necessary to accomplish performance goals; (3) participation in review sessions to assess goal progress; and (4) recycling through the goal-setting phase.

It can be reasonably assumed that individuals with a performance history justifying DAP can benefit from the implications of developmental appraisal. Participation in goal setting allows for the establishment of meaningful and challenging goals. Participation in review holds few of the dangers of distortion identified above because the individual is already a high performer. Finally, there is relatively little potential conflict between developmental and evaluative aspects in DAP since the manager can assure the performer that he or she will receive favorable organizational rewards. Indeed, a successfully implemented DAP will generally lead to promotion or increased responsibility through job enrichment.

Maintenance Action Program

For most employees an appraisal focused on a maintenance action program (MAP) will be appropriate. MAP is applicable for individuals who are not likely to improve their performance because of ability or motivational constraints, or on jobs that do not allow for meaningful goal setting and performance enhancement. The focus, therefore, of MAP is on maintaining performance at the currently acceptable levels.

Emphases, and therefore the processes, of MAP and DAP differ substantially. In a MAP the supervisor and the technology of the job will be primarily responsible for the establishment of work goals and objectives. Review of work performance is the supervisor's responsibility. While reviews should be scheduled in accordance with the completion time of the assigned tasks, frequently the timing of reviews is determined by the calendar, that is, the employee's anniversary date with the organization.

We recognize that the premises of MAP (and remedial action programs, discussed below) are contrary to the humanistic ideal of universal potential for growth and development. Certainly employees should not be relegated to a MAP until several appraisals point consistently in the same direction. Nevertheless, employees do reach growth limits or are placed on jobs which constrain further development. Attempts to develop such employees in their current roles is wasteful to the organization and potentially frustrating, if not threatening, to the employee.

If an individual on a MAP performs at a consistently high level, he or she should be considered for a DAP. Such a possibility may require that the employee be assigned to a job allowing for greater performance variability. Regression from MAP is, of course, also possible. In that case the employee should be considered for a remedial action program.

Remedial Action Program

The most troubling employees for managers are those whose performance has been consistently marginal or unacceptable and are, therefore, candidates for a remedial action program (RAP). A RAP is aimed at performance improvement through close supervisory controls. Failing that, termination of the employee is the aim. Thus, a RAP must provide specific supervisory feedback on performance deficiencies. Frequent examples of behaviors reflecting acceptable and unacceptable behaviors are desirable. Clearly, self-appraisal is undesirable in a RAP given the findings discussed above concerning the effects of self-feedback.

A RAP also should include specific programs for improved performance *imposed by the supervisor* which include the explicit identification of performance measures and time perspectives for review. Moreover, the review intervals should be of very short duration; at least until performance levels begin to improve.

If performance fails to improve or declines after the initiation of a RAP, the manager is obligated to initiate an explicit sequence resulting in a final step of termination. Ideally, the aim of such a sequence is either the return of performance to an acceptable level or the voluntary separation of the employee. Such a sequence must be explicit and formal in the sense that the employee understands that he or she has moved into this phase of the RAP. Such knowledge is not only an ethical requirement but will undoubtedly be necessary if the terminated employee takes legal action.

TABLE 3
Appraisal Programs and Dimensions of Feedback

	Development Action Program	*Maintenance Action Program*	*Remedial Action Program*
Nature of feedback	Future-oriented Implied goals Self-generated Implies job scope expansion	Past-oriented General focus on exceptions System-generated Implies no change	Past- and future-oriented Detailed focus on method System (boss)-generated Implies punitive action
Amount and frequency of feedback	Task-specific Intensive feedback Frequency highly influenced by performer	Time-paced Medium feedback	Nearly continuous monitoring Intensive feedback—decreasing frequency only if performance improves

IMPLICATIONS

There are a number of important implications which follow from the three systems proposed. From a managerial point of view, the most important may well pertain to the nature, amount, and frequency of feedback suggested by each system. An attempt to summarize these is presented in Table 3. The three appraisal programs are arrayed horizontally and the dimensions of feedback are displayed vertically.

In a DAP, the temporal orientation is toward the future, with an explicit emphasis on what needs to be done to develop the performer to the limits of his or her present capabilities or to expand those capabilities. Feedback should imply goals or areas of performance within which goals are appropriate for expansion. At least initially, the feedback will be primarily self-generated, with the superior playing the role of organizational reality tester. The essence of feedback in a DAP is the implication that the performer's task is always expandable and that the job is to be seen and designed as an arena for self-growth.

Feedback in a DAP should be task-specific. It should probably focus on the opportunities available for performer growth *and* on the constraints that the performer sees as inhibiting maximum performance. That is, feedback should include information concerning changes in technology and the nature of the work flow that would remove barriers to improved effectiveness as perceived by the performer. The feedback should be paced according to critical incidents, both positive and negative, in the performance pattern and should not be placed by the calendar. Finally, the frequency of feedback should be primarily under the control of the performer. Questions should be answered and opportunities explored when the performer sees the need.

In a MAP, feedback should be primarily past-oriented. The predominant emphasis is on maintaining the past pattern and level of performance. The essential theme is that "what has been is good enough for the future." Feedback should be used to focus on the exceptions or deviations from an established pattern of stable, acceptable performance. Feedback is generated from the managerial control system. This control may be provided by a superior or a technology such as an accounting system or a quality control instrumentation. The performer in a MAP should not be expected to generate feedback about his or her performance as a part of the formal appraisal system. The essence of feedback in the MAP is that "no news is good news" to the performer, and the underlying managerial assumption is that change is unnecessary most of the time. The system should be designed to highlight exceptions but should not attempt to monitor the majority of employee behaviors or performances. Only when major deviations from standard behavior patterns occur and on the occasion of the time-paced reviews (such as once per year) is feedback likely to be an efficient strategy of control.

In a RAP the time orientation is toward both past and future. Emphasis is placed on the necessity for immediate improvements beyond past performance. In addition, the focus of the evaluation is on what, *in the eyes of the superior,* must be done to improve performance. The feedback should emphasize the exact, proper methods to be used to execute satisfactory performance. In addition, considerable detail needs to be provided concerning the specific deficiencies that exist. The feedback must be system-generated, usually by the immediate superior with possible inputs from functional specialists in personnel or technical specialties directly related to the nature of the task. Clearly, the implication of a RAP is that punitive action lurks and that unless measurable, tangible performance improvements are quickly forthcoming, termination is the likely outcome.

Nearly continuous monitoring and feedback of performance is required in a RAP. Feedback must be intensive, certainly weekly, and possibly daily. Feedback is stretched only if performance improvements begin to appear and seem to be stabilized. Consideration can then be given to the advisability of shifting to a MAP. The desired goal of a RAP is performance improvement. Short of that attainment, an acceptable outcome would be the voluntary termination by the performer.

In summary, the three systems proposed here represent an improvement beyond typical performance appraisal systems as they operate in most organizations. They should encourage an efficient use of managerial time since the majority of employees in most jobs will best fit a MAP, which requires the least managerial attention. MAP's operate essentially on a management by exception principle. In addition, the three systems serve to separate development and evaluation in the sense that DAP is primarily developmental in orientation while MAP is evaluative and RAP is clearly evaluative with some focus on immediate performance improvement.

Finally, implicit in the operation of the three systems is that every performer must be reviewed periodically. Without this systematic monitoring of performance, the three systems could lead to a performance caste system wherein employees become locked into a single appraisal categorization. Clearly, that is not the intent of an effective evaluation system.

Developing Life Plans

by Gordon L. Lippitt

Many organizations are trying to cope with the problems created by increasing anti-establishment feelings, a mobile working population, a shorter work week and job obsolescence caused by technological and knowledge explosion. These problems are accentuated by a desire on the part of individuals to actualize their own potential. A new concept of the training and development responsibilities of organizations is needed and is here proposed.

It seems apparent that a fundamental way to be of service to people in organizations it to help them examine their life goals and plans as a means of achieving their own potential. Tests and counseling services are used for youth in career planning, but it is rare to find such a service for adults. Some counseling clinics and individual therapy for adults exist, but this is usually conducted in a clinical setting where the individual goes to a professional counselor out of major concern for some problem confronting him. This new concept suggests that organizational training and development practitioners make available individual and group experiences that will assist employed and productive persons in their organizations to review, evaluate and examine their life plans.

There are several reasons why a company, agency or organization should assume such a responsibility for its employees:

1. To demonstrate the larger *social responsibility* of a mature organization.
2. To indicate to adult employees that the organization *cares* about them as individuals.
3. To more effectively *release the potential* of the individual in behalf of the organization.
4. To help the individual prepare for *change* in society, the organization, and himself.
5. To strengthen the psychological contact between the individual and the organization.
6. To plan more effectively the learning experiences the individual will require to achieve his life goals.
7. To focus on the person as a whole individual whose total life inter-relates.

How are these goals achieved? First, let us examine the objectives and rationale of the design.*

1. To help participants look at themselves, to decide what is important to them, and to develop projects for the future which will provide them as much individual need satisfaction as possible.
2. To build a climate of trust in a three to six person group.
3. To present an opportunity for practice in giving and receiving help.

*I was first introduced to some of the group methods in life planning by Dr. Herbert Shephard, a pioneer in this kind of work during the past five years. The design explained in this article, with some modifications, is taken from an exercise conducted by Dr. Shephard at Bethel, Maine in July 1969 for the participants in a Program for Specialists in Organizational Training and Development. This program was sponsored by the NTL Institute for Applied Behavioral Science.

The rationale of the design, stated simply, is:

Personal objectives for the future are almost impossible to state without first doing some "getting in the mood" kinds of activities. In this design, these activities aid a person to display a number of important aspects of himself to himself. Of special help to the participant is an inventory of aspects of himself that help him to understand where he is at this point in his life and what are some of his rather immediate expectations. Once these are displayed, the choice of future actions, plans and projects becomes easier.

The "sharing" parts of the design are aimed at revealing one's self to others and through "joint sharing" to generate more self-growth goals than one could achieve through self-insight alone. The gradual revelation of self, during one or more sessions, builds trusting relationships as well as acceptance of self and others.

INTRODUCTORY PHASE

Trainer presents the objectives to the group as outlined above. He then gives a rationale for the experiences the group will share. He points out that stating objectives for the future is a difficult task for all of us; that the experiences will assist each participant to review his own feelings about his own self-concept and his plans for achieving or revising that self-concept; that as a result of these experiences the choice of future actions, plans and projects will be easier for each participant to achieve.

If necessary, the trainer may wish to have the group set time limits, physical arrangements, and other details to lessen the effects of any unknown time or physical restraints. Prior to the session the trainer should prepare instructions (given below) on separate sheets and distribute them at the appropriate time.

It helps to get the consent of the group involved before starting. A question can be asked, such as "Would you be willing to spend some time looking into the future and making some plans for yourself?" This question, if answered fully, should promote enough response to determine if there is active resistance. Individuals who actively resist probably will not get involved enough to gain from the experience and, if they wish, should be excused. An alternative would be to assess the degree of readiness in individual interviews prior to group meeting.

A. WARM-UP PHASE

Divide groups into natural work groups or previously established learning groups. Four participants in a group appears to be an optimum number. The trainer now helps the group "get into" the experience. He can explain as follows:

"Today we will look at where we are, who we are, and what we like, and try to spread these out in front of ourselves. Then with this information available, we can look to the future and try to fit it in as best we can to our own plans, objectives, and growth. Everyone will need a pencil and about 15 pieces of paper."

"The results of this experience will mainly be for your own use."

The trainer then gives his first instruction to the small groups:

Line-Drawing Activity

Trainer: "Your first task is to—draw a horizontal line from left to right representing your life—put a check on it where you currently are now—spend a few moments discussing with your group why you drew the line as long as you did, and why you put the check where you did—ask any questions about it you want. Focus on age or growth, whatever you choose." (Place emphasis on importance of this step.)

After group appear to have discussed this sufficiently the trainer then introduces the next activity:

Who Am I Activity

Trainer: "It is a part of our culture to explain things chronologically. Therapy deals with the past, while sensitivity training deals with the present, the here and now. Probably the most important thing about behavior that is occurring here and now is that it has consequences for here and now, plus past explanations, and future eventualities. So, today, we will work on the right hand side of the check mark you have made on your life line, and look at that part of your life that hasn't happened yet. We will investigate the right hand side of your line as much as we can, rather than slip back to the left side. Write—on ten separate pieces of paper—ten separate answers to the question, 'Who am I?'

"You have your own way of thinking about yourself. You may think of yourself in terms of your role, or in terms of qualities that you have. You may think of yourself in terms of your negative attributes. Or you may think of yourself as a mixture of all of these different frameworks. Whatever framework your life has had, try to find different answers to the question, 'Who am I?' and write them down. When you are done, I want you to review the ten answers and think about what you would be if you eliminated any one of them."

Wait until all have finished.

"When you have finished writing, rank order them. At the top of the rank order, put those self-descriptions that are most essentially you, and at the bottom of the rank order put those self-descriptions that you could most do without and still not lose your most essential qualities."

Trainer should check for understanding by the group.

"After you have finished your rank order, share these with one another, and discuss them freely."

After giving the group a chance to discuss their cards with each other, the next warm-up activity can be introduced.

Autobiographical Activity

Trainer: "Next, move all the way over, almost to the right end of your life line, and write a brief autobiography that might appear at that point in time in *Who's Who.*

"Don't write this autobiography as an obituary. Write what you would like to have written about you and what you might be able to accomplish. It should be a statement you like to read, and contain accomplishments that are possible. It should be realistic, but still things about yourself you believe are really conceivable. Now share your autobiographical sketch with the rest of your team, and discuss it. Then go back to your list of ten 'Who Am I?' statements and add any additional statements that would further explore what you would like to be."

At the end of this time period it would be appropriate to schedule a break, or it may be appropriate to adjourn the first session, if that is the nature of the development activity schedule.

B. LIFE INVENTORY PHASE

In this phase of the design, the participants should more fully examine their aspirations, assets, inadequacies, and expectations. It is helpful if the trainer has forms ready for displaying the cost of the inventory items explained below; but if not, he should list these items on a chalkboard or chart pad so the group can refer to them as they make their individual lists.

> *Trainer:* "This next step is quite hard work. Something called a *life inventory.* To look at all the things that you do and would like to do. It will help you to display all of yourself in terms of your activities and values. It ends up as a map of your life in terms of a number of elements which may or may not be overlapping. I am going to write down these elements for you."

1. The first element is entitled— *"Peak Experiences."*

   Trainer: "This definition is broad enough so that they are not necessarily the most exquisite moments you have had. These are or have been your 'kicks'—the moments in your life that are remembered as having been really great; the times when you have felt you were really living and enjoying living. These are the moments that have made you feel living is worthwhile. It is a list of the events that have mattered to you in terms of making you feel you are glad you are a human being and glad you are alive."

2. The second element is— *"Things I Do Well."*

   Trainer: "Some of these probably are things that are very meaningful to you. There may be duplication with your first list. Some of the things you do well may be things that bore you to death. This is a hard list to compile because it competes with our cultural norm of being modest. Try to overcome this inhibition."

3. Next, *"Things I Do Poorly."*

   Trainer: "This list should contain things you want to do or you have to do, but not necessarily things in which you have no interest. It should be a list of things you do poorly that for some reason or another you need to do. You may play the violin poorly, but if you have no interest in or need to do it, don't include playing the violin."

4. The next element is, *"Things I Would Like to Stop Doing."*

   Trainer: "This might or might not be things that you have to do but would like to stop doing. Someone else in your team might be able to suggest some things that it would be good for you to stop doing—now, or in the future. Some of the things on this list may be things you would like to do but that you know you do poorly. Others might be things that you hate to do, but for some reason feel you have to do."

5. Next, *"Things I Would Like to Learn to Do Well."*

   Trainer: "This might be a list of desired skills that you would like to include in your personal and potential life. It might be related to an avocational activity or a new skill in your present job."

6. Our sixth element is, *"Peak Experiences I Would Like to Have."*

   Trainer: "These are the kinds of things you imagine you would like to have happen to you but which have not."

7. The next element is, *"Values to be Realized."*

   Trainer: "This element is less clear than the others. Values means many things to many people. It might be being rich, having deep friendship, or being with young people. They can be tangible, but most probably are not."

8. Our last element is, *"Things I'd Like to Start Doing Now."*

   Trainer: "The objective here is to explore some of the things you may have been putting off, but which you really want to start doing. It might be growing a beard, becoming more aggressive, asking for more responsibility on your job or a number of other similar items."

Following completion of listing the elements on a chalkboard or chart pad, the trainer will want to set some guidelines and time limits.

Trainer: "Let me also suggest a procedure. It's best for the person whose inventory is being taken to be free just to think and respond, and not have to write in detail. If other team members will serve as consultants, interviewers and recorders, the person being inventoried will not have to bother writing down things and can be free to respond. Don't beat it to death. Get down those things that are revealed spontaneously, and move on to the next person. Move at a lively pace, then go back and add those things that people want to add to their lists. It's best to spend 10 minutes or so with each individual, but you can also take each element in order among all the members of the group."

This phase of the experience will take at least an hour. This may be a good time for another break so that the participants can relax before omving on to the "action planning" phases of the design.

C. PROJECT PLANNING PHASE

The objective here is to help each individual establish goals and plans by identifying projects that can lead him toward desired achievements. Some of these will involve his personal life or his job, while others may relate to new arrangements in his life.

Trainer: "The next phase begins the formulation of projects that combine a number of the desires expressed in the life inventory. This is difficult, and there are few procedures or patterns. Instead of thinking of goals with a separate set of strategies, think of projects that provide opportunities to allow you to learn what you want to learn or that move you towards the peak experiences you want to have. In each project, try to realize as many of these values, goals and desires as you can. Try to develop an overall picture that lets you feel alive and satisfied. I can make these three suggestions:

a. Think of vocational or avocational projects to which you are already committed. Consider the parts of these projects that provide you opportunities to learn what you want to learn, that move you toward the peak experience you want, or that allow you to reach the values, goals and desires you want. Think about these projects in terms of what you can add or subtract from them so they will provide you with increased fulfillment.

b. Then list projects that you have in mind to which you have not yet made a commitment. Consider these in terms of those which are likely to be most fulfilling for you. Make some plans for these.

c. Another thing you might do is brainstorm possible projects with your group. Make a list without evaluating each item. Rotate around the team, first one person and then another. After the list is made, each person can evaluate each project for himself."

This phase of the process is where the "pay off" will take place. This part of the design will take at least one hour or more. At the end of this time the trainer may want to have some general discussion with the total group on such questions as:

- Which aspects of the design seem to be most difficult?
- Which aspects of the design seemed most meaningful?
- What surprised you the most?
- What are some of the obstacles you might encounter in accomplishing your projects?

This will provide a valuable release, evaluation and channeling of the learning experience to their ongoing life experience.

CASE EXAMPLES OF LIFE PLANNING DESIGN

The heart of a life planning design is the individual, his present relationship to his own life, and his current value system. When used with a work group in an organization, a major ingredient that must be added is information relevant to the organization's current needs and the expectations of that particular work group. Consideration should also be given to the timing of such an "informational input" so it will be available to the participants before their plans and projects are developed.

The work group in this case is a staff of management and organization development specialists in a large cooperation.* It is composed of the staff supervisor, four staff managers, and one secretary. The group had been involved in joint objective-setting for a year and a half. However, all previous activity had evolved from an examination of the group's responsibilities and translation of these into mutually agreed upon objectives for the group. These group objectives were then carried out by members who volunteered to undertake them or, by natural division of talents, certain projects went to certain members. Admittedly, the staff supervisor felt that he and the other members were ready to individualize all the objectives for the year 1970. He publicly shared his search for a method or resource that would accomplish this goal. He accepted the life planning and inventory idea, as modified to include some input of company goals, needs, and expectations for the coming year.

The work group met at an interference-free location, handling other concerns in the morning and began the design in the afternoon. The "warm-up phase," described earlier, was conducted in the afternoon. As a general reaction the participants favored the exercise and indicated that they were in the mood for further life planning and inventory. Some comments were: "I've never really taken

---

*I wish to acknowledge the valuable contribution of Charles F. Fitzsimmons to this phase.

this kind of time to look at myself," "My rank-ordering of the 'Who-am-I?' cards changed a couple of times and the others helped me examine this quite closely"; "The conditions seem ripe for this and I'm getting plenty of personal help"; and "I'm hooked on this, now."

The design was halted at this point to allow time for the superior of the work group's leader to spend an hour discussing, from the viewpoint of his position in the organization, the outlook for the coming year. His talk included some areas where his boss thought work was needed as well as some general priorities. Ample time was allowed for questions, clarifications and probings from the work group. After he left, the work group leader offered some of his own reactions and priorities of a general nature. The work group agreed to meet the next morning to continue the design.

At the next morning session, the "Life Inventory" phase of the design was conducted. This is the most time-consuming section, but also the most productive in terms of generating a vast amount of information for each individual regarding his present mood and some foreseeable expectations. At this point the participants felt they had enough to think about and asked for time to assimilate and understand what they had learned.

Two days later the work group reconvened to try the "Project Planning" phase. Points of clarification were handled first. Re-establishing the proper mood was not a problem because a review and discussion of the information obtained earlier helped regenerate enthusiasm. Projects and plans were tentatively laid out and a priority assigned. Then a reality testing period was proposed and each member individually began to test his plans against the time available for the next year. There were more plans and projects than there was time available for the testing. A best accommodation was made by placing the items in order of priority.

The session ended with a commitment to meet again in two weeks. Each participant committed himself to bring with him his plans and projects for the coming years in a "Management by Objectives" format. In addition, these objectives would include earlier developed criteria such as: desirable, attainable, satisfying, measurable, legal, moral, ethical, positive, accounting for known internal blocks, written, and flexible enough to allow for unknown essential priorities.

Group reactions to this design ran like this: "It helped me to understand my own priorities in terms of personal growth," "I've never done any long-range planning before, but after I realized the satisfaction of some previous plans, I was anxious to affect my own future with some present planning"; "It provided me with more insight into myself than I've ever had before"; "It helped me understand how I can realize a couple of goals in one project where before I thought something had to give," and "I'm anxious to get on with some of the ideas I have now."

VALUES OF THIS KIND OF LEARNING EXPERIENCE

One way of evaluating this learning design is to compare its applicability to some of the emerging trends in training and development.* As we examine these trends in the light of this general design for life planning, the following observations are relevant:

1. It is more desirable to *improve performance* than merely to increase individual knowledge. This design was used to increase individual knowledge about one's self, but mainly to help the individual make better career plans for himself. Perhaps nothing will have a more profound impact on individual performance than the kind of commitment and enthusiasm that can be generated by this kind of learning experience.
2. *Group training situations* are more important than only improving the skills of an individual. The design in the case example discussed above was focused almost wholly on solving the problem of what the group would do next year and where its time would be spent. This was the first time such a design had been used with a work group in this organization. It seemed to improve the work climate and goal orientation.
3. Such training should be viewed as the *way management wants to get its job done* and not solely as a function of a training department. In the case example cited this was not really a factor since it was a training group using its own resources. It was seen as a step toward organizational achievement, however, and the same design can be used with similar work groups with advantageous results.
4. It is better to build *"in-house capabilities"* than to depend upon outside experts or resources. In the case example, Dr. Shepard's design was adapted to a specific work group's development. Certainly, this is a development of *"in-house capabilities."* Also, four other training managers are now familiar with the design and can adapt it to other situations when it seems appropriate.
5. Management should insist on evaluation of training instead of accepting the results on faith. There was no real test of the results achieved by the work group in the case example, except that the "bosses" were pleased and thought the time was well spent. In 12 to 18 months this criteria can and should be more realistically assessed.

*See Gordon Lippitt, "Emerging Trends in Training and Development," *The Training and Development Journal,* Feb. 1969.

6. Training activities should be focused on *"learning how to learn."* This fits with the design I have discussed, because the activities facilitated learning how to learn about oneself. There is also some built-in learning in that evaluations will go on throughout the year with each project's activity and as each plan unfolds.
7. The present trend is to move away from training that is unrelated to the *learner's* experiences or his *organization's* needs. In the case application this design was specifically meant for the learner's experiences and the organization's needs. In heterogenous settings the application to an organization, per se, might be somewhat less.
8. There is a tendency away from didactic, non-participative approaches to learning and *more action-learning.* This design is wholly participative and resulted in real action plans.
9. There is substantial value in providing reinforcement and a follow-up experience for trainees, so that learning is enhanced by application. In work group situations the reinforcement and follow-up will naturally develop throughout the year as objectives are individually tracked and progress periodically reviewed at team meetings.
10. More is accomplished by learning that is *self-motivated* by the learner rather than imposed upon by him. By its very nature this life planning design is self-motivating because there is the reward of objective achievement. Also, the data generated provides a means for each individual to personally plot his own growth.
11. Instead of the vague assurance that training will be "good for you," there is greater emphasis on *goal orientation.* The use of the life planning design, as applied in the case example, had a very specific goal in mind, both for the individual and the organization.
12. There is an advantage in achieving greater *homogenity in training groups,* so that people learn to function together in their organizational relationships. Work groups should be trained together, and the life planning design can be used exactly that way in as much as a part of its purpose is to build trust and to initiate practice helping. Increases in these two areas will yield great benefits to an organizational work group.

Despite this favorable comparison with a list of criteria and the favorable reactions from the participants in the case reported, real evaluation will only come in time. At least a year must pass before a true measurement of results can be taken. Only if subsequent performance improves over a period of time can a training design be considered successful. At this point, however, my observation and experience indicates that this life planning design will produce positive results.

OVERVIEW

This kind of design and its application in organizations is not to be implemented without caution, nor is it devoid of problems to be overcome. I would not recommend it for a work group that is not ready for it. Such readiness can be assessed by answering these questions:

- Is the group already a fairly cohesive one rather than one that needs elementary team building? This design is far more advanced than mere application for team building. It should not be used in a work group that has more fundamental problems. Such a group probably would have difficulties that would prevent the participants from leveling to the degree needed or that would cause them to revert to dealing with old problems rather than focusing on future activities and goals.
- Is the group somewhat experienced in objective setting to see this as a legitimate endeavor? This design should not be used as an initial try at objective setting, the process is too complicated. The danger here is that it wouldn't be taken seriously, thus ending in a game.
- Is the leader of the group ready for such an activity and is he willing to support it after he understands what is involved? He must be convinced that this will be helpful because he has to live with it for a year.

Are the organization's general priorities available and can they be worked in as an input? This seems especially critical since the whole effort will fail if the organization surprises the members with roadblocks to their plans and projects. Realistically, the members need to know where the boundaries are in order to develop realistic expectations.

Does the work group seem responsible and mature enough to make individual growth plans that are consistent with their resources? The key here is their past record and a diagnosis of their present psychological status. The members of the group discussed in the case example above were specialities within the organization and they were able to identify with a professional field valued by the organization. This may not be true in other work groups that have less definable patterns of personal growth and development.

As this kind of activity is considered for an already overworked training and development department and staff, a question arises as to whether it might be worth the effort, money and time. Will it really benefit the organization? The conditions of personal and organizational life of the 1970's and beyond seem to indicate to me that such an approach is not only needed but essential:

People feel today that the modern organization is too large, too impersonal and too complex. Such an activity and design will lessen this feeling.

People at work today possess multiple loyalties to themselves, their families, their community, their recreational group and their work group. The organization that helps a person see the inter-related relevance to these multiple loyalties, and does not try to command loyalty only to itself, will be seen as a creative force.

With the increased mobility of people in work forces, it is desirable to optimize their contribution to the organizations to which they belong. Life planning efforts may increase the duration of a valuable employee's tenure with an organization.

Young people's increasing expectations of quick promotion to an organization is creating a pressure on those now in middle management. The possibility of discovering new opportunities and career for experienced workers may open up vistas for them, and simultaneously provide opportunities for the upward striving youth.

New technological advances will make some jobs obsolete. Rather than keeping people who have become "obsolete" on the work force out of kindness and thereby causing them to feel unneeded, it is far better to help them find new, revitalizing challenges so that they may be useful to themselves and others in a meaningful way.

Life planning is closely allied to the well-known concept of management by objectives. In this instance, however, the objectives are one's life plans and not just work assignments. In many instances the process of management by objectives can be combined with life planning experiences. An enlightened management, a training and development staff or an aware manager can creatively confront the changing needs and motivations of people in today's society by seeing the relevance of life planning experiences as a new way to optimize the potential of people in the organization of tomorrow.

PART TWO
QUESTIONNAIRES

Questionnaire 1
ATTITUDES TOWARD PERFORMANCE APPRAISAL

- Assesses attitudes towards the performance appraisal systems that people have been using. Useful for training and for analysis of the appraisal system.

Questionnaire 2
A SAMPLE SELF-APPRAISAL FORM

- A series of questions to help a person do a self-appraisal in preparation for an appraisal session with the supervisor.

Questionnaire 3
GENERAL IDEAS ABOUT PERFORMANCE APPRAISAL

- A general assessment of attitudes towards appraisals, the reward system, and usefulness of performance appraisal results. Good for analysis of the general organization or needs assessment for training sessions.

Questionnaire 4
PERFORMANCE MEASUREMENT AND REVIEW

- Self-test for understanding of accurate measures. Useful for individual learning. Excellent for generating group discussions on accurate measures.

Questionnaire 5
SETTING GOALS AND APPRAISING PERFORMANCE

- Questionnaire for generating group discussion on the performance appraisal process. General enough to fit any organization.

QUESTIONNAIRE 1
ATTITUDES TOWARD PERFORMANCE APPRAISAL

Indicate your opinion of the performance appraisal system you have been using by completing each of the following statements. Circle your responses.

	The Performance Appraisal System...	*Agree*	*Not Sure*	*Disagree*
1.	...measures all relevant dimensions of performance.	A	?	D
2.	...is objective.	A	?	D
3.	...is accepted as legitimate and important by the organization.	A	?	D
4.	...is constructive and enhances employee development.	A	?	D
5.	...is an integral part of managing.	A	?	D
6.	...is useful in the planning and job staffing processes.	A	?	D
7.	...is uniform across the organization.	A	?	D
8.	...is clearly understood by those who use it.	A	?	D
9.	...is useful in performing supervisory responsibilities.	A	?	D
10.	...is regularly used as a basis for various personnel actions.	A	?	D

QUESTIONNAIRE 2
A SAMPLE SELF-APPRAISAL FORM

The questions below are designed to stimulate your thinking, and to help you prepare for the appraisal session and get maximum benefit from it. Think about your own personal performance, progress, and plans for future improvement. Appraise yourself. When finished, this form may be given to your superior or retained by you.

1. What do I consider to be the important abilities which my job requires?
2. What are some aspects of my job that I like best? That I like least?
3. What are the ways in which my superiors can help me to do my job better?
4. In what aspects of my job do I feel I need more experience and training?
5. What are my major accomplishments for the past year?
6. What have I done for my personal and/or professional development?
7. Are there any changes I would like to see made in my job which would improve my effectiveness?
8. Are all of my capabilities being utilized in my present position? If not, how can they be better utilized?
9. What are specific things I need to do in the next year for my own development?
10. In what ways would my present position better prepare me for assuming more responsibility?
11. What are my long range plans? What type of work do I see myself doing five years from now? How am I preparing myself for this work?

QUESTIONNAIRE 3
GENERAL IDEAS ABOUT PERFORMANCE APPRAISAL*

The following items ask your opinions about performance appraisal in general and as it is carried out within your organization as a whole. For these items, please indicate the extent to which you agree or disagree with each by circling the number which most closely corresponds to your opinion.

	Strongly Disagree	Disagree	Slightly Disagree	Neither Disagree nor Agree	Slightly Agree	Agree	Strongly Agree
1. Performance appraisal cannot be objectively and unemotionally carried out by managers.	[1]	[2]	[3]	[4]	[5]	[6]	[7]
2. Few people really understand what the objectives of performance appraisal are.	[1]	[2]	[3]	[4]	[5]	[6]	[7]
3. Most people have a real understanding of how performance appraisal results are used in my organization.	[1]	[2]	[3]	[4]	[5]	[6]	[7]
4. In my organization, *salary* decisions *are* based on performance appraisal results.	[1]	[2]	[3]	[4]	[5]	[6]	[7]
5. In my organization, *promotion* decisions *are* based on performance appraisal results.	[1]	[2]	[3]	[4]	[5]	[6]	[7]
6. Supervisors and subordinates pretty much agree on what constitutes good or poor performance.	[1]	[2]	[3]	[4]	[5]	[6]	[7]
7. Current performance appraisal practices provide accurate feedback to the subordinate.	[1]	[2]	[3]	[4]	[5]	[6]	[7]
8. Most supervisors are not rewarded for doing performance appraisal well.	[1]	[2]	[3]	[4]	[5]	[6]	[7]
9. Most managers would not carry out performance appraisal of their subordinates unless the organization required them to.	[1]	[2]	[3]	[4]	[5]	[6]	[7]
10. Most subordinates would not participate in performance appraisal unless the organization required them to.	[1]	[2]	[3]	[4]	[5]	[6]	[7]

*Developed by Edward E. Lawler III, Steve Kerr, Chuck Maxey, Monty Mohrman, Bruce Prince, Janet Schriesheim, Department of Organizational Behavior, Graduate School of Business Administration, University of Southern California, Los Angeles, California 90007.

QUESTIONNAIRE 3 *(continued)*

	Strongly Disagree	Disagree	Slightly Disagree	Neither Disagree nor Agree	Slightly Agree	Agree	Strongly Agree
11. Performance appraisals are fairly and honestly done in this organization.	[1]	[2]	[3]	[4]	[5]	[6]	[7]
12. Performance appraisal motivates individuals to improve their performances.	[1]	[2]	[3]	[4]	[5]	[6]	[7]
13. It wouldn't make much difference to our business if performance appraisals were not done.	[1]	[2]	[3]	[4]	[5]	[6]	[7]
14. Performance appraisal typically leads to productive changes in the subordinate's behavior.	[1]	[2]	[3]	[4]	[5]	[6]	[7]
15. Overall, subordinates, (i.e., appraisees) are satisfied with our performance appraisal system.	[1]	[2]	[3]	[4]	[5]	[6]	[7]
16. Overall, supervisors (i.e., appraisers) are satisfied with our performance appraisal system.	[1]	[2]	[3]	[4]	[5]	[6]	[7]
17. Performance appraisals lead to better supervisor and subordinate understanding of what the subordinate's role should be.	[1]	[2]	[3]	[4]	[5]	[6]	[7]
18. Salary decisions *should* be based on performance appraisal results.	[1]	[2]	[3]	[4]	[5]	[6]	[7]
19. Promotion decisions *should* be based on performance appraisal results.	[1]	[2]	[3]	[4]	[5]	[6]	[7]
20. A subordinate's self-appraisal *should* be an important part of the performance appraisal process.	[1]	[2]	[3]	[4]	[5]	[6]	[7]
21. Performance appraisals *should* be based on goals previously agreed to by the supervisor and subordinate.	[1]	[2]	[3]	[4]	[5]	[6]	[7]
22. Performance appraisal *should* be done *only* for the subordinate's personal development.	[1]	[2]	[3]	[4]	[5]	[6]	[7]

QUESTIONNAIRE 4
PERFORMANCE MEASUREMENT AND REVIEW

Read the sample measure and then in the column mark a yes or no indicating whether the statement could be considered an accurate and descriptive review of performance.

	Is statement an accurate and descriptive review of performance? (Yes or no)
1. Manager indicates she will be requesting maternity leave next year.	______
2. Park superintendent completes performance appraisals using the BARS approach as recommended by the Department. Appraisals are done on time and include a self-appraisal done by the employee.	______
3. Manager is an excellent leader.	______
4. Lawyer doesn't delegate properly.	______
5. Fifteen of twenty employees report dissatisfaction with a supervisor's conduct towards them. They report supervisor is abusive, demands overtime from them, and refuses to assist.	______
6. Bank officer met an objective to develop scheduling procedures for ABC account which was useable by purchasing, contract administration, and field personnel.	______
7. Public official gave presentation explaining the budget to City Council. Presentation was unorganized, visuals were poor, official was unable to answer questions.	______
8. I've heard the clerk wastes paper when making copies.	______
9. Doctor's clothing tends to be brightly colored and red.	______
10. Secretary made four errors on a letter.	______
11. During the year the receptionist wasn't courteous to visitors.	______
12. School superintendent has trouble coping with stress. Arrest record and family problems indicate problems extend beyond the job.	______
13. Bookkeeper didn't crosscheck XYZ report with balances in accounts. Error resulted in lost interest.	______
14. Manager gives most assignments to one subordinate, thereby creating one overloaded subordinate while the other subordinates have little to do.	______
15. Salesmanager's spouse insulted three of the organization's best employees at a dinner party.	______
16. Researcher doesn't accept assistance from others very well.	______

QUESTIONNAIRE 5
SETTING GOALS AND APPRAISING PERFORMANCE

Instructions: Please put a check in either the "Yes" or "No" column depending on whether or not you agree with the statement.

1. When talking about performance it is a good idea to include a summary evaluation so that the subordinate knows exactly where he or she stands and how he or she rates compared to others.

   Yes ________ No ________

2. An appraisal of performance about once a year is usually about right. It's predictable—employees can count on it and it doesn't overly interfere with their freedom to get the job done.

   Yes ________ No ________

3. When giving feedback on performance, it is usually best to focus on and be specific about those areas where improvement is necessary.

   Yes ________ No ________

4. Praise has a very good effect on a subordinate during an evaluation and motivates even better performance.

   Yes ________ No ________

5. Because performance appraisal is so closely tied in with salary and compensation it is good, if possible, to discuss the two together.

   Yes ________ No ________

6. The subordinates being appraised are most concerned about your evaluation of their performance. The discussion, therefore, should focus not only on what they have accomplished but on what you think about it.

   Yes ________ No ________

7. When appraising performance you should focus on past performance. You should start by providing the subordinate with the information you have about his or her performance. You should then try and focus on what was done right or wrong so that the individual can learn from past experience.

   Yes ________ No ________

Revised from a form developed by Alan Frohman, Frohman Associates, Lexington, Massachusetts.

PART THREE
ROLE-PLAYS

Instructions for Role-Plays on Performance Management
- Brief instructions on how to work with triads in role-play situations.

Role-Play 1
- Role-play dealing with a poor performer.

Role-Play 2
- Role-play dealing with a high performer who has problems working with others.

Role-Play 3
- Role-play dealing with a long term employee whose motivation is down.

Observer Worksheet for Managing Performance Feedback
- Structured observation sheet for role-plays. Asks questions about each of the stages of a performance appraisal interview.

Play Well Thy Part
by William H. Cooper
- Outlines a role-play training program.

INSTRUCTIONS FOR ROLE-PLAYS ON PERFORMANCE MANAGEMENT

1. Break the group into triads.
2. Each group is to decide who will be manager, employee, and observer for the first round.
3. Hand out role-play #1 and instructions to participants on "How to Role Play."
4. Each group does the role-play. Observers fill out the "Observer Worksheet for Managing Performance Feedback."
5. At the end of the role-play observers feed back observations to the total group. Total group identifies and discusses the hardest part of the performance review.
6. Participants rotate roles.
7. Hand out role-play #2 and repeat steps 4, 5, and 6.
8. Hand out role-play #3 and repeat steps 4 and 5.
9. Summarize key points.

Note: We have also found it very productive for participants to choose a real problem to role-play rather than those provided. One participant will briefly describe a performance problem in which he/she is involved. Another participant will assume the role of a second person in the performance situation described. The second participant should play the role of an individual receiving performance feedback. A third participant acts as an observer. The procedures for observation and feedback remain the same. After the description of the situation the participants engage in the role-play similar to any other role-play.

ROLE PLAY 1
MANAGER'S ROLE

One of the employees you supervise has been working in your organization for three years. This employee's performance has consistently been low. You have consistently mentioned the lack of motivation and interest that the employee displays but it doesn't seem to have had much of an effect. Recently the employee's performance has almost totally ruined three major projects.

You had established goals:

a. to complete the survey of customer needs in two months;
b. to increase sales by thirty percent in one year;
c. to reduce cost of recruiting each engineer from $450 to $250 while meeting requisition totals and dates in six months.

No progress has been made on any of these goals to date and one month has passed.

ROLE PLAY 1
EMPLOYEE

Your manager really seems to have it in for you. You have been working for this manager three years. During that time your manager has never seemed willing to give you responsibility for anything. All you seem to get is work no one else wants to do. It is often quite boring. At first you couldn't really figure out what you were supposed to be doing. When you figured it out you really didn't want to do it.

You had established goals:

a. to complete the survey of customer needs in two months;
b. to increase sales by thirty percent in one year;
c. to reduce cost of recruiting each engineer from $450 to $250 while meeting requisition totals and dates in six months.

You are currently way behind on all of them after one month. You don't even want to do them!

ROLE PLAY 2
MANAGER'S ROLE

One of the employees working for you has been with the organization for about a year. This employee is full of energy, is bright, and has done well on all assignments. The employee literally tears into any assignment and comes on like gang-busters to get it done. The only real problem you have noticed is that the employee seems totally to lack any sort of tact. The employee seems to have offended more than a few of the other employees to the point that some of them would really rather not work with this employee. Some have said that the employee is too pushy. You have decided you have to raise these problems with him/her.

During the last performance period, the goals have been:

a. to complete and implement product introduction plans by October 1 for:
   - shared display
   - PCT
   - vortex

b. to obtain a thirty-percent sales growth by October 1;

c. to obtain a twenty-percent ROA by October 1.

All of these goals have been met. In fact, sales growth was thirty-five percent and ROA was twenty-eight percent. It is October 15, and time for the annual review.

ROLE PLAY 2
EMPLOYEE'S ROLE

You have been working in the organization for about a year. It's been a good experience. You have had numerous different assignments and have done excellently on them all. You're hoping a promotion is coming soon. If you're going to make it up the administrative ladder to where you want to be, you are going to have to move fast. You have no real complaints about your job. The one frustration you have had is that everyone seems to be too involved in politics. They let their feelings and interpersonal attitudes get in the way of performance. You've had to straighten a few of your co-workers out. Tell them to forget the bickering and get on with the job. Once they realized you meant to complete the assignments and do a top-notch job, they seemed to kick it in gear and really perform.

During the last performance period your goals were:

a. to complete and implement product introduction plans by October 1 for:
   - shared display
   - PCT
   - vortex
b. to obtain a thirty-percent sales growth by October 1;
c. to obtain a twenty-percent ROA by October 1.

All of the goals have been met. In fact, sales growth was thirty-five percent and ROA was twenty-eight percent. It is October 15, and time for your annual review.

ROLE PLAY 3
EMPLOYEE

You have been with the organization for four years. You've survived three top administrators and six department heads. Things never change. They're still as messed up as they were twenty years ago. Why try? You do your job and you do it well but you're not about to go sticking your neck out any more. Let the younger people fight the system. You'll be glad to work an honest forty hours a week but you're not about to get ulcers and worry about work at home. Life's too short. Let the managers do the worrying. That's what they're paid for.

Goals for this performance period were:

1. to achieve an average age of accounts receivable not to exceed twenty-five days by June 1;
2. to complete training of three replacements for key positions in shipping by June 1;
3. to complete design specifications for the new inventory system by June 1.

You have completed the specifications. You tried a couple of times to get the accounts receivable problem solved but no one wants to cooperate. Training the three replacements has been hard because they don't have the right background and are kept so busy doing other things they never have time to sit down and learn. It is now January 1.

ROLE PLAY 3
MANAGER

One of the employees you supervise has been with the organization for eight years in various positions. This employee probably knows more about the organization and people than anyone around. The employee has been on the present job for four years. Any job you give the employee gets done—not spectacularly or particularly fast but it gets done. The employee is well respected in the organization and often serves as an informal counselor to younger workers with personal problems. You have tried numerous times to get the employee more involved in the organization. You think if the employee was ever willing to help out on some of the decisions by making recommendations and/or participating it would really help. As it is, the subordinate tends to wait for a specific assignment and then do it. The employee doesn't seem to be able to get the big picture and help solve some of the problems or decide what needs to be done.

Goals for this performance period were:

1. to achieve an average age of accounts receivable not to exceed twenty-five days by June 1;
2. to complete training of three replacements for key positions in shipping by June 1;
3. to complete design specifications for the new inventory system by June 1.

It is January 1; you suspect that subordinate lacks self motivation. Nothing is done on the training and accounts receivable. The design specifications are already done. You suspect the subordinate is waiting for specific instructions.

OBSERVER WORKSHEET FOR MANAGING PERFORMANCE PROBLEMS

1. Clarification of purpose
   a. Was the purpose of the discussion made clear in the beginning?

   b. Was the problem to be addressed described in specific terms?

2. Preview of topics

   After the purpose of the discussion is clarified, the person being interviewed will usually be asking him/herself "What kind of information does he/she want?" Rather than let him/her guess as the discussion goes from question to question, it is best to lay out the topics initially and suggest a way of talking about them.

   a. Was it clear what topics were to be discussed?

   b. Did the participants have a chance to talk about how to conduct the discussion?

3. Motivation of interviewee

   The person interviewed must be involved. His/her views are important and a commitment to the solution is critical. A good way to assess how involved the interviewer gets the other person is to consider the types of questions that were asked and how much listening the interviewer did.

   a. Did the interviewer ask relevant questions? Did the interviewer spend too much time trying to give answers and tell the other person what to do?

   b. Did the interviewer listen? Did the interviewer spend too much time talking?

   c. Did the person interviewed have a chance to participate in defining the problem?

4. Body of the discussion
   a. Did the participants jump too quickly to try to solve the problem before it was accurately described?

   b. Did the participants agree on what the problem was?

5. Summary
   a. Did the participants reach a conclusion?

   b. Did both participants leave with a clear understanding of what each was going to do (action plans) to solve the problem?

   c. Did they set times for completing the actions and getting back together? Were feedback mechanisms put in place?

"PLAY WELL THY PART"
by William H. Cooper*

Managers continue to have difficulties conducting effective performance appraisal interviews. Symptomatic of these difficulties are frequent reports that managers and subordinates leave the interview with little exchange of usable information, fail to set agreed-upon goals and objectives,[1] feel anxious about the interview, produce little change in subsequent behavior, and not infrequently fail to even hold an interview—the "vanishing performance appraisal" phenomenon.[2]

These symptoms are not new, nor have they gone addressed by those interested in improving the skills of managers. Hundreds of thousands of manager hours have been devoted to trying to help managers overcome their appraisal skill deficiencies. These hours have been spent listening to lectures, discussing interviewing problems, viewing videotaped interviews and on a variety of other methods. Of all the methods used, the role play has probably been the most prominent method used to train managers in this area. Its popularity is based on the belief that classroom practice is an effective method of learning how to conduct an appraisal interview. Despite its popularity, managers who have conducted one or two role playing appraisal interviews continue to have problems conducting effective appraisal interviews.

STANDARD ROLE PLAYING EXERCISES

The model for most appraisal interview role playing exercises is the Stanley-Burke exercise developed by the late Norman Maier.[3] In this exercise, one person is given the role description for George Stanley (an engineering department section head), another the role of Tom Burke (a supervisor reporting to Stanley), and a third acts as an observer. Once the actors have studied their respective roles, the Stanley-Burke interview takes place, followed by feedback on the effectiveness of the interview.

The Stanley-Burke exercise is useful in highlighting the dynamics of mutual information exchange, the role of goal and objective setting in appraisal interviews, and the ease with which a manager can fail to pick up on job problems the subordinate may have. In my experience it is an effective method of *sensitizing* managers to performance appraisal interview problems. Coupled with videotaped and observer-to-Stanley feedback, it can help prepare managers to change the ways they conduct appraisal interviews.

A problem with the Stanley-Burke interviews is that it does not take the manager *far enough.* For example, thoughtful managers used to conducting a "Tell and Sell"[4] interview may attribute the apparent failure of this method in this role play to the peculiarities of the role information, or to the idiosyncrasies of the person playing the Burke role. This is essentially the problem of any one-shot training session. It may alert the manager to a need for change, or at least raise doubts about the universal applicability of their present approach to the appraisal interview, but it isn't enough to change behavior. For skill acquisition, repeated practice is a necessary condition.[5]

Two follow-up methods are described in this article. Both methods avoid the dual problems of boredom inherent in doing several standard role plays and the lack of involvement that may result from simply watching videotaped interviews. The first is the use of an "advisory role play" in which a group of managers provide advice to the person who will be conducting the appraisal interview. The second is a "transcript writing exercise"

---

[1]Robinson, J. C., and Robinson, L. C. Modelling techniques applied to performance feedback and appraisal. *Training and Development Journal,* January 1978, *32,* 48–53.

[2]Hall, D. T. *Careers in organizations.* Pacific Palisades, Calif.: Goodyear, 1976, p. 68.

[3]Maier, N. R. F. *The appraisal interview: Three basic approaches.* La Jolla, Calif.: University Associates, 1976.

[4]Maier, *ibid.*

[5]Rackham, N. The coaching controversy. *Training and Development Journal,* November 1979, *33,* 12–16.

in which the manager puts himself/herself in the role of both manager and subordinate and writes the anticipated dialogue for the upcoming interview.

Explicit is the belief that one source of interviewing problems is managers' attempts to use the same interviewing method in all situations. In my experience, a characteristic of those managers who get results from appraisal interviews is that they tailor their method to the situation.

The Advisory Role Play

The advisory role play (ARP) attempts to capitalize on the sensitization frequently observed among managers after they have gone through a standard role playing exercise. The ARP makes use of this sensitization by providing a vehicle for managers to give their advice to a fellow manager about to conduct an appraisal interview, as well as a chance to be involved observers of an interview they have played a role in designing.

The procedure is simple. All managers in the training group, as well as the role players, are asked to read a case which portrays the setting for the interview and the events leading up to it. The interviewer and interviewee are given the usual role descriptions in advance of the interview. After the whole group and the interviewer have given some thought to the upcoming interview, and while the interviewee is absent, the group advises the interviewer about how to conduct the interview. At the outset the advice is typically quite general—conduct a tell-and-listen interview, or tell the interviewee what you think about his/her performance, etc.—but this quickly turns into more specific advice about how to open the interview, what to do if he/she fails to get a response, etc. If the group waffles about giving such concrete advice, the trainer can remind the group that one of their peers is soon to be "on the line." Following the advice-giving phase, the interview takes place. After this the interviewer can give an evaluation of his/her performance, followed by the interviewee's evaluation and then a group critique of the interview.

Selection of the interviewer is of some importance. It should be someone the trainer has identified as being flexible and able to improvise, but should not be someone who is clearly an "all-star," because this may reduce the transfer value of the exercise. Choosing among several volunteers may be the most convenient method of doing this. The critical element is that the interviewer be able to incorporate *some* of the advice from the group. Experience with this technique has shown that it is most effective when the interviewer has been able to incorporate some of the advice from the group, since then group members get a chance to see what might happen if someone else put their advice into practice.

To summarize, the advisory role play is a training method in which the group provides advice for an upcoming interview, some of the advice is incorporated by the interviewer, the interview takes place and a critique of the interview follows. The ARP is an economical device that provides a common interview for all group members to discuss, while involving them to a greater extent than is true when they simply watch (or watch a videotape of) an interview.

Transcript Writing Exercise

A second technique is the transcript writing exercise (TWE). The TWE can be used separately, or in tandem with the advisory role play. Essentially, the TWE tries to move the manager from the position of interviewer to a situation in which s/he plays both roles. The purpose is to have the manager think about the interview as a mutual information exchange setting, rather than the simpler manager-to-subordinate frame of reference. This is not easy because it is not the way we are accustomed to thinking. As a result, some "hand-holding" is required.

The assignment given is the following: X will be conducting an appraisal interview with Y. Provide a script for X to follow and explain your rationale for conducting the interview in this way. We are primarily interested in how well you, as X, will handle this interview, but we also expect you to provide realistic responses for Y.

The TWE is made easier if the group has read transcripts before. The ones provided by Maier[6] have been the ones I've used and they help to make the TWE seem less unusual.

Figure 1 shows excerpts from a transcript written for a case called Dominion Acceptance[7] in which a trust company regional manager (Keast) is conducting an appraisal interview with a branch manager (Snell) whose

---

[6]Maier, *The Appraisal Interview.*

[7]Dominion Acceptance Company Ltd. (ICCH 9-474-701). Boston: Intercollegiate Case Clearing House, 1974.

FIGURE 1
Exerpts from a Transcript Written for the Dominion Acceptance Company Ltd. Case.

Keast:	Good morning, Ron. As you know we're here to review the performance of this branch. The improvements in the operations since my last visit have been noted and are appreciated. However, there remain many problems still outstanding and we have to get them cleared up today.... Frankly, Ron, these are the areas that worry me: your relationship with the staff, your non-adherence to the procedures manual, the number of new accounts, and authority delegation in the office.
Snell:	Excuse me, Mr. Keast, I understand what you are saying, but I feel that in all fairness you should realize that all those problems stem from the inadequacies of the staff I have....
Keast:	The procedures manual states that the manager should do extensive field work. However, your new accounts have declined and you are hardly ever out of the office. Could you tell me why this has happened?
Snell:	As I said, it depends on the personnel. How can I leave the office if I'm not sure the assistant manager is capable of running it in my absence?
Keast:	I can understand this when Jerry was here, but do you have any doubts about De Coste's abilities?...
Keast:	But are they realistic? We try to pay competitive wages. The collection officers here are making substantially below the average for collection officers with similar lengths of service. The salaries will have to be brought into line. Now, I still don't understand the business of the dinners and breaks. Why did you feel this was necessary?
Snell:	I felt I had to tighten up in order to discipline a non-performing staff. I was controlling the expense side.
Keast:	What effect do you think this had on the workforce?
Snell:	They got used to it.
Keast:	Ron, this really hurt. The employees feel gypped, especially when some breaks are mandatory. That is one reason why it is important to adhere to the procedures manual. Ron, what I hear you saying is that you were controlling costs "to tighten up." But this has really cost the branch in longer-run performance. Is that close?
Snell:	Yes. I thought it was what you would want me to do.
Keast:	This puzzles me. When I look at the records, the change crops up first about June of last year. Is there some factor which would account for this sudden decline?...

performance decline is apparent to Keast, but the *causes* are unclear. The sample is representative of what the transcripts look like. Further examples may be found in Dominion Acceptance Teaching Note.[8]

To summarize, the transcript writing exercise requires managers to confront the uncertainty about mutual information exchange they take into an appraisal interview setting by having them write both parts of an interview. While the focus is primarily on what they should say as the interviewer, they also have to provide what they anticipate to be realistic responses from the subordinate.

A TWO-DAY WORKSHOP

The sequential use of standard role playing exercises, the advisory role play and the transcript writing exercise can now be described. Prereading for the workshop could include papers by Maier,[9] and Cummings and Schwab.[10] Figure 2 provides an outline for an intensive two-day workshop incorporating the elements described above. The schedule is based on a training group of 15 to 20 people.

The sequence begins with a standard role play, transcript reading, and a second standard role play on the first day, with the TWE and ARP on the second day. An alternate sequence is to substitute the ARP for the second standard role play on the first day, and move the second standard role play to the afternoon of day two.

The first day begins and ends with discussions of performance appraisal interview problems, with the two standard role play exercises providing the central focus. The one used here are the Stanley-Burke and Jones-Marshall[11] exercises. Both are conducted in the usual way, followed by feedback from both the observers and

[8]Dominion Acceptance Company Ltd. Teaching Note. (ICCH 5-480-614.) Boston: Intercollegiate Case Clearing House, 1980.

[9]Maier, N. R. F. The appraisal interview and its objectives. In Maier, *The Appraisal Interview,* pp. 1–20.

[10]Cummings, L. L., and Schwab, D. P. Systems for appraisal and development. In *Performance in organizations: Determinants and appraisal.* Glenview, Ill.: Scott, Foresman, 1973, pp. 118–130.

[11]In Hall, D. T., Bowen, D. D., Lewicki, R. J., and Hall, F. S. *Experiences in management and organizational behavior.* Chicago: St. Clair Press, 1975, pp. 231–232.

FIGURE 2
Outline for a Two-day Appraisal Interview Training Workshop

Day One	
Introduction	1 hour
Assignment and reading of roles for Stanley-Burke Exercise	¼ hour
Stanley-Burke Exercise	½ hour
Feedback (from videotape and/or observer)	½ hour
Coffee	¼ hour
Discussion of Stanley-Burke Exercise	1 hour
Reading Maier Transcripts	1 hour
Lunch	1 hour
Discussion of Maier Transcripts	1 hour
Assignment and reading of roles for Jones-Marshall Exercise	¼ hour
Jones-Marshall Exercise	½ hour
Feedback (from videotape and/or observer)	½ hour
Discussion of Jones-Marshall Exercise	¾ hour
General Discussion, Case A distribution, role assignments and assignments of Transcript Writing Exercise	1 hour
	9½ hours
Evening of Day One	
Individual reading of Case A and Transcript Writing Exercise	2–3 hours
Bar service	
Day Two	
Review of Day One	½ hour
Case A Advisory Phase of ARP	¾ hour
Case A Role Play Phase of ARP	½ hour
Coffee	¼ hour
Discussion of Case A Role Play	¾ hour
Assignment of roles, distribution and reading of Case B	1 hour
Group Transcript Writing Exercise for Case B (lunch scheduled in)	2 hours
Case B Advisory Phase of ARP	¾ hour
Case B Role Play Phase of ARP	½ hour
Discussion of Case B Role Play	½ hour
General Discussion, Goal Setting, Summary and Conclusions	1½ hours
	9 hours

videotapes, if available. The post-feedback general discussions can proceed by having each Stanley/Jones describe how they had planned to conduct the interview, followed by the observers' accounts of the interviews and the Burke/Marshall statements of what they thought the outcomes of the interviews were.

In between the two exercises are the Maier interview transcripts,[12] which are based on the Stanley-Burke roles. A useful method is to discuss one each of the tell and sell, tell and listen and problem solving transcripts, focusing on *when* each might be used. Group members may propose initial models as to when each method might be most appropriate. One that frequently emerges at this stage is a two-factor model; the first represents the current level of employee performance and the second is how much knowledge the supervisor has about the source of the employee's performance problems.

---

[12]Maier, *The Appraisal Interview.*

Problem solving is frequently suggested for the high performer, while a tell and sell is suggested for the poor performer when the supervisor has a good understanding about the source of the performance problem. When these conditions are not met, a tell and listen interview is often recommended. Additional factors such as employee preferences, type of manager-subordinate relationship, etc., can also be argued for. Whatever models emerge, the point is to have managers recognize that the same method will not be universally effective. If time permits, the initial models may be revised during the general discussion that ends the first day.

After the points from the two exercises have been summarized, the trainer then distributes Case A, which will form the basis of the transcript writing exercise. The TWE may then be described, the role players for the advisory role play selected and the first day wrapped up. A case that works well here, and for which there are role descriptions and sample transcripts, is the Dominion Acceptance[13] case mentioned earlier.

The evening of the first day is devoted to the TWE. Even when the Maier transcripts have been read, some "hand-holding" will be necessary for some managers. Stress should be placed on the process, not the exact wording. Managers should be discouraged from dwelling on the details of the subordinates' responses. During the evening the trainer will also want to go over the roles of the players with them. Characteristic responses of the subordinate should be discussed with him/her, while the planned method of the supervisor should be reviewed in some detail.

The first day is long. A bar service around 10 p.m. would be welcomed and provides a vehicle for idea exchange about Case A and the TWE.

Day Two

The review of day one which opens day two may be used to restate the working models and/or as a setting for surfacing managers' feelings about the previous day. Following this, the Case A advisory role play is conducted, followed by the distribution of Case B and the assignment of roles. The transcript writing exercise which is incorporated with Case B may switch to a group exercise or continue with the individual TWE. The group exercise may be preferable because by that time most of the managers have gotten accustomed to arguing their viewpoints with each other, and natural groups have formed. During the transcript writing period the role players can again be coached.

In order to increase the transfer value of the training and to widen the range of interviews experienced, a broader case may be desirable. A case such as the case of the plateaued performer[14] fills such a need in that the interview is between a president and his vice-president of marketing over what to do with a young sales manager whom the vice-president wants to transfer because of alleged inexperience.

An alternative which has worked well (but which is nevertheless risky) is a case called Karen Lappin.[15] This case centers around the personal lives of an assistant trust company manager and his head cashier, whose affair is causing work problems. The branch manager has to decide whom to interview and how. A third option is the Peter Hoskins case[16] which focuses on the problems of managing a consultant who has become unreliable, has health and family problems, and who has not been appraised for some time. Whatever case is chosen, the trainer should attempt to broaden the context of the training to increase its transfer value to more than standard appraisal interview settings.

Following the second ARP, the trainer needs to tie the preceding two days together. Depending on his/her skills, preferences, and goals, the trainer may want to elaborate a more complex model, or draw one or more from the group. Whatever method is used, the point is to reinforce the idea that exclusively using a single method will frequently result in a mismatch with the situation faced by managers. The absence of a validated prescriptive model should be openly confronted.

The standard and advisory role plays and the transcript writing exercise permit managers to both practice and see a variety of interviewing methods. The intention is to develop the idea that having a repertoire of methods and some guides to their uses will improve appraisal interviewing. Practice in using the methods is provided, as well as opportunities to be an involved observer of others' interviews. As a result, managers should go beyond the

[13]Dominion Acceptance Company Ltd., (ICCH 9-474-701).

[14]Warren, E. K., Ference, T. P., and Stoner, J. A. F. Case of the plateaued performer. *Harvard Business Review,* January-February, 1975.

[15]Karen Lappin (ICCH 9-479-733), and Karen Lappin Teaching Note (ICCH 5-479-734). Boston: Intercollegiate Case Clearing House, 1979.

[16]The Case of Peter Hoskins. In Lorsch, J. W., and Barnes, L. B. *Managers and their careers: Case and readings.* Homewood, Ill.: Irwin, 1972, pp. 12–23.

sensitization stage and decrease the frequency of a given manager's interviewing method failing to match the interview situation. Hence the prediction made is that the interview problems identified at the beginning of this article should decline following training, compared to either managers with no training or those receiving standard role play training.

Evidence from performance rating training[17] and handling employee problem training[18] suggests that when role playing is coupled with extensive feedback and modelling opportunities, the results are stronger than when more standard methods are used.

SUMMARY

Role playing exercises are a widely used method of improving managers' appraisal interviewing skills. Two methods which build on and extend the basic role play are described. The advisory role play allows managers to see an interview conducted in which the interviewer uses some of their ideas. The transcript writing exercise places the managers in the role of both interviewer and interviewee, thereby increasing their sensitivity to the information exchange aspects of appraisal interviews. A two-day workshop was described which utilizes standard role plays, the advisory role play, and the transcript writing exercise as part of a package, the purpose of which is to broaden and sharpen a manager's skills in conducting appraisal interviews.

---

[17]Latham, G. P., Wexley, K. N., and Pursell, E. D. Training managers to minimize rating errors in the observation of behavior. *Journal of Applied Psychology,* 1975, *60,* 550–555.

[18]Latham, G. P., and Saari, L. M. Application of social-learning theory to training supervisors through behavioral modeling. *Journal of Applied Psychology,* 1979, *64,* 239–246.

PART FOUR

CASE STUDIES

Case Study Guidelines

- A series of questions useful for analyzing performance cases. Focuses the analysis on performance appraisal as a continuing part of performance management. Also, provides suggestions on how to guide the discussion.

Case 1: The Poor Performer

- Situation involves an energetic performer who is receiving little administrative help.

Case 2: Sam Higgins

- Case considers how the organization is managing performance.

Case 3: The Unhappy Guest

- A sequential dialogue between an employee and her managers. Shows how poor communication causes performance problems. Can be analyzed using the questions in Reading 16: *Nonevaluative Approaches To Performance Appraisal* by Les Wallace.

Case 4: Sam Carrons

- A dialogue between an employee and his supervisor showing what happens when job responsibilities are not clear.

Case 5: Mary Lou Petrillo

- Sequential case of mismanagement of performance problems.

CASE STUDY GUIDELINES

LEARNING OBJECTIVES

1. To identify that performance includes long-run and short-run objectives; human resource as well as production objectives; and maintenance as well as growth objectives.
2. To reinforce the importance of the total performance planning and management process.
3. To recognize that both the superior and subordinate have responsibilities for managing performance.
4. To identify the skills necessary to manage performance.

Cases are written to provide a basis for discussion and a method for generating further involvement of a group. You should use them to reinforce the importance of each component of the performance management cycle and identify the skills necessary to manage performance. We suggest you facilitate case analysis by asking the following questions:

1. *How is performance defined?* You should help the participants start thinking about types of performance goals are mentioned by asking "what other things are important to help maintain performance?" This should lead into a discussion of long-term versus short-term performance goals, human resource goals, development versus production types of goals, etc.
2. *How is performance being managed?* The participants should understand that just focusing on goals and not becoming involved in the rest of performance management does have its advantages or people wouldn't do it. It's more direct and allows the manager more psychological control. It is simpler because there is a tendency to focus on short-term results, etc. However, the costs in lost performance usually outweigh these gains. Involve the participants in sharing their own experience. Focus particularly on those who have had positive experience. One way to focus on the positive is to ask the question "Describe the best boss you ever had." In answering this question participants will usually list all of the components of the performance management cycle included in Part V.
3. *What are the responsibilities managers and employees have in managing performance?* The purpose of this question is to reinforce the point that both parties are equally responsible. It is often too easy in organizations to adopt the "too bad I have such a bad manager" attitude. Have participants recognize that the employee can initiate, implement, and use the performance management cycle. They don't have to wait for the manager. Both are responsible.
4. *What skills do managers and employees need to manage performance?* Use this question as a chance to have participants identify the skills they would like to focus on in the training. You can broaden the question by asking the participants to think about skills they feel they need to manage performance. You could conclude the discussion with a list of skills they as participants would like to focus on in the training. You could then use this list to emphasize and modify the training so it fits the group you are working with.

CASE 1
THE POOR PERFORMER

"It's not fair!" said Dave to his supervisor at his third bi-monthly performance review. "I'm working harder than anyone else. I've been in here every weekend for the past three weeks doing work my people don't seem to be able to do, and yet, here I get another lousy performance rating from you. I don't know what to do!"

Recent college graduates are selected each year by the large Metro Hospital to participate in their 12-month administrative training program. The program, created two years ago as a device to provide a continuous flow of administrative talent to the rapidly growing needs of the hospital, is widely known as being rigorous and competitive, providing ground for future hospital management personnel. The program is marked by bi-monthly performance reviews and a final retention review; not everyone who enters the program is retained by the hospital. While the other hospitals in the region are often willing to accept those who fail to make it at Metro, the pressure to remain in the program is intense.

"Unfortunately, Dave, the hospital cannot reward effort alone," said the supervisor solemnly. "We have to face up to the reality of poor performance when it happens. It's simply a matter of results, I'm afraid." The supervisor was holding the computer-generated "score card," which listed the late rates and error rates for the four administrative processing teams.

The rating given Dave during his last review was not good, and Dave knew that subsequent negative reports would pretty much eliminate his chances to get a position at Metro. As a result of his last review, Dave had redoubled his efforts and made great demands on his staff of four to reduce their error rate and to decrease their processing times. This increased pressure drove one person to transfer to another department, and another person had developed into a chronic absentee case. A week prior to this third review, Dave had received a replacement for the transferred clerk.

Dave's supervisor referred to the performance rating sheets in front of him. "Although your initiative remains high, Dave, and I've given you another 8 on that, I simply cannot in all fairness give you more than a 5 on 'quantity of work accomplished' and 'quality of work accomplished.' Your error rates and processing times are still both higher and longer respectively than any of the four processing teams. I'm sure with your abilities you will find a way to do better during this coming rating period. I have to say that if things don't improve, it doesn't look good for you here at Metro."

1. From what you read about the Metro training program, is their performance review mechanism helping insure that the best managers are retained by the hospital? If not, what changes would you suggest?

2. For on-the-job training programs in general, what objectives would you set and how would you insure that you were meeting them?

From *Motivational Dynamics II*, Organizational Dynamics Incorporated, 16 New England Executive Park, Burlington, MA, 01803. Reprinted with permission.

CASE 2
SAM HIGGINS

Sam Higgins, Production Manager, has been with Semco for about five years. Although his formal training is as an engineer, Sam enjoys the challenges of the production environment. However, at present, Sam feels caught in the rapid increase in production demands.

"The end of the quarter is like hell around this place. They tell me I should be concerned about percentage of batch yield, turn around process time, operator training certification. Some quarters I feel lucky just to get those circuits out the door on time."

Victor Mennan has been with Semco for about a year, as Production Engineer assigned to one of the more complicated operations. Victor's job requires fast-paced skills and independent spot quality decisions. Sam has just finished telling Victor he is a "marginal performer."

"You know, he called me into the office and told me my work was not good, that too much of my output was being sent back for rework. He never told me anything was wrong. I figured I was doing okay, you know. I even figured I ws doing pretty good, for not getting much help. The first three months I was here, this guy who was real good, helped me along. But, then he was transferred and, with all the new people, I was supposed to be the more experienced. So, I did the job I thought I was supposed to do."

Sam's current problem, he feels, is hiring and training people. His staff has mushroomed by sixty percent in this last year alone. "I'd like training to be an integral part of my job. I've been trying to find information about career possibilities for myself and for people like Victor, but I gave up because it made my boss so upset. The financial goals of the company always seem much more real and tangible than the human resource needs."

Every year, Sam receives his performance goals, based on the production demands of his division. Sam remembered the time when there was mutual goal setting, but now he receives from his manager Tom Hartley the production quotas necessary to meet corporate growth figures.

According to Tom, "You do what you have to do to meet ROI and growth figures. I don't have time for all that management stuff. My biggest problem is finding people to fill th eopen requisitions. People here have a high degree of control over what they are responsible for. Job descriptions and specific responsibilities just don't make sense, given the fast pace."

"This is an easy climate. People are accepted for their competence without the pressure to conform, and there is a great degree of flexibility in working toward corporate goals. Unfortunately, what happens is that any kind of negative feedback, especially about individual performance, is given too late. It's very easy under the growth crunch to smooth over conflicts for fear of expending too much time arguing and not producing."

"I know that I could use some help in management training and I wish there was some way this environment would be more supportive of our human resource needs."

Written by Lynn Isabella.

CASE 3
THE UNHAPPY GUEST

Jerry Smith is in charge of handling complaints for the Grand Hotel in St. Louis. His office is part of the Public Relations unit of the organization. Guests of the Hotel leave their complaints on forms which the Hotel leaves in every room. Mr. Smith and his two subordinates are supposed to compile the complaints, and take appropriate action.

Recently the President of the Grand Hotel received a letter from an angry guest who had asked, on his complaint form, that a letter be sent back explaining why room service had been slow. The guest also wanted to know what steps would be taken to correct the situation. But the guest claimed to have received no letter at all. Hence his new complaint—this time to the President's Office.

Since the Hotel is divided functionally into two wings, Mr. Smith knew from the guest's room number that the subordinate who hadn't responded to the complaint was Kathy Bleer, in charge of the East Wing. Jerry approached Kathy at lunch one day in the Cafeteria.

SCENE I

Smith: Say, Kathy, I want to talk to you about something.
Kathy: Yes?
Smith: There's a real problem here. The President's Office has gotten a letter from an angry guest saying that you hadn't written back as he'd requested.
Kathy: What?
Smith: This guest was quite upset, and you know that doesn't make us look good in the President's eyes.
Kathy: I really don't know what you're talking about.
Smith: Come on, Kathy, this is really serious. Now let's talk about it.
Kathy: Let's not! (Walks out of the room.)

SCENE II

(Mr. Smith approaches the Director of Public Relations, Ms. Scott.)
Scott: What is it, Jerry?
Smith: I'm having a problem with Kathy Bleer. The President got a letter from a guest saying that Kathy hadn't written to him as he'd requested on his complaint form. Now the President is all upset. And when I approached Kathy to talk to her, she wouldn't say anything to me. She just walked right out of the room.
Scott: What in the world did you say to her?
Smith: Nothing, really. I just raised the issue, and she got all huffy and walked out on me. It was humiliating. There were other people around. I can't deal with her when she's put me in that kind of position.
Scott: Well what do you think I can do about it?
Smith: Maybe you could just talk to her. I don't seem to have any clout.
Scott: If that's what you want, Jerry, I'll see what I can do.
Smith: Yes, I wish you'd try it. Thanks.

From "Performance Review," *The Applied Management Series,* Organizational Dynamics Incorporated, 16 New England Executive Park, Burlington, MA, 01803. Reprinted with permission.

SCENE III

(In Ms. Scott's Office.)

Kathy: Did you want to see me, Ms. Scott?

Scott: Yes, Kathy. I understand there's been some trouble between you and Mr. Smith . . . something about an unanswered request from a guest. Would you like to tell me your side of the story?

Kathy: There's nothing to tell. I don't kow what this is all about. He just came over to me in the lunch room, and started getting all hot under the collar about a guest. What was I supposed to say? He could have waited until regular worktime to do that.

Scott: Perhaps so, Kathy, but this really could be a serious problem. I think it might look like Mr. Smith was being too strong in his criticism, but he really has the best interests of all of us in mind.

Kathy: Best interests? He just lit into me out there—and he didn't even explain himself.

Scott: Well, let me try to explain for him. You see, Kathy, it may not seem serious that some guest writes to the President. I know we have some pretty nutty people stay here, and they want the moon. But the President's Office is very sensitive to complaints like this, and it looks bad for all of us when he gets one.

Kathy: I do a good job, Ms. Scott. I handle complaints as well as anybody would. I don't even know who this guest is. He's probably one of those people who scribble something at the last minute, and you can't even read it.

Scott: You mean you wouldn't respond if something were hard to read?

Kathy: No, Ms. Scott, I don't mean that. I mean that some of them are just impossible to answer. You can't read them.

Scott: Well, Kathy, that's not a good attitude. It just won't do. Kathy, I can't stress enough to you that we are in a very sensitive position. We have to take the flack for everybody else's mistakes, and it's very hard sometimes. But a few oversights like the one you made, and we could be in serious trouble.

Kathy: Ms. Scott, it's not fair to ask 100% perfection. That's impossible on this job. I do the best I can. It's not fair.

Scott: Don't get upset, Kathy. I know you work hard. But look at Mr. Smith's position. He puts his head on the block when you make a mistake. We just have to be an *extra* bit more careful to do everything—including processing those illegible complaints—because what looks like a minor complaint here looks like a major problem at the top. That's just how it is, Kathy.

Kathy: I don't know what you want me to do.

Scott: Just try a little harder to realize that your actions are very important, and have consequences for all of us. I know you're a good worker, and I'm sure you'll be able to do better.

Kathy: O.K.—I understand, Ms. Scott.

Scott: Good, Kathy. Thanks for coming in.

CASE 4
Sam Carrons

For the past ten years Sam Carrons has been employed as an area representative for Wesley-Salk, Inc., a large manufacturer of insulating products. Sam has always done well as a salesman. He has always been able to meet or exceed his quota; and overall has been a hard working, loyal, and apparently satisfied employee. Certainly Arthur Miyakawa, Regional Sales Manager and Sam's boss, never had cause for serious complaint.

In the last six months, however, something has changed. Sam's attitude has seemed to deteriorate. He doesn't come in with a friendly word for the staff as he usually had; he doesn't seem to want to get into conversations about himself or anything else except the United Fund Drive, a cause which has always been close to his heart.

Even worse, Sam doesn't seem to have the same hold on his market that he has had in the past. His sales orders have begun to slip. One large customer has requested a different representative. Art's only consolation is that he hadn't lost that business entirely.

Art has been mulling over the situation for several days. He sees Sam in the Cafeteria line, and asks Sam to sit with him at a quiet table in one corner.

Art: How are you, Sam?
Sam: Fine.
Art: I thought it would be good to touch base.
Sam: (Nods.)
Art: Uh, how are things going, Sam?
Sam: O.K.
Art: You're looking a little low today.
Sam: What?
Art: Just not up to your usual self?
Sam: Well, I have been a little tired. I've been working really hard on the United Fund Drive.
Art: Yes, I know.
Sam: Well, the Drive's really going well. We'll probably exceed our goal. I think the President's Office is really going to be pleased. So, how are *you* doing?
Art: . . . Listen, Sam, there's something bothering me. I—uh—I'm really concerned about your performance lately. You've been slipping, Sam, and it's time to do something about it.
Sam: Slipping? Damn it, Art, I've been working as hard as ever.
Art: There's no doubt about it, Sam. I have your latest sales figures right here.
Sam: Listen! You know you can't judge from those figures. They don't take into account the recession. I'm not the only one who isn't doing so well these days.
Art: Look, Sam, I hate to say it, but we're concerned with *your* problem here, not what anybody else is doing. I'm afraid you're going to be in serious trouble if your record continues this way, and I don't intend to see you go down hill. You've been a friend of mine too long for me to let that happen. Now maybe if you tell me what's going on, I can help you.
Sam: Gee, Art, there's nothing going on. It's been hard lately, that's true—but for everybody, not just me. I know I haven't been doing so well, but it's just a temporary situation.
Art: Temporary? Sam, we're talking about six months. Don't try to get out of it. What's wrong with you?
Sam: There's nothing wrong with me! The pressure has really increased since we merged with Acme. There's too much paperwork now with that Coordinating Office to report to in addition to you.
Art: But Sam, don't you see that we're now more crucial to the success of this whole company than we ever were before the merger? That puts extra responsibility on us. We've got to meet it. Listen, Sam, the way I see it, you're not using your time wisely.

From "Performance Review," *The Applied Management Series,* Organizational Dynamics Incorporated, 16 New England Executive Park, Burlington, MA, 01803. Reprinted with permission.

Sam: Oh?

Art: That's right, Sam. You spend an awful lot of time on the Fund Drive.

Sam: Well, it takes time, but not really so much, and it's only once a year.

Art: I know, but it's a beginning. Don't you think if you put less of your energy into the Fund and more into your work, we'd do better?

Sam: Art, the Fund Drive is very important, and it needs my participation!

Art: You see, Sam, that's just what I mean. This Fund Drive is overly important to you. I know it's important, and I'm all in favor of it—but look at it this way; if we don't meet our sales quota, there won't be money for the Fund Drive or anything else. We've got to put first things first.

Sam: Well sure, Art, but... oh, I don't know....

Art: Don't let it get you down. We can find somebody else to do your work on the Fund. We need you more doing the real sales. I know... Jennie Morales could take over some of that work. She's not a very high producer anyway. Then we can have you where we really need you.

Sam: Jennie Morales? I don't think she'd be very good.

Art: Well, Sam, let's give it a try, and see how it works. And I want you to come in and see me every Friday for a few weeks. Let's keep track of how you're doing. You've always been a crackerjack salesman, and there's no reason why you can't be in the future. We'll get this United Fund business straightened out, don't you worry.

Sam: You really think I can do better? We're having hard times you know.

Art: Sam, I *know* you can. Now get out there and hustle. I'll see you in a week.

Sam: O.K.—boss. Gotcha!

CASE 5
MARY LOU PETRILLO, PART A

Mary Lou Petrillo has been employed by Bowes Shoes for twelve years. She has done nearly everything that can be done in production. She has worked in Cutting, Stitching, Dyeing, Tooling and Last Making. Now, with the expansion of Bowes Shoes, Mary Lou's supervisor, Annie Santos, has put Mary Lou in charge of the entire cutting room.

As part of the expansion, Cutting has taken on three new people. None of them had much experience in the shoe business before they came to Bowes. Mary Lou has had to put in a great deal of time training and supervising these new employees, teaching them how the unit functions and how to do their jobs.

During a regular production meeting, Annie found herself having to call Mary Lou "on the carpet" for the low output of the cutting room, and the low quality of the goods that were produced there. Annie dropped the subject when tension between them began to mount, but she had to face the issue again the next week during the regular performance review.

After the review, Annie was no more satisfied than she had been at the outset. The cutting room still could not keep up with the other phases of the operation which depended on them, and return rates from retail outlets were still far too high. Annie began to wonder whether she'd been wise to put Mary Lou in charge of the Cutting Room. She didn't seem to understand her responsibilities as a supervisor, and Annie felt that Bowes might be better off without her.

QUESTIONS FOR ANALYSIS

1. How do you think the three new cutters are really affecting production?

2. What could Annie Santos have done to be sure Mary Lou Petrillo correctly understood her responsibilities?

3. If you were Annie Santos, what would you do now?

From "Performance Review," *The Applied Management Series*, Organizational Dynamics Incorporated, 16 New England Executive Park, Burlington, MA, 01803. Reprinted with permission.

CASE 5
MARY LOU PETRILLO, PART B

Mary Lou:	I'm tired of hearing you complain about how the cutting room is doing.
Annie:	*You're* tired of it? What do you expect me to do?
Mary Lou:	You can't squeeze blood from a turnip. We're doing the best we can.
Annie:	Well you're output doesn't show it. And the retailers are returning all the shoes.
Mary Lou:	That's too bad. But we've got these three rookies in the room. I'd sure like to know how the bozos in personnel ever picked them out if they expect...
Annie:	It's your job to run the room and get the stuff out right. Don't tell me it's personnel's fault.
Mary Lou:	You think I would ever hire clowns like those? Personnel has no idea what it means to supervise people that don't know anything. Let them come down and do it themselves.
Annie:	Nobody said it's your responsibility to be a babysitter.
Mary Lou:	How do you think they'll ever get the work done, if I don't help them?
Annie:	I don't care how they do it! Just get it done!

QUESTIONS FOR ANALYSIS

1. How do you think the three new cutters are really affecting production?

2. What could Annie Santos have done to be sure Mary Lou Petrillo correctly understood her responsibilities?

3. If you were Annie Santos, what would you do now?

PART FIVE

TRANSPARENCY MASTERS/ OVERHEADS*

---

*The assistance of Dr. William E. Beusse, U.S. General Accounting Office, Washington, D.C., is greatfully acknowledged.

MASTER 1
STRATEGIC PLANNING AS A PREREQUISITE OF PERFORMANCE APPRAISAL

STRATEGIC PLANNING I

1. Why are we here?
   - Whom do we serve?
   - What do we do for them?

2. Who are we?
   - What are out strengths?
   - What are out weaknesses?

3. Where are we going?
   - Where are we now?
   - What opportunities exist?
   - What problems do we face?
   - What do our clients need?

STRATEGIC PLANNING II

- Top level
- Input from below

1. Analyze external environment
   - Identify opportunities
   - Identify problems

2. Assess strengths and weaknesses
   - Human
   - Financial
   - Technological
   - Physical facilities
   - Other

3. Devise programs to take advantage of strengths and opportunities and minimize impact of weaknesses and problems

4. Convert programs to resource needs, budgets, and plans

MASTER 2
WHAT IS PERFORMANCE APRAISAL?

The Appraisal Process:

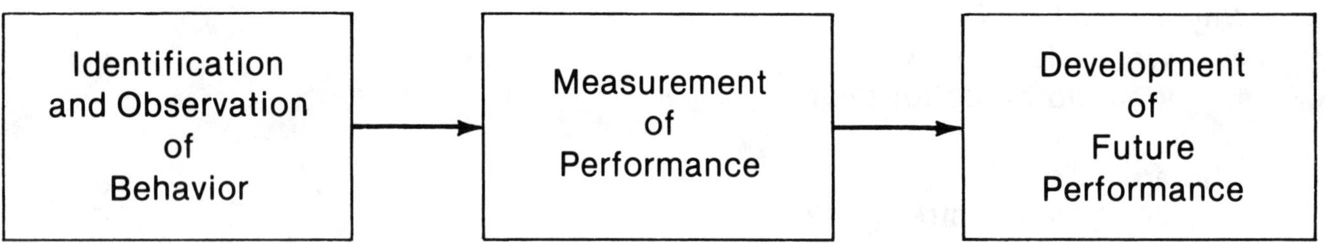

MASTER 3
OBJECTIVES

COMMUNICATION
- WORK TO BE ACCOMPLISHED
- PERFORMANCE EXPECTATIONS
- FEEDBACK

EMPLOYEE DEVELOPMENT
- WHAT THE *EMPLOYEE* CAN DO TO . . .
- WHAT *DIGITAL* CAN DO TO . . .

REPRESENT KEY INPUT TO
- SALARY ADMINISTRATION
- CAREER PLANNING
- WORK PLANNING
- INDIVIDUAL CAREER ASPIRATION
- BACK-UP PLANS
- TIES TO CAREER SYSTEM

MASTER 4
USES OF APPRAISALS

Subsystem Elements	*Interface With Appraisal Subsystem*	*Viewpoint*
Staffing:		
Recruitment	Identifying Current Inadequacies	Developmental
Selection	Criteria for Selection Predictors	Developmental
Placement		
Transfer	Individual Skills for New Assignment	Developmental
Promotion	Identifying Outstanding Performer	Judgmental
Termination	Identifying Inadequate Performer	Judgmental
Human Resource Inventory	Skill and Potential Data	Developmental
Rewarding:		
Benefits		
Salary Structure		
Merit	Comparative Data on Performance	Judgmental
Intrinsic	Motivation Through Objective Setting, Feedback, & Participation	Developmental
Changing:		
Organizational Climate	Appraisee Evaluation	Developmental
Organizational Structure		
Management Styles	Identify Need For General Change	Developmental
Policies	Two-Way Feedback	Developmental
Communication	Two-Way Feedback	Developmental
Developing:		
Rotating	Judgments on Learning	Developmental
Training	Identifying Individual Upgrading Needs	Developmental
	Evaluating Previous Training	Developmental
Counseling	Career Planning Basis	Developmental

MASTER 5
THOROUGH PERFORMANCE APPRAISAL PROCESS

A. *MANAGERS SHOULD:*

1. TRANSLATE ORGANIZATIONAL GOALS INTO INDIVIDUAL JOB OBJECTIVES/ REQUIREMENTS.
2. COMMUNICATE THEIR EXPECTATIONS REGARDING EMPLOYEE PERFORMANCE.
3. PROVIDE FEEDBACK TO THE EMPLOYEES.
4. COACH THE EMPLOYEES ON HOW TO ACHIEVE JOB OBJECTIVE/ REQUIREMENTS.
5. DIAGNOSE THE EMPLOYEE'S RELATIVE STRENGTHS AND WEAKNESSES.
6. DETERMINE A DEVELOPMENT PLAN FOR IMPROVING JOB PERFORMANCE AND ABILITY UTILIZATIONS.

B. *EMPLOYEES SHOULD GET THE ANSWERS TO:*

1. WHAT AM I EXPECTED TO DO?
2. HOW WELL AM I DOING?
3. WHAT ARE MY STRENGTHS, WEAKNESSES?
4. HOW CAN I DO A BETTER JOB?
5. HOW CAN I CONTRIBUTE MORE?

C. *THE CORPORATION SHOULD:*

PROVIDE EMPLOYEES WITH A CLEAR UNDERSTANDING OF WHAT IS EXPECTED OF THEM, ESTABLISH DIRECTION BY SETTING OBJECTIVES AND PRIORITIES, MONITORING RESULTS, AND RESPONDING TO PROBLEMS TO ENSURE THAT ALL ASSIGNED OBJECTIVES ARE MET ON TIME.

MASTER 6
WHAT IS JOB PERFORMANCE?

Behavior is simply activity on the job.	BEHAVIORS:	Checking all sick leave balances, preparing a tabular summary, distributing to entire staff with new leave policy statements.
Which is evaluated or appraised by the organization according to set of criteria and termed performance.	PERFORMANCE:	Leave balances are checked accurately and distributed in a timely manner.
Which results in any one or more of several, observable outputs.	RESULTS:	Leave report written.
Which can result in desired unit or organizational outcomes and hence effectiveness.	EFFECTIVENESS:	Report proves useful, as leave and associated costs have been reduced.

MASTER 7
KEY ELEMENTS OF THE PERFORMANCE APPRAISAL

1. THE PROCESS SHOULD BE KEPT SIMPLE.
2. FOR EACH JOB FAMILY CLUSTER, APPROPRIATE JOB CHARACTERISTICS SHOULD BE DEVELOPED.
   A. SEPARATE AND REPRESENTATIVE OF EACH JOB FAMILY CLUSTER.
   B. CLEARLY DEFINED.
   C. FLEXIBLE TO ALLOW FOR SELF EXPRESSION.
3. RATING SCALE SHOULD:
   A. BE FLEXIBLE FOR SELF EXPRESSION BUT STRUCTURED.
   B. RATE THE EFFECTIVENESS AND IMPORTANCE AS WELL.
4. THE SYSTEM SHOULD BE EASY TO ADMINISTER (POSSIBLY COMPUTERIZED).
5. SHOULD BE MODULAR TO:
   A. ALLOW FOR GRADUAL INTRODUCTION TO THE ORGANIZATION.
   B. ALLOW FOR FUTURE POSSIBLE USES.
6. IT SHOULD CONSIDER THE EXISTING MANAGEMENT CAPABILITIES AND ABILITY TO CONDUCT THE APPRAISAL.
   A. EASY TO OPERATE (SIMPLE AND FLEXIBLE).
   B. EASY TO EXPLAIN (TRAINING AND EXPLANATORY MATERIAL).
   C. EASY TO MAINTAIN (SUPPORT RESOURCES: TRAINING, DIRECTORY OF ACTIVITIES).
   D. EASY TO ADMINISTER (COMPUTERIZED).
7. SHOULD BE CONSISTENT WITH LEGAL DEMANDS AND IMPLICATIONS.
8. SERVE AS PART OF A TOTAL SYSTEM.

MASTER 8

STEPS OF A PERFORMANCE APPRAISAL

A. Subordinate initiates the appraisal by reviewing with his supervisor the results of his performance.
   1. The subordinate has evaluated his or her own performance against predetermined goals and identifies where he or she has fallen short, reached, and surpassed the goals.
   2. The supervisor assesses the subordinate's goal accomplishment prior to the appraisal.
   3. The supervisor must work very hard to set a climate where subordinates feel that they can honestly and objectively evaluate themselves without cutting their own throat.

B. At the meeting the supervisor *coaches,* not criticizes, the subordinate. They try to agree on reasons why goals were not achieved or why problems developed. No one tries to blame the other, for *both share responsibility for the subordinate's success or failure. A full, complete flow of information must occur; neither should hold back.*

C. Obstacles to reaching goals and obstacles which are causing problems are identified. Plans are made to overcome or avoid these obstacles. Both the supervisor and the subordinate contribute to the development and carrying out of these plans.

D. New goals are set.

Developed by Alan Frohman, Frohman Associates, Lexington, Mass.

MASTER 9
SOURCES OF PROBLEMS IN PERFORMANCE APPRAISAL AND THEIR CONSEQUENCES

Performance Appraisal Problem Sources	→	Result in Negative Rater and Ratee Perceptions and Feelings About the Appraisal System	→	Result in Ineffective, Biased and/or Inaccurate Appraisal Data	→	Result in Ineffective Organizational Decisions
The Person: Bias and errors in human judgement Stereotypes and prejudices Failure to use all available relevant information on performance The Job: Ambiguous criteria Incompleteness of criteria Irrelevant criteria The Situation: Lack of rewards for conscientious appraisals Lack of rewards available for those receiving high ratings Lack of attention to the individual's needs for feedback and development		"The appraisal system is a waste of time" "The appraisal system is too time-consuming." "The appraisal system is too ambiguous, subjective, and biased." "The appraisal system is not really used in promotion decisions." "We never know what the organization considers important." "We never know where we stand." "Appraisal is not really part of my job. I need to get the job done." "Each supervisor seems to have different standards."		Subjective opinions on overall performance not specific strengths and weaknesses Lenient appraisals Failure to complete appraisals Biased ratings		Failure to recognize excellent performance Failure to recognize potential Promotion selection decision errors Grievances due to subjectivity and bias Failure to adequately staff jobs with proper skills mix Failure to build skills through training

MASTER 10
PERFORMANCE MEASUREMENT AND GRADE LEVEL

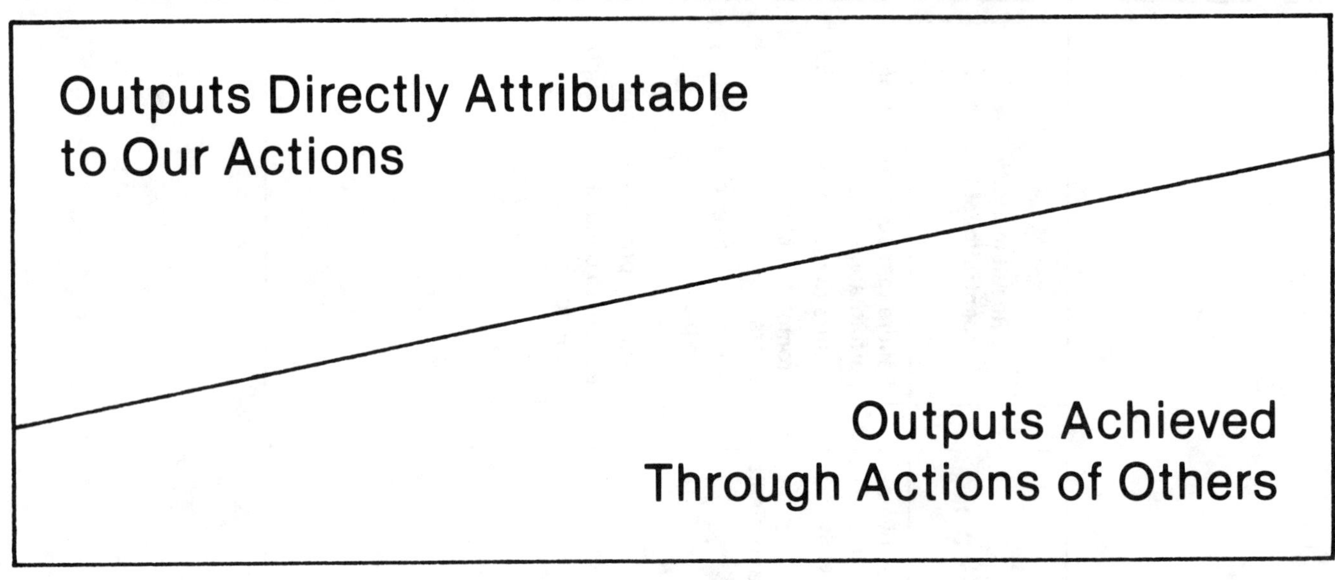

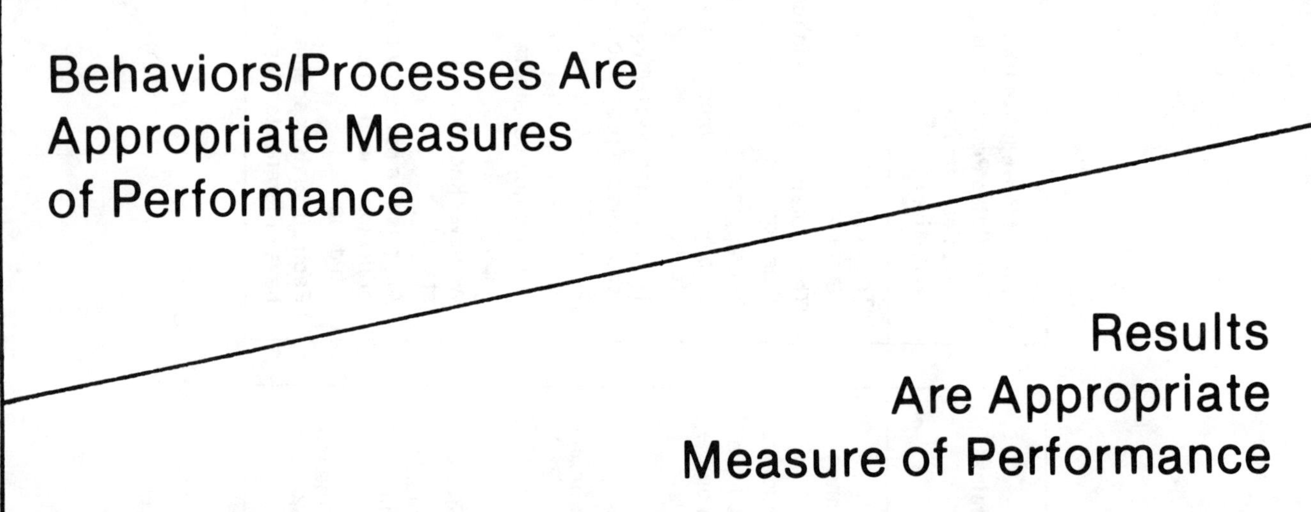

MASTER 11

DETERMINANTS OF THE EFFECTIVENESS OF AN APPRAISAL SYSTEM (NECESSARY CONDITIONS)

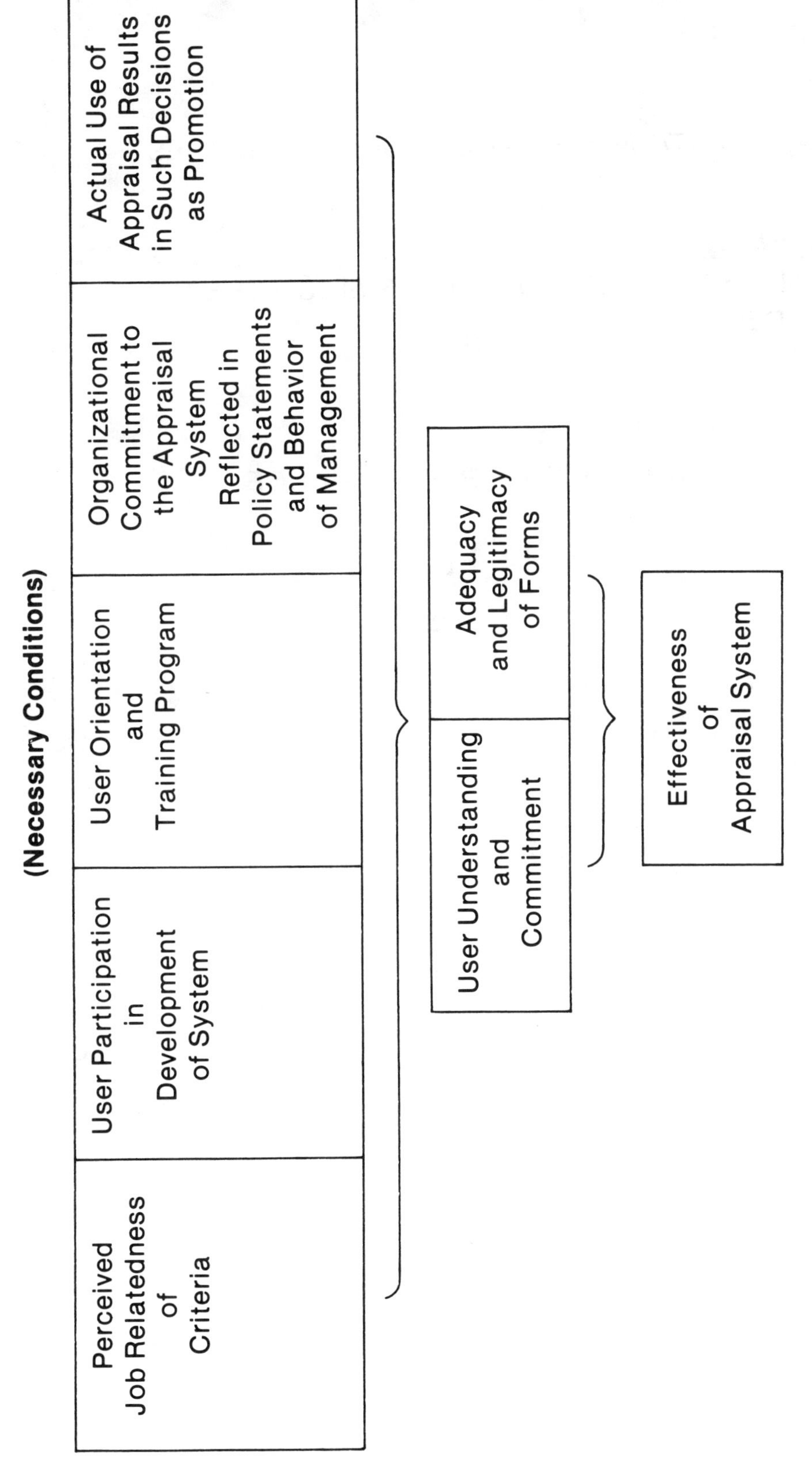

MASTER 12
PROBLEMS TO BE AWARE OF IN ANY PERFORMANCE APPRAISAL SITUATION

1. *HALO EFFECTS*

2. *PERSONAL RELATIONSHIPS* AND RESULTING BIASES

3. *CENTRAL TENDENCY*
   - RATING DIFFERENT INDIVIDUALS MUCH THE SAME EVEN IF THEY ARE DIFFERENT.

4. *LENIENCY OR STRICTNESS*
   - VARYING STANDARDS OF PERFORMANCE

MASTER 13
BEHAVIORAL ANCHOR SHEET

Job title:

Job dimension:

Behavioral Anchor Statements:

Instructions: On this sheet please provide three or more behavioral anchor statements for each performance level. You will complete one "Behavioral Anchor Sheet" for *each* job dimension for the job.

1. Excellent performance:

2. Very good performance:

3. Good performance:

4. Fair or average performance:

5. Poor performance:

6. Very poor performance:

7. Unacceptable performance:

From *Personnel Administration, An Experiential/Skill-building Approach,* Addison-Wesley Publishing Company, Reading, Mass., 1981, p. 137.

MASTER 14
SUGGESTIONS FOR WRITING USEFUL BEHAVIORS

1. Use specific examples of behavior, *not conclusions* about the "goodness" or "badness" of behavior.
   - *Use this:* This supervisor tells a secretary when the work was to be completed, the degree of perfection required, the amount of space it must be typed within, and the kind of paper necessary.
   - *Not this:* This supervisor could be expected to give very good instructions to a secretary. Instructions would be clear and concise.
2. Avoid using *adjective qualifiers* in the anchor statements; use descriptions of actual behavior.
   - *Use this:* This supervisor understands employees such that the supervisor can repeat both the employee's communication and the intent of the message. They also make certain they talk in private when necessary and do not repeat the conversation to others.
   - *Not this:* When supervising associates, this supervisor does a good job of understanding their problems. This supervisor is kind and friendly.
3. Avoid using anchors that make assumptions about employee *knowledge* about the job; use descriptions of behavior.
   - *Use this:* This employee performs the disassembly procedure for rebuilding a carburetor by first removing the cap and then proceeding with the internal components, gaskets, etc. If in doubt about the procedure, the mechanic will refer to the appropriate manual.
   - *Not this:* This mechanic knows how to disassemble a carburetor and will do so in an efficient and effective manner.
4. Avoid using frequencies in anchor statements, use descriptions of behavior.
   - *Use this:* This officer performs the search procedure by first informing those arrested of their rights, asks them to assume the search position and then proceeds to conduct the search by touching the arrested in the prescribed places. When the search is complete, the officer informs the arrested and proceeds to the next step in the arrest procedure.
   - *Not this:* This officer always does a good job in performing the search procedure.
5. Avoid using *quantitative values* (numbers) within anchors.
   - *Use this:* This accountant submits reports on time which contain no misinformation or mistakes. If discrepancies occur on reports from the last period, this accountant identifies the cause.
   - *Not this:* This accountant could be expected to meet 90% of deadlines with 95% accuracy.

From *Personnel Administration, An Experiential/Skill-building Approach.* Addison-Wesley Publishing Company, Reading, Mass., 1981, p. 111.

MASTER 15
A CHECKLIST FOR OBJECTIVES

1. SUPPORTIVE OF GAO AND/OR DIVISION GOALS? (i.e., A MEANS TO THOSE ENDS?)

2. DEALS WITH IMPORTANT ASPECTS OF THE JOB?

3. MEASURABLE WITH QUALITATIVE OR QUANTITATIVE CRITERIA?

4. RESULTS-ORIENTED?

5. SPECIFIC?

6. CLEARLY WORDED?

7. TIME-BINDING?

8. ACHIEVABLE?

9. CHALLENGING?

10. SUPPORTED BY AUTHORITY AND RESOURCES?

11. BACKED BY AN ACTION PLAN?

MASTER 16
SETTING OBJECTIVES

1. Review sources of objectives:
   a. Organization/unit plans, objectives, strategies
   b. Objectives of next higher level
   c. Key results areas
   d. Job or position descriptions
   e. Discussion with supervisor, subordinates, clients, etc.
   f. Organizational problems and opportunities
   g. Previous performance plan and objectives

2. List major types of objectives which could be established within each of the key results areas.

3. Review the list with supervisor (and subordinates) to clarify their meaning and priority and preliminary thoughts on specific objectives.

4. Develop one or more draft objectives, including those of a continuing and project nature for each key results area.

5. Identify criteria and a rough action plan for each objective.

6. Omit/revise any objective for which no criteria exist, no practical action plan is possible, or which does not comply with the "Objectives Checklist."

7. Break objectives into subobjectives or components if required.

8. Note any conditions outside your control which would influence the attainment of the objectives.

9. Determine which objectives are critical.

10. Review the objectives, criteria, action plan, etc. with your supervisor.

11. Make any modifications necessary after supervisor's review.

12. Develop detailed action plan for each objective.

13. Begin to carry out action plans.

14. Periodically review sources listed in step 1, revising objectives, criteria, conditions, action plans, etc. as necessary and reviewing changes with supervisor and subordinates.

MASTER 17
THINGS TO REMEMBER ABOUT PERFORMANCE DISCUSSIONS

1. Obtain, prepare, and thoroughly familiarize yourself with any necessary data on the subject.
   a. *Collect* information on organization goals and objectives. What programs have the greatest impact? Where can the state-of-the-art be advanced?
   b. *Think* about the job. What are the routine tasks? With whom does the subordinate have working relationships?
   c. *Review* typical days. How does the employee spend the time? For what is the employee held accountable?
   d. *Select* the major responsibilities. Should something be eliminated? Is it essential work?

2. Fix in your own mind the objectives to be accomplished during the discussion.

3. Prepare mentally to engage in the discussion.

4. Enter the discussion as a "joint venture" in problem-solving.

5. Explain reasons for note-taking, if you expect to do it.

6. Establish a climate which encourages an employee to express thoughts without fear of being viewed critically.

7. Be ready to "hear" a problem and the subordinate's attitude and feelings without pre-evaluation or pre-judgement.

8. Resolve any barriers to effective communication.

9. Clearly state and mutually agree upon the specific results of the discussion.
   a. *Set* priorities. What is the best allocation of time? Which objectives are most important?
   b. *State* specific objectives. What are the expected results (why do it) and what is the present status vs. the desired result (how to measure success)?
   c. *Identify* courses of action. What is the recommended path or course of action to follow? What are the alternative possibilities?
   d. *Determine* indicators of results. What are the areas for measurement? How can you tell if you are achieving the intended results?
   e. *Plan* for improvement. Do the goals focus attention on improvement? Does the employee need to learn new skills or technology?

10. Plan for the follow-up to the discussion.

MASTER 18
PERFORMANCE IMPROVEMENT METHOD (DISCUSSION GUIDE)

A. *Develop a careful definition first if there is a problem.*
   1. State what it is. View a problem as a deviation from the standard.
   2. How do you know that it's a problem? What are the signs that indicate a problem?
   3. Determine how much the problem is costing the organization in terms of:
      a. Work not being done
      b. Work not being done on time
      c. Problems being caused in other parts of the organization.

B. *Try to determine the cause of the problem.*
   1. Is something preventing the work from being done?
      a. Does the employee have the right tools to do the job?
      b. Are organizational policies/procedures hindering performance? (confusion, conflicting goals, complicated procedures, lack of money, time, etc.)

   2. Does the employee have enough knowledge to do the work?
      a. Does he know why it should be done a certain way?
      b. Does he know how his work contributes to the work of the organization?
      c. Does the employee possess enough knowledge about the work and how it is to be done to be able to do it?
      d. Has he ever been told that his work is not meeting acceptable standards?

   3. Try to determine if the job (task) itself has a built-in problem that leads to poor performance.
      a. Is the work too difficult for one person?
      b. Is the work so disagreeable that it is avoided?
      c. Is there no reward or sense of satisfaction in doing the particular task?

C. *Accurately record the results of the session.*
   1. Prepare a rough draft and let the employee review it.

   2. Include all expected changes that should occur.

MASTER 19
SOLVING PERFORMANCE PROBLEMS

Problem		*Try*
1. Something prevents the work from being done	a.	Supply more or better tools
	b.	Change policy/procedures, if possible
2. Employee doesn't have enough knowledge	a.	Tell him why the job should be done a certain way
	b.	Tell him how the job contributes to the work of the organization
	c.	Instruct the employee in the skills needed. Determine a training or developmental experience that will help provide the skill needed
	d.	Inform the employee about the specific shortcomings of his work
3. The work itself has a built-in problem	a.	Assign the task to more than one person
	b.	Rotate a disagreeable task among other employees so one person isn't stuck with it all of the time
	c.	Provide an incentive for overcoming built-in problems and doing the job (Recognition, appreciation, greater variety of rewarding work, more independence, etc.)

PART SIX

SAMPLE TOPICAL OUTLINES FOR BRIEFINGS AND WORKSHOPS

The readings included in this book will give you the proper background to lead workshops and presentations. In the outlines in which questionnaires, role-plays, or cases are suggested, select those that are most appropriate for your organization from the ones provided in this book or from other sources you have available.

TOPICAL OUTLINE FOR PRESENTATIONS AND BRIEFINGS

This outline will be useful for presentations to top management, discussions in departments on performance appraisal problems, development of new appraisal systems, evaluations of present systems, etc.

Introduction
- Why the orientation/briefing was scheduled
- Why those in attendance were invited
- Very brief overview of agenda
- Objectives of orientation/briefing

Specific Problems/Areas Which Would Benefit From An Improved Performance Appraisal System.
- Managing people and units—through an added emphasis on performance itself, identifying, defining, and measuring it
- Planning—through setting objectives for the organization, subunits, and individuals
- Staffing—through articulating requirements of each grade/position
- Selection—through a set of specific, valid criteria for success on each job
- Wage, salary and award administration—through a more rational, logical, equitable distribution of reward, based on merit
- Training and development—through identification of strengths and weaknesses
- Morale and motivation—through tying rewards to performance

What Is Performance Appraisal?
- Not just measurement or evaluation
- Must include defining desired performance as well as imposing/developing it
- More than forms
- Not just a once-a-year activity

Necessary Conditions For An Effective Appraisal System
- A set of organizational policies which reinforce the importance of appraisal and spell out its intended uses
- Commitment—in their own words and behavior—of top management to the success of the system
- Allocation of required resources
- Communication to managers that appraisal is a vital, continuing part of their management responsibilities and that effectiveness in this area is a criterion in their own appraisals.
- Participation of users in system design
- Orientation, training, monitoring, and follow-up for users
- Adequate forms
- System monitoring, evaluation, and redesign

The Next Steps (Any Or All Of The Following May Be Applicable).
- Set up a task force, committee, etc. to take charge of design and implementation
- Management of each unit has responsibility for design and implementation, but receives technical assistance from staff group or consultant.
- Assess feasibility of contracting with consultants to design system
- Develop overall prototype for organization, with each unit making appropraite modifications
- A group or person develops a detailed plan, including financial and human resources required and target dates, for further discussion

Questions And Answers

OUTLINE OF A WORKSHOP ON CONDUCTING PERFORMANCE APPRAISAL

This type of workshop would be useful for training managers to conduct meaningful performance appraisal which will result in improved motivation and performance. The workshop will fit any type of performance appraisal instruments. Modify, expand, or shorten the outline to fit your own situation and time constraints. This sourcebook has numerous alternatives which can be used very effectively. This is only one sequence we have found useful. As proposed the workshop would take one or two days.

Preparatory Reading

- Have participants review the reading *What Is Performance Appraisal?* by Schneier and Beatty (pages 4-11) before coming to the session.

Introduction To Program

- State clearly purposes of program—use Overheads
  - 2: *What Is Performance Appraisal* (page 232).
  - 3: *Objectives* (page 233).
  - 5: *Thorough Performance Appraisal Process* (page 235).

Discussion Of What Performance Appraisal Is

- Administer Questionnaire 1: *Attitudes Toward Performance Appraisal* (page 193).
- Discuss results—identify common problem areas.
- Emphasize importance of all the characteristics in the questionnaire by showing how performance appraisal relates to other management systems. Use overhead 4, *Uses Of Appraisal* (page 234).

Discussion Of Problems In Appraising Performance

- Explain problems of documentation (see the reading *Documenting Employee Performance* by Smith (pages 94-97). If necessary administer test on documentation included in the article or Questionnaire 4: *Performance Measurement And Review* (page 197).
- Discuss rating errors
  Overhead 12: *Problems To Be Aware Of In Any Performance Appraisal Situation* (see procedures explained in the reading *Training Approaches And A Workshop To Minimize Rating Error* by Latham and Wexley (pages 85-91) if more training on rating is needed).

Examples Of How To Analyze Performance Problems

- Emphasize the importance of analyzing performance before feedback is given by reviewing concepts in the reading *Human Performance Problems And Their Solutions* by Rummler (pages 165-172).
- Review questionnaire *A Guide For Troubleshooting Performance Problems* (pages 170-172) in the reading *Human Performance Problems and their Solutions* by Rommler or Overhead 18: *Performance Improvement Method* (page 248).
- Use Case 1: *The Poor Performer* (page 220) or Case 2: *Sam Higgins* (page 221) to show how the questionnaires can be used to analyze performance problems.

Case Study On Giving Performance Feedback

- Have participants review the reading *Nonevaluative Approaches To Performance Appraisals* by Wallace (pages 97-101).
- Discuss Cases 3 (page 222) and 4 (page 224) by seeing how closely they followed the guidelines of good performance feedback presented in the article.

Discussion Of Principles Of Good Performance Interviews

- Use Overhead 17: *Things To Remember About Performance Discussions* (page 247) to review the proper preparation for a performance review.
- Discuss principles presented in the reading *Performance Interview Guidelines* by Mahler (pages 101-105) and/or *Observation Worksheet For Managing Performance Feedback* (page 208).

Role-Plays On Giving Performance Feedback

- Role-plays as explained in *Play Well Thy Part* by Cooper (pages 210–215).
- Observers give feedback on role plays using *Observer Worksheet For Managing Performance Feedback* (page 208) or *Performance Interview Checklist* (pages 103–105) in article *Performance Interview Guidelines* by Mahler.

Summary Of Learning

- Have participants develop action plans of how they will implement what they have learned.
- Review *key points* of workshop.

OUTLINE OF A WORKSHOP ON DEVELOPING, IMPLEMENTING AND EVALUATING PERFORMANCE APPRAISAL SYSTEMS

This type of workshop would be useful for people responsible for making the performance appraisal system work. The workshop covers all of the steps: developing, implementing, and evaluating. Depending on your particular needs and the state of your performance appraisal system, you may wish to condense certain portions of the workshop and enlarge others. As proposed the workshop would take about two days.

Preparatory Reading

- Have participants review the reading *What Is Performance Appraisal* by Schneier and Beatty (pages 4-11) before coming to the workshop.
- Have participants review the reading *Appraising Appraisal: Ten Lessons From Research For Practice* by Sashkin (pages 120-128) before coming to the workshop.

Introduction

- State clearly the purposes of the workshop—use Overheads
  2: *What Is Performance Appraisal?* (page 232).
  3: *Objectives* (page 233).
  6: *What Is Job Performance* (page 236).

Discussion Of Purposes Of Performance Appraisal

- Administer Questionnaire 3: *Evaluating Performance Appraisal Systems* (page 195) or *Organizational Performance Appraisal.* Questionnaire Evaluation in *Appraising Appraisal: Ten Lessons From Research For Practice* by Sashkin (pages 122-123). You may want to have participants complete this questionnaire(s) prior to the workshop.
- Discuss areas of agreement and disagreement.
- Review the many uses of performance appraisal by 1) reviewing Overhead 4: *Uses of Appraisal* (page 234) and 2) having participants analyze Case 2: *Sam Higgins* (page 221). Use the *Case Study Guidelines* (page 219) to help the participants analyze the case.

Review Problem Areas In Performance Appraisal

- Present common problem areas—use Overhead 9: *Sources Of Problems* (page 239).
- Have participants identify problem areas that exist in the performance appraisal system in use in the organization.
- Have problem-solving groups prioritize the problem areas and identify solutions. Develop action plans for the solutions.

Define Performance

- Review the steps for criterion development as presented in the reading *Essentials Of Criterion Development* by Cascio (pages 24-27).
- Have participants examine how well existing measures in the organization have been developed.
- A common problem at this stage is that job analyses have not been done. You might want to do training in how to conduct a job analysis which can be the basis effective appraisal. (See the reading *Job Analysis and Performance Appraisal* by Beatty (pages 33-42).)

Choosing The Proper Format

- Present samples of alternative formats—the reading *Types Of Performance Measures* by Cascio (pages 42-51) has samples of all the most popular formats.
- Participants should review advantages and disadvantages of each type. (See the reading *Performance Appraisal: Match The Tool To The Task* by McMillan and Doyle (pages 65-70).
- Practice developing criteria—have participants read any of the cases in the case section and develop standards of performance, critical incidents, behavioral anchors, or whatever matches the format you have chosen.
- Examine the criteria developed using the characteristics of good criteria presented in the reading *Criteria For Appraisal Effectiveness* by Kane and Lawler (pages 129-134).

- Examine the criteria based on how useful they will be in the organization (See Overhead 4: *Uses Of Performance Appraisal* (page 234).)
- Revise the formats based on the critiques.

Performance Review And Feedback Skills

- Have participants review proper documentation by having them complete the questionnaire in the reading *Documenting Employee Performance* by Smith (pages 94–97).
- Conduct role-plays using *Observer Worksheet For Managing Performance Feedback* (pages 208–209).
- Based on experience have participants design training sessions for implementing performance appraisal. These will be sessions the rest of the organization participates in. They should read *Training Approaches And A Workshop To Minimize Rating Error* by Latham and Wexley (pages 85–91) and *Play Well Thy Part* by Cooper (pages 210–215) before designing the training sessions.

Performance Appraisal And Equal Employment Opportunity (EEO)

- Have participants review the reading *Performance Appraisal: Legal Aspects* by Odom (pages 108–115).
- Have participants develop a list of requirements that the organization's performance appraisal system must comply with to meet legal requirements. Use Overhead 7: *Key Elements Of The Performance Appraisal* (page 238) to summarize the discussion.

Develop Action Plans For Implementing An Effective Performance Appraisal System

- Summarize *key points* of workshop.
- Develop plan for implementation.